LITTERAE ORGANI:
ESSAYS IN HONOR *of*
BARBARA OWEN

Zacharias Hildebrandt: Störmthal *(1723)*
1989 Westfield Center study-tour: *Organs of Bach's Era in Thuringia and Saxony*
Photo by Robert Cornell

LITTERAE ORGANI:

ESSAYS IN HONOR *of*

BARBARA OWEN

Editors

JOHN OGASAPIAN

SCOT L. HUNTINGTON

LEN LEVASSEUR

N. LEE ORR

OHS PRESS
RICHMOND, VIRGINIA
TWO THOUSAND AND FIVE

Library of Congress Cataloging-in-Publication:
Litteræ Organi: Essays in Honor of Barbara Owen.
ISBN 0-913499-22-6
1. Beach, Giles, 1826-1906. 2. Buck, Dudley, 1839-1909. 3. Organ Music
– Interpretation (Phrasing, dynamics, etc.) 4. Organ (musical
instrument). 5. Organ (musical instrument) – Conservation and
Restoration. 6. Organ (musical instrument) – Mexico. 7. Organ
Recordings. 8. Organ Tuning. 9. Owen, Barbara. 10. Piano. 11.
Rosales, Manuel. 11. Thayer, Eugene, 1838-1889.

ML55.O94 2005

*This publication was designed using a Macintosh G5 computer and
Adobe Creative Suite 2 software. The book was set using Adobe
Bembo, a typeface based on the work of Venetian scholar and printer
Aldus Manutius (1449 –1515).*

The Publications Governing Board of the Organ Historical Society affectionately dedicates this volume to Barbara Owen in appreciation of her outstanding contributions to the Society and its goals. As scholar, author, restorer, musician, founding member of the Society and its first president, Barbara Owen has been a tireless advocate of historical organs in America and abroad. We offer these essays on the occasion of the Society's fiftieth anniversary with gratitude for her inspiring leadership.

— Laurence Libin, on behalf of the
Publications Board of Governors of the OHS Press

Scot L. Huntington, *Chair*
Gregory Crowell, *Director of Publications*

Allison Alcorn-Oppedahl
Lynn Edwards Butler
Michael Friesen
Sebastian M. Glück
Len Levasseur
Laurence Libin
Orpha Ochse
Andrew Unsworth
William T. Van Pelt

CONTENTS

ILLUSTRATIONS

FORWARD

OCTOBER 11ᵀᴴ 1961 was a particularly propitious day for C. B. Fisk as Barbara Owen walked through the doors of the old shop to begin work. Barbara was already well known as an organ scholar, her interest in the instrument having been kindled while growing up in New Haven, Connecticut and developed more fully at Westminster Choir College. She had played an important role in founding the Organ Historical Society in 1956 and in 1959 had accompanied E. Power Biggs, his wife Peggy, and a recording engineer on an extensive tour of early American organs. Barbara wrote the comprehensive notes for the resulting seminal recording, *The Organ & Music of Early America*. She had tremendous knowledge of antique organs and a great circle of friends and acquaintances.

Charles Fisk certainly knew of Barbara, both by reputation and through their many mutual friends. Well aware of the current organ scene in the Boston area, Barbara would have known of Charles Fisk as well. He was gaining a reputation for his innovative work and his pursuit of historic organbuilding practices. In the summer of 1961 he had left the Andover Organ Company where he had been both president and owner, and moved to Gloucester to establish C.B. Fisk, Inc. with three employees, now four with the arrival of Barbara. C.B. Fisk was located in an old building near the center of Gloucester, a former ropewalk which had flourished during the days of fishing schooners. By 1961 the building had fallen into severe disrepair: when it rained the roof leaked and in the winter the building was freezing cold. Barbara settled in on this new frontier with characteristic vigor.

Soon known affectionately as "The Barbar," she readily pitched in to help the fledgling company. Her Control Center was an old walnut roll-top desk which she had carefully refinished. She established office procedures that would go on to grow as the shop grew and the workforce expanded. Her knowledge and contacts throughout the organ world enabled her to offer invaluable advice when inquiries arrived. Many a church discovered new aspects of its own history when Barbara was called upon. The company could forge ahead, charting new territory, as she reassured potential clients that they would be well served taking the (then) bold step of ordering a tracker organ.

As the office began to run smoothly, Barbara left her roll-top desk afternoons and moved out into the workshop. With past experience in organ maintenance and tuning, she was eager to participate more in the building of organs. Initially making and assembling small parts, she was soon laying out windchests and pre-voicing flue pipes. She conferred on design of the instruments, always advocating space for the organ tuner – *please leave enough room to inch by!* Before long Barbara had become a voicer and during her tenure did much of the shop flue voicing and finish voicing. She taught many of her colleagues the secrets of maintenance and tuning – of organs and organists alike. A maintenance trip with Barbara was an educational expedition that might well include an organ crawl to a nearby instrument or a near-death experience as she careened through Boston traffic!

In 1975, just after C.B. Fisk had moved to the new shop on Kondelin Road, Barbara took a leave of absence to spend more time on a book she was researching and writing. After publication of *The Organ in New England* she returned to the shop, but her new career as an author had been launched and the demand for her as a scholar, consultant and champion of historic American organs was ever increasing. Her last project with the shop was the final tuning for the new organ at House of Hope Presbyterian Church in St. Paul in 1979.

We at C.B. Fisk are grateful to Barbara Owen for the nearly twenty years she gave to the development and vision of this workshop. Her hard work during the infancy of the company helped to assure its success, and the gifts she freely shared with us continue to guide our work. We join the Organ Historical Society in honoring her for her devotion to the study of the best of American pipe organs, for educating people about them, their maintenance, restoration, and preservation.

Your colleagues at C.B. Fisk

BARBARA OWEN

⚜

Biography

BARBARA OWEN was born January 25, 1933, in Utica, New York. She received her Bachelor of Music degree from Westminster Choir College in 1955, and her Master of Music degree in musicology from Boston University in 1962, as a student of the eminent scholar Karl Geiringer. She pursued advanced study in Europe at the North German Organ Academy and the Academy of Italian Organ Music. In 1963, she began a distinguished forty-year tenure as Director of Music at the First Religious Society of Newburyport, Massachusetts. Between the years 1961 and 1979, she worked with the leading American organbuilding firm, C.B. Fisk as a pipe voicer.

As a young woman in her early twenties during the 1950s, Ms.Owen defined and mapped a new subdiscipline in American musical scholarship: the study of Anglo-American organs, organ design, and organ music. In 1956, she and a handful of others founded the Organ Historical Society, of which she became founding president; that organization now counts some 4000 members internationally, and publishes a quarterly journal as well as a series of books, monographs and editions. Ms. Owen was honored with its Distinguished Service Award in 1988, and designated an Honorary Member in 1998, in recognition of her contributions both to the Society and to scholarship. The American Musical Instrument Society honored her with its prestigious Curt Sachs Award in 1994.

Over the past half-century, a flood of publications – essays, reviews and books – has poured from Ms. Owen's pen, typewriter, and computer. She has edited several volumes of organ and choral literature from various eras. The most significant items in that formidable bibliography are listed elsewhere in this volume. Her most recent work explores continental Baroque and Romantic organ music as well as Anglo-American subjects.

Perhaps most characteristic of Barbara Owen is her unfailing generosity. She has selflessly advised and aided other researchers with her encyclopedic knowledge about her subject, and the voluminous files of material she has collected. Over the years, she has inspired and encouraged countless other music historians (the compilers among them), and fostered scholarship in American church music and organ literature among students and seasoned scholars alike.

Now in semi-retirement from church music, Ms. Owen continues her scholarship without slackening in pace and level of quality. She is curator and founder of the Organ Library of the Boston American Guild of Organists located at Boston University. Her work is internationally known and respected, and she is generally regarded both here and abroad as one of the top half-dozen scholars in her field.

It is thus fitting on this fiftieth anniversary of the Organ Historical Society's foundation, that a group her friends and colleagues from America and Europe offer her, as the Society's founding president, as a respected scholar, and as a beloved friend, this collection of original scholarship in her honor. As editors, we have intentionally endeavored to preserve the international character of the collection by leaving unchanged the distinctive spellings and citation formats customary to each contributor and his or her scholarly tradition.

JOHN OGASAPIAN

EXPLANATORY NOTES

1 | ABBREVIATIONS USED IN TEXT AND TABLES

b.	born
b./bb.	bar/bars (in Peter Williams)
c.	copyright
ca.	circa
d.	died
cf.	*confer:* compare
cm	centimeter
ed.	editor(s)
e.g.	*exempli gratia:* for example
et al	*et aliæ:* and others
ff.	folios
fol.	folio
idem	previously mentioned
Ibid.	*ibidem:* in the same place
i.e.	*id est:* that is
MS	manuscript
m./mm.	measure/measures
mm	millimeter
n.a.	not available
N.B.	*nota bene:* note well

n.p.	no pagination
p./pp.	page/pages
r.	reign
sc.	*scilicet:* that is to say; namely
sic	intentionally so written
st(s).	street(s)
s.v.	*sub verbo:* under the word (for dictionary entries)
vol.	volume
w.p.	wind pressure

2 | COMPASSES

Much confusion can arise from the diversity of systems in common use for describing key compasses. For this book, we have adopted the universal German system:

CC (16-foot) – C (8-foot) – c° or c (4-foot) – c¹ (2-foot) – c² (1-foot) – c³ (½-foot) - c⁴ (¼-foot)

These refer to the keys (and pedals) of the organ, not to the pitch of the registers.

3 | ACKNOWLEDGEMENTS

The following are gratefully thanked for their editorial assistance in the production of this volume: Gregory Crowell, Rollin Smith and Andrew Unsworth.

We would like to thank C.B. Fisk, Inc., and in particular Virginia Lee Fisk, Steve Dieck and Mark Nelson for their generous assistance in the production of this book.

CONTRIBUTORS

JONATHAN AMBROSINO is a consultant, journalist and tonal finisher, concentrating on twentieth century American organs. He was elected President of the Organ Historical Society from 1999-2001, after having served on the Society's National Council from 1993 to 2001. He has carried out tonal restoration on well-known Aeolian-Skinner organs such as those at the Groton School and Church of the Advent in Boston. His consulting practice involves both restorations and new instruments, for such diverse institutions as Harvard Memorial Church and Washington National Cathedral.

STEPHEN BICKNELL lives in retirement in London. He worked at a senior level for the English organ builders Mander and Walker and is the author of *The History of the English Organ*.

LYNN EDWARDS BUTLER, organist and organologist, has pursued her interests in historic organs and performance practices since 1976. She is currently researching the history of Central German organ building in the first half of the eighteenth century. Her all-Bach program recorded on the newly built Richards & Fowkes organ in Deerfield, Massachusetts, is about to be released by Loft Recordings.

DANA HULL has degrees from Bowling Green State University (Ohio) and the University of Michigan (Ann Arbor). She moved out of the library profession into restoration of historic tracker organs in the late 1970s. An organist herself, Dana has endeavored to stem the increasing tide of destruction of old organs, returning them to their original state whenever possible. Examples of her efforts are concentrated in Michigan, but can also be found coast to coast.

SCOT L. HUNTINGTON established the organ building firm of S.L. Huntington & Co. in Stonington, Conn. in 1988. Specializing in the restoration of historically significant instruments and the construction of mechanical-action organs in historic styles, the firm built a chamber organ for Dartmouth College in the style of the seventeenth-century English builder "Father Smith", for which Barbara Owen provided invaluable assistance. He is serving a second term as Vice President of the Organ Historical Society in which capacity he worked to create the OHS Press He is presently Chair of the Publications Board of Governors.

LEN LEVASSEUR is the founder and Executive Director of Kid-Start, Inc. a not-for-profit child care services program in Lawrence, Massachusetts. Between 1991 and 1997, Len published *The Northeast Organist Magazine,* and currently serves on the Publications Board of Governors of the OHS Press.

LAURENCE LIBIN is Research Curator at The Metropolitan Museum of Art, where he directed the Department of Musical Instruments from 1973 to 1999. He travels extensively for study and as an academic lecturer and consultant to cultural institutions worldwide, including recently in Japan, Mexico, Italy, and Russia. He is a Life Fellow of the Royal Society of Arts, a member of the Comité International des Musées et Collections d'Instruments de Musique, and a Governor of the American Organ Archives of the Organ Historical Society.

ORPHA OCHSE is Professor of Music Emerita at Whittier College (California). Her books and articles have spanned a broad range of topics related to organs, organ performance and organ builders. She was named Honorary Member of the Organ Historical Society in 1991, and was given recognition awards by the American Institute of Organbuilders in 1980 and 2002.

JOHN OGASAPIAN is Professor of Music History at the University of Massachusetts, Lowell. He was editor of the Organ Historical Society's quarterly journal, *The Tracker,* from 1991 to 1999. The Society has designated him an Honorary Member, and he was a recipient of its Distinguished Service Award. He is a contributor to *The Encyclopedia of Protestantism, American National Biography* and the *New Grove Dictionary of Music.* His most recent book is *Music of the Colonial and Revolutionary Era.*

N. LEE ORR is Professor and Chair of Academic Studies in the School of Music at Georgia State University in Atlanta. He writes on nineteenth-century American choral and organ music. His most recent works are a volume of Dudley Buck's choral works for the *Music in the United States of America* series and a biography of Buck for the University of Illinois Press.

UWE PAPE is a professor of computer science at the Technical University in Berlin, director of Pape-Verlag, specializing in organ-related publications, and director of the ORDA project (Organ Documentation in North Germany). He is the author of *The Tracker Organ Revival in America* and serves regularly as a consultant for historical organ construction and restoration projects, most recently the Marienkirche in Berlin, Frauenkirche in Dresden, and Nicolaikirche, Spandau.

STEPHEN L. PINEL holds two degrees in Sacred Music from Westminster Choir College in Princeton, New Jersey, and did further graduate work in Historical Musicology at New York University. He currently serves as Archivist for the Organ Historical Society, and often contributes writings on American organ history to journals both here and abroad.

JOHN SPELLER was born and educated in England where he obtained degrees from the Universities of Bristol and Oxford. As an organbuilder he has worked for James R. McFarland & Co., Columbia Organ Works, Inc., and Quimby Pipe Organs, Inc. He lives in St. Louis, Missouri, and is a frequent contributor to *The Tracker* and *The Diapason.*

SUSAN TATTERSHALL has been closely involved with the Mexican organ-building tradition from 1980 to the present. She has hosted over a dozen organ tours to Mexico, published many articles about the Mexican organ, and from 1994-1997, served as director of the Organos Historicos de Mexico workshop. She resides in Denver, Colorado, and travels to Mexico frequently for maintenance work on restored organs, and to research and document work on unrestored instruments.

NICHOLAS THISTLETHWAITE is Canon Precentor of Guildford Cathedral, Surrey, UK. He is a former Secretary and Chairman of the British Institute of Organ Studies, and has written extensively on the history of the organ and of choral foundations in the British Isles. He is the author of *The Making of the Victorian Organ*. Dr. Thistlethwaite also acts as an organ consultant; his projects include Birmingham Town Hall, Eton College Chapel, Chelmsford Cathedral, Buckingham Palace, St. John's College, Cambridge, and Christ Church, Spitalfields.

PETER WILLIAMS, whose first book was *The European Organ* (1966), is emeritus Arts & Sciences Professor at Duke University, and former Dean of Music, University of Edinburgh, where he was also Director of the Russell Collection of Harpsichords. An early harpsichord pupil of Thurston Dart and Gustav Leonhardt, Peter Williams was Music Scholar of St. John's College, Cambridge, and is currently Chairman of the British Institute of Organ Studies (BIOS) and Vice-President of the Royal College of Organists (RCO).

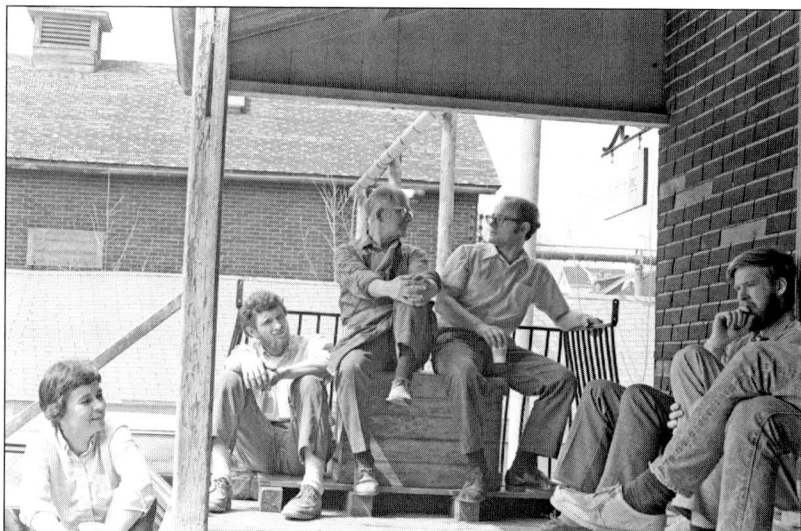

Barbara Owen, Lou Dolive, Joe Grace, Nick Atwood and Jerry Lewis
at the old C.B. Fisk shop

Charles Fisk and Barbara Owen on her 39th birthday, 1972
Photo by Robert Cornell

FROM WULFSTAN OF WINCHESTER TO THE LAUDIAN REMNANT

ASPECTS OF THE OLD ENGLISH TRANSPOSING ORGAN

John L. Speller

A GOOD PLACE TO BEGIN is with the Latin word *organa*, which generally occurs in the plural. There is of course a parallel old English plural usage,
organs – as in "a pair of organs," referring to a single instrument but using *pair*
in a way analogous to "a pair of scissors" or "a pair of trousers." This plural use
occurs in English down to Elizabethan times and beyond. As far as the Latin
is concerned, however, perhaps the greatest difficulty in studying the medieval
organ from literary sources has been the problem of determining precisely
which references to *organa* refer specifically to pipe organs. This is because
there is considerable uncertainty among historians of the organ in the earlier
part of the medieval period as to whether the Latin word *organa* refers to the
pipe organ in particular or to musical instruments in general.

   The terminological confusion over the word *organa* has arisen largely because of two passages in Augustine of Hippo's *Commentary on the Psalms*. In
Jerome's Vulgate translation of the Bible, Psalm 150:4 reads, "Laudate eum in
chordis et organis." At first sight this might mean, "Praise him on the strings
and organ," but Augustine quite rightly points out that *organa* here is to be
taken in its Greek sense, meaning musical instruments in general, rather than
the pipe organ in particular. For the last two hundred years or more historians
have taken this statement of Augustine's to mean that until the later middle
ages – and there is some argument about precisely when – we cannot be certain whether a reference to *organa* refers to a pipe organ or not. I wish to be-

gin, however, by taking issue with this. What Augustine in fact says is that in Ps. 150:4 *organa* "is a Greek word ... applied generally ... to all musical instruments," but that "being called *organ* is a Latin and conversational usage".[1] Similarly, commenting on Psalm 57:9, Augustine states that in this Psalm "... *organa* is the word used for all instruments. Not only is that called an organ, which is great, and blown into with bellows."[2] It is difficult to understand how anyone could think that these passages mean that the Latin use of the word *organa* was in any way ambiguous. If in Latin *organa* did not normally mean a pipe organ, why on earth would Augustine find it necessary to explain to his readers that the Greek usage meant something else? My first point, therefore, is that the force of Augustine's argument is that the normal meaning of the word *organa* in Latin is "pipe organ," and that Ps. 150:4 and Ps. 57:9 represent an unusual use of Greek terminology on the part of Jerome in his Vulgate translation. If *organa* does normally mean "pipe organ," then it follows that medieval references to *organa* should be taken to refer to organs unless the context specifically demands otherwise. Once this point is grasped it simplifies the task of studying early references to the organ considerably.

As a starting point for studying the organ in medieval England there is an excellent discussion of the early history of the English organ from the tenth to the sixteenth centuries in Stephen Bicknell's book, *The History of the English Organ*.[3] He begins with an account of the organ at Malmesbury Abbey and other instruments associated with St. Dunstan (909-988), Archbishop of Canterbury, who according to William of Malmesbury may himself have had some skill as an organbuilder. William of Malmesbury also mentions another archbishop who dabbled in organbuilding – Thomas of Bayeux (d. 1100), the first Archbishop of York after the Norman Conquest. Thomas built organs, played upon them himself, and encouraged his clergy to do likewise. He also adapted many secular minstrel airs to church use in much the same way as the Wesleys did in the eighteenth century.[4] Whether built by archbishops, saints or sinners, however, one thing all early English organs seem to have had in common was that they were transposing instruments in a sense analogous to the way that a B-flat horn is a transposing instrument. The pipe organ was a transposing instrument in F. The lowest note that on a modern keyboard would be C in fact played the F pipe. Thus the instrument transposed down a fifth throughout its compass. Organists played organ music on the keyboard as written, but in Renaissance times when the organ began to be an accompanimental instrument, it was necessary to transpose either down a fourth or up a fifth in order to bring music to a pitch at which a choir could sing with it. This was actually considerably easier to accomplish than might at first appear. All that was necessary was for an organist to be familiar with the treble, bass and alto clefs. He or she would then be able to transpose simply by reading one clef as though it were another. Thus, to transpose up a fifth the player would pretend that what appeared in the music as an alto clef was in fact a treble clef, and so forth, *mutatis mutandis*. For an organist trained on the transposing organ this would have been second nature.[5] It is important to remember, nevertheless, that in medieval times the organ was normally used *alternatim* with plainsong chant, rather than as an accompanimental instrument. Organists before the Reformation period would therefore not normally have needed to accompany a choir at all. It was probably because of the rise of the practice of accompanying choral music on the organ that transposing organs were phased out. An intermediate stage seems to have been to include one or more stops in unison with the choir in what was otherwise a transposing instrument. Robert Dallam thus included in the Chaire Organ of his 1632 instrument at York Minster "1 recorder of tynn, unison to the voice".[6] This may also have been the purpose of the mysterious "antheme stop" included in Dallam's 1662 proposal for a new organ at New College, Oxford.[7]

The fact that English organs used to be transposing instruments, explains quite a bit about the later form of the English organ. Unlike Continental organs, where the main unison stop is often a *Principal* of 8-foot pitch, in old English organs, the *Principal* is invariably a 4-foot stop. This is a consequence of the habit of playing transposed down a fifth, whereby the *Principal* became the unison stop and the *Open* or *Stopped Diapason* became a sub-unison stop. It is interesting in this context, as Martin Renshaw has pointed out,[8] that the sub-octave strings on the arch-lute are still referred to as *diapasons*. J. Bunker Clark further points out that Thomas Morley used *diapasons* to mean notes doubled an octave beneath in the bass.[9]

The lowest note of the organ keyboard, playing F, was generally described as five-feet long (for the *Principal*) or ten-feet long (for the *Open Diapason*). This so-called "Quire Pitch" represented an extraordinarily high pitch by modern standards.[10] After the Restoration of the Monarchy in 1660, few new transposing organs were built and most surviving instruments were converted to normal pitch. In order to retrofit an old organ, a new, non-transposing keyboard and mechanism was provided, and the FF pipe was changed into the GG pipe, resulting in a lower pitch and thus the G-compass organ became the norm in the English-speaking world down to the middle of the nineteenth century. One curious legacy of the transposing organ, however, was that a ten-foot case front continued to be the norm in English organbuilding until the 1830's.[11]

The transposing organ rapidly disappeared from England in the second half of the seventeenth century – after the Civil War, during which English organbuilders in exile had grown used to the non-transposing organs of the Continent. There had also been transposing organs in continental Europe, but they had disappeared around a century and a half before they did in England. In retaining them for so long, England was probably something of a conservative backwater. At the time transposing organs were phased out on the Continent, organs were still mostly of the *Blockwerk* type, with few if any individual stops. This meant that European stop nomenclature mostly developed after transposing organs were abandoned. Thus the Continental stop names avoided the English system of using *diapasons* for the naming of unison stops. Furthermore, because transposing organs disappeared from the Continent so long ago, there is less evidence of them remaining, and correspondingly little interest is shown in them. There is nonetheless some evidence for transposing instruments found in paintings like the Van Eyck panel of 1425 in Ghent, or the Hugo van der Goes painting of 1476 at Holyrood Palace, both of which clearly show instruments where the lowest pipe is the right length to sound an F and the lowest key on the keyboard appears to be C. There is also literary evidence of transposing organs, such as that in Trier Cathedral, built by P. Briesger of Koblenz in 1537, with a compass of FF-a^2 (49 notes), in which FF sounded C.[12] However, there has been remarkably little interest shown even in determining which early European organs were in fact transposing. The swallow's nest organ at the Laurenskerk at Alkmaar, built by Jan van Covelen in 1511, has apparently always had a compass of FF-a² (50 notes) and currently the keyboard functions normally with the C key sounding a C pipe. However such is the lack of interest in the subject, that the question of whether this organ was originally a transposing instrument does not even seem to have been discussed at the time of the organ's most recent restoration.

Fortunately English musicologists have shown a little more interest in the subject. Among recent developments, musician and scholar John Harper has been one of the originators of an *Early English Organ Project* aiming to re-create two small instruments in the style of the sixteenth century. These are based on the remains of a windchest found in use as a door at Wetheringsett, Suffolk, and the remains of another windchest surviving in the church at Wingfield, Suffolk.[13] Stephen Bicknell discusses both these artifacts in his recent book on the English organ.[14] The organbuilders Martin Goetze and Dominic Gwynn of Worksop, Nottinghamshire, have carried out the work of constructing the two small organs, typical of English instruments built around 1530, one of seven and one of five stops. The choice of builder was a good one, since Martin Goetze and Dominic Gwynn have taken a considerable interest in the transposing organ. Both have authored scholarly articles on the subject.[15] The instrument based on the Wingfield chest is a small instrument of five stops, all of open wood pipework, with only rudimentary casework. The instrument based on the Wetheringsett chest has seven stops, one a stopped wood rank but all the rest metal, and includes a regal and a rather more elaborate case. The two contrasting styles of Wingfield and Wetheringsett effectively illustrate the differences between small and medium-sized instruments of the early-sixteenth century.

It is interesting to ask how long the organ had been a transposing instrument *before* it ceased to be so in seventeenth-century England. While this question may not admit of any precise answer, it is at least fair to say that transposing organs were in use for a very long time. One phenomenon that may shed light on the earlier history of the transposing organ is the choral practice known as *organum*. This of course was the idea of singing plainsong in two parts at a constant interval – usually a fourth or fifth – and was one of the earliest forms of harmony, in use from the ninth century to around 1250 C.E. Before the seventeenth century, the tenor voice was the dominant choral voice, so that singing a fourth or fifth lower in *organum* would have been a comfortable arrangement for basses.[16] But where does the word *organum* itself come from? A glance at most large dictionaries will show that etymologists believe the word is related to our old friend *organa*.[17] Does it not seem strange that a choral technique should be named after a musical instrument? Could it be that the choral technique is named after the pipe organ because the this instrument, like the choral technique, operates a fourth or fifth away from unison pitch? In other words, was *organum* a choral technique that originated as an imitation of the transposing organ? The etymology suggests that this might in fact have been the case. If so, the organ must have been a transposing instrument since at least the ninth century and possibly long before that. It must be remembered, however, that it was only around the twelfth century that the balanced keyboard was reinvented, so that the earliest transposing organs would have been worked by pulling sliders on and off. Furthermore, until around 1500 the organ would have been a *Blockwerk* without separate stops. As the transposing organ appears to antedate both the reinvention of the keyboard and of individual stops, the earliest examples must have been very primitive indeed.

Some details of the form of a late tenth-century organ may be gleaned from Wulfstan's account of the organ in Winchester Cathedral in around 990 C.E.[18] There were actually three well-known Wulfstans in England at this period – Wulfstan of Worcester, Wulfstan of York and Wulfstan of Winchester – and it is important not to confuse them. Wulfstan of Winchester was a monk who seems to have had a good deal to do with the music of Winchester Cathedral and who may have occupied some position analogous to the present-day post of Precentor. Winchester was an important musical center at the time, as evidenced by the existence of the eleventh-century musical collection known as the *Winchester Troper*,[19] notwithstanding the apparently insuperable difficulties of interpreting its notation. One choral composition surviving from the period is Wulsftan's own free organum anthem, *Alleluia, te martyrum*. Wulfstan was evidently a man of many parts, and as a scholar he is best known as the author of a *Life of St. Æthelwold.*[20] He also wrote a musical treatise entitled *De Harmonia Tonorum.*[21]

According to Wulfstan's description, the organ at Winchester Cathedral in the late tenth century had four hundred pipes. A reference to forty *linguæ,* (tongues), each with ten holes, suggests a *Blockwerk* of ten ranks with a compass of forty notes. Forty notes seems an extraordinarily large compass for the time, especially bearing in mind that few accidentals were called for in the music of the period, and that therefore there were probably fewer notes in an octave than the twelve in the chromatic scale of a modern instrument. The longest pipe would have been ten feet long – or possibly even twenty, which might go some way toward explaining both the large compass and the number of people required to pump the organ. In either case the lowest note would probably have sounded an F. The word *lingua,* (tongue), may suggest a wide slider-like strap of leather pierced with holes. An advantage of this would be that leather would have sealed in the crudely made chests of the time rather better than wood. Reference is made to two brothers working harmoniously together to play the instrument, and it is possible that the two organists sat on opposite sides of the organ, one pulling the tongues on and the other taking them off. Most commentators have suggested that the sliders were worked by levers and that the two organists sat side by side, one working at the bass end of the compass and the other at the treble. It must remembered, however, that the custom of the time would have been to improvise the versets comprising most of the organ music played *alternatim* with the choir. It is difficult to see how two organists would have been able to play together *ex tempore*, however much they were "in harmony" with each other. On the other hand if one organist were merely responsible for pulling off the sliders, it would have been a relatively simple matter for the principal organist to signal to his assistant when this should be done. The winding system must have been extremely inefficient, since the organ had twenty-six bellows on two different floors, operated by no fewer than seventy men. These men, however, may have operated in shifts, perhaps only working for a few minutes and then resting as others took over. Pumping the extremely primitive winding system of the organ must have been very arduous work.

Acquiring balanced keyboards and stops, the organ gradually developed into something more like its modern form over the ensuing centuries. By around the year 1530, England probably contained more pipe organs than it ever would again until at least the middle of the nineteenth century. Most large and medium-sized parish churches and monastic foundations contained at least one organ, and large cathedrals and abbeys often contained several. In the largest churches it was normal, for example, to use the main organ on the Pulpitum or Quire Screen only during major festivals, including the Great Fifty Days of Easter, and the instrument's painted doors would remain closed for the rest of the year. A smaller instrument would be played for the normal services, and often a large church would have a third instrument for festivals associated with the Blessed Virgin Mary. All the organs would of course remain silent during the penitential season of Lent.

According to an ancient source quoted by Rimbault, the arrangements at Durham Cathedral, which had five organs, three of them in the Quire, seem to have been rather different:

> There were three pair of organs belonging to the said quire, for maintenance of God's service, and the better celebrating thereof. One of the fairest pair of the three stood over the quire door, only opened and played upon the principal feasts, the pipes being all of the most fine wood, and the workmanship very fine, partly gilt upon the inside, and the outside of the leaves and covers up to the top, with branches and flowers finely gilt, with the name of Jesus gilt with gold. There were but two pair more of them in all England of the same making, one in *York*, and another in *[St.] Paul's [Cathedral, London]*. Also there was a lantern of wood like unto a pulpit, standing and adjoining to the wood-organs over the quire door, where they had wont to sing the nine lessons in the old time, on principal dayes, standing with their faces towards the high altar. The second pair stood on the north side of the quire, being never played upon but when the four doctors of the Church were read, viz., Augustine, Ambrose, Gregory and Jerome, being a pair of fair large organs, called the *Cryers*. The third pair were daily used at ordinary service.[22]

The London organbuilders John Howe, Sr., and his son, John Howe, Jr. (*alias* John Heweson) are possible contenders for the distinction of having built the York, St. Paul's and Durham organs mentioned in the passage quoted above, since they are known to have worked at York Minster in 1485, 1531 and 1536.[23] According to Burney, however, the builder of the organ in Old St.

Paul's Cathedral was not one of the Howes but William Beton of King's Lynn in Norfolk,[24] and if so Beton might have built the organs at Durham and York as well. We may note that the finest organ used for major festivals and positioned above the door into the Quire (i.e., on the Pulpitum) had wooden pipes. Wooden pipework was very popular among old English organ builders, some of whom seem to have used wood in preference to metal, resulting in a characteristically sweet-toned instrument. On her death in 1509, Lady Margaret Beaufort left her three organs to Christ's College, Cambridge, of which she had been the founder. These were described as "a payre of Organs the pypis of wayndskott," a "lesser payre," and an "olde payre with an olde case."[25] This again suggests the superiority of the organ with wooden pipes, in this instance of wainscot (oak). It seems curious that there was an organ for playing only on days when the Four Doctors of the Church were read and yet that there was apparently not one for feast days of the Blessed Virgin Mary. This may have been a local peculiarity of Durham Cathedral. There were actually quite a few days when passages were read from the Doctors of the Church in the medieval breviary,[26] so the instrument would have been used quite frequently, presumably *alternatim* with the plainsong chanting. The name, *Cryers*, for one of the organs is somewhat mystifying, unless it refers to the original donor of the instrument. "Cryer" does indeed appear to have been a fairly common surname in Durham.

The zenith of the pipe organ in early-sixteenth century England coincided with a period of great prosperity before the disastrous policies of King Henry VIII led to economic decline. Exactly how many instruments there were in England in the early-sixteenth century will probably never be known, since many of them would have been in abbeys and other monastic foundations whose records have long since been destroyed. The extent of disruption which the Dissolution of the Monasteries caused can hardly be overstated. Documentation suggests that the closing of Glastonbury Abbey alone put more than twenty-thousand people in the County of Somerset out of work – not just the monks, but grocers, construction workers, farm workers, clothiers and many others whose secular livelihood depended on the business generated by the vast monastery and its estates. Much of what existed before the Dissolution of the Monasteries has vanished without trace. Glastonbury Abbey, the largest monastic foundation in Britain, has at least left its legacy for posterity in the form of a picturesque ruin. Of other places there is even less to see. Only minor vestiges remain of Taunton Priory, one of the two or three largest monasteries in the country, and it is no longer even certain precisely what site this monastery occupied. Thomas Cromwell, known as "The Hammer of the Monks" since he was King Henry VIII's agent for the Dissolution of the Monasteries, was actually the Member of Parliament for the Borough of Taunton. Taunton was a Puritan stronghold, but however popular Cromwell's policies may have been with his Puritan constituents, these policies would have cost a goodly number of them their jobs and fortunes. So far as the organs are concerned, the occasional reference that has survived only whets the appetite to know what else has been lost. Another picturesque ruin is Fountains Abbey in Yorkshire, and here we know at least that the Treasurer's Roll for 1446-1458 records that "Thomas Swynton, monk, was paid 20d., and four sheepskins for the organ, 19d.," and again that later there was another "Item pro Organis, 11d."[27] In most other cases we do not possess even such minimal information as this with regard to what existed before the 1530s. Even fewer records from convents have survived than from monasteries, and we now know almost nothing of the organs these convents contained, nor of the nuns who played them. In some cases monastic organists moved to non-monastic churches after the Dissolution of the Monasteries. A noteworthy example is Thomas Tallis, organist of Waltham Abbey, who went on to become an organist of the Chapel Royal in the Elizabethan period.

It was not just economic decline that led to a reduction in the number of pipe organs in sixteenth-century England. Another reason was that most organbuilders were thoroughly opposed to the breach with the Church of Rome and the Dissolution of the Monasteries. It is not hard to see why since it ruined their livelihood. Some of them like the Dallam and Harris families were *Recusants* or Roman Catholic loyalists. Henry VIII therefore regarded organbuilders – and, by extension, organs – as a dangerous focus of dissent. As early as 1531, the King clearly considered the threat sufficient to dissolve the Worshipful Company of Organ Makers, the guild for organbuilders in the

City of London. Nonetheless, in order to exercise any trade within London a craftsman had to belong to one or other of the trade guilds, so if the Worshipful Company of Organ Makers no longer existed, organbuilders needed to find another guild. Thus we find entries such as this one of August 29, 1531 in the register of the Worshipful Company of Skinners:

> Fforasmuche as this court is credeblye informed that the olde name and company of organ makers ys nowe consumed and dyssolved, wherefore now at the speciall request of John Howe ye yonger, organ maker, he ys transposed to the mistery and company of skynners.[28]

Organbuilding involves quite a bit of leatherwork, mechanism, and metalwork, and so it was natural that most organbuilders took refuge in the skinners', clockmakers' or blacksmiths' guilds.

A third reason for the decline in organbuilding in sixteenth- and seventeenth-century Britain was the growth of Puritanism, which in many cases involved a complete rejection of instruments of music in Christian worship, a situation that continued in Scotland right down to the nineteenth century. Archbishop Thomas Cranmer of Canterbury is said to have discouraged the use of the organ in St. Paul's Cathedral, London, as early as 1552. Queen Elizabeth I was a little more favorably inclined toward the organ, but nevertheless a combination of economic hardship, Puritan opposition, and a feeling that the organbuilding trade was politically suspect led to a massive decline in the number of organs in England during the sixteenth century. It is impossible to know what the extent of this would have been, but it would not be surprising to find that more than nine-tenths of the church organs in England were lost during the course of the century.

The organ nevertheless continued to be popular as an instrument of merriment in taverns and important private houses. This secular use was in part responsible for the unpopularity of the organ as an instrument of worship among the Puritans. Unfortunately, however, because few records have survived, it is impossible to know much about the extent of the instrument's secular use either. In some cases, organs went from being sacred to secular instruments and ended up in private hands as part of the spoils from the Dissolution of the Monasteries. In spite of all this, in some churches however,

there seems to have been a certain degree of loyalty toward individual organbuilders. W. L. Sumner, for example, notes how many churches in London
continued to tune and maintain their organs until John Howe, Jr., died in
1571. They then simply allowed them to fall into disrepair until they became
unplayable and were finally sold as scrap.[29] Perhaps some organs fell into disrepair because there was no longer anyone skilled enough to repair them. A
few neglected instruments managed to last a very long time, and it would be
interesting to know just how many of them were still existing even by the
end of the eighteenth century.

The story was not however, entirely one of decline. There does appear
to have been at least a modest increase in the output of the organbuilding
industry during the first third of the seventeenth century, in the years leading
up to the English Civil War. Nonetheless, the number of instruments involved
may have been relatively small in comparison with the way things had been
before the 1530's. This modest resurgence of organbuilding took place under
the influence of what is generally called "The Laudian Revival." The place of
the organ in the Laudian Revival has been chronicled in various places and is
the subject of the fifth chapter of Stephen Bicknell's aforementioned book.[30]
The designation "Revival" is not perhaps an entirely satisfactory one, since in
many ways the period during which William Laud (1573-1645) was Archbishop of Canterbury represented not so much a revival as the last gasp of the the
anti-Puritan party in the Church of England before the Civil War. Archbishop
Laud's circle was a small and closely-knit remnant of perhaps only a few doz-
en important families who vainly held out for High Church values – including organs – against a hostile and Puritan-dominated society. They should not,
though, be thought of as mere reactionaries, since in many ways Laud was a
radical espousing the progressive views of Dutch theologian Jacob Arminius
(1560-1609) in opposition to the prevailing Calvinism of the times. In this
he was opposed by his predecessor as Archbishop of Canterbury, George Abbot (1562-1633), and a large majority of the Puritan-dominated Church of
England.[31] The members of the Laudian remnant probably appreciated that
they were fighting a losing battle and that, at least for the time being, Puritanism was likely to triumph. The Laudian faction are often portrayed as stub-

born and obdurate, but they were probably not so much this as determined to hold firm to the end and to go out in a blaze of glory. That in a sense, is what Archbishop Laud himself did — preaching a lengthy and eloquent sermon at his own execution and praying on the scaffold that God would "bless this kingdom with peace and charity, that there may not be this effusion of Christian blood amongst them."[32]

One of the more remarkable instruments from the end of the Tudor period was a mechanical organ-clock, the organ part of which Thomas Dallam built in 1599-1600, which was constructed as a gift from Queen Elizabeth I to the Sultan of Turkey. One might wonder whether or not this may have been a transposing instrument. A drawing of the Sultan's organ appeared in *The Illustrated London News* for October 20, 1860, and Andrew Freeman reproduced this in an article he wrote about the instrument in the 1940s. Freeman remarks that although the illustration appears authentic the anonymous contributor to *The Illustrated London News* may have misappropriated the original drawing of *ca.* 1598, executed on parchment and preserved "among the unnoted treasures of our national manuscripts," since it appears to have disappeared.[33] Perhaps the anonymous contributor was Dr. Edward Rimbault, a notorious book thief as well as a noteworthy historian of the organ.[34] In any event, examination of the drawing of the organ reveals that there appears to be a keyboard of three octaves, c^0 to c^3, with the longest façade pipe two-feet long. The instrument was not, apparently, a transposing organ, but that was just the beginning of a further line of research. First of all, one is struck how similar, architecturally speaking, the casework of the Sultan's organ was to the Jacobean screens in the Parish Church at Croscombe in Somerset and in Wadham College Chapel, Oxford. On looking up Croscombe, one finds that the screen there seems to be contemporary with the pulpit in the church, which bears the date 1616. Furthermore, from the same general period there is a reference in the churchwardens' accounts for 1627-28, to the building of an organ at Croscombe by a builder named Halgar.[35] "Halgar" is probably a misreading of Halyar, a Bristol organbuilder who is also known to have built organs about the same time in the parish churches of Pilton and Yatton in Somerset.[36] Croscombe Parish Church has monuments from the early-seventeenth century commemorating

James Bisse, who died in 1606, and William Bisse, who died in 1625.[37] Perhaps, a member of the Bisse family was responsible for obtaining Croscombe's Halyar organ? Next, looking up the Wadham College screen, it is found that this dates from around the year 1613. Next to the screen there is a stained-glass window, the work of Bernard van Ling, 1622, which includes the arms of the Wadham, Strangways, Petre and Bisse families.[38] What an interesting coincidence that the Bisse name should crop up once more! A little further research shows that the Venerable Philip Bisse, D.D., Archdeacon of Taunton, who died in 1611, left his extensive library to Wadham College. To understand how close all this was to Archbishop Laud, it is only necessary to remember that William Laud himself was at this very time President of St. John's College, Oxford, just the other side of the street from Wadham. Returning to Somerset, we find that in 1600 Wells Cathedral was planning a new organ:

> Touching the makyng of a new organ, the chapter wholy referr themselves to Mr. D[octor] James Bisse, now master of the fabrick, for the finishing of that business, and what he shall doe therein they doe promise to retify and allowe of it.[39]

This was the same James Bisse whom I have already mentioned as the subject of a memorial of 1606 at St. Mary's, Croscombe, five miles up the Shepton Mallet road from Wells. There is no record of whether the Rev. Dr. Bisse ever got round to making any recommendations about the new organ for Wells Cathedral, but it took the Dean and Chapter until 1620 to get around to purchasing a new Dallam organ. I include this little *excursus* as an illustration of the point I have already made, namely that the Laudian Remnant in the church consisted of a very closely-knit group of families, and of how easily connections may be drawn between them.

As part of her attempt to reintroduce Roman Catholicism in the 1550's, Queen Mary had made an unsuccessful attempt to reestablish monasticism in England. The nearest that the Church of England came to reestablishing monasticism in the Laudian period was an experiment in communal living undertaken by Nicholas Ferrar (1592-1637). Ferrar founded his community at Little Gidding, Huntingdonshire in 1626. It consisted largely of family members and a few friends. The community is the subject of one of T.S. Eliot's

Four Quartets. On his arrival in the village Nicholas Ferrar found the medieval church at Little Gidding in use as a barn and restored it, providing a new font, lectern and organ. The organ seems to have played a prominent part in the life of the community, though unfortunately no details of the instrument have survived, and its maker is unknown. It was probably very small and may have been similar to the early seventeenth-century chest–organ that survives at Knole House in Kent. The Knole House instrument is not a transposing organ. The Little Gidding instrument may or may not have been. The Little Gidding community engaged in a constant vigil of prayer, sang Matins and Evensong in the church daily, taught the local children to read and write and otherwise ministered to the villagers. King Charles I thought highly of the community and visited it on three separate occasions. After Nicholas Ferrar's death in 1637, his brother continued the community. The Puritans scorned it, referring to it as the *Arminian Nunnery*.[40] In 1646, Cromwell's army broke up the community and desecrated the church. Needless to say, the organ was destroyed.

A good example of a small organ of the Laudian period is the instrument that Eton College procured from Thomas Dallam of London in 1613-14 at a cost of just over £117. This was an "organ contayning fyve stops,

1. a diapason of tynn fyve foot longe stopped
2. a principall of tynn a open stopp fyve foot longe
3. a fflute unison with the principall fyve foote long of tynn
4. an octavo to the principall of Tynne
5. a ffyfteenth of tynne.

As there was already "an octavo to the principall," it seems likely, as Stephen Bicknell points out, that the "ffyfteenth" was a *Fifteenth* to the *Principal,* i.e., two octaves above the pitch of the *Principal,* or what we normally call a *Twenty-Second*.[41] There seems also to have been a "shakeinge stop", of which more anon. A further expense is included, "It. to Mr. Dallam for blewe painted paper v *s.*"[42] This may suggest that, like many European organs, some old English organs had their bellows, chests, etc., covered with a special blue paper, similar to that now used on matchboxes, etc., to seal the knots in the woodwork and to protect against moisture. As in most instruments, the carved casework was contracted for separately. This little instrument represents in the early seventeenth century an organ similar in scope to the Wetheringsett instrument of a century before.

A much larger example of an early-seventeenth-century transposing organ was the two-manual instrument built in 1618 at St. John's College, Oxford. This was the college where William Laud was President from 1611 to 1621, a few years before before he became Archbishop of Canterbury. The royal physician, Sir William Paddy (1554-1634), who was an alumnus of the college, donated the instrument. The organbuilder was Thomas Dallam of London, who had recently completed an instrument at Worcester Cathedral with the following stoplist:

"The particulars of the great organ

Two open diapasons of metall CC fa ut a pipe 10 foot long
Two principals of metall
Two Smal principals or 15ths of metal
One twelfth of metal
One recorder of metal, a stopt pipe

In the Chaire Organ

One principal of mettal
One diapason of wood
One flute of wood
One Small principal or fifteenth of metal
One two and twentieth of mettal."[43]

The St. John's College organ had the same stoplist as the Worcester Cathedral instrument. Doubled ranks on the Great – in this case two Open Diapasons, two Principals and two Fifteenths – were characteristic of English organbuilding right down to Ward's York Minster organ built in the early-nineteenth century. The idea probably came from placing organs on the Pulpitum or Quire Screen, which involved having two façades – one facing the Nave and the other facing the Quire. As well as providing bidirectional tone and a modicum of additional volume, the use of the two Open Diapasons separately or together had the advantage of creating a variety of timbres. From having two Open Diapasons, the doubling of ranks became popular for the higher-pitched stops as well, so that in the St. John's College instrument the Principals and Fifteenths were also doubled. The "diapason of wood" in the Chaire Organ would have been a *Stopt Diapason,* while there were also contrasting flutes – the capped metal *Recorder* in the Great and the wood *Flute* in the Chaire. The Chaire *Flute* was also probably stopped, since open flutes were comparatively rare in English organs before the nineteenth century. Both flutes were presumably of 5-foot pitch, playing unison with the Principals. Until the nineteenth century, flutes were predominantly solo rather than accompanimental stops, but after the abolition of the transposing organ the flutes ceased to be 5-foot unison stops and became 4-foot octave stops. Nevertheless, they obdurately remained solo stops, resulting in some rather "flighty" eighteenth-century *Voluntaries for the Flute* in which no unison stops were used. The "two and twentieth" may, like the extant example in the Adlington Hall organ of *ca.* 1670, have been in essence a one-rank mixture – starting as a twenty-second in the bass but breaking back to a twelfth after several octaves. To add to their expressive *vocale* quality, old English organs were generally voiced to the point at which the pipes were almost overblowing, and then starved somewhat of wind through the use of narrow windtrunks to the windchests.

The St. John's College organ was a remarkably large instrument by the standards of the time. The college chapel is only a small building, and would not be expected to house a large instrument. Indeed, the present organ in the chapel is only slightly larger than its seventeenth-century cousin. Furthermore, Sir William Paddy's generosity to his old college was not limited to the organ, since he also endowed the Paddy Organ Scholarship, as well as giving the college library many valuable books and manuscripts. Among the early organists of St. John's College was Robert Lugge, organist from 1635 to 1639. He was the son of John Lugge, organist of Exeter Cathedral 1603-45 and composer of a *Voluntary for Double Organ.*[44] Robert Lugge was followed in 1639 by William Ellis, also an organist of Eton College, who continued as organist of St. John's after the Restoration of the Monarchy and died in 1674. The college seems to have been very proud of its music in the Laudian period and commissioned a number of choral works including an anthem by Michael East (*ca.*1580-1648), then organist of Lichfield Cathedral. The Dallam organ at St. John's survived until it was replaced by a new Byfield & Green instrument in 1769. The new organ incorporated the *Sesquialtera* and *Trumpet* that Byfield's father had added to the Dallam organ.[45] This suggests that the Dallam organ underwent a substantial rebuild some time before 1769, and that it was probably no longer a transposing instrument. The Worcester Cathedral and St. John's College, Oxford, organs would provide good models for a rather larger "Early English Organ Project" involving a *Double Organ* – as two-manual instruments were termed in the Laudian period. Such was the instrument of Tallis, Byrd and Gibbons. Another great musician of the time, Thomas Tomkins, presided over the Worcester organ. Coming down to the twenty-first century, however, there is currently no entirely authentic medium for the performance of works such as Orlando Gibbons's *Fantasia for Double Organ* or John Lugge's *Voluntary for Double Organ,* and the best that can be done is to use instruments from later in the seventeenth century, notably the Adlington Hall organ, or the Dallam instruments in France.

Further light is shed on the instruments of the Laudian period by the meticulous accounts that King's College, Cambridge, kept in connection with the building of their new Dallam organ in 1606. Rimbault reprints extracts from these as an appendix.[46] The Dallam organ is, of course, the instrument whose magnificent case still graces King's College Chapel today. Unfortunately the precise stoplist does not seem to have survived. Among the accounts one reference is at first puzzling: "Item for brass for the shaking stoppe iiiis."[47] It has often been suggested that the "shaking stoppe" was a form of tremulant, but it is difficult to know why brass would have been required for one of these, except as part of a type of spring. The most common early form of tremulant would have been the *Tremblant Doux*, consisting simply of a weighted wooden flap hanging in the windline. More light is shed on the nature of the Shaking Stop by what is known of the still partially extant Loosemore organ in Nettlecombe Court, Somerset. The 1665 contract for this organ, built by John Loosemore for Sir George Trevelyan at Nettlecombe Court, includes a *Trumpett* and a *Shaking Stopp* as two of the registers. The "Shaking Stopp" still existed at the time when organ historian C.A. Edwards visited the organ in the nineteenth century, and he reported unequivocally that it was not a tremulant but a reed stop forming the bass to the *Trumpet*.[48] If so, it was probably a reed stop of fractional-length, and possibly of the regal variety. In an article on the development of reed stops in English organs, Dominic Gwynn refers to the fact that a non-original label on the *Regal* stop at Blair Atholl reads "Trumpet" and also that, writing on old English organs in the early-eighteenth century, the Hon. Roger North referred to the inadequacies of the "trumpet-regall."[49] Perhaps we are dealing with something akin to these. Only the *Shaking Stop* is mentioned in the King's College accounts as requiring brass. If the *Shaking Stop* was a reed, brass would have been necessary for its tongues, and probably also for its shallots unless wood shallots were used. It is certain at least from this that there were no other reeds in the King's College instrument. Reeds were comparatively rare in English organs before the Civil War, and it will be noted that even quite substantial instruments like those at Worcester Cathedral and St. John's College, Oxford, apparently had only flue stops. The stop list for the Dallam organ in Eton College, already mentioned, specifies five stops, and there is no mention of a *Shaking Stop* in the contract. However, an entry of 1626-27 mentions a payment of twelve shillings to "one that mended the shakeinge stop," and while this might suggest that the *Shaking Stop* was a tremulant that did not count as one of the five speaking stops, other references suggest that the *Shaking Stop* may have counted as a something analogous to the "traps" or "toy-counter" of a modern theatre organ. Thus, Dallam's Turkish organ, already mentioned, contained "five whole stops of pipes" – though only four are actually listed, "viz. one open principal, unison recorder, octavo principal, and a flute." The account then continues that there were "besides [i.e., in addition to these four stops] a shaking stop, a drum and a nightingale."[50] This does seem to suggest that the *Shaking Stop* was, like the drum and nightingale, something akin to a theatre "trap". Perhaps it was not included in the list of "*whole* stops of pipes" because it was a short-compass bass-only reed, like the one at Nettlecombe Court.

Two further points are worthy of notice. First, the winding systems of early English organs were probably sufficiently unstable that a tremulant would in most cases have been totally unnecessary – the wind would have been shaky enough without one! Furthermore, if as in many early organs the wind was raised by pulling up a wedge-shaped bellows with a rope slung over a pulley, it would be possible to obtain a tremolo effect by tugging on the rope – something that I myself have accomplished on the 1787 Tannenberg at Lititz, which has a similar sort of winding system. A further reference does, however, suggest that the *Shaking Stop,* if not a tremulant, did at least perform some kind of undulant function. This is in a seventeenth-century treatise on the viol, where a bowing technique for gracing or ornamenting music is compared to the *Shaking Stop* on the organ:

> Some also affect a Shake or Tremble with the Bow, like the Shaking-Stop of an Organ, but the frequent use thereof is not (in my opinion) much commendable.[51]

This then, is the last link in the puzzle. If the *Shaking Stop* was an early and primitive bass reed, it would invariably have been out of tune – perhaps even deliberately so – resulting in a resonant celeste-like effect. Having an octave of trumpet-regal type pipes in the bass would have produced an undulant bass reed capable of producing this "shaking" effect in any key. At 8-foot (or possibly even at 16-foot or 32-foot) pitch, a slightly out-of-tune regal-type stop might have produced a thunderous effect, capable of shaking the building. In all likelihood, one can conclude, such was the old English *Shaking Stop.*

The mention of King's College, Cambridge, the Hon. Roger North and John Loosemore all together in the preceding paragraph brings to mind another connection. The Loosemore family lived for centuries at Kerscott Farm in Bishops Nympton, Devon. One member of this family, possibly a brother of John Loosemore, was Henry Loosemore. Henry Loosemore is best remembered today for his anthem, *O Lord, Increase our Faith,* for a long time erroneously ascribed to Orlando Gibbons. Henry Loosemore was organist of King's College, Cambridge, from 1627 until his death in 1670. He was also resident organist to the North family at Kirtling Hall, near Newmarket. Kirtling Hall was the country house where the Princess Elizabeth, later Queen Elizabeth I, had been kept under house arrest during the reign of her sister Mary. Loosemore's second job at Kirtling Hall may have supported him in the lean years of the Commonwealth when the organ in King's College Chapel was out of operation. The college paid organbuilder Henry Jennings of Cambridge for dismantling the King's College organ in 1642-43, and in 1644, following an Order in Council requiring the removal of organs, an artisan by the name of Ashley received a further three shillings for taking down the organ case.[52] Loosemore's feeling of despondency at the loss of his instrument doubtless gave way a couple decades later to one of joy when the organ was re-erected after the Restoration of the Monarchy. The old Chaire case was replaced by a new one, and it is unclear how much of the old pipework, if any, was re-used in Lancelot Pease's organ of 1661. But it is nice to think that the main case originally built for Thomas Dallam's transposing Double Organ of 1606 is still there to house the college's organ four centuries later.

:: N O T E S ::

[1]   *St. Augustine on the Psalms,* Psalm CL, section 5. *The Nicene and Post-Nicene Fathers,* ed. Philip Schaff and Henry Wase, Series I (Edinburgh, 14 vols., 1986-1989), 8:157.

[2]   *St. Augustine on the Psalms*, Psalm LVII, section 14. *The Nicene and Post Nicene Fathers,* 8:64. Another early Christian writer, Dio Cassius makes the same point when commenting on the same passages of the Psalms.

[3]   Cambridge, 1996, 11-25.

[4]   Edmonstoune Duncan, *The Story of the Carol* (London, 1911), 38.

[5]   This is explained in considerable detail in the most comprehensive account of the transposing organ to have appeared to date, J. Bunker Clark, *Transposition in Seventeenth Century English Organ Accompaniments and the Transposing Organ.* Detroit Monographs in Musicology, Number 4. (Detroit, 1974), see especially p. 9ff. Clarke concentrates particularly on the musical use of the transposing organ, but his monograph also contains some data on the form of the instrument itself. Also useful in this context is Stephen Bicknell, "The Transposing Organ," *BIOS Journal* 9 (1985), 79-81, as well as the first five chapters of his *The History of the English Organ.* On the musical use of the instrument, see also William Reynolds, "Chirk Castle Organ and Organbook: An Insight into Performance Practice involving a Seventeenth-Century

'Transposing Organ'," *Journal of the British Institute of Organ Studies* 21 (1997), 28-55.

⁶   Clark, *Transposition in Seventeenth Century English Organ Accompaniments and the Transposing Organ*, 33.

⁷   cf. Bicknell, *The History of the English Organ,* (Cambridge: 1996), p. 110f.

⁸   Martin Renshaw, "Documents relating to three Organs in Lichfield Cathedral," *Journal of the British Institute of Organ Studies* 26 (2002), 149.

⁹   Clark, *Transposition in Seventeenth Century English Organ Accompaniments and the Transposing Organ,* p. 28, citing Thomas Morley, *A Plain and Easie Introduction to Practicall Musicke* (1597), ed. R. Alec Harmon, London, 1952), 166.

¹⁰   On the question of pitch in the Tudor period see, for example, Roger Bray, "More Light on Early Tudor Pitch", *Early Music* 8:1 (January 1980), 35-42. Bray argues that early Tudor Quire pitch was so high that music from the period needs to be transposed up about a minor third to bring it to its original pitch.

¹¹   Jo Huddleston, "In Search of Tudor Scaling," *BIOS Reporter*, 24:4 (October 2000), 9.

¹²   The specification is given in Peter Williams, *The European Organ 1450-1850* (London, 1966), 62.

¹³   See John Harper, "Rediscovering the Sound of the English Tudor Organ," *Church Music Quarterly*, (September 2001), 11-12.

¹⁴   Bicknell, *The History of the English Organ,* 28-36.

¹⁵   Martin Goetze, "Transposing Organs and Pitch in England," *FoMRHI Quarterly*, 77 (January 1995), 61-67. See also, Dominic Gwynn, "The Early English Organ Project: Rediscovering the Sound of the Sixteenth Century", *Organ Building: Journal of the Institute of British Organ Building* 2 (2002), 70-77.

¹⁶   See, for example, *The Oxford Companion to Music,* ed. Percy C. Scholes (London, 9th. ed., 1955), 447.

¹⁷   See, for example, *The Shorter Oxford English Dictionary* (Oxford, 3rd. ed., 1973), 2: 1463.

¹⁸   The Latin text with a parallel English translation by J. McKinnon is given in Peter Williams, *A New History of the Organ from the Greeks to the Present Day* (London, 1980), 39f.

[19] Corpus Christi College, Cambridge, MS 473.

[20] Wulfstan of Winchester, *Life of St. Æthelwold*, edited and translated by Michael Lapidge and Michael Winterbottom (Oxford University Press, 1992).

[21] William Sayers, "Irish Evidence for the *De Harmonia Tonorum* of Wulfstan of Winchester", *Mediaevalis* 14 (1991, for 1988), 22-38.

[22] Davies of Kidwelly, *Ancient Rites of Durham*, cited by Edward F. Rimbault, *The Early English Organ Builders and their Works, from the Fifteenth Century to the Great Rebellion; An Unwritten Chapter in the History of the Organ; A Lecture delivered before the College of Organists, November 15th., 1864.* (London, 1865; reprinted by Positif Press, Oxford, 1996), 27f.

[23] Bicknell, *The History of the English Organ*, 53.

[24] Cited by William L. Sumner, *The Organ: Its Evolution, Principles of Construction and Use* (London, 3rd. edition, 1962), 106; see also, James Boeringer, *Organa Britannica: Organs in Great Britain 1660-1860* (3 volumes, Lewisburg, 1983-89), 2:152.

[25] Quoted by Nicholas Thistlethwaite, *The Organs of Cambridge: An Illustrated Guide to the Organs of the University and City of Cambridge* (Oxford, 1983), 22.

[26] The breviary in use at Durham does not appear to have survived in its entirety, but a typical English breviary of the time was the *Hereford Breviary*. This was reprinted at the turn of the last century by the Surtees Society. *The Hereford Breviary,* edited from the Rouen edition of 1505 with collation of manuscripts by Walter Howard Frere and Langton E.G. Brown. Volume I, Surtees Society Publications, vol. 26 for 1903 (London, 1904.) Volume II, Surtees Society Publications, vol. 40 for 1910 (London, 1911.) Volume III, Surtees Society Publications, vol. 46 for 1913 (London, 1915.) The Surtees Society has also published the *Durham Collectar*, which however only lists the prayers (collects) used as part of the breviary – *The Durham Collectar (Durham, Cathedral Library, MS A.IV.19)*, edited by Alicia Corrêa, Surtees Society Publications, vol. 107 for 1991 (London, 1992.) Passages from the Doctors of the Church (of whom there are now considered to be thirty-three rather than just the four of medieval times) are still read in course as part of the Roman Catholic breviary.

[27] *Memorials of Fountains Abbey,* Surtees Society, volume 130 for the Year 1918 (London, 1918), 230-232, citing the Treasurer's Memorandum Book for 1446-1458, fols. 115v. and 117r.

[28] Cited in Cecil Clutton and Austin Niland, *The British Organ* (London, 1963), 47.

[29] Sumner, *The Organ,* 111.

[30] Bicknell, *The History of the English Organ,* 69-90.

[31] George Abbot is today mostly remembered for having shot and killed a gamekeeper while out hunting. This was generally felt to have been the gamekeeper's own fault, since everyone had been told beforehand that the Archbishop was a rotten shot and warned to keep out of his way.

[32] Peter Heylin, *Cyprianus Anglicus* (London, 1668), 537.

[33] Andrew Freeman, "Thomas Dallam's Turkish Organ," *The Organ,* 25 (October 1945), 60. The illustration appears on p. 61.

[34] See Percy Young, "The Notorious Dr. Rimbault (1816-1876)," *Journal of the British Institute of Organ Studies* 22 (1998), 126-139. Among other things, Dr. Rimbault is known to have stolen valuable musical manuscripts from the Library of Christ Church, Oxford and sold them to the British Museum. I certainly do not see any reason, as some have done, to suggest that the drawing is not genuine.

[35] National Pipe Organ Register, on the British Institute of Organ Studies website at <http://www.bios.org.uk> entry No. [N05556].

[36] Sumner, *The Organ,* 108.

[37] A.K. Wickham, *Churches of Somerset* (Dawlish, 1965), pl. 76; see also Nikolaus Pevsner, *North Somerset and Bristol,* The Buildings of England, vol. 13 (Harmondsworth, 1958), 178.

[38] Royal Commission on Historical Monuments – England, *An Inventory of the Historical Monuments in the City of Oxford* (London, 1939), 121.

[39] Roger Bowers, L.S. Colchester and Anthony Crossland, *The Organs and Organists of Wells Cathedral* (8th. ed., Wells, 1987), 3.

[40] *The Arminian Nunnery: Or, A Briefe Description and Relation of the late erected Monasticall Place, called the Arminian Nunnery at Little Gidding in Huntingdonshire. Humbly recommended to the wise consideration of this present Parlia-*

ment. The Foundation is by a Company of Farrars at Gidding. London: Printed for Thomas Underhill, 1641.

[41]   Bicknell, *The History of the English Organ,* 80.

[42]   Sumner, *The Organ,* 116f.

[43]   The stoplist of the Worcester organ is quoted by Bicknell, *The History of the English Organ,* 78 from Colin Beswick, *The Organs of Worcester Cathedral* (Worcester, 1967), 6.

[44]   Clark, *Transposition in Seventeenth Century English Organ Accompaniments and the Transposing Organ,* 69.

[45]   Robert Pacey, *The Organs of Oxford* (Oxford, 1980), 77; see also, Boeringer, *Organa Britannica,* 3:12.

[46]   Rimbault, *The Early English Organ Builders,* 78–86.

[47]   *Ibid.,* 79.

[48]   C.A. Edwards, *Organs and Organ Building* (London, 1881), 14, 119, cited by Michael Wilson, *The English Chamber Organ – History and Development 1650-1850* (London, 1968), 86.

[49]   Dominic Gwynn, "The Development of English Reeds from Robert Dallam to John Gray," *Journal of the British Institute of Organ Studies* 19 (1995), 123.

[50]   Stanley Mayes, *An Organ for the Sultan* (London, 1956), 79.

[51]   Christopher Seymour, *The Division-Viol, or The Art of Playing ex tempore to a Ground* (London, 1665), 10.

[52]   Thistlethwaite, *The Organs of Cambridge,* 51.

ORGANS AND ARMINIANS IN SEVENTEENTH-CENTURY CAMBRIDGE

✺

Nicholas Thistlethwaite

ACCORDING TO THOMAS FULLER, in his *History of the University of Cambridge* (1655), it was during the academic year 1633-4 that the University began to be 'much beautified in *buildings*'. He continued:

> But the greatest alteration was in their *Chappels*, most of them being graced with the accession of Organs. And, seeing Musick is one of the Liberal Arts, how could it be quarrelled at in an University, if they *sang with understanding* both of the matter and manner thereof: Yet some took great distaste thereat as attendancie to superstition.[1]

Fuller's question is ingenuous (or more likely mischievous). In 1630's Cambridge, the introduction and use of a pipe organ had a symbolic value which transcended any purely musical function. It was a political statement: a touchstone of religious orthodoxy or heterodoxy (depending on one's attitude). In an age when religious questions were the dominant intellectual issues of the day, liturgical forms and their accompanying apparatus expressed a point of view. Hence, in the eyes of many, the installation of an organ was a provocative act, not to be ignored.

Those who promoted organs (and altars, stained-glass windows, choirs, the wearing of the surplice, bowing at the Name of Jesus, kneeling to receive the Sacrament, the lighting of candles, and the hearing of confessions) were usually known to contemporaries as 'Arminians'.[2] The term is imprecise and invites confusion with the followers of the Dutch theologian Jacobus Arminius (1560-1609), whose programme and teachings were different, though clearly related. Both branches of the movement took issue with the Calvinism which had dominated the Dutch and English churches for half a century. They questioned Calvinist teaching on predestination ('the mother of faith', in John Calvin's words) with its insistence that God had from eternity destined each human being either to life or to death. In Calvin's scheme of things, the elect were assured of forgiveness and salvation: Christ had died for them, and for them alone, and it was impossible for the elect to forfeit the justifying faith which they had been given. In the same way, the reprobate were helpless to resist their fate which was destruction: neither good works nor repentance availed one jot.

It was a hard doctrine but logical: Calvin's purpose was to insist on the sovereignty of the will of God, which was not to be deflected by human endeavour. He was inspired by passages such as chapter eight of the Epistle to the Romans:

> Moreover whom he did predestinate, them he also called: and whom he called, them he also justified: and whom he justified, them he also glorified. (8:30)

Because Calvinists believed that the die had already been cast (although they would scarcely have welcomed the metaphor), any human intervention designed to provoke repentance or provide a sacramental channel for divine grace was superfluous. It was sufficient for the elect to hear the word of God preached, and to have the assurance that they were saved. Hence ceremony, music, most forms of ecclesiastical art and the use of vestments were rejected. (Another reason was their close identification with the Catholic liturgies which Protestants had cast out as idolatrous and therefore offensive to God.)

Most of the Elizabethan bishops were Calvinists. In the universities, too, Calvinism prevailed. But by the closing decade of the sixteenth century, a few brave spirits were questioning the received wisdom. Grace, they maintained, was not the sole preserve of the elect, as Calvinists believed, but was God's instrument for (potentially) the saving of all mankind, and grace could be channelled through the sacraments. It followed that the celebration of the sacraments, and of divine service generally, should be accompanied by the sort of ceremony and ornament which would do honour to God and awaken the worshipper to its spiritual efficacy. Hearts might be turned and souls saved by the evocation of 'the beauty of holiness'. Tyacke has summarised it thus:

> … the English Arminian mode, as it emerged in the 1630s, was that of com-
> munal and ritualized worship rather than an individual response to preaching
> or Bible reading … Building on the Prayer Book, English Arminians elabo-
> rated a scenic apparatus in which the sacrament of holy communion had a
> key role. The altar, railed in at the east end of churches and often set on a dais,
> became the focal point of worship … As Archbishop Laud put it, "in all ages
> of the Church the touchstone of religion was not to hear the word preached
> but to communicate".[3]

The subject is complex, and its study is not helped by the fact that a broad spectrum of anti-Calvinists were abused by contemporaries as 'Arminians'. Yet its significance for our present purpose is twofold. First, the anti-Calvinists took a much more liberal view of the use of music and organs in worship than their opponents, and, secondly, Cambridge was the forum for some of the most significant skirmishes in the debate between Calvinists and Armin-ians, and the eclipse of the former, and rise of the latter, is, in part, reflected by the re-appearance of organs and (in some cases) choir music in the col-lege chapels, beginning in the 1590s. Many of those who paved the way for the full-blooded Arminianism of the 1630s – men such as Lancelot Andrewes (1555-1626),[4] John Overall (1560-1619)[5] and Richard Neile (1562-1641)[6] – had strong Cambridge connections, and were involved in anti-Calvinist controver-sies that blew up there, in 1595 and 1599, for example.[7] Through their teaching, and their devotional and liturgical practice, they influenced the rising genera-tion of Cambridge Arminians, among them, Richard Montagu (1577-1641),[8] John Cosin (1594-1672)[9] and Matthew Wren (1585-1667),[10] all of whom were associated, directly or indirectly, with the re-introduction of organs.

This is the background to the phenomenon, often described but not al-ways (in its theological aspects) understood: namely, the renaissance of chapel music in early-seventeenth-century Cambridge.

The first three decades of Elizabeth's reign (from 1558) had been barren years as far as organs were concerned. Evidently King's still had two chapel organs in use in 1564-5 when eight pence was paid 'for ij lynes for the greate organs and ij lynes for the lesse organs'.[11] Further payments were made for

'roopes', and 'pullies', and for mending 'the bellowes of ye organes' in succeeding years,[12] but then in 1570-1 the Mundum Book records the receipt of one
hundred shillings 'pro Organis', and 45s 10d 'for thold organ pipes'.[13] Many
years later, the Puritan-inclined Provost Goad reported that 'at his first coming to be Provost [March 1570] the commissioners, appointed by authority
from the queen's majesty, viz. the then Bishop of Ely, my lord of Canterbury
his grace, & others coming into the College Chapel, did appoint & command
[him] to have them [sc. the organs] taken away, & sold to the College use,
which was done'.[14] This is all very mysterious: there was no general order to
remove organs; but both Richard Cox, the Bishop of Ely, and Goad himself
were strong Calvinists, who would have favoured silencing them. Although
the choir was maintained at King's during the Elizabethan era, it is likely that
no organ was heard again in the chapel until the early years of the following
century.[15]

Nor was the picture brighter elsewhere. Various colleges disposed of organs
at this time – Pembroke in 1567,[16] Queens' in 1570,[17] Jesus in 1582-4[18] – and
it seems likely that during the years of the Calvinist ascendancy, between the
mid-1560s and the 1590s, organs were not used in the chapels. Where a choir
was maintained (King's, Trinity) simple homophonic music and metrical psalms
would have been sung unaccompanied; elsewhere, just the psalms.[19]

A change of mood is discernible by the 1590s. The stricter Calvinists
('precisians' or, more usually, 'puritans') had over-played their hand, and with
the defeat of the Spanish Armada in 1588 the likelihood of a successful Catholic invasion receded. Elizabeth herself maintained a Chapel Royal in which
music and ceremony figured prominently, and a more conservative approach
to liturgy lingered, too, in some of the cathedrals – it is surely significant that
many pre-Reformation clergy (canons and former monks) survived as members of cathedral foundations well into Elizabeth's reign.[20] During the 1590s,
Cambridge witnessed the first serious assaults on the Calvinist position: by
William Barrett, in a sermon in Great St. Mary's in 1595, which aroused great
controversy, and in the lectures of Peter Baro (Lady Margaret Professor of Divinity) and John Overall (Regius Professor of Divinity), respectively in 1596
and 1599.[21] Although the establishment held firm, and the offenders were duly

reprimanded, notice was given that Calvinist orthodoxy would no longer go unquestioned.

So it is not surprising that the same decade provides the first evidence of an attempt to raise the musical profile of chapel services in Cambridge, in defiance of the Puritan faction's disapproval of such 'superstitious' innovations.

In 1593, Dr. Thomas Nevile was appointed Master of Trinity College. Nevile (who in 1597 also became Dean of Canterbury, where he inspired a similar revival in the musical life of the cathedral)[22] was a man of immense wealth. In the year following his appointment, he recruited John Hilton to be Organist and Master of the Choristers (Trinity's foundation included six lay clerks, ten choristers, and the organist), and Ian Payne has gathered convincing evidence for the vitality of the college's musical life under Hilton (1594-1609) and his successors, Thomas Wilkinson (1609-12) and Robert Ramsey (1615-44).[23] There is some slight suggestion that an organ may have been in use before Nevile's advent,[24] but the accounts for 1593-4, and the two subsequent years, provide firm evidence of a campaign to renovate an old chapel organ or perhaps install a new one.

1593-4	to Hughe Rose for the Organe		vi^{li} xiij^s iiij^d
	to Andrewe Chapman for	}	
	the frame of the Organe	}	xxiiij^{li}
	for mr Pooleys organe		iij^{li}
	nayles &c for the Organe		iiij^s vi^d
	for yron worke belonginge to	}	
	the Organe as appeareth by	}	xlvij^s ii^d
	a byll of particulars	}	
1594-5	to Hughe Rosse for the Orgaines		v^{li}
1595-6	to Hughe Rose for fynishing ye Orgaines		v^{li}

These slight records are difficult to interpret. By far the largest payment was to the college carpenter (Chapman) for 'the frame of the Organe'. Was this a case? But if so, why not use the term? (which was in common currency at the time). It seems at least as likely that it describes the main structure of the instrument – perhaps even including the soundboard and actions – such as a skillful carpenter might make under the direction of someone with a working knowledge of organs. And who was Hugh Rose? Three payments totalling a little over £16, spread over three years, suggest neither great ambition nor rapid progress. Could this be the college carpenter and a colleague with some knowledge of instruments[26] setting to, and building or renovating an organ in an existing case? Finally, what of 'Mr Pooleys organe'? Was this a temporary hire, or the purchase of an instrument to be dismembered for parts?

Further work was undertaken in 1603-4:[27]

| It: to the Organ mender for tuninge, makinge } | iij^{li} |
| the bellowes, and tuninge of the Stopps } | |

It: to the Joyner for a Perriment on the }	
topp of the organs wth the Scrowles and }	xlj^{s} viij^{d}
7 bowles for the same }	

| It: henges for the newe doore and a lock } | ij^{s} x^{d} |
| wth a crowes foote for the topp of ye Organes } | |

The comparatively modest sum paid for the addition of a pediment, scrolls and urns to the case implies an instrument of no great size, but only six years later a more ambitious project was underway:[28]

Item paid to John York for his owne work and }	
his mans about the mending of the ould organ }	
and for tynn, lead and other newe (*illegible*) }	xlij^{li}
by him for that work as may appeare by his }	
byll	

Item paid to Russell ye painter for painting }	
and guilding ye ould organ-pypes & the }	viij^{li} x^{s}
Case therof }	

| Item paid to the Sawyer for sawing the Clapbord } | |
| and making a lather for the use of the organ } | viij^{s} |

Item to the smythe for Ironworke for the organs }   xxx[s]

Item to John York for making the newe chaire }
orgaine   }   xl[li]

Item to Knuckle the painter for painting & }
guilding therof   }   xiij[li] vj[s] iiij[d]

The expenditure of more than £100 on a major reconstruction of the chapel organ in 1609-10 argues for a serious commitment to the college's musical foundation (and probably also exemplifies a wish not to be outdone by King's, where a completely new organ had been provided in 1605-6 at enormous expense). York[29] reconstructed the old organ and provided a new chair organ in its own case – it is interesting that the two organs were still spoken of as two separate entities, although (presumably) playable from keyboards placed one above the other: organs with two keyboards were still a novelty in England. Informative, too, is the fact that the decoration of the two cases accounted for more than twenty per cent of the cost: a reminder of the later decorative schemes that still survive in part at Stanford-on-Avon and (concealed) at Tewkesbury.

Over the next few years, more money was expended on the organ. York received £4 'for mendinge the organs' in 1611-12, and two labourers received 33s 8d for assisting him. The joiner was paid 10s, and 12s was given 'for six deales for stopps' (stop rods, perhaps?).[30] In 1613-14 more repairs were needed. 'John' (York, presumably) received 33s 10d for 'him selfe and his man for twentie dayes and for parchement leather glewe &c', and two further payments of 13s 4d 'for mending the organe againe'; he also had 2s 6d 'for mending the smale organe', and nine shillings 'for 60[li] of leade for the Organ'.[31] During the following year (1615) King James I visited the college. It may have been in connection with this royal visitation that £25 was spent on 'mending ye organs'; the work was undertaken by Stephen Brittaine, who received a further £4 ('this yeares allowance') in 1617-18.[32] The series of accounts then breaks until 1637.

The construction and maintenance of organs at Trinity College is clear evidence of a desire to promote a less austere, more 'theatrical' style of worship, in which choir music, organs and possibly viols featured.[33] Payne has also noted increasing expenditure on the external trappings of worship at this time.[34] Although it is necessary to be cautious about identifying these innovations of the 1590s and 1600s as 'Arminianism' (they were certainly not 'Laudianism'), there is no doubt that they prepared the way for the changes of the 1620s and 30s that were to prove so controversial.

The other Cambridge college to follow a similar path at this period was King's. The mysterious silencing of the chapel organs by the commissioners in 1570 has already been mentioned. When a further episcopal visitation took place in 1603, Roger Goad was still Provost – an elderly survivor of Elizabethan Calvinism. It was probably a sign of the growing confidence of the anti-Calvinist party that they felt able to engineer a challenge to Goad about the college's failure to fulfil its statutory obligation to maintain an organ. The result was the commissioning of the Thomas Dallam organ of 1605-6.

The new organ took nearly fourteen months to make and cost the enormous sum of £396 3s 9d. Dallam moved his workshop to Cambridge, and he and his men were paid wages of thirty shillings each week by the college. The accounts[35] record further payments for their bedding, laundry, 'dyett in the hall', and (additionally) 'bread and beer'. They also reveal that the college supplied the materials required to make the organ, all of which are carefully itemised in the schedule. Some of the details are suggestive: 'ebony for kayes' [sc. keys], 'packthred to bynd the pypes', 'flannell clothe to laye under the kayes', 'fustian to cast the mettell uppon' (so the pipes were made on site), 'chalke to lay upon the fustian', and 'brasse for the shaking stop' (i.e. a tremulant); but although the accounts confirm that the organ consisted of 'greate' and 'chayre' organs, housed in separate cases, they cast no further light on its musical design.

Dallam was not the only contractor involved in the construction of this instrument. A Cambridge carpenter was paid £16 for 'the frame of tymber whereon the organs [stand]', but a specialist contractor, one Hartop, was brought in to make the cases. He and his men were engaged on the job for ten months and the college paid for the carriage of his tools to and from the town. When the cases were complete they were embellished by 'Knockle the

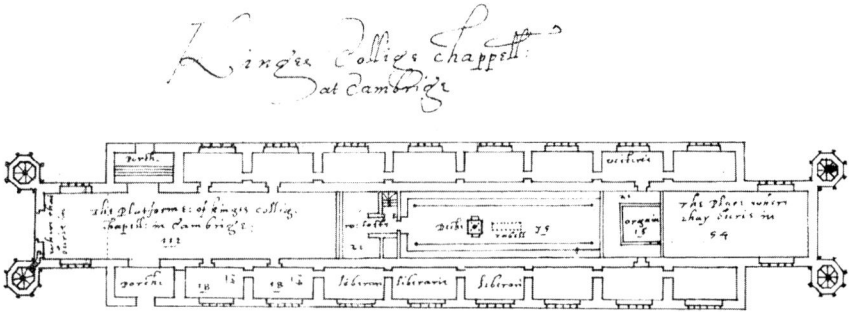

Figure 1 – Plan of King's College Chapel, *ca.* 1609, showing the Communion Table ('tabell) placed on the east-west axis between the stalls, and the 'orgain" to the east, where the mediæval altar had stood. *R.I.B.A. Drawings Collection, Smythson no. 1/4 (1), reproduced by kind permission of the Royal Institute of British Architects.*

Limber' (probably the same man who was paid for similar work at Trinity in 1609-10) with gilding and colour. Four pipes in the Chayre and five in the Great Organ were embossed, and Knockle also gilded two stars and the '2 figures or pictures that stand in the greate Organ'.

It is a common misconception that the present main case on the screen at King's dates from 1605-6. This is extremely unlikely. Dallam's organ stood to the east of the choirstalls, on the site of the pre-Reformation altar. It is shown in this position on Robert Smythson's plan of *ca.* 1609 (Figure 1).[36] The communion table was placed between the stalls – the usual liturgical arrangement in the Jacobean Church. Consequently, there would only have been one front, and (as Bicknell has shown)[37] the accounts suggest that it had five towers, including a large 'middle tower'. The present main case with its receding perspective and small centre tower is likely to date from after 1660. The 'frame of tymber' mentioned in the 1605-6 accounts may have been a low gallery or platform, intended to raise the organ above the floor. However, it had been moved to the screen by 1632-3 when the communion table was set 'altar-wise' against a new eastern screen in the third bay of the chapel.[38] It seems possible that the move occurred as early as 1613 when Dallam was paid £30 for unspecified work 'circa Organ'. He and his men were in Cambridge for eight weeks, and (significantly) Chapman the carpenter was paid £7 10s for associated work.[39]

Street plan of Cambridge during the reign of Queen Elizabeth I:
one of the contemporary versions of the Braun and Hogenberg map of *ca.* 1575.
Reproduced by permission of the Syndics of Cambridge University Library.

When it was completed in 1606, Dallam's instrument must (surely) have created quite a stir in conservative Protestant circles in the University. An ambitious organ (was it the first in England to have two keyboards?) of considerable visual splendour, it would have been an affront to Provost Goad and his fellow Calvinists. Perhaps it was intended as a snub to the old man by his opponents within the Fellowship.

With the installation of organs in Trinity and King's, the first chapter in their reintroduction to Cambridge came to an end. Both colleges had choral foundations, and so there was a certain practicality in the provision of instruments – at least to more liberal minds – but the succeeding phase of the story was to see organs installed in chapels which had no choral forces (or had to create them) and in which their introduction was part of an aggressive anti-Calvinist policy intended by its promoters (the Laudian bishops and college heads) to alter the character of the Established Church. There can be little doubt that this policy helped to foment the discord that led ultimately to the tragic conflicts of the 1640s and 50s.

A manuscript entitled 'Innovations in Religion & abuses in Government in ye University of Cambridge'[40] casts light on the ways in which worship had changed in the college chapels by the early-1640s. At Christ's College, for example:

> on Surplice dayes they sing the severall parts of divine service save y[e] chapters [lessons], and in theire singing of hymnes [canticles] and anthemes they use organs & sing alternatim. Many things in their service is [sic] performed non-intelligibly to men not acquainted with pricksong [polyphony] ...[41]

Something similar was going on at Queens':

> the Confession is sung by all on Sundayes & holy dayes.

> At y[e] repetition of y[e] doxologie & creeds all stand up with theire faces toward the East.

> Anthemes are used instead of singing of psalmes with y[e] Organs.[42]

Meanwhile, at St John's:

> At ye west end are a paire of organs set up by D[r] Beale, in y[e] wainscot of wch is a hollow place capacious enough for an image [though it appeared not to have one] just above y[e] entrance into y[e] Chappell ...

> Singing of [metrical] psalmes in ye usuall & accustomed way of ye Church is thrust out of the chappell and in ye roome thereof Anthems are brought in …

> At ye second service [Communion or Ante-Communion] three officiate, the principall Minister, Epistler & Gospeller, all three bowe together three severall tymes before they begin that part of service …[43]

Jesus (with 'a lately erected paire of organs on ye back of wch are these three letters gilt IHS …')[44] and Pembroke ('Organs wth anthemes are used insteed of ye singing psalmes')[45] were guilty of similar innovations, but the greatest offender of all, in the eyes of this particular observer, was Peterhouse:

> On solemne dayes a pot of incense is set upon ye steps of ye Altar, and as ye smoke abounds the Organs & voices in ye Chappell are raised …

> The service is sung or said in severall places, the second service at ye Altar wth diverse bowings & cringeings. The Letany [sc. Litany] on Sundayes & holy dayes is sung by two kneeling before ye Altar. Latine service on comon [common or Communion?] dayes is used.

> In ye Inner chappell hang divers novel orders wch are vigourously imposed, as noe wearing of gloves in ye chappell, noe sneezing, noe blowing of noses, noe scratching of ye head, noe yawning, noe spitting upon ye pavement & ye like …

> The Schollers in ye Colledge are exceedingly imployed to learne pricksong to ye great losse of theire time & prejudice of theire studdyes …[46]

The author has a great deal more to say about the ornamentation of college chapels with hangings, painted ceilings, stained glass, altar rails, altar coverings, candlesticks, marble floors, and carpets, to the introduction of which – under the influence of the Arminians, emboldened by royal patronage and the advancement of Laud to the Archbishopric of Canterbury in 1633 – the various college account books bear witness. What becomes clear, however, is that one of the most significant (and, to Calvinists, objectionable) results of the triumph of the anti-Calvinists was the installation of organs in at least eight chapels.[47]

With one notable exception, the documentation of these organs of the 1630s is poor. The earliest may have been the instrument commissioned in

1634 for Jesus College. Under the Mastership of William Beale (appointed in 1632) worship in the college chapel had begun to move in a Laudian direction, with the purchase of hangings and Latin service books.[48] He departed for St. John's in 1634, and his successor, Richard Sterne (a leading Arminian, who was to attend Laud on the scaffold) continued his policy. On 18 October of that year the college made an agreement with Robert Dallam of Westminster (son of Thomas) for a new organ costing £200. It was sealed two days later. Dallam's work was evidently complete by 27 July 1635, when it was noted

Datae sunt Roberto Dallam per Praesentem et majorem partem Sociorum duodecim librae ultra summam de qua pepigerant.[49]

£12 have been given to Robert Dallam by the President and senior fellows over and above the sum which they had agreed.

Although it is not strictly germane, it is worth pausing here to correct a myth. Ever since Robert Willis and John Willis Clark in their monumental *Architectural History of the University of Cambridge* (1886) published an abbreviated version of this particular entry in the college archives, and mis-read 'per Praes' as 'pro Peds',[50] there has been speculation that Robert Dallam's organ had a set of pedals.[51] However, there is no doubt about the correct reading. Those searching for the earliest English pedals must now start with the remains of toe pedals at Adlington Hall (*ca.* 1693?)[52] and the documented examples at St Paul's Cathedral (1720-1) and St Mary Redcliffe, Bristol (1726).[53]

Jesus remained in the forefront of Laudian endeavours in Cambridge. The organist's post was funded by a levy on all college members except the sizars (poor scholars)[54] and the Puritan commentator of the early-1640s noted the existence of an altar 'with stepps to it and rayles before it', blue hangings behind, 'Cherubim heads gilt' above, and a cloth embroidered with gold thread thrown over it.[55] Unfortunately, nothing further is known about Dallam's organ, except that he was paid five shillings for tuning it in May 1638, and 'wire for the clock and organ' was purchased in June 1640 for 1s 10d.[56]

Having proved himself an energetic promoter of Arminianism, William Beale was rapidly promoted. There was a disputed succession to the mastership of St John's in 1634. The King took the opportunity to impose Beale.[57] A programme of Laudian reforms began almost at once, with stained glass, hangings, cushions for the altar, the painting of the ceiling and the introduction of a series of sixteen sacred pictures placed around the walls of the chapel. On 28 July 1635 an agreement was made with Robert Dallam for a new organ. It survives, and as it is the only pre-Commonwealth document to describe the musical specification of a Cambridge organ, will be quoted in full.

> Articles & Covenants of Agreem[en]t indented made & agreed upon the eight and twentieth day of July A[nn]o d[o]m[in]i 1635. Annoq[ue] Regni Regis Caroli Angliae &c. undecimo. Betweene William Beale doctor of divinity & Master of the Colledge of St John the Evangelist in the University of Cambridge the Fellowes & Schollers of the same Colledge on the one p[ar]t & Robert Dallam of the Citty of Westminster Organmaker on the other p[ar]t as followeth. Viz\[t],
>
> Imprimis the s[ai]d Robert Dallam for him his executors & adm[inistrat]ors doth covenant and grant to & with the s[ai]d M[aste]r Fellowes & Schollers and theyr successors by these p[rese]nts in maner & forme following. That is to say that he the s[ai]d Robert Dallam his executors & assignes for the consideration hereafter expressed shall & will at his & theyr owne proper costs & charges make & finish one payre of organs or Instrum[en]t to conteyne six severall stoppes of pipes every stoppe conteyning fortynine pipes (viz) one diapason most part to stand in sight one Principall of Tynne one Recorder of Wood one small Principall of Tynne one two & twentieth of Tynne with sound boords Conveyances Conducts Roller boord Carriages & keyes two bellowes & wind trunkes with the case & carving onely with all other necessaries thereunto belonging finding all maner of stuffe both of yron brasse Tynne Timber & wainscoate incident to the making & finishinge of the s[ai]d Instrum[en]t w[hi]ch he the s[ai]d Robert Dallam shall make up & finish & sett up in the Chappell of St Johns Colledge afores[ai]d betweene the day of the date of these pr[esen]ts & the first day of July now next ensuing. 1636
>
> In consideration of wh[ic]h worke and organs to be made finished & sett up as is afors[ai]d the s[ai]d M[aste]r Fellowes & Schollers doe covenant grant & agree for them & theyr successors to & with the s[ai]d Robert Dallam his executors adm[inistrat]ors & Assignes by these pr[esen]ts that they the s[ai]d M[aste]r Fellowes & schollers shall & will well and truely pay or cause to be payd unto the s[ai]d Robert Dallam his executors adm[inistrat]ors or Assignes the sume of Nine score & five pounds of lawfull money of England in maner & forme following (viz) Fower score pounds at the sealing & delivery of these presents, and forty pounds more at the delivry of the materialls be-

longing to the s[ai]d Instrument And the rest at the full Conclusion & finishing of the s[ai]d worke And also that they the s[ai]d M[aste]r Fellowes and
Schollers and theyr successors shall beare & defray the charges of Carriage of
these Organs & materialls thereof from the Citty of Westminster to St Johns
Colledge afores[ai]d and all tooles incident thereunto & of Recarriage of the
same from thence back againe to Westminster. In witness whereof as well the
s[ai]d M[aste]r Fellowes & Schollers theyr Com[m]on seale as also the s[ai]d
Robert Dallam his seale to these pr[esen]ts Interchangeably have putt the
day & yeare first above written[58]

It is interesting to note that the parties to the agreement clearly expect
the new organ to be made in Dallam's London workshop; it provides specifically for him to find all the 'stuffe' (materials) for the construction of the organ – unlike his father's instrument for King's, thirty years earlier – and almost
half the contract price is to be paid on sealing the agreement so that he can
get to work. A further major installment will be due when the organ parts are
delivered to the college: by that stage, the instrument will be well on the way
to completion. The stop list is, of course, of the greatest interest, though the
picture is slightly confused by the reference to 'six severall stoppes' preceding
a schedule of just five. Possibly a stopped diapason was omitted or taken for
granted.[59]

The contract appears to include the provision of 'the case and carving', although the wording ('onely') is ambiguous. Until recently, it had been widely
assumed that the main case which survived in the chapel until 1868, when a
new chapel was built, and was then transferred to Old Bilton, was the Dallam
case.[60] This assumption now seems less secure. It has marked affinities with
Cambridge cases of the later-seventeenth century, and its survival through the
years of the Commonwealth rests on no documentary evidence. It now seems
possible that no pre-1642 Cambridge cases have come down to us.

The college accounts refer obliquely to the installation of the organ:
there are various payments for the construction of an organ loft and stairs
between January and June 1636 (a total of £21 13s 3d);[61] but none of the payments to Dallam appear. However, some light is cast by a college order that
'old and uselesse' pieces of college plate should be 'sould att London', and that
the money raised 'should goe towardes the Organs which since was wholy

payd for with Mr Bouthes money' (this seems to have been a legacy). The sale raised £52 10s 6d.[62]

Dallam returned to repair and tune the organ in August 1637 (forty shillings) and March 1639 (£2 6s 8d, plus 1s 4d for his 'entertainment'), although the following year the college recruited a local man, Henry Jenings, to undertake the (annual?) tuning for thirty shillings.

Beale attempted to create a chapel choir, supported by endowments, at St. John's but failed.[63] Down the road at Peterhouse, John Cosin (Master of the college from 1634, and the most notorious of Cambridge Arminians) was more successful.

The new chapel had been built by Cosin's predecessor, Matthew Wren, between 1628 and 1632. Cosin, however, was determined to introduce the full panoply of Arminian liturgy, and within a short time, the services at Peterhouse were 'noted above all the Towne for popish superstitious practises'.[64] Cosin's innovations included an organ. Documentation is scanty, and is confused by the fact that the college seems to have acquired two organs during the 1630s, one for the chapel ('organum pneumaticum') at a cost of £140, and another smaller instrument, given by Cosin's friends John and Alice Peyton, 'that the Scholars might practise sacred music in the Parlour'.[65] In 1635-6, £8 was spent on building an organ loft, and in November 1637 £5 was paid for the organ case. This second entry may relate to the decoration of the case, for a schedule of desiderata survives in Cosin's hand and includes 'ornatus organi pneumatici'.[66] The same paper (which is undated) records a donation of £200 by the Master and Fellows 'ad organum Pneumaticum et Libros corales', so, in all probability the organ was installed in the period 1635-7, but lacked the sort of painted and gilded casework that the organs at King's and Trinity exhibited. The reference to 'Libros corales' brings us back to Cosin's choir. Ian Payne has described in detail the evidence for the creation of a choral foundation at Peterhouse during the 1630s.[67] If the surviving Peterhouse part-books represent the choir's repertoire, this was an ambitious undertaking, and the organ would have played a critical part. Unfortunately, no record survives of its maker, but Robert Dallam must be a strong candidate given his connections with the royal court and with Cambridge.

The other three colleges known to have used organs at this period may be dealt with more briefly, in the absence of significant documentation. The Christ's College accounts show evidence of work on the organ loft and payments to an 'organist' (organ maker?) in 1636-7. Not all the entries are specific, but those most likely to relate to the organ amount to just over £60.[68] It is, of course, possible that other payments were made by individuals, and not recorded in the college's books, as happened elsewhere.[69] Under Edward Martin, Laud's former Chaplain, Queens' became one of the more ritually 'advanced' colleges. In January 1637 the sum of £114 8s 1d was allocated 'for the Organs', and later that year the organ 'wheele' was mended and a 'Ring & Pin' purchased at a cost of 3s 4d.[70] In November 1637 5s 6d was paid 'for 2 brasen pulliss for ye Organ, & a bonfire Nov: 5th'; in the following month Henry Jennings was paid fifteen shillings 'for cleaning & tuning ye Organ'.[71] The following February 'Fr: Wright' was paid for half a day's work 'to help ye joiner set ye Cover over ye Organ'.[72] Whether this was temporary protection while building work went on, or an ornamental (or acoustic?) feature is unexplained. Finally, of the 'organes' said to be in use at Pembroke College in *ca.* 1640 not a trace survives in the records.[73] But given the college's Arminian pedigree, their existence is wholly possible.

By the late-1630s, the ascendancy of the anti-Calvinists in Cambridge was evident to all. The Puritan foundations of Emmanuel and Sidney Sussex maintained an old-fashioned Calvinist style of worship, and a number of other colleges seem to have made only half-hearted gestures in the direction of the new orthodoxy, but a combination of royal patronage used to place 'sound' men in influential posts, and the aspirations of the ambitious to please their masters, lent an Arminian complexion to (probably) a majority of colleges. Laud's plans to make a visitation of the University *ca.* 1636 undoubtedly spurred some on (although the visitation never took place): at Trinity College, for example, the communion table was moved to the east end and railed in that year, and £50 was spent on 'paynting and guilding the Organ'.[74]

Organs were undoubtedly potent symbols of the triumph of Arminianism, and so when that movement went into eclipse, organs were highly vulnerable. The religious tensions exacerbated by Laud and his minions contributed in a major way to the outbreak of war in 1642. Cambridge was a prize waiting to fall into the lap of Parliament because of the strength of opposition to the Crown in Eastern England. Beale was arrested in September 1642, Cosin accompanied the queen into exile in France, and by 1643, Cromwell was in control of Cambridge and had requisitioned St John's College as a prison for miscreants. Later that year, the notorious iconoclast, William Dowsing, was given a commission to purge Cambridge of its idols. He began at Peterhouse.

Dowsing would certainly have included organs among the 'monuments of superstition and idolatry' that the Parliamentary ordinance of August 1643 required him to remove.[75] But in the college chapels, he found none. They had been spirited away. The college accounts reveal something of the story. At Peterhouse, Anthony Fawkner was paid 9s 6d on 23 April 1643 'for worke about the frames for the blew hanging done in the Chapple & remooving the organ pipes'.[76] Fifteen shillings was spent at Jesus College 'for taking down the Organs'.[77] St John's paid Henry Jennings £1 1s 'for taking down the pictures and the orgens and whiting the wall' early in 1643, and then a further four shillings 'for taking downe the litle organ' (were there two organs in the chapel?).[78] More than a year later 6s 8d was paid 'to old Dowsy when the Organ case was taken away'.[79] Jennings was also employed at King's during Lent 1643, when 'Mgro Gennynge' received £2 for 'taking downe le Organ', and an unnamed joiner who assisted him was paid £1 1s. In the summer of 1644, 'Ashley' received three shillings 'pro taking downe the Orgaine case' (which, presumably, Dowsing had spared when he visited in December 1643).[80] The ubiquitous Jennings surfaces also at Trinity, where he was paid forty-five shillings in 1642-3 'for taking downe ye Organ pipes', and George Woodruffe (carpenter) fifteen shillings 'for taking downe ye organs & hanginge'.[81] It is interesting to note that three colleges (and possibly more) went to the trouble of employing an organ builder to dismantle and (presumably) store their instruments: evidently they were hoping that the time would come when they could be reinstated.

That time would indeed come — although it is not entirely clear how many organs survived to be reinstalled.[82] For the moment, the Arminians were routed, and the Calvinists (with the temporary support of an unstable coalition of sectaries and millenarians) had the upper hand. Not only the organs but the episcopal Church of England itself was dismantled. Robert Dallam emigrated to Brittany. But he, and the spiritual heirs of the Arminians, would be back.

ACKNOWLEDGEMENTS

The author wishes to express his gratitude to the custodians of the various college archive collections referred to, both for their assistance and for permission to quote from material in their care. They, and the staff of Cambridge University Library, have been invariably helpful.

: : N O T E S : :

[1]   Thomas Fuller, *The History of the University of Cambridge since the Conquest*, (London, 1655), 167.

[2]   For a long time, historians preferred the term 'Laudian', thus identifying the movement with one of its leading exponents. However, it was not in contemporary usage, and a good many Arminians had reservations about Archbishop Laud's strategy and character. The term 'Laudian' also tends to focus on ceremonial innovations to the exclusion of doctrinal issues. 'Arminian' is to be preferred.

[3]   Nicholas Tyacke, *Anti-Calvinists: The Rise of English Arminianism ca.1590-1640*, (Oxford, 1987) 246.

[4]   Master of Pembroke Hall, 1589; Dean of Westminster, 1601; Bishop of Chichester, 1605; of Ely, 1609; of Winchester, 1619.

[5]   Fellow of Trinity, 1581; Regius Professor of Divinity, 1595; Master of St. Catharine's College, 1598; Dean of St. Paul's, 1602; Bishop of Coventry and Lichfield, 1614; of Norwich, 1618.

[6]   Matriculated at St. John's College 1580; Dean of Westminster, 1605; Bishop of Rochester, 1608; of Coventry and Lichfield, 1610; of Lincoln, 1614; of Durham, 1617; Archbishop of York, 1632. There is some evidence that Neile was a comparatively late convert to Arminianism (early 1600s), but like all

converts, he compensated for his late awakening by his zeal for the cause (Tyacke, *Anti-Calvinists*: 110).

⁷   On Cambridge at this period, and the religious controversies which coloured the life of the University, see, H.C. Porter, *Reformation and Reaction in
Tudor Cambridge*, (Cambridge, 1958), (reprinted 1972). Tyacke, *Anti-Calvinists*, is
the foremost modern treatment of the subject generally.

⁸   Fellow of King's College, 1597; Dean of Hereford, 1616; Bishop of
Chichester, 1628; of Norwich, 1638.

⁹   Canon of Durham, 1625; Master of Peterhouse, 1635; Dean of Peterbor-
ough, 1640; Bishop of Durham, 1660.

¹⁰   Master of Peterhouse, 1626; Dean of Windsor, 1628; Bishop of Hereford,
1634; of Norwich, 1635; of Ely. 1638.

¹¹   King's College Archives (KCA): Mundum Books, vol. 15 (1565-9)
[KCAR/4/1/16]: Custos Ecclesiae, 1564-5 [no foliation or pagination].

¹²   KCAR/4/1/16: Custos Ecclesiae, 1566-7, 1567-8, 1568-9.

¹³   KCAR/4/1/17: Custos Ecclesiae, 1570-1.

¹⁴   Cited in, Ian Payne, *The Provision and Practice of Sacred Music at Cambridge Colleges and Selected Cathedrals ca. 1547 - ca. 1646*, (New York & London,
1993), 56. The original is said to be in a MS Volume of Visitations [May 1603]
in KCA.

¹⁵   References in the Mundum Books from 1583 onwards to the purchase
of chords for the organ, noted by Payne (idem), do not appear in the chapel
account, and almost certainly refer to an instrument elsewhere in the college.

¹⁶   Ian Payne, 'Music at Jesus College, Cambridge, ca. 1557-1679' [sic], in,
Proceedings of the Cambridge Antiquarian Society, [PCAS] (1987), 76:102; cites
Pembroke College Archives, B: 184 as source.

¹⁷   Payne, *Provision and practice*: 57.

¹⁸   Payne, 'Music at Jesus College', *PCAS*, 99.

¹⁹   Payne's *Provision and practice* is the principal modern study of chapel
music in Cambridge during this period, and casts much light on a previously obscure subject. It should be noted, however, that his accounts of organs
in particular chapels do not in every case exhaust the documentary evidence
(e.g. Trinity College in the early-1600s).

[20]   The last monk of Durham Priory survived as a minor canon of Durham Cathedral until the 1590s.

[21]   Porter, *Reformation and Reaction*: 281-2, 376-90, 398-407.

[22]   Patrick Collinson, Nigel Ramsey and Margaret Sparks (eds.), *A History of Canterbury Cathedral*, (Oxford, 1995), 439-41.

[23]   Ian Payne, 'The musical establishment at Trinity College, Cambridge, 1546-1644', in, *PCAS* (1985), 74:53-69.

[24]   Trinity College Archives [TCA], Senior Bursar's Accounts [SBA], 1585-6, fol. 46v: 'To Hughe mending the instrume[n]t and virginalls at the audit [5 shillings]'. This could be the chapel organ, but it could equally well have been a chamber organ or another type of instrument altogether.

[25]   TCA: SBA 1593-4, fol. 263r; 1594-5, fol. 286r; 1595-6, fol. 307r.

[26]   See the reference to the 1585-6 repair by 'Hughe' in footnote 24 above.

[27]   TCA: SBA 1603-4, fol. 60r.

[28]   TCA: SBA 1609-10, fols. 172v, 173r.

[29]   'York' also did small repair work to the organs of Magdalen College, Oxford on a number of occasions between 1616 and 1637, as well as other minor works around the chapel there. It may be the same man. See, John Harper, 'The Dallam organ in Magdalen College, Oxford', in, *BIOS Journal* 9 (1985), 60-1.

[30]   TCA: SBA 1611-12, fol. 198r.

[31]   TCA: SBA 1613-14, fol. 226v.

[32]   TCA: SBA 1614-15, fol. 256r; 1617-18, fol. 329r.

[33]   Payne, 'Trinity College, Cambridge, 1546-1644', in, *PCAS* (1985), 74:61-2.

[34]   *Ibid.*, 62, 64.

[35]   The accounts survive in the mundum books: KCAR/4/1/23 (1605-6): no foliation. They were first published in *The Ecclesiologist* (vol. 20, December 1859: 314ff), and then in Edward J. Hopkins and Edward F. Rimbault, *The Organ, Its History and Construction* (2nd edition, London, 1870), 62-6.

[36]   R.I.B.A. Drawings Collection, Smythson No. 1/4. Reproduced in, Trevor Cooper (ed.), *The Journal of William Dowsing*, Woodbridge 2001: plate 23.

37 Stephen Bicknell, *The History of the English Organ*, (Cambridge, 1996), 74.

38 The accounts yield no evidence of significant expenditure on the organ at the time of the removal of the altar, although Robert Dallam was paid £22 0d 6d for unspecified work in 1635 – KCAR/4/27: 1634-5.

39 Other significant payments at this period included £10 to Dallam in 1617 for repairs, £11 13s 4d to 'Mro. Hamlin' for further repairs in 1622, and £22 0s 6d to [Robert] Dallam in 1635, again for repairs [KCAR/4/24: 1616-17; KCAR/4/25: 1621-22; KCAR/4/27: 1634-5].

40 British Library, Harleian 7019: fols. 52-93.

41 *Ibid.,* fol. 84.

42 *Ibid.,* fol. 78.

43 *Ibid.,* fol. 74.

44 *Ibid.,* fol. 80.

45 *Ibid.,* fol. 81.

46 *Ibid.,* fols. 71, 73.

47 Trinity, King's, Peterhouse, Pembroke, Christ's, Queens', Jesus and St. John's. As far as is known, Caius, Emmanuel, Magdalen, Clare, Corpus Christi, Sidney Sussex, St. Catharine's and Trinity Hall did not have organs in this period, although some of these are criticised in Harleian MS 7019 for musical or liturgical innovations.

48 See, Payne, 'Music at Jesus College, Cambridge, c1557-1679', in, *PCAS* (1987), 76:99.

49 Jesus College Archives: COL 1.1: 20 October 1634, 27 July 1635.

50 Robert Willis and John Willis Clark, *The Architectural History of the University of Cambridge,* (Cambridge, 1886), 2: 142, note 4.

51 See, for instance: B.J. Maslen, 'The earliest English organ pedals', in, *Musical Times*, vol. 101 (1960): 579; Nicholas Thistlethwaite, *The Organs of Cambridge*, (Oxford, 1983), 46; Bicknell, *History of the English Organ*: 86.

52 John Mander, 'Some notes on the organ in Adlington Hall', in, *BIOS Journal* 10 (1986), 67-8.

53 Nicholas Thistlethwaite, *The Making of the Victorian Organ*, (Cambridge, 1990), 14.

[54] Payne, 'Music at Jesus College': *PCAS* (1987), 76:99. The first organist was George Loosemore (1635-41); he was probably a younger brother of Henry and was later Organist of Trinity College (1660-82).

[55] BL Harleain MS 7019: fol. 80.

[56] Jesus College Archives, A/C 1.3: 943, 964.

[57] Edward Miller, *Portrait of a College* (Cambridge, 1961), 21-2.

[58] St John's College Archives [SJCA]: Lease Book 1627-48 [C8.2]: 253.

[59] For discussion of compasses and stop lists at this period, see, J. Bunker Clark, *Transposition in Seventeenth Century English Organ Accompaniments and the Transposing Organ*, (Detroit, 1974), 23-37; Bicknell, *English Organ*: 69-90.

[60] See, for example, Cecil Clutton and Austin Niland, *The British Organ* (London, 1963), 175, 184.

[61] Rentals Book, 1634-49 [SJCA, SB4.5]: f.49v.

[62] *Ibid.,* f.58r.

[63] Payne, *Provision and practice*: 108.

[64] Lucy Hutchinson (ed. J. Sutherland), *Memoirs of the Life of Colonel Hutchinson,* (Oxford, 1973), 25; cited in Cooper (ed.), *William Dowsing*: 156.

[65] Thomas Alfred Walker, *Peterhouse* (Cambridge, 1935), 57. According to Francis Blomefield, the Peytons' gift was recorded on a Table of Benefactors in the chapel, which noted that the organ was valued at £40; see, Blomefield, *Collectanea Cantabrigiensia* (Norwich 1750): 155. An entry in the accounts recording the expenditure in 1635 of £4 4s 1d for two journeys to Doddington 'circa organum ... ex dono Dominae Peyton' probably refer to this parlour organ (PA, Bursar's Roll, 1635).

[66] Walker, *Peterhouse*: 128.

[67] Payne, *Provision and practice*: 94-100.

[68] Christ's College Archives, Accounts 1622-39 [sic]: fols. 372 & 373.

[69] The accounts are in any case incomplete at this period, with none surviving for 1638-45.

[70] Queens' College Archives (Cambridge University Library), QC 27: 14; Journale 6: fols. 73 & 74.

[71] QCA, Journale 6: fol. 76.

[72] QCA, Journale 6: fol. 77.

[73] BL Harleian MS 7019: fol. 81. See also Payne, *Provision and practice*: 108-109.

[74] Payne, *Provision and practice*: 93-4.

[75] On Dowsing, see, the introductory essays in (ed.) Cooper, *William Dowsing*.

[76] Cited Payne, *Provision and practice*: 165.

[77] JCA A/C 1.3: 1030 (1642-3).

[78] SJCA: Rentals 1634-49, fols. 226v, 230r.

[79] *Ibid.,* fol. 252v. 'Dowsy' is unlikely to refer to William Dowsing, but it is not impossible.

[80] KCA KCAR/4/1/28: 1642-3; KCAR/4/1/29: 1643-4 (Custos Ecclesiae).

[81] TCA SBA 1642-3: fol. 59v.

[82] See, Nicholas Thistlethwaite, *The Organs of Cambridge* (Oxford, 1983), passim.

SOME OBSERVATIONS ON THREE KEYBOARD-COMPOSERS

FRESCOBALDI, J.S. BACH AND DOMENICO SCARLATTI

Peter Williams

WHAT FOLLOWS IS A MIXED SERIES OF OBSERVATIONS on certain keyboard pieces of three exceptionally gifted keyboard-composers. Two particular aspects of Frescobaldi are looked at. First, his verifiable influence on a pair of distinguished successors, Froberger and J.S. Bach; and secondly, his skill in handling certain thematic material that would have offered models to any organist coming into contact with his central, formative, and dominating publications. Thirdly, a major work of Bach is looked at in the light of a different kind of speculation: how biographical details could, and then perhaps should, affect one's whole approach to it. And finally, a different kind of speculation: how the means by which we know a major repertory − i.e. the nature of its transmission between the composer and a player today − bear on intimate details for the performer today.

What these speculations have in common is that they are prompted by a keyboardist's responses to exceptional music, and are all practical in origin. I have come across them all in day-to-day playing at the keyboard. No grand theory or hermeneutic scheme is behind the items, only the belief that music is (in a sense peculiar to itself) a 'language', constructed from particular 'vocabularies' and 'grammars' which are in themselves pleasing, always historically located and, in important cases, exercising a strong influence on the later speakers of that language.

FRESCOBALDI'S IDIOM

In the opening movement of the *Fiori musicali* (pub. 1635) – a little Toccata – there appears, as if slipped in, a tiny melodic cell that is unmissable on a well-toned organ or harpsichord and yet is not a grand gesture of any kind (see Example 1). This whole Toccata is a masterpiece in miniature, succinct and yet incorporating a whole range of ideas suitable for toccatas and much longer preludes. It is a veritable fund for the improvising organist. Quite how a few notes can have such a melodious affect is hard to say, and they pass by without any further reference, almost as if Frescobaldi had taken such little felicities for granted. But probably not very long after their publication, J.J. Froberger appears to have spotted them, for we get the following in the Elevation toccata of his book of 1649 (see Example 2). Whether this comes from more than a buried memory is hard to know, but I imagine composers thinking so much in terms of specific genres and what belongs to them that such little details crop up naturally. If Example 2 was not also a toccata but, say, a capriccio, one could suspect a conscious allusion.

As to genres: can one not say whether a much later work, Bach's *Canzona* BWV 588, is directly imitating the particular canzona that appears in the same book of Frescobaldi, complete with triple-time *Abgesang* (see Example 3), or whether it is alluding more generally to the type. But when Froberger uses the Chromatic Tetrachord as a theme in his *Canzona,* FbWV 302, direct influence of Frescobaldi is more than likely. In the case of Bach, seeing that several of his many other themes bear a resemblance to previous music of respected organists – the Passacaglia theme (Raison, both halves), the Fugue, BWV 574 (Legrenzi), the *Allabreve in* D (Corelli), the c minor Fantasia (Grigny), the *Pièce d'Orgue* (Boyvin?), the slow movement of the Fifth Brandenburg (Marchand) – a good case can be made for some definite connection with Frescobaldi too. The closer this connection, the more likely that Bach's *Canzona,* far from being his only organ fugue to begin with a pedal subject, as popularised in inauthoritative editions, is in fact *senza pedale.* So there may be practical implications behind such similarities as these. Biographical implications too, for the *Canzona* must date from at least a decade before Bach is documented as owning a copy of the *Fiori musicali.*

SOME OBSERVATIONS ON THREE KEYBOARD-COMPOSERS

EXAMPLE 1

EXAMPLE 2

EXAMPLE 3

Froberger's "quotes" are those of a composer used to taking but altering themes, purloining but reworking, such as German organists were brought up to do. (Handel's lifelong habits, generally improving on what he purloined, should doubtless be seen against this background.) One of Froberger's most striking alterations of Frescobaldi – surely a much more dominating influence over him than either Scheidt or Sweelinck – is to take his common-property hexachord theme CDEFGA and chromaticize it, slipping in chromatic accidentals to create a new and promising fugue-subject. Froberger's familiarity with Fresobaldi's other books is also clear, but by the time of mature Bach, who is less likely to have known them, the Frescobaldi-Froberger-Louis Couperin line of free toccatas is no longer to be traced: they had died out.

On the other hand, the *Fiori musicali* appears to have exercised a long-lasting influence on Bach, over thirty or more years, doubtless thanks to its sheer musical quality. Perhaps the *Art of Fugue* is in d minor because, as *tonus primus*, it was recognized as fundamental, the "exemplary key for exemplary collections", one amply demonstrated in Frescobaldi's book. Similarly, *Clavier-Übung III* is planned as a kind of *Fiori musicali* writ large, with a *toccata avanti* (the Prelude in E-flat) and *canzon post communione* (the Fugue in E-flat), Kyries in *stile antico*, various kinds of fughetta, both pure *cantus firmi* and *cantus*-derived imitation, and a set of movements following a liturgical or hymnological order. All this is as in Frescobaldi's book.

And then, if Bach was working on the *Goldberg Variations* shortly after *Clavier-Übung III,* or even partly at much the same time, it is all the likelier that the final 'Quodlibet' is in some degree a response to, or some subconscious allusion to, the "Bergamasca" in *Fiori musicali*. This Bergamasca is not only something of a quodlibet itself, and likewise follows on a mighty collection of 'serious' movements, but has a theme rather similar to one in the *Goldberg*. It is also in the same key of G major (see Example 4).

It is true that Bach's final years saw several essays in *stile antico* of a kind very like the classical accounts of it in Fux's *Gradus ad Parnassum* and in some Dresden court-music of the period. (One thinks especially of the Mass in b minor.) But the *stile antico* of *Clavier-Übung III* seems to me more specific than this, close to the keyboard counterpoint of the 4/2 movements in Frescobaldi,

EXAMPLE 4

though on the grander scale of a later composer than he: a 'successor' vying with a 'precursor'.

FRESCOBALDI'S CHROMATICS

One should distinguish between the Chromatic Tetrachord (as in A-C-C♯-D or E-C♯-C♮-B) and the Chromatic Fourth (as in A-B♭-B♮-C-C♯-D or D-C♯-C♮-B-B♭-A). Both have a history, and it may well be that the latter, as a theme in its own right and as a convenient progression in vocal or instrumental counterpoint, was somehow derived from the former – from having its 'gap' filled in by half steps.[1] Notice that in both cases, the progression is essentially from dominant to tonic or vice-versa, and so makes both themes particularly useful to composers of 'the great diatonic period' evolving in the later sixteenth century. There is really nothing modal about either of them, although strangely enough, in organ music well into the nineteenth century, the tendency would remain to use them in the organist's first, second and third tones (*primus, secundus, tertius*), i.e. d minor, g minor and a minor. Originally, this

EXAMPLE 5

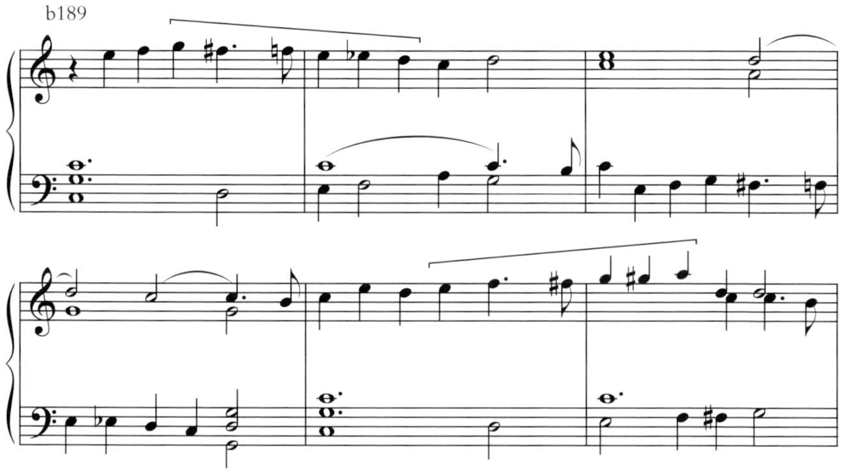

EXAMPLE 6

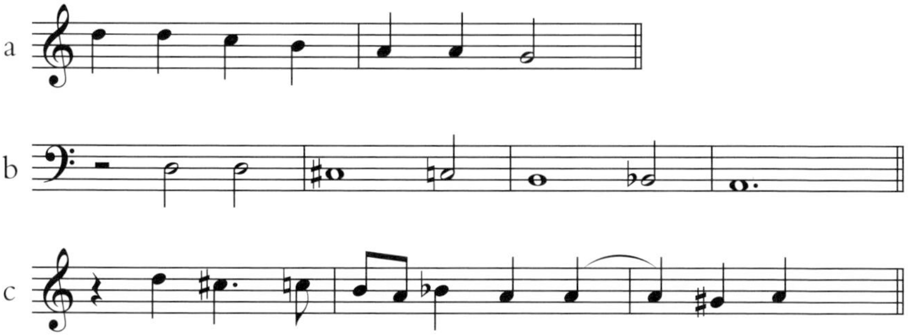

EXAMPLE 7

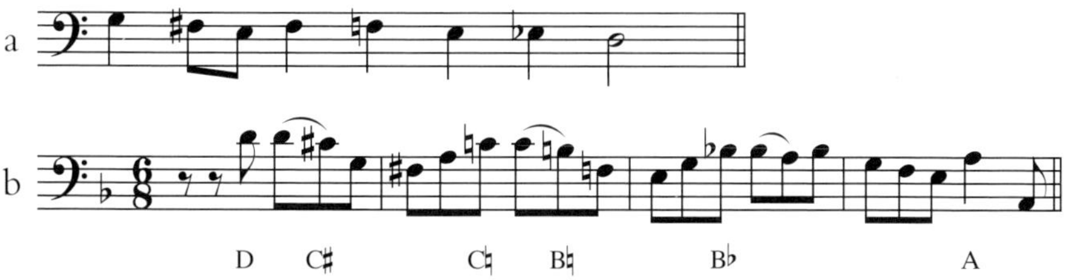

must have been for reasons connected with meantone temperaments and their 'good keys', but habits remain longer than the need for them.

In his "Cento partite sopra passacagli" (*Toccate*, pub. 1637) Frescobaldi has already discovered that the Chromatic Fourth need by no means be restricted to the dominant-to-tonic progression: in Example 5 it moves in C major from G-to-D or E-to-A, strangely anticipating the freedom with which Domenico Scarlatti will introduce the theme a century later. Of course, in Example 5 it is decorative, without harmonic function, but in this regard too – using the phrase for decorative purposes – Frescobaldi was also ahead of his time and again anticipating Baroque and even Classical use and usage. In the *Fiori musicali,* however, Frescobaldi is beginning to find an even more significant application of the Chromatic Fourth, i.e. using it in the form of a paraphrase (see Example 6). Here, (a) is the Bergamasca theme, (b) a triple-time chromatic version, (c) "paraphrased" with an extra note.

This is a modest example, with the chromatic line barely changed; but a whole new area of thematic invention was opened up when a Chromatic Fourth was "paraphrased" by weaving it into a longer and more developed line. The following excerpts show how the idea could develop, either directly through the line Frescobaldi-Froberger-Bach or more indirectly through the persistent search amongst great composers for new ways to treat traditional themes (see Example 7), where (a) is Froberger's *Capriccio* FbWV 506 and (b) Bach's *Magnificat* chorale BWV 648. After such "paraphrasing" as Bach's, so many later appearances of the Chromatic Fourth, from 1750 to 1950 approximately, are simpler, more naive, more conventional in their allusion, and thus less original.

BACH'S ORGELBÜCHLEIN AND HALLE

Unlike the music discussed above, this famous collection of chorales seems to have no true antecedents – the settings are only remotely similar to chorale-variations – and thus raise questions of what they are and what they are for.

In recent scholarship, there have been two dating schemes proposed for the original movements numbered BWV 599-644. If we accept the various hypotheses made some time ago about the chronology of Bach's Weimar manuscripts, the earliest entries in the album would have been made during Advent 1713.[2] But more recently, "the thought of setting a beginning ... closer to the early Weimar period, approximately 1708 to 1710 ... becomes tempting", if the so-called 'Neumeister Chorales' are authentic precursors of the *Orgelbüchlein* and therefore not too removed from them in time.[3] The problem then, however, is musical, because more than a few years (ten at least?) need to have elapsed before the immature figural counterpoint of 'Neumeister' could possibly have blossomed into the rich, polished idiom of BWV 616 or 628.

For the *Orgelbüchlein* to have begun in late 1713 – i.e. as a self-contained album using, in part, some earlier works – either Bach would have intended to use them on the Weimar organ after its then current rebuilding-work, or he would have planned them to suit the organ and the musical practices of the Liebfrauenkirche, Halle, where towards the end of 1713 he was invited (or said he was) to succeed F.W. Zachow, Handel's teacher. This was some eight months after work started on the Weimar organ and about the time that the contract for a new and unusually large three-manual organ was signed in Halle, for the town's major church.

Not only do the *Orgelbüchlein* preludes' expressiveness and even their succinctness fit in with the pietism associated with Halle but they seem to conform to the church's contract-requirements laid out in December 1713:[4]

langsam ohne sonderbahres coloriren mit vier und fünff Stimmen und dem Principal andächtig einzuschlagen, und mit iedem versicul die andern Stimmen iedesmahl abzuwechseln, auch zur qvintaden und Schnarr wercke, das Gedackte, wie auch die syncopationes und Bindungen...

(to play in a devotional manner, slowly without exceptional decoration in four and five parts [voices? stops?] and with the Principal [alone? or with whatever else was drawn?], and at each verse to alternate the other stops every time, also to apply to the Quintadena and reed-stops the Gedackt, as too the syncopations and suspensions...)

Such specifics are rare, suggesting one of several things: that the "Low church"priorities of the clergy were to govern the organist, or that Zachow had not always played discreetly, or that he had and the tradition must be maintained. Perhaps all three. Though the clerk was unsure of his terms, what the committee wants is clear: discreet registration, rich harmony and recognisable melody. The new 65-stop organ, approved and inaugurated in 1716, may already have been in the mind of the committee, for although earlier and smaller organs in the church doubtless had the four specified stops, the new one was to do so on a luxurious scale: four Principals, two Quintadenas, eleven reeds, two manual Gedackts, big pedal. One can imagine a certain apprehension amongst any church committee.

Another important point is that the new Halle organ seems to have had chamber pitch and a "tolerably good temperament",[5] for these alone could explain both the high pitch and distant keys of some of the settings in the *Orgelbüchlein*. Perhaps some of them were used when Bach examined the completed new organ in 1716: certainly, a warm registration centred on the organ's 8-foot tone matches the rich harmonic spectrum of almost all of the chorale-settings themselves. Now if all this is a plausible picture, the Halle connection would go some way to 'explain' how such unusual settings as those in the *Orgelbüchlein* – really unlike anything else – came about in the first place.

Furthermore, if the collection was begun with Halle in mind, its special manner of harmonizing straight through without inter-line interludes could also reflect the style of hymn-singing in this town church. Inter-line interludes are familiar both from hymn-settings presumed to be earlier, such as Bach's so-called *Arnstadt Choräle* (see BWV 715), and from those known to be later, such as Kauffmann's *Harmonische Seelenlust* (Leipzig, 1733). But the "Low church"convictions of Halle would require simpler or less distracting forms of chorale, something more expressive than usual, replacing the formality of standard-hymns-with-interludes (which tend to be either "neutral" or merely "pictorial") by more discrete, individual settings, simple in shape, expressive, warm in *Affekt* and warmly registered on the new organ.

While Bach's new duties as *Konzertmeister* at the Court of Weimar from March 2, 1714 need not have meant leaving the *Orgelbüchlein* project as incomplete as in fact it is, finishing it was surely much less urgent. Even if he continued to play for services in Weimar, which is not certain, one can easily imagine that the settings suited both Halle's expressive, sentiment-laden style and its large parish congregation better than the aristocratic formality of a duke's chapel such as Weimar. The settings could still have served as teaching material, of course, demonstrating a range of techniques and styles, illustrating how to compose figural harmony and enabling an organist's pedal-playing to progress from simple left/right alternation (BWV 612) through partial alternation (BWV 615) to less and less (BWV 622).

It came about that the unfinished album received a title page some years later, when Bach was in another position (Köthen) and even perhaps about to move to yet another (Leipzig). From the period of the title page, and hence of the pedagogic aims it put into words, could also have come the album's directions for two manuals and even, in most cases, for the pedal. The recognition, already there in Spitta,[6] that the pieces are (mostly) earlier than the title means that the title page can say nothing about their original purpose or nature. For example, the idea that here was a collection of organ chorales for the young Wilhelm Friedemann is based on the new title page and the analogy it offers to other collections of the period, in content (*Clavierbüchlein W.F. Bach*, 1720) or title page (*Well-tempered Clavier* I, 1722 and *Inventions*, 1723). While it has to remain possible that the composer did intend all along to give it this name, it is nevertheless unlike the other didactic works for Friedemann and much more like an organist's hymnbook, one that would have joined or matched older collections of organ-chorales in the Bach circle.[7]

On the question of the title page and its implications: fuller than the *Clavierbüchlein's,* the *Orgelbüchlein's* may well allude to E.N. Ammerbach's *Orgel oder Instrument Tabulatur* (Leipzig, 1571).[8]

Orgel-Büchlein

Worinne einem anfahenden Organisten

Anleitung gegeben wird, auff allerhand

Arth einen Choral durchzuführen, an-

bey auch sich im Pedal studio zu habi-

litiren, indem in solchen darinne

befindlichen Choralen das Pedal

gantz obligat tractiret wird.

SOME OBSERVATIONS ON THREE KEYBOARD-COMPOSERS

Dem Höchsten Gott allein zu Ehren,
Dem Nechsten, draus sich zu belehren.

Little Organ Book, in which guidance is given a beginning organist in how to set a chorale in all kinds of ways, and at the same time to become practised in the study of pedalling, since in the chorales found therein the pedal is treated completely obbligato.

For the highest God alone Honour,
For my Neighbour, that he may instruct himself with it.

Ammerbach, 1571 Edition
Orgel oder In-
strument Tabulatur.
Ein nützlichs Büchlein, in welchem notwendige erklerung der
Orgel oder Instrument tablatur, sampt der Application, auch fröhliche
deutsche Stücklein [etc] zubefinden [etc]
Jetzund aber der Jugend und anfahenden dieser
Kunst zum besten in Druck vor-
fertiget [etc]

Organ or Harpsichord tablature. A useful little Book in which will be found necessary explanation of [keyboard] tablature, together with its application [rudiments, fingering], also jolly German pieces [etc]. N.B. now best prepared in print for young people and beginners in this art

Ammerbach, 1583 edition
Orgel oder In-
strument Tabulaturbuch, in sich
begreiffenden eine notwendige unnd kurtze anlai-
tung, die Tabulatur und application zuverstehen [etc]
Jetzund aber, der Jugend und anfahenden diser kunst zu gutem,
mit fleiß zusammen gebracht [etc]

Organ or harpsichord tablature-book, containing within it a necessary and short introduction to understanding tablature and its application [etc] N.B. now carefully brought together for the good of young people and beginners in this art

If the *Orgelbüchlein's* title page does allude to these, which are the first collections of keyboard music published in Leipzig, perhaps it does so to acknowledge the city to which the composer was by then hoping to move. This would mean interpreting Dadelsen's dating for the title page (something "he wrote in the last Köthen years")[9] as meaning early 1723, the period of Bach's election to the cantorate of Leipzig.

SCARLATTI'S CHALLENGE TO HIS COPYISTS

Equally without antecedents appear to be Domenico Scarlati's sonatas, but here there is a different range of questions. Although the musical and geographical context, in which he achieved perhaps the most intimately idiomatic music ever written for harpsichord, removed him from the usual dominating influences north of the Pyrenees and Alps, it is possible to find points of comparison with other repertories. Such comparisons do not suggest actual influences but arise when one idiosyncratic body of fine music can, in the mind of the player, call up another.

For example, Scarlatti sometimes created a binary-form sonata in which the second subject is not only the same as the first but, on its return in the tonic in the second half, brings with it a distinct feel of 'the Recapitulation'. I do not see how the origins of (or reasons for) Sonata Form in the period of Haydn and Mozart can be fully traced without taking into account a significant group of Scarlatti sonatas and the effect he achieved with the tonic-dominant relationship. And not only Scarlatti himself: that he influenced composers quite unconnected with him is suggested by similar first and second subjects in binary movements of the late-classical French composer Duphly. Again, in attempting to describe Scarlatti's deftness, his sheer panache in creating original music from the simplest ingredients, interesting comparisons can be made by considering how he handles themes also used by other composers of the time.

Some examples: Sonata Kk 334 opens like J.S. Bach's C major Prelude for Organ, BWV 547 (the '9/8 prelude'); Sonata Kk 103 opens like the prelude to Bach's A major English Suite; Sonata Kk 184 has a the sequence of diminished 7ths found again in the Gigue of Bach's Partita in B-flat; Sonata Kk 54 closes with much the same line that opens the canons of *Vom Himmel hoch*, BWV 769.

Without exception, in all such instances Bach is more "thorough" and single-minded, and as such the comparisons are very instructive. After all, these are qualities that in Bach can and sometimes do tend towards a *nimiety* ("excess, redundancy" – *Oxford English Dictionary*), a "thoroughness" all too easily replacing art by artifice, especially when one compares his treatments with Scarlatti's. The latter can seem thoughtless by comparison, and yet the musical skill with which he can turn necessity into virtue – as when a narrow C-compass forces him to alter a bass sequence in the g minor Fugue Kk 30 (bb. 136) – is never inferior.

For "deftness" and "sheer panache", a more appropriate comparison for Scarlatti is Frescobaldi, not least in their way of treating the six-note phrase of rising or falling semitones, the so-called 'chromatic fourth.' Both compos-ers can be quite conventional in their use of this phrase in fugal counterpoint, which is not surprising since it can so easily be adapted as a countersubject, whatever the character of the fugue as a whole. Frescobaldi slips it into the popular Bergamasca tune to give a sudden harmonic shading (see Example 6); Scarlatti prepares for a second subject by a preparatory chromaticism. These little chromatics also imply a difference in articulation for the left hand: *legato* before the inevitable *détaché* that follows, as in Example 8, from the Sonata in B-flat, Kk 441 (slurs added). It is hard to imagine Bach being so 'deft' with it: a work of his that might use much the same motif as Example 8's left-hand, for example the Prelude in a minor *WTC2,* is much more likely to hammer it home, exhaustively, ingeniously, with invertible counterpoint, etc.

One problem, however, is that in the absence of autograph sources for Scarlatti's sonatas, editions rely on a few early prints and on sets of copies pro-fessionally prepared during the eighteenth century, though under whose su-

EXAMPLE 8

pervision has never been established. It is likely that the copyists, including the early engravers, sometimes misunderstood a detail, or it was ambiguously written in the source they were using (perhaps "some kind of shorthand" copy)[10] or simple errors were made in transcribing; and each editor will have made suggestions appropriate to a particular edition's aims. The Appendix below offers a few suggestions for the "first" 30 sonatas, the *Esercizi*, in the knowledge that though some of them have been suggested before, yet others are possible. In general, the questions one might have about Scarlatti copies, that is to say the sonatas as we know them, fall into categories of the following kind:

possibly wrong notes (e.g. when a sequence is inconsistent and there is 'no obvious reason' why it is so)

possible or probable omissions (as when a copyist misreads his source, which may be unclear, or when the source itself, autograph or otherwise, made a mistake)

possibly missing accidentals (occasionally through a "forgetting" of the key-signature or previous flat/sharp/natural, but perhaps more often when chromatic implications have not been recognized by the copyist)

ambiguous or possibly mistaken first and second-time bars (in most cases, the result of conventions as found in other Italian or italianate music, whereby it is left to the player to use common sense with respect to the halfway and final cadences)

ambiguous or possibly mistaken notation (as for the dividing between rh/lh: considering the importance of this both to the player's performance and to the composer's intended rhetoric, the ambiguity can surely be attributed to copyists' imprecision or misunderstanding?)

The Appendix makes no claim to be exhaustive about Kk 1–30 or even, strictly, to be editorial corrections at all, representing instead the kind of questions raised about the transmission of these unique pieces. Each point raised here is in a sense guesswork, and questions remain about many individual notes, including accidentals and (especially) missing ties. By no means would the works of Frescobaldi and J.S. Bach yield many fewer quesions, and in that respect, each of this essay's approaches to a corpus of music could be applied to the work of each of its composers.[11]

APPENDIX: NOTES TO SCARLATTI'S SONATAS KK1-30

For the convenience of players, the page-numbers in the first volume of Kenneth Gilbert's edition (Paris: Heugel, 1971-1984, with revised reprints) are given, but the suggestions can apply to all editions, including facsimiles, and are not meant as "corrections" to Mr. Gilbert's indispensable edition, nor as a further set of annotations to other editions. Reference to "the engraving" denotes the *Essercizi* (London, 1738 or 1739)

Kk	Page	Bar	
1	2	7	judging by the similar sixteenth-note runs in bb. 11, 17 and elsewhere (bb. 8, 10, 15, 16, 27-29), there is a missing lh b-natural in the first beat: copyist/engraver read it as the tail of the first note?
	2	13	was this lh/rh distribution also intended for b. 31? Or this final phrase is intended in both cases for the rh alone?

4	8	5	the original key-signature of one flat caused all four e's in this bar to have a flat by them in the engraving, but the second (rh beat 2) surely should be natural?
	9	39	if the second rh beat is *reliably* different from that in b. 21, at least the c's should be tied?
5	10	21	cf. b. 68: is there a missing slur in b. 21 and does that in b. 68 indicate rh *glissando* (with c-natural)?
	10	30	if there is a missing rh appoggiatura, does that suggest all other trills in the Sonata are not upper-note?
6	12	29	last bass note A-flat?
		33-6	cf. bb. 72-4: are the lh differences intentional (latter preferable)?
		36-7	cf. bb. 74-5: does the rh beaming (a) reproduce Scarlatti's and (b) imply that rh continues through to the final trill(s)?
7	14ff		a distinction between upper-note and main-note trills intended throughout?
	14	9ff	since the engraving indicates rh at 9 and lh at 31, it is safe to assume lh indication at 9 omitted. But note: corresponding bars in second half (95, 117) are the same, with the same "omission"
		32	alto c² (plus ornament in engraving) then g¹: should be a chord as in b. 34 etc?
	15	37	c³? – and rhythm as b. 127?
	16	74-94	every first beat should have an ornament, alternating between hands?
8	19	36	tenor d¹ (and b-flat in b. 39) tied?
		47	no final bar in the engraving: so first-time bar b-flat, second-time b-natural (so a major chord)?
9	21	42	last rh note g¹?
		45	rh second beat had no accidentals, so c²-natural, b¹-flat?
10	22-3		why are all the scales slurred in the engraving, but only two in Kk 9?
	22	36	appoggiatura with a fermata in the engraving: a misread slur?
	23	44	appoggiatura to b¹ with a fermata in the engraving: misreading for double appoggiatura (i.e. with g¹-sharp, cf. b. 20)
11	24		missing tempo word in engraving: insufficient space between the staves for 'Allegro'?
		14	cf. b. 28: fermatas over rests unusual

	25	19	hands cross back on third beat (as in engraving)?
12	26	1	on repeat, lh begins on g⁰?
		5-6	rh b¹-natural after c²-sharp?
	27	25	2nd-time bar ends with rh e¹-natural (key-signature); last lh b is natural?
	28	32	perhaps the d-flat in the lh was not an error, and bb. 32, 25 and 5-6 intended augmented seconds to be heard?
	29	49	alto second beat, missing b-flat and a. Is final b flat or natural?
13	30	17	why the engraving omitted D is unclear, but it includes the alto c²-sharp in b. 51
15	36	1-2	beaming consistent (bb. 1-2, 5-6, 55-6, 59-60): meaning?
		9-40	presumably crossed hands, though a change at b. 28 possible (similarly second half, bb. 72-99, and b. 87): lh cued each time.
16	40	19	slurring different from b. 21 through lack of space in engraving
	41	50	the appoggiatura surely produces the same rhythm as b. 52: did the composer (as a convention) avoid leaping up to an appoggiatura
17	45	45	cf. b. 120ff: nothing in the notation to suggest that (or where) the lh takes over the triplets. Alternating?
	46	80	perhaps a repeat of b. 76 or more likely (as in engraving) the same as b. 65
18	49	16	unclear why last rh note sharpened
	50	31	unclear why second alto note g¹ not f¹
20	57	41-3	since the engraving has a key-signature of three sharps it is not certain that the d²-naturals are intended
21	60	38	cf. b. 42: neither have c²-natural in the engraving (nor sharps in b. 43) and would imply rallentando; but bb. 114, 118 have f¹ natural. Does the duplication in each case suggest that the original source did not write out the repetition?
	60/63		in each case are there missing slurs and ties between the penultimate chord (BCEG, EFAC) and the final?
22	64	16	e²-natural (not in engraving) after f²-sharp?
23	68	6	does the similarity of the lh motif to that in K.22 (b.14) suggest a pair of sonatas, different in other respects (mode, metre etc.)
24	72	4ff	the three sets of rising scales alternate hands as well as the arpeggios?

	74	37	engraving has rh first, then lh each time – in error?
		39	should the first 3 rh B's be sharp, then 4 natural B's?
	74	45	should beat four be a chord with b and g-sharp?
25	78	58	the engraving's reading of the rh (g^2 sharpened, a^2 sharpened, g^2) is unambiguous:
27	85	18	should the tenor's a be b-natural? (cf. b. 20)
		20ff	cf. b. 65ff: was it understood that lh took over when the run reached its stave (c^1-sharp)?
28	88	10ff	as elsewhere, the halving of a triplet's note-values (plus slurs) seems to be for the sake of visibility (cf. J.S. Bach's autograph of *In dulci jubilo* BWV 608)
29			the absence of rh/lh indications at b. 28ff, 70ff (simple melody) and b. 16ff, 57ff (melody plus alto) suggest regular distribution at these points. Otherwise, left over right, even including final bars of each half?
	92	44	Is the engraving's omission of lh notes in beats 2 and 3 for a c^3-compass harpsichord?
30			The only 'Moderato' sign in the *Essercizi:* so a slower beat than e.g. Kk 9?

REFERENCES

G. von Dadelsen, 'Zur Entstehung des Bachschen Orgelbüchleins', in ed. A. A. Abert and W. Pfannkuch, *Festschift Friedrich Blume zum 70. Geburtstag* (Kassel, 1963), 74-79.

Dok I = *Bach-Dokumente,* Vol. I, ed. Werner Neumann and Hans-Joachim Schulze (Kassel etc, 1963).

Dok II = *Bach-Dokumente,* Vol. II, ed. Werner Neumann and Hans-Joachim Schulze (Kassel etc, 1969).

H.-H. Löhlein, *Orgelbüchlein, Sechs Choräle von verschiedener Art* (Schübler-Choräle), *Orgelpartiten* = *NBA* [Neue Bach-Ausgabe] IV/1 KB (Kassel, 1987).

P. Spitta, *Johann Sebastian Bach,* 2 vols. (Leipzig, 1873, 1880).

C. Wolff, *Bach: Essays on His Life and Music* [collected writings] (Cambridge MA, 1991).

: : N O T E S : :

[1]   For a fuller account of the whole topic, see my *The Chromatic Fourth* (Oxford: Clarendon Press, 1997), especially pp. 7-12 (the distinctions in practice) and pp. 37-42 (examples in Frescobaldi).

[2]   Löhlein 1987, 85-95 (NBA).

[3]   Wolff 1991, 299.

[4]   Dok II, 50.

[5]   Dok I, 150.

[6]   Spitta I, 818.

[7]   The *44 Choräle zum Präambulieren* of Johann Christoph Bach (1642-1703) and the so-called 'Neumeister Chorales' of J.S. Bach.

[8]   Cf. Löhlein 1987, 106-7.

[9]   Dadelsen 1963, 77.

[10]   The phrase is from Frederick Hammond, 'Domenico Scarlatti. A la recherche des autographes perdus', ed. François Seydoux, *Fiori musicologici. Studi in onore di Luighi Ferdinando Tagliavini* (Bologna: Patron, 2001), 275-96, here p. 288. This essay makes several points relevant to the Appendix given here.

[11]   For an earlier, but I think lone and unchallenged, attempt to list a few similar questions about transmission of Bach, see my 'The Snares and Delusions of Notation: Bach's early Organ Works', in ed. George Stauffer and Ernest May, *J.S. Bach as Organist* (Bloomington: Indiana U. P., 1986), 274-294.

JOHANN GABRAHN'S ORGANIZED PIANO IN CONTEXT

Laurence Libin

HISTORICAL RESEARCH ABOUT ORGANS mostly targets sizable instruments installed in churches, concert halls, and other public venues. With some notable exceptions, scholars have paid comparatively little attention to small domestic organs, although these were once quite numerous and widespread. Although their repertoire lacks glamour and although many extant examples are anonymous, poorly preserved, or of unimpressive workmanship, small organs nevertheless deserve serious study for their often idiosyncratic designs, unfamiliar tones, and important social functions. Hybrid, or combination, chamber instruments are especially interesting because they display intimate links between organ building and the sister crafts of harpsichord and piano making. Many inventive organ builders of the eighteenth century and later built pianos as well as organs and experimented with combined types.

One of these hybrids, the "organized piano" or *fortepiano organisé* epitomized by the work of Johann Gabrahn described below, typically combines a small organ with a so-called square piano.[1] Its antecedent, a positiv organ incorporating a harpsichord or spinet, today usually called a *claviorganum*, existed in many forms since at least the sixteenth century.[2] Frequent mention of organ-harpsichord combinations by practical writers from Praetorius to Adlung shows these to have been more familiar during the baroque era than the few surviving examples might indicate. The claviorganum's colorful tonal palette allowed a single performer to contrast or join the prolonged notes of pipes with the sparkle of plucked strings. Usually, organ and harpsichord components could be played separately or together, but disparities of tuning and loudness might have made coupling problematic. (Similarly, in modern performances, piano and organ played simultaneously often sound out of tune and unbalanced.)

Among the most elaborate and innovative baroque claviorgana is Michele Todini's "machine of Polyphemus and Galatea," constructed in Rome about 1670 and now in The Metropolitan Museum of Art, New York. Its richly carved and gilded outer case is flanked by original, nearly life-size sculpted figures of Polyphemus and Galatea playing respectively a *sordellina* (bellows-blown bagpipe) and an invisible lute. According to Todini's description, the very large harpsichord (length 270 cm) mimicked the sounds of Galatea's lute while concealed pipes gave voice to the cyclop's bagpipe.[3] Evidently Todini intended not only to provide varied tone colors but also, through them, to evoke contrasting characters or affects, an important consideration both for solo and continuo playing. Todini's inclusion of unconventional pipes, probably reeds, specially made for him by two unnamed brothers from Naples, is intriguing, but no trace of the organ remains; perhaps it was never completed. The surviving elements, however, exemplify the visual and aural theatricality of many early keyboard instruments, and point to the necessity of studying these ingenious showpieces from a broadly humanistic viewpoint.

During the eighteenth century, claviorgana achieved considerable popularity in elite musical circles. Handel may have played one to accompany his oratorio *Saul* (1738) and composed a concerto for it in 1739.[4] A much altered, two-manual example in harpsichord form, built in Hannover by Herman Willenbrock perhaps for the Elector Georg Ludwig (later King George I of England), dates from 1712, when Handel visited Hannover and might have performed upon this richly decorated instrument, now also in The Metropolitan Museum of Art. Johann Mattheson, Handel's friend in Hamburg, recommended claviorgana for continuo use in church cantatas,[5] an expedient that saved space, personnel, and money by having one instrument take the place of two; the same economic considerations applied in theaters and so might help explain Handel's supposed usage.

After about 1760, pianos gradually replaced harpsichords as the claviorga-num's preferred stringed element, bringing to the instrument the additional advantage of naturalistic dynamic expression, a hallmark of neoclassical musi-cal style. Novel and ingenious, organized pianos appealed strongly to Enlight-enment sensibilities, and the cleverly designed instruments were widely of-fered for sale, mainly to well-to-do amateurs. An early advertisement for what seems to have been an organized piano with a flute stop appeared in the 1764 *Danziger Anzeigen und Nachrichten* (no. 32, p. 212): "Es wird denen respectiven Liebhabern zu wissen gethan, daß bey dem Orgelbauer F.R. Dalitz auf dem dritten Damm, ein Forte Piano mit der Flaut=Travers, und gut conditioniert, zu verkaufen steht. Kauflustige können es Nachmittags von 4. bis 5 Uhr in Augenschein nehmen." (If the term "fortepiano," used here without qualifica-tion, refers to a square model as is likely, this advertisement contradicts the no-tion that Johann Zumpe invented this form of piano in London about 1766.[6]) Similar advertisements by other little-known Danzig makers such as Georg Wilhelm Rasmus further demonstrate the presence of organized pianos in that port city, a fact of some importance relative to the spread of these instruments across the Baltic region and to the work of Johann Gabrahn in particular.[7]

Conceptually related to Dalitz's earlier work, the *Melodika* that Johann Andreas Stein built in 1772 comprised a rank of pipes under expression that could be attached to another clavier. Stein reportedly sold his Melodika in Paris in 1773. Later, he exhibited in Augsburg a *clavecin organisé*, believed to be the two-manual organized grand piano sold by Stein about 1781 to a Swedish amateur and now stored in the Göteborg municipal museum. The presence of such an ambitious instrument in Sweden along with organized instruments by, among others, Johannes Klein (1771) and Pehr Lundborg (1772 and later) both preserved in Stockholm's Musikmuseet, and one (now lost) made by Friderick Beenick in Copenhagen, further illustrates the late-eighteenth-century vogue for such hybrids in states bordering the Baltic Sea.[8]

In his comprehensive treatise *L'art du facteur d'orgues*, Dom François Bedos de Celles describes and illustrates the construction of a two-manual *fortepiano organisé* that the French court organ builder Adrien Lépine had presented be-fore the French Royal Academy of Sciences in 1772.[9] Dom Bedos shows a three-rank organ compactly fitted beneath a German-action (*Prellmechanik*) square piano. Lépine's organ is noteworthy for including one divided rank of 8-foot reed pipes in addition to a full-compass 8-foot *bourdon* and a treble-compass 8-foot *ouvert*. These two half-ranks of reeds, respectively called *basson* and *hautbois*, have differently shaped resonators and stand at the rear of the organ below a pedal-operated swell flap that recalls the expressive intent of Stein's contemporaneous *Melodika*.

Very few extant organized pianos have reed stops, so their musical effect has not been much explored. A lost English example by Crang Hancock reportedly included a trumpet stop as well as percussion devices; we can imagine that the dramatist and entertainer Charles Dibdin, who owned this instrument until 1805, would have appreciated its versatility for instance in battle pieces and similarly lively, quasi-pictorial music.[10] Another reed-equipped instrument, made in Vienna by Franz Xaver Christoph about 1785 (Kunsthistorisches Museum, Vienna; ex coll: Prince Liechtenstein) and recently restored, has three split ranks: two gedeckts and a reed called *Zunge*, remarkably sounding at 16-foot pitch. The piano has a normal five-octave range, FF-f^3, but the organ compass extends only from C to f^3 and is divided between c$^{\sharp 1}$ and d^1. A short compass and divided ranks typify organs in such instruments.

Dating from the same year as Dom Bedos's publication, 1778, is an English organized piano acquired in 1811 by the Musée National des Techniques, Conservatoire des Arts et Métiers, in Paris. The London workshop of Johannes Zumpe and Gabriel Buntebart (in partnership 1769-1778) built the piano part of this instrument but its organ is anonymous and was probably subcontracted, as was becoming common practice. Several prominent London manufacturers followed Zumpe's lead in producing composite organized pianos. One in The Metropolitan Museum of Art combines a Longman & Broderip piano with an organ by Eaton Pether, dated 1786; this member of the Pether family seems otherwise unknown. (Presumably Michael Arne played an instrument like this in performing a theater concerto for organized piano in 1784.)[11] Coincidentally also in 1786, John Geib, a German immigrant organ and piano builder who like Eaton Pether and William Gater was a subcontractor for Longman & Broderip, patented a so-called English double action for pianos that strikingly resembles Johann Gabrahn's piano action, mentioned below. Numerous other organized pianos by Longman & Broderip now in museum collections (for example in Berlin, Brussels, Stockholm, and Vienna), might contain so-far unidentified work of minor builders who, like makers of clock organs, deserve more study.

By about 1790, organized pianos had appeared in the New World. The only such instrument depicted anywhere in an independent work of art appears in a privately owned portrait of about 1792 by the Puerto Rican artist José Campeche, showing María de los Dolores Martínez de Carvajal, daughter of a mayor of San Juan, standing by an evidently prized *piano organizado*. Campeche, besides being colonial Puerto Rico's foremost painter, was an important church musician, music teacher, and organ technician. He was appointed deputy organist of San Juan's cathedral in 1783 and later directed music at the Carmelite convent of San José. In 1801 that convent received a bequest for the purchase of a *piano organizado* (perhaps the one shown in the portrait) and for a stipend allowing Campeché to teach the prioress to play the instrument, which reportedly remained in use into the 1840s. Coincidentally also in 1801, the cathedral chapter of Seville, Spain, purchased a 14-year-old organized piano by Zumpe's former partner Gabriel Buntebart and his obscure associate Sievers, whose first name is unknown. Clearly, then, such instruments were considered appropriate for playing in Spanish Catholic churches (even during Lent when ordinary church organs were silent), by nuns, and by gentlewomen who observed the strictest decorum. An advertisement in the *Gaceta de México* (2 July 1793) for a four-stop organized piano built by Don Mariano Placeres, principal organist of Durango cathedral, together with a local clock maker, further connects organized pianos both to Hispanic church music and to clock making, a theme that recurs in the work of Johann Gabrahn.[12]

After immigrating to New York, John Geib advertised in the *Spectator* (19 March 1800) to make organized pianos independently; he claimed, untenably, to be the first to do so in America. Apparently a good potential market existed for these instruments in the young United States, for in Boston on 11 July 1804 the piano maker Benjamin Crehore entered into a short-lived partnership with the organ builder William Goodrich to produce them, presumably for home use; at this time few New England churches had organs of any kind. No example by Crehore and Goodrich is known, but one made in Boston by Goodrich and Alpheus Babcock about 1828-29, now in Boston's Museum of Fine Arts, shows the type persisting well into the nineteenth century, when they were supplanted by piano and reed organ combinations.

Like the derelict Babcock & Goodrich and typical Longman & Broderip instruments, most organized square pianos look graceless as furniture even by standards of their own day, and survive in poor condition due to mishandling. Their weight made them hard to move safely, and their crowded interiors made maintenance awkward. Remarking on a "piano with a flute attachment" played by one Herr Palzow in St. Petersburg in 1802, Ludwig Spohr remarked that "the tones . . . of the strings and of the flute had together a very bad effect."[13] The only extant Pennsylvania German organized piano, built about 1810 by John Wind (collection of Raymond Brunner), has had its piano gutted, probably because it was unfeasible to maintain. Eventually, transport and tuning were greatly eased and manufacturing costs were lowered by replacing conventional flue and reed pipes with small, relatively stable free reeds of the modern plate-mounted type employed in melodeons and harmoniums and adopted in the celebrated "aeolian attachment" patented in 1844 by Obed M. Coleman (U.S. patent no. 3548).[14]

⁂

The earlier introduction of free-reed stops to European organs owes much to experimental builders of organized pianos active in the Baltic region as early as the 1780s, a subject only now being seriously explored.[15] Undoubtedly the finest and most interesting such instrument incorporating a free-reed rank stands essentially unaltered in the palace of Paul I, son of Catherine the Great, at Pavlovsk near St. Petersburg (Fig. 1). Several publications mention it but it has never been fully and accurately described because of restricted access for examination. This is apparently the only organized piano remaining in Russia and one of very few extant eighteenth-century Russian keyboard instruments of any kind. Its near-miraculous survival (the palace was practically destroyed during World War Two) testifies to the diligence and devotion of Russian curators, whose reluctance to expose their treasures to handling by strangers must be viewed sympathetically.

Inscribed in ink on the soundboard is the maker's mark, "Gabrahn./St: Petersburg An[n]o 1783," the last number in pencil (Fig. 2). It might seem strange that such an important commission should have been entrusted to a craftsman so obscure today, but Johann Gabrahn was obviously highly experienced and surely enjoyed skilled assistance, for example in executing the lavish marquetry that decorates the instrument's case inside and out (Fig. 3). When the composer and virtuoso Jan Ladislav Dussek performed at court in St. Petersburg in 1785, he might well have played on this extraordinary and historic instrument.

Johann Gabrahn's birthplace is uncertain, but about 1774 in Mohrungen (Morag) near Danzig, a clavier maker named Gabrahn, probably the same person, was accused of working without a license in a lawsuit brought by the local organ builder Johann Gottfried Fischer.[16] The unusual surname Gabrahn still occurred in Danzig in the early-nineteenth century, but today in German telephone directories the name exists only in Bensheim and Villingen-Schwenningen. Conceivably, Johann Gabrahn left the vicinity of Danzig in reaction to a decline of trade after Prussia seized the city in 1772; his name first appears in St. Petersburg newspaper advertisements in 1775. (The organ and clavier maker Johan [sic] Christian Gronenberg left Danzig for Copenhagen perhaps about the same time.) Under Russian patronage Gabrahn enjoyed more freedom to experiment and certainly a wealthier clientele than he would have had in Mohrungen, where guild and civic rules evidently constrained his activity.

Because the Russian Orthodox Church does not admit organs, Gabrahn could not have expected to build many large instruments in St. Petersburg; he would have had to concentrate on chamber and clock organs, working in collaboration with furniture and clock makers. The celebrated, nearly four-meter-tall "mechanical orchestra" and astronomical clock produced by Johann Georg Strasser in St. Petersburg between 1793 and 1801, probably intended for the Mikhailovsky Castle of Paul I but now in the State Hermitage Museum, incorporates components by Gabrahn that exemplify this aspect of his creativity. Originally this magnificent clock organ had thirteen barrels programmed with works by Haydn, Mozart, and Anton Eberl.[17]

Figure 1 – Organized square piano by Johann Gabrahn, St. Petersburg, 1783;
Pavlovsk, Palace of Paul I

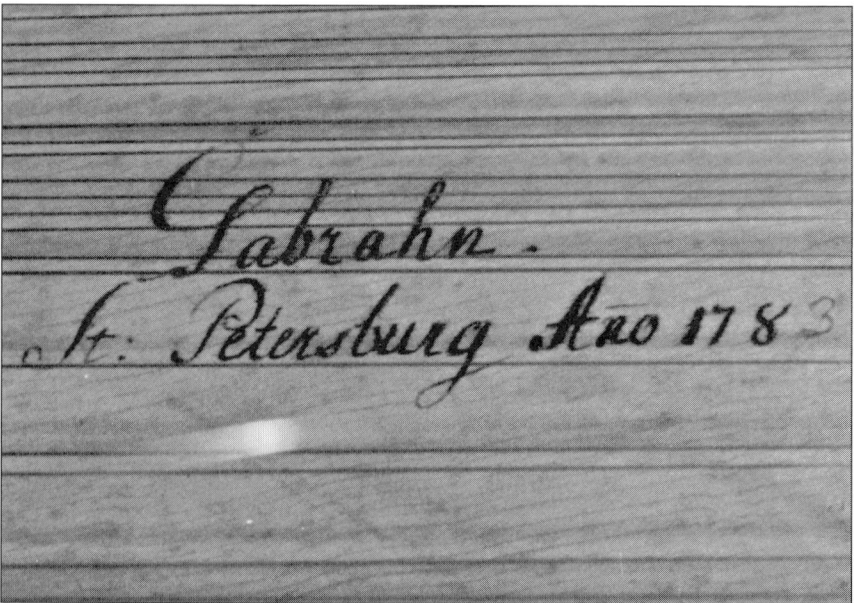

Figure 2 – Signature of Gabrahn on piano soundboard

Organized pianos were evidently popular among wealthy musical amateurs in St. Petersburg; numerous references to them and to normal pianos, mostly imported, appear in local advertisements during the reign of Catherine the Great (r. 1762-96).[18] These fashionable keyboard instruments, ubiquitous in upper-class households, reflect the Empress's enthusiastic embrace of modern European and especially British arts and technology. That Russian aristocrats esteemed English pianos is shown by the presence, also in Pavlovsk, of a splendid Zumpe & Buntebart square piano, dated 1774, designed expressly for Catherine by the famed British architect Robert Adam, with casework probably executed in Thomas Chippendale's workshop.[19] I believe Catherine gave this extraordinary piano to her first daughter-in-law, Grand Duchess Natalia Alekseevna (the former princess Wilhelmina of Hesse-Darmstadt), the first wife of Paul I.

Gabrahn's organized piano far outshines even the imperial Zumpe & Buntebart piano. According to its custodians at Pavlovsk, Catherine gave Gabrahn's masterpiece to her former lover Grigori Alexandrovich Potemkin, a connoisseur of music who owned many fine instruments and who was named prince of Tauris in 1783, the date on the piano's soundboard. But belief in Potemkin's ownership rests only on the instrument's supposedly having been stored in a palace once owned by him, called Tavrichesky (Tauride), which however was completed but still unfurnished in 1790. Legend relates that at some uncertain time the Gabrahn was taken from Tavrichesky to another palace, Gatchina, and thence, after World War Two, to Pavlovsk.

This story needs some explanation. After Potemkin's death in 1791, Catherine herself briefly occupied Tavrichesky, but after her death her son Paul I dispersed the palace's contents. After Paul's death in 1801, his widowed second wife, Maria Fyodorovna, began to restore Tavrichesky and occasionally lived there. Later, Alexander I returned some of the dispersed furnishings, but under Nicholas I, Tavritchesky became practically a furniture warehouse from which, in the mid-nineteenth century, some pieces were sent to Gatchina along with some objects from the Hermitage. Gatchina was built between 1766-81 by another of Catherine's lovers, Grigori Grigoryevich Orlov. After Orlov's death in 1783, Catherine gave Gatchina to Paul I and Maria Fyodorovna. So Gatchina, rather than Tavrichesky, could have been the original home of the Gabrahn instrument, or it could just as well have come to Gatchina in the nineteenth century from the Hermitage or elsewhere.

As an alternative to the supposed Potemkin provenance, I suggest that Catherine might have given the Gabrahn organized piano to her second daughter-in-law, Grand Duchess Maria Fyodorovna (the former Princess Sophia Dorothea of Würtemberg) on the occasion of her and Paul's moving into Gatchina in 1783. Perhaps Catherine meant both this and the Zumpe & Buntebart piano to help alleviate the boredom and stress suffered by both of her daughters-in-law. Catherine herself was no musician but recommended music to Natalia Alekseevna as an "improving" pastime. Maria Fyodorovna was an accomplished performer; among other instruments she reportedly owned an elaborately encased square piano by David Roentgen and Peter Kinzing (Neuwied, 1785) that was used both at Gatchina and Pavlovsk and auctioned at Sotheby's in New York on 16 May 1987.

I tentatively base my suggestion of Maria Fyodorovna's ownership of the Gabrahn instrument on two chamber works dedicated to her about 1790 that specifically call for organized piano: a septet composed by her Ukrainian music master, Dmitri Bortnyansky (1751-1825), and a sextet by Domenico Cimarosa (1749-1801); these compositions are the only ones known to me that explicitly require an organized piano. Bortnyansky, a pupil of Baldassare Galuppi, became a Russian imperial court composer in 1779. When Giovanni Paisiello, Maria Fyodorovna's music teacher, left St. Petersburg after seven years in 1783, Bortnyansky took over Paisiello's teaching duty and was also named. *maestro di cappella* to Paul I, whose regular music teacher was Vincenzo Manfredini. In addition to composing keyboard sonatas and chamber music for Maria Fyodorovna, Bortnyansky wrote much liturgical music and several operas premiered at court in the 1780s.

Bortnyansky's septet in B-flat major, perhaps an arrangement of a lost quintet from 1787, is entitled on the manuscript score (St. Petersburg, Saltykov-Shchedrin National Library), "*Sinfonie Concertante pour le fortepiano Organisé, L'harpe, deux Violons, viola di Gamba, Basson, et Violoncelle Composée pour Son Altesse imperiale Madame La Grande Duchesse de Russie par D. Bortniansky 1790*" [capitalization as in original]. On the title page the copyist first

Figure 3 – Marquetried piano case interior

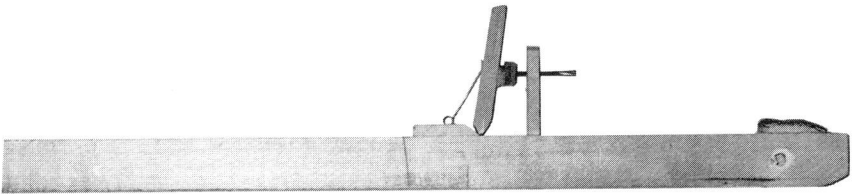

Figure 4 – Piano escapement mechanism

wrote "*L'harpe*" last of the instruments but then rewrote it directly after "*forte-piano Organisé*," displacing the violins, probably in order to elevate the harpist's status. Either the harpist was a friend of Maria Fyodorovna's and the Grand Duchess herself played the keyboard part, or they might have taken turns, since Maria Fyodorovna also owned and presumably played a harp now in the Hermitage collection. The score does not specify organ registrations, but perhaps directions appeared in the (missing) performance parts.

Cimarosa served as imperial court *maestro di cappella* between 1787 and 1791 and presented operas at Gatchina and the Hermitage. His sextet in F requires nearly the same odd ensemble as Bortnyansky's septet; its manuscript score (Bodleian Library, MS. Tenbury 1047) is entitled, "*Sestetto Per il Piano-forte Organizzato Con Arpa, Violino, Viola da Gamba, Violoncello, e Fagotto Composto espressamente per Sua Alt:za Imp:le La Gran Duchessa di tutte le Russie Da Domenico Cimarosa*" and in another hand, "*Ed alla medesima Altezza Sua dedicato*".[20] On the first page of music the keyboard is designated only as *Piano-forte* and on the third page as *Cembalo*, but these terms were conventionally interchangeable, and registration indications for *Flauto, Clarinetti*, and *Cembalo aperto* in the keyboard part of the *Allegro maestoso* movement (only) show that Cimarosa intended the organized piano. (Clarinet, understood here in its original sense of a small clarino or trumpet, gives an idea of the desired tone quality of the reed rank.)

The peculiar instrumentation and simple textures of Bortnyansky's and Cimarosa's works suggest that both were meant to amuse a particular ensemble of amateurs, including at least one man because a woman was unlikely to have played the bassoon. In this connection it would be useful to know who in St. Petersburg still played the viola da gamba as late as 1790.

Whatever the provenance of Gabrahn's organized piano, he was obviously well prepared to construct it, albeit certainly with expert assistance. Whether Gabrahn originated its clever design is uncertain; he might have modeled it in part after a Baltic prototype, perhaps by the Danish organ builder Franz Kirsnick, an early experimenter with free reed pipes, active in St. Petersburg after about 1780. In any case, Gabrahn's instrument exhibits better workmanship than that of the 1774 Zumpe & Buntebart piano, which however, it resembles in being marquetried inside and out, notably under the lid where its striking fan medallion recalls those under the lid of the piano. Also as in the Zumpe & Buntebart, a wide ribbon formerly held its lid back at more than a 90-degree angle; no prop sticks were provided, so the lid either stood wide open like a clavichord's or stayed closed during performance.

Gabrahn's sumptuous FF-f^4 keyboard features mother-of-pearl-covered naturals with vermilion score lines and ebony arcades, and accidentals covered with tortoiseshell – opulent materials that recall the rich decoration of instruments by earlier Hamburg makers such as Johann Adolph Hass and Joachim Tielke. The keys from C to f^4 have padded blocks on the underside that depress the organ's stickers beneath; these stickers pass through a slot in the piano's thick bottom and then through a guide rack, described below. The piano is double-strung throughout, has a single undivided bridge without backpins, and overhead dampers to the top note. The damper arms hinge to a removable panel secured in the spine by elegant pins and clasps.

A brass knob on the left key cheek pulls the hammer rail slightly forward, probably for an *una corda* effect.[21] Two other brass-knobbed levers within the well to the left of the keyboard raise the damper rail and mute batten respectively. It is not clear how to disengage the hammers in order to play the organ alone; the *una corda* stop could not have had this function. The tuning pins, grouped at the right side of the case rather than along the spine as in John Broadwood's patent of 1783, are identified between each pair of pins by German-style inked pitch letters and wire gauge numbers. From treble to bass, the gauge numbers specify three notes at no. 5, fifteen at no. 4, twelve at no. 3, ten at no. 2, seven at no. 1 (the lowest pair marked *Mass.* for *messing*, indicating a switch from iron to brass wire), two at no. 0, two at no. 00, and two at no. 000; the remaining eight overwound bichords lack gauge numbers.

Most astonishing is the piano's sophisticated English double-action mechanism with back checks, intermediate levers, and screw-adjustable escapement jacks recalling those patented in London by John Geib in 1786, three years *after* the date on Gabrahn's soundboard. The fine-threaded brass escapement screws are inserted from the back, necessitating key removal for adjustment (Fig. 4). Brass wire springs return the jacks. Possibly this type of action origi-

Figure 5 – Lion-head handles for lifting the piano;
note rear extension of base containing the organ

Figure 6 – Piano removed, showing guide rack for dowel stickers
(one in place) above intermediate levers

Figure 7 – Wind system assembly

Figure 8 – Inscription "Fagot bass"

nated in Germany and was only developed in London by Geib rather than invented there by him. In any case the action appears to anticipate those in pianos built by Geib for Longman & Broderip in the late 1780s.

To allow access to the top of the organ, the entirely independent piano can be lifted off its base by ornate handles at its sides (Fig. 5). The rectangular, cloth-paneled base containing the organ is deeper than the piano; a board covers the extra depth at the back, where Dom Bedos showed a swell flap. In the base just beneath the slot in the piano's keybed, a sliding guide rack holds the short dowel stickers, which start at note C; these dowels depress long back-hinged intermediate levers that in turn depress longer stickers that fan out to the windchest beneath (Fig. 6). It is not clear how the player shifts the rack to engage and disengage the stickers, as no coupler control is evident. A disconnected pedal lever at the right end of the base allowed an assistant to pump the feeder, which occupies the bottom right side of the base (Fig. 7). Unlike many organized pianos, no provision exists here for the player to pump; this effort would have been inconvenient and undignified, especially for a noblewoman.

Four brass stop knobs, one above the other beneath the keyboard on either side, control the two pipe ranks, both of which are divided bass and treble. The upper knobs govern unnicked, stopped wood flutes; the lower knobs control the reed rank. German stop names are inked on extensions of the slides where the stop rods connect (Fig. 8):

Floet Bass   *Flo: 8 fus disca[nt]*
Fagot Bass   *Rohr c. dis:*

An iron pedal at the front beneath the bass end of the keyboard seems meant to shift the lower of two superimposed flute sliders and simultaneously to open swell panels that enclose the reeds, but this double function is uncertain and could have been altered. The largest wood pipes lie horizontally, as usual, in two stacks of seven at the back of the base behind a stack of six tenor pipes; the flute trebles stand vertically in front of these tenors, and in front of the trebles lie another five horizontally stacked flute pipes, all this behind the fanned stickers.

In front of the stickers stand the reed pipes, which, most unusually, occupy a small swell box enclosed front and back by two pairs of perforated
panels. The outer, sliding panels have rectangular perforations and the inner,
fixed panels have triangular openings (Fig. 9). This arrangement, which closely
resembles that in the restored, *ca.* 1802 George Christoffer Rackwitz organized piano in Stockholm (Statens musiksamlingar, Musikmuseet), ensures a
gradual increase of loudness, since as the outer panels slide sideways, only the
tips of the triangles are exposed at first. Springs at the top treble side of the
swell box close the outer panels when the pedal is released. If the sticker guide
rack above the swell box is removed, the whole box can be unhooked and
lifted up and out of the base.

The reed pipes have rectangular wooden blocks and boots gasketed at
their joint with white leather and held together by small white leather tabs
(Fig. 10). Brass tuning wires penetrate the blocks. The rectangular toes fit
snugly into their toe holes. These pipes have double-conical resonators except in the extreme treble where the resonators are funnel-shaped (Fig. 11).
Dom Bedos shows similar double-conical resonators on Lepine's *basson*, surely
no coincidence. Unfortunately the pipes are disordered and at least eight are
missing, along with most of the brass reeds and shallots. Nevertheless, the resemblance of these unusual pipes, believed to be the oldest extant free-reeds
in any European instrument, to those in the later Rackwitz organized piano
further indicates a close connection between Gabrahn and Rackwitz.

No less impressive than its working parts is the instrument's spectacular,
colored wood and ivory marquetry, the product of a highly skilled artisan employed by a patron of great wealth and refined taste. One element of the marquetry deserves special attention: Short passages of clearly legible music notation appear on the top of the lid and also centered on the piano's nameboard.
The tune on the nameboard (Fig. 12) repeats one of two untexted tunes notated on the lid over an inscription in Latin letters, "by Ulk [Ulrick?] Tideman."
(Fig. 13). Use of the Latin alphabet and the English "by" rather than "von" or
"van" or the Russian equivalent reflects the English vogue at Catherine's court.
Although painstakingly clear, the notation is not entirely accurate. The time signature of the first tune, "No. 6" in G major, is given as ¾ although the meter is

Figure 9 – Cloth panel removed, showing sliding swell panels in front of reeds

Figure 10 – Swell panels removed, showing reeds, many out of order

Figure 11 – Treble reed pipe

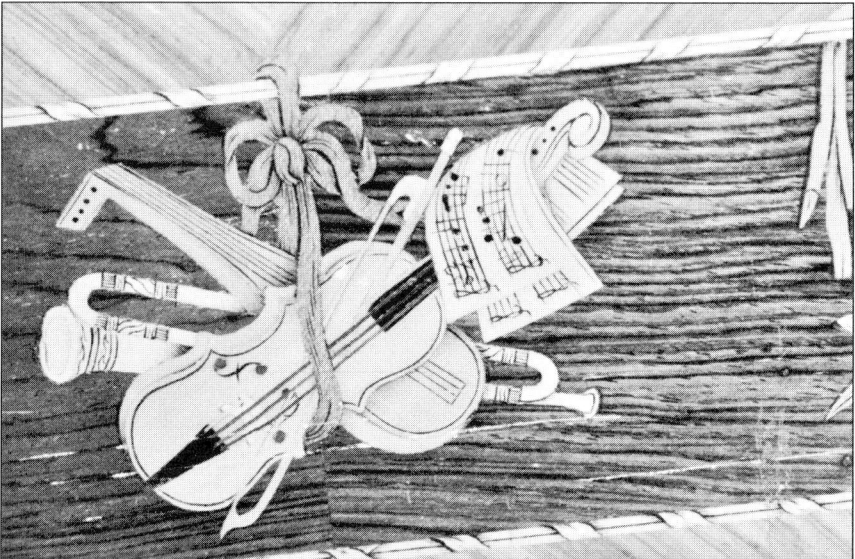

Figure 12 – Inlaid music notation on nameboard

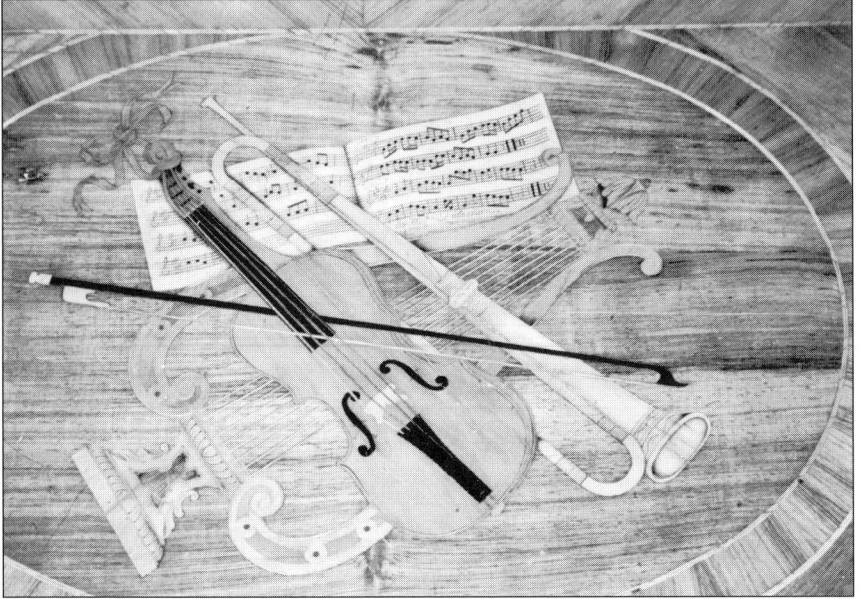

Figure 13 – Music notation in trophy on top of lid

really ⅔. The second melody, "No. 7" in g minor, in ¾ meter, is today associated with a well-known Russian folk song, "Kak u hashego shirokogo dvora" ("Wie bei unserem großen Hof" or "We are sitting in our big yard"). Conceivably, Tideman composed this tune, and this may be its earliest notation, though as its appearance here suggests, perhaps it was copied from a manuscript containing at least five preceding tunes.

Ulrick Tideman has not yet been identified; his surname and variants (Tiedemann, Tidemann, Tijdman) were common in eighteenth-century Britain and northern Europe. An organist named Albert Tidemann resided in Koenigsberg (Kaliningrad) in 1631 and Koenigsberg's proximity to St. Petersburg suggests a family connection to Ulrick, but the dates are far apart.[22] Perhaps Theodor Tiedemann, who built organs in Riga about 1778-1806, was related. However, possibly Ulrick Tideman was not a musician but instead executed the marquetry. The Imperial archives on Pskovskaia Street in St. Petersburg reportedly holds his request for Russian nationality, but these archives are currently closed to outside researchers.

While Gabrahn's organized piano testifies to an exceptional level of taste, ingenuity, and craftmanship, it also poses many questions. For example, its intended pitch and temperament have not yet been determined; this information, possibly obtainable through analysis of the flue pipe dimensions, would have implications for musical performance practice at the Russian court.[23] Indeed, the whole issue of correlations between pipe and string scalings and tunings might well be addressed by study of organized pianos like Gabrahn's.

One hopes that in the future, with cooperation from Pavlovsk's administrators, specialists will be able to document this important instrument thoroughly and guide its conservative restoration. Accomplishing this goal might allow the little-known chamber works of Bortnyansky and Cimarosa, and perhaps still undiscovered music intended for the organized piano, to be heard again as its composers intended.

: : N O T E S : :

[1]   The square piano, or *Tafelclavier*, which derives its rectangular shape from the clavichord, was introduced in the mid-eighteenth century and quickly became the prevailing model, greatly outnumbering grand and upright pianos in amateur use until the late-nineteenth century. Few organized pianos exist in grand or upright forms, although some large, twentieth-century theater organs incorporate grand pianos.

[2]   Wilson Barry, "Preliminary Guidelines for a Classification of Claviorgana" in *The Organ Yearbook* XV (1984), 98-107.

[3]   Michele Todini, *Dichiarazione della Galleria armonica* (Rome: Tizzoni, 1676; reprint, Lucca: Libreria musicale italiana, 1988).

[4]   Peter Williams, article "Claviorgan" in *The New Grove Dictionary of Musical Instruments*, ed. Stanley Sadie (London: Macmillan, 1984), 1:430; further on these instruments see Peter Williams, "The Earl of Wemyss' Claviorgan and its Context in Eighteenth-century England" in *Keyboard Instruments: Studies in Keyboard Organology, 1500-1800*, ed. Edwin M. Ripin (New York: Dover, 1977), 77-87.

⁵ Johann Mattheson, *Der vollkommene Capellmeister* (Hamburg: C. Herold, 1739), 484.

⁶ Michael Cole, *The Pianoforte in the Classical Era* (Oxford: Clarendon Press, 1998), 57. Cole offers a useful survey of combination instruments as well as descriptions and illustrations of various piano action types; see especially "Organized Pianos," 250-253.

⁷ The Danzig advertisements are cited by Benjamin Vogel, "Pianos of Gdańsk until 1815" in *Muzyka Fortepianowa XII* (Gdańsk, 2001), 346-361.

⁸ See Dorthe Falcon Møller, *Danske Instrumentbyggere 1770-1850: en erhvervshistorisk og biografisk fremstilling* (Copenhagen: Gad, 1983). Beenick was associated with the Danish organ and clavier builder and luthier Johan Nicolai Scherr, whose son Emilius Nicolai Scherr established himself as a maker of organs, pianos, and guitars in Philadelphia in 1822.

⁹ Dom François Bedos de Celles, *L'art du facteur d'orgues* Part IV (Paris: L.F. Delatour, 1778), chapter 5, 634-640 and pls. cxxx-cxxxiii.

¹⁰ Cole, *The Pianoforte*, 252-253.

¹¹ Williams, "Claviorgan," 430.

¹² Another *clave organisado* was advertised in Cuba in 1792. Further on Campeche and organized pianos in Latin America, see Laurence Libin, "Music in paintings of José Campeche" in *Music in Art: Iconography as a Source for Music History (Proceedings of the Ninth Conference of the Research Center for Music Iconography, 5-8 November 2003)*, forthcoming.

¹³ Ludwig Spohr, *Autobiography*. English translation, (London: Longman, Green, Longman, Roberts & Green, 1865), 44.

¹⁴ For an early American piano-reed organ combination see Laurence Libin, "A Unique Organized Piano from Pennsylvania" in *The Organ Yearbook* XVIII (1987), 95-108.

¹⁵ See Niclas Fredriksson, "Free Reeds in Organochordia towards the end of the 18ᵗʰ century" in *ISO Journal* 14 (July 2002), 36-42; 15 (November 2002), 20-40; 16 (March 2003), 62-76. Mr. Fredriksson kindly shared with me his notes on Gabrahn's instrument prior to publication.

¹⁶ Herbert Heyde, *Musikinstrumentenbau in Preußen* (Tutzing: Hans Schneider, 1994), 148.

[17] For an on-line description of this work see <www.hermitagemuseum.org>.

[18] Vladimir V. Koshelev, "Gabrahn and his 'piano organisé'" in *Almanac IV, St. Petersburg International Music Festival 2001*, 64–69.

[19] Laurence Libin, "Robert Adam's instruments for Catherine the Great" in *Early Music* (August 2001), 355–367. A piano by Buntebart & Sievers, 1784, remains in the instrument collection of the St. Petersburg State Museum of Theatre and Music.

[20] This manuscript is bound with another Cimarosa sextet, also in the composer's hand but written on different paper with different ink. The volume formerly belonged to the eminent church musician Frederick Arthur Gore Ouseley, founder of the College of St. Michael and All Angels at Tenbury, whose father was Ambassador to Russia and an amateur musician.

[21] An *una corda* stop appears in an organized piano built in 1784 by John Joseph Merlin in collaboration with R. & W. Gray; its piano hammers are disengaged by a separate stop. See C.F. Colt with Antony Miall, *The Early Piano* (London: Stainer & Bell, 1981), 32–33.

[22] Robert Eitner, *Biographisch-Bibliographisches Quellen-Lexikon der Musiker und Musikgelehrten* … (Leipzig: Breitkopf & Härtel, 1898-1904; reprint, New York: Musurgia, 1947), vol. 9. The name Ulrick Tideman appears with no additional information in the Danish genealogical website <www.sadolins.com/onetree101.html> (accessed 3 August 2004).

[23] Pavlovsk curators Alexei Guzanov and Alexandra Vasilyevna Alexe'eva and my colleague V.V. Koshelev kindly assisted me during several brief visits to inspect Gabrahn's instrument, but museum policy precluded a thorough study. Niclas Fredriksson's independent investigation was likewise incomplete. It would be particularly useful to compare Gabrahn's pipework with that in the related Rackwitz instrument, which Fredriksson has exhaustively documented.

OAXACA'S AMAZING ORGAN CULTURE

✸

Susan Tattershall

IT WAS A DELICIOUS ESCAPE from the blazing Oaxacan sun, ducking into the church of Tlacochahuaya, a transition made even more savory by the fact that an organ was rumored to be there. Momentarily blind in the darkness, I fixed my eyes on what I believed must be the *coro*, and waited, as if for a developing Polaroid snapshot, as a shadowy outline transformed into an organ – but what an organ!

"May I go up and see it?" I asked, pointing (a familiar routine).

"It doesn't work."

A few moments later, (thanks in great part to the cuteness of the baby astride my hip), Daniel, the sacristan, and I were old buddies, and we were ascending the steep, dark circular stairway of the bell tower, like the blind leading the blind.

Thus began a rich relationship with the pipe organs in the state of Oaxaca and the efforts to protect them. That day in June 1983, I found myself facing a thing of unusual beauty; a medium-sized organ, case and façade pipes painted with flowers and leaves of exuberant colors. This organ was already known among art historians, since its appearance in Pal Keleman's book *Baroque and Roccoco in Latin America*. But to see it with my own eyes brought a catch to my throat. Who could have imagined that this lovely organ was just one among many?

Today, 21 years from that encounter, there is a mountain of information about the organs in the state of Oaxaca, a big, complex accumulation of facts that desperately needs sorting and organizing. A catalogue of 39 Oaxacan or-

gans was produced in 1999 by Gustavo Delgado and Ofelia Gomez, with funding for the six-year project provided by Banamex.[1] By 2002, only two years
into its existence, the newly formed Instituto de Órganos Históricos de Oaxaca [IOHIO, pronounced "yoyo"] had documented some 26 more. The restoration of the organ in Tlacochahuaya took place during 1990 and 1991, and was
the first in the state of Oaxaca. Between 1996 and 2001 another five restorations were accomplished. A total of 67 pre-twentieth century organs in Oaxaca
have now been documented, and they raise more questions than they answer.

To drive around the *Mixteca Alta* to the north of Oaxaca City, or the Zapotec villages to the south and to look in the churches is to be amazed by the
number and quality of extant pipe organs. The earlier instruments are particularly enchanting, notably the finely painted cases in San Andrés Zautla and
Tamazulapan, and the sweet, more rustic painting found in Santiago Ixtaltepec
or Santiago Tlazoyaltepec[2]. Their cases carry saints, archangels, and generic
musician angels. Their façade pipes are adorned with painted faces (*máscaras*)
in the Spanish tradition and also with painted flowers. Their mouldings and
back-panels are awash in swirls of decorative flourishes in green, gold, black
and white. Occasionally, as in the small case in Coixtlahuaca, even red. These
painted cases fell out of style in the late-eighteenth century, and later organs
like those of Teotitlán del Valle and Zaachila, have cases of natural, unvarnished,
wood. The dating of these organs is in its infancy, and the broad outline which
places unpainted cases into a later period is based mainly by dating backwards
from the group of large, unpainted organs which we know to be from the
late-nineteenth century.

Given the small number of surviving procession organs in Western Europe (approximately four or five) it is amazing to note that there are seven
extant processional organs in the state of Oaxaca alone and another six in the
rest of the Mexican Republic (two others were unfortunately destroyed in the
1990s). In addition, there are another seven organs in Oaxaca of an interesting
"hybrid" type. These instruments are not floor positives, but like the processional organs, sit atop tables. However, these tables are much lower, and the
instruments larger than processional organs, based as they are on a four-foot
open principals. They are winded by pairs of bellows larger in size than those

of the processional organs and which are often placed on a frame beside the organ rather than on a table and directly behind the organ. This makes these "hybrid" instruments too bulky and heavy to move about easily. There exists in the state of Tlaxcala two organs which are of this hybrid type.

In the summer of 1990, the restoration of the Tlacochahuaya organ began, thanks to the patronage of the *Fundación Pichiquequiti*, aided by the Business Bureau of Oaxaca and the village *tequio* – a sort of Public Works Committee comprised of men who wish to volunteer their time for the good of the village (and by so doing, enter the village power structure). José Luis Falcón, a young man from Mexico City and now an organbuilder in his own right, served as apprentice. The project was designed to respect and to manifest three overarching principles. The first was that the community participate as meaningfully as possible so as to engender an emotional investment which would continue to protect the organ after the projects completion. The second was to preserve and incorporate back into the organ, every scrap of old material found within the instrument. The third principle was to meticulously document every material part of the organ, the processes used, as well as every social aspect of the restoration process.

The villagers' enthusiasm was heightened because the restoration was to take place in the organ loft, and they would get to experience the pride and excitement of observing and participating in the process. The opportunity to get to know this organ intimately was exciting to me, notably, as one of the earliest notices we have of an organ in the New World comes from Oaxaca in an account book for the village of Santa Catarina (now known as the *Codice Sierra)*. In 1553, a certain Diego Gutierrez went to Mexico (the city) to fetch "a case of flutes," and the glyph that accompanies this entry in the book depicts organ pipes. Other entries suggest that Diego was the village cabinetmaker. Clearly he would have learned organbuilding from an established builder, and the existence of a Zapotec word for organ *("pichiquequiti")* in a sixteenth-century dictionary suggests that organs were being built and played routinely in Oaxaca during the sixteenth century. Oaxaca was evangelized by the Dominican order. Presumably therefore, the Dominicans had established an organ workshop or a series of workshops by the end of the sixteenth century.

The case of the Tlacochahuaya organ displays the most distinguishing characteristic of Oaxacan organ cases – they have "hips". Among floor positives in Oaxaca, (i.e. neither processional organs nor hybrid-organs) there is an architectural element intrinsic to all of them. Just below impost-height, the organ cases have protuberances left and right – sometimes a simple half-circle, sometimes a complex set of curves – which have no musical, mechanical, nor pneumatic function. At the time of the restoration in Tlacochahuaya, I suggested to a fellow restorer for the Mexican government that, looking at the organ from the front, they appeared to be "hips" (*caderas*). The name stuck. This curvaceous detail actually gives the organs a somewhat feminine appearance, and even in hybrid-organs, an exaggerated moulding around the base of the organ case just above the table, seems an extension of this idea. There are four basic "hip" profiles into which nearly all organs fall as well as several maverick "hip" designs. Some of the earlier and larger organ cases (La Soledad, Yanhuitlan) not only have substantial "hips" but the design of the front of the lower case contains painted lines which repeat the curve reinforcing the visual idea. Some later eighteenth-century organs (Tlacolula, Teotitlán) have small, circular hips, as if the builders felt they were requisite, but couldn't remember why. Organs built in the very late-nineteenth century and early-twentieth century have huge, exaggerated "hip" profiles (the large organs in Coixtlahuaca and Tamazulapan).

For many Oaxacan organs, the case is the only element extant. In Tlacochahuaya, however, slightly over half of the pipes still remained. I asked Daniel during my first visit there if he had ever heard the organ. He said that no one had heard it since the Revolution (1911–1920), because Carranza's troops came through the village and took over the church. They kept their horses below, in the nave, and the soldiers lived in the organ loft. The community believes that the soldiers stole the organ pipes and melted them down for bullets, because apparently, once the soldiers left, the organ no longer functioned. To be accurate, it appears that Carranza never came through Oaxaca, however, some set of troops did. In Oaxaca, horror stories of troops pillaging churches during the Revolution are plentiful, and indeed, the smaller pipes were the ones missing – a fact which supports the ploughshares-to-swords theory. Such wartime tragedies happen in many countries, but in Oaxaca, (and Mexico in general), no one seemed able to pick up the pieces and put the organs back together again when the hostilities ended. The organ culture of Mexico has always been fragile, entrusted to a very few players and builders, and the Church was devastated financially by Juarez's Reform Laws of the 1860s. During the insecure and unstable years of the Revolution, Mexico's grand tradition in organbuilding largely disappeared. Occasionally, inscriptions can be found in organs left by repairmen who worked on the organ in the years after 1920, but no domestically-built pipe organs dating after the Revolution have been found in the country.

For the villagers in Tlacochahuaya, the organ restoration was an object of intense curiosity and scrutiny. A representative of the *tequio* arrived every morning to offer assistance, be it in cleaning sheepskin off the chest or toe-boards, bringing buckets of water, or sweeping the mountains of bat guano out of the organ and off the organ's roof. The council of village authorities also arrived each morning around 10:30 to check on the progress of the work. This was an important part of their duties, as they are responsible to their constituency for any robbery from or damage to the church, as well as the failure of a project from which the church would have benefited. Several of the counselors had never gone up to the loft. All of them spoke Zapotec as their primary language, and a few spoke Spanish. At first, they assembled themselves in a line, facing me, and asked a series of formal questions: "Was the organ any good? Could it really be restored? When would it be finished? Who was going to pay for what? Would they be given an organist to play it?" Each question necessitated a prelude and postlude in Zapotec, among themselves, as they reached consensus as to what I had said, and what the proper response should be. As weeks passed, the questions became more personal, although the questioning, with clarification sessions in Zapotec before and after each inquiry, never waned in intensity: "How much did an airplane ticket from New York cost? Is organbuilding really a profession? Is it a job or is it a hobby? Are there other people who fix organs?" Finally, having established a certain rapport, they asked us if we liked mescal, the regional alcoholic spirit. We promptly responded in the affirmative. The Zapotec debriefing ensued,

Figure 1 – The façade of the organ at Tlacochahuaya

one of the men left the room, and reappeared shortly, bottle of mescal in hand. At this point we became co-conspirators in their search for a morning social hour. Each morning after that, the visit from the village authorities included a shot of mescal, and lots of laughs.

There was a very irritating question, however, that was raised constantly by visitors to the loft. Locals would constantly ask if the organ was *bueno,* i.e. "good." Upon receipt of the affirmative, the automatic reply was, "ahhh, sure, the organ came from Germany, right?" Needless to say, there is nothing whatsoever to link this very region-specific organ to anything in the German tradition, and yet there seemed to be a conviction among the local populace that anything special and unusual must have come from Germany. When a local reporter asked me the question for a newspaper interview, he received a tirade about the unquestionable capacity of Oaxacan craftsman to make such instruments, and the utter lack of relationship between the German organ and Oaxacan organ. The article that appeared the next day stated that the organ was absolutely Zapotec, and was being restored by a German organbuilder. Somehow, the German thing had to get in there.

One glance will tell you that the classic Oaxacan organ is very different from its Northern European counterpart, and a bit of digging will affirm that it is also very distinct from organs in the rest of Mexico. Decoratively, they are unique – not only are grotesque faces painted around the pipe mouths of the façade pipes, (a characteristic related directly to the Iberian organ), but flowers are often painted along the whole length of the pipe (Figure 1). Organ cases from the eighteenth century are painted as well, sometimes with bright flowers – like the Tlacochahuaya case. In other instances, one finds cases with leafy green, white and black decoration and bordered with gold curliques. Even in the cathedral, whose lower case was changed nearly one hundred years ago to a natural wood finish, florid decoration in red and green was found during the restoration of the organ in 1997. Processional organs and hybrid organs, which usually have doors, display paintings of saints, archangels, and musician-angels (Tamazulapan, Santiago Ixtaltepec, Zautla). As a comparison, the processional organ of Santa Anita Huiloac, Tlaxcala, built in 1714 by the Poblano builder Bernardo Rodriguez, has doors containing paintings of musician-angels on the interior surface, but is decorated with vases of flowers, rather than saints, on the outside. As further comparison, no other organ on the *altiplano* is painted in an exuberantly decorative style, though some cases are painted in a solid color while others are decorated in *faux-bois.*

As we began to take the Tlacochahuaya organ apart and do battle with the calling cards left by bats, mice, birds, and squirrels, at the same time holding our breath against the intense stench of bat urine which had penetrated the toe-boards, sliders, chest table and leather, we began to see how beautifully made the organ is. The chests are scribed neatly, holes are drilled cleanly and accurately, and the pipes are made carefully to scale. This was a treat and worth the olfactory assault. The woods employed are ayacahuite (*pinus ayacahuite*, related to Southwestern white pine) and tropical red cedar (*cupressus lusitanica*), both of which are resistant to wood-eating insects. Ayacahuite looks like common pine, and it is not unusual for organbuilders to make the mistake of using pine, thinking it is ayacahuite; thus, we had several portions of the case which had been attacked by woodworm.

There are empty mortises in the sides of the case that align with the sliders, a witness to an earlier incarnation of the organ when the sliders protruded through the case on either side – the organ's sole stop mechanism. Today, the organ has stop knobs at the console, and because the bellows are now on the right side, it would be impossible to reach the mortises to change stops. This brought up the question of dating the organ, as the organ could not possibly have been in its present configuration yet at the time having the sliders poking through the sides of the upper case. While the painting on the lower case matches in color and design the painting on the vault of the church, the painting on the upper case is slightly different in content and effect. Our friends in the village told us that the loft was added to the church in 1730. Clearly then, at one point the organ was below, its bellows being set behind it, stops were manipulated by pulling and pushing the ends of the sliders which protruded from the sides of the organ case. Possibly, it had either a different lower case, or the lower case was painted in a dissimilar style.

Layer upon layer of the organ was taken apart and brushed off, wiped, and scraped. In the case of the channel boards that fed the façade pipes and

the *batalla*, (owing to the depth of bat urine penetration and the stench it produced), we were compelled to plane off several millimeters of urine-soaked
wood. All the leather skins lining the chest table, the underside of the toeboards, and the channelboards were ruined – permeated with animal excre-
tions. Mireya Olvera, a painting restoration expert, worked on cleaning the
painted surfaces of the case. The largest pipe of the *Bardón* had a cross and
the date 1735 inscribed upon it. The *Bajoncillo* on the left side sits in a wood-
en block, fastened to a channel board which connects to the toeboard and is
opposite an abandoned *pajarito* stop on the right-hand side. It is cobbled together, improvised, though ingeniously. Conclusion: at the time the organ was
brought up to the newly-finished loft, the *Bardón, Bajoncillo* and the *Trompeta
en Batalla* were added, and new stop action was installed.

Inscriptions found on some pipes indicated that interventions occurred
during the nineteenth century. Indeed, the character of the keyboard indicated that it was newly made for the organ in the late 1800s. It was not worn
enough to have been original equipment, and the octave scale, the key length,
and the fact that the keys were mounted with pins as hinges at the tail (not
the usual sheepskin hinges found in Mexican organs) made a date of later
manufacture certain. When the bellows was examined, it likewise had been
radically altered. The usual wooden-rib-and-sheepskin-hinge arrangement had
been replaced by a set of internal frames, onto which an enormous hand-sewn
bag of cowskin had been tacked with upholstery nails. The sewing was impec-
cable, given the thickness of the cowhide, and the upholstery nails held firmly.
When open, it looked like an enormous smithy's bellows, though rectangular,
and yet when closed, it hid its true nature so discreetly that I had failed to notice it when writing up the work plan.

A tell-tale strip of white fuzz and old glue around the rim of the bellows
covers made it clear that the cowhide arrangement was a later creation, and
that a reconstruction of the ribs-and-hinges system was in order. The realiza-
tion that good *ayacahuite* was going to be needed to restore a set of ribs to the
bellows put me in a state of mild panic. A quick consultation with the state
authorities (who provided us with a driver to and from the village each day)
resulted in a Sunday excursion to a remote village in the *sierra* above Gue-

latao, birthplace of Benito Juarez. We bargained hard for a few thick planks of *ayacahuite* which that village had harvested, milled and air-dried for seven years, earmarked for the restoration of their altars which had been pillaged and burned during – what else? – the Revolution. Out-bargained to the tune of 20% over expected price, we returned in the pickup with our prized *ayacahuite* only to have the truck break down in the most classic situation possible – on a curve of the high-speed two-lane road, in the dark, in the pouring rain.

Good luck returned a few days later when we found a milling operation in Oaxaca which agreed to cut the planks into boards one centimeter thick, for free. Final planing and cutting was done in the loft, provoking a discussion with the village authorities about the qualities of men and women. It is worth noting that, in 1990 and 1991, Tlacochahuaya had no paved streets, two automobiles and only one telephone, (a public phone located in a small store), with unpredictable hours. With such limited access to the outside world, it had never occurred to our Zapotec friends that women were capable of working with hand-planes and saws, and they weren't sure it was "right" in the cosmic scheme of things. However, they were unanimous in agreeing that the female is the stronger sex, and concurred wholeheartedly that they would not wish to belong to *that* half of humanity which gives birth. Today, the village has phones, several computers, paved streets, a sewer system, cars, and a handful of two-story houses. When I return to Tlacochahuaya for maintenance visits, the sacristans and authorities don't bat an eyelash when I head up to the loft with my toolbox, and no one bothers to make the long climb up to stare at me working.

In an effort to procure leather for the bellows, and to disseminate the news of our project beyond the town limits of Tlacochahuaya, we pulled ourselves out of bed early one Sunday morning to bargain for skins in the Tlacolula market, some 45 minutes from Oaxaca City. The market is a frenzy of Zapotec villagers all buying and selling raw materials: skins and the meat of the animals the skin once belonged to; fruits, vegetables, chilis, cactus ears, mescal, and any other edible commodity imaginable; saddles, blankets, tools and building materials; herbs, pomades, potions and candles for witches and healers. Naturally, we were out-bargained there too, thanks to the *gringa* factor, but my very obvious presence in the market produced a flood of people coming to Tlacochahuaya during the following week, in cars and on donkey back, with skins for sale.

There is a row of tanneries along a stream in Oaxaca City, and it was easy to find a tanner to cure the skins for us. The traditional alum tawing process of sheepskins appeared to be unknown to the tanners, though extant bellows and chests suggest that in the past, this was a common technique of preserving skins for organbuilders' use. Eager to please us and secure our business, the tanner promised the skins earlier than he could actually deliver them, and the skins were finally delivered to us, still damp, the very last day of the first stage of the project. I had to leave Oaxaca for New York, and José Luis stayed to finish leathering the bellows, and to await Joaquín Wesslowski, the pipemaker from Mexico City contracted to restore the old pipes and to make the new ones. It was clear from the quality of the tanner's work that I was going to need to bring a few gusset skins from the States when I returned for the second stage of the project (luckily, I had brought good sheepskins for re-lining the chest with me).

The day after I left, a sub-director of the Instituto Nacional de Antropología e História (INAH) arrived, claiming not to have been notified about the project (in fact, the head of the INAH had been invited to the kick-off event, and had declined to come). José Luis summoned the village authorities, but no amount of arguing or protesting was sufficient. Mr. *Queso Grande* from the INAH declared the project "suspended," put a padlock on the choir doors, and stormed off in a self-righteous cloud of dust. Joaquín Wesslowski arrived the next day to the bad news that the pipes were padlocked in the *coro*. José Luis brought him to meet the village authorities, who, at first, engaged in their usual huddle-then-talk routine, and then went into plenary huddle mode. Ultimately, José Luis and Joaquín were instructed to go to the *coro*. A few minutes later, the authorities arrived with a big bolt-cutter, and with an air of great satisfaction, cut the padlock off the door. Just to be safe, they waited until nightfall to haul the pipes down to Joaquín's van. They needn't have worried, however, the INAH never returned to the scene of the crime.

Back in New York, I was able to reflect on the unusual disposition of the organ:

Left Hand:	*Right Hand:*
Bardón (Stopped Flute, 8′)	Bardón (Stopped Flute, 8′)
Flautado (Principal, 4′)	Flautado I (4′)
Octava (Principal, 2′)	Flautado II (4′)
Quincena (Principal, 1′)	Octava I (2′)
Diez y Novena (Principal, ⅔′)	Octava II (2′)
Veinte y Dosena (C-B ½′; c⁰-c¹ 1′)	Docena (c$\sharp^1$ – c², 1⅓′; c$\sharp^2$ – c³, 2⅔′)
Bajoncillo (Trumpet, 4′)	Trompeta en Batalla (8′)
	Pajaritos

There are no wood pipes, and all ranks save the *Bardón* and reeds are principal-scaled. Such a disposition, with the doubled pitches in the right hand, seemed unusual, to say the least. My secret fear was that it would be a boring-sounding organ (anyone who has heard it will tell you emphatically that it is not). Subsequently, during the following summer and stage two of the project, we had the opportunity to travel to San Andres Zautla, a village on the other side of Oaxaca City in the hills to the west of Etla. The organ there has five ranks of unaltered, homogeneous pipework, and, though missing the keyboard and bellows (which the community burned one year to create "holy" ashes for Ash Wednesday), was missing only sixteen pipes. It has an exterior decoration strikingly similar to that of Tlacochahuaya. Its disposition is the following:

Left Hand:	*Right Hand:*
Flautado (4′)	Flautado I (4′)
Octava (2′)	Flautado II (4′)
Quincena (1′)	Octava I (2′)
Diez y Novena (⅔′)	Octava II (2′)
22nd/15th (C – B ½′; c⁰ – c¹ 2′)	Docena/Quinta (c$\sharp^1$– c² 1⅓′; c$\sharp^2$ – c³ 2⅔′)
Tambor	Pajaritos

It was comforting to realize that the disposition in Tlacochahuaya was not an oddity, but was representative of a local style. During the second stage of the restoration, as the voicing and tuning work went forward, it became apparent what this doubling of pitches in the right hand was all about – the effect is to give the soprano tessitura a strong, brilliant sound such that the organ effortlessly maintains the same intensity from bass to treble. It represents a consciously chosen aesthetic, one which bestows depth, force and color to the upper registers of the organ, without shrillness or screechiness. A strong sound in the treble of an organ would have been essential for another aspect of Oaxacan musical culture – brass bands are everywhere in the villages, and often enter the church and play along with the organ.

The result, of these peculiar dispositions, perhaps unintended, is that each octave of the organ has a different disposition, creating a plenum that functions like a large mixture, recalling a *Blockwerk* organ disposition. In the case of Tlacochahuaya the octave-by-octave disposition is the following:

$C - c^0$: $8', 4', 2', 1', \frac{2}{3}', \frac{1}{2}'$, Bajoncillo $4'$
$c\#^0 - c^1$: $8', 4', 2', 1', 1', \frac{2}{3}'$, Bajoncillo $4'$
$c\#^1 - c^2$: $8', 4', 4', 2', 2', 1\frac{1}{3}'$, Clarin $8'$
$c\#^2 - c^3$: $8', 4', 4', 2', 2', 2\frac{2}{3}'$, Clarin $8'$

In the case of San Andres Zautla:

$C-B$: $4', 2', 1', \frac{2}{3}', \frac{1}{2}'$
$c^0 - c^1$: $4', 2', 1', \frac{2}{3}'$
$c\#^1 - c^2$: $4', 4', 2', 2', 1\frac{1}{3}'$
$c\#^2 - c^3$: $4', 4', 2', 2', 2\frac{2}{3}'$

Interestingly, there exists a later organ (1772) in San Andres Huayapan, a village suburban to Oaxaca City, with relatively homogenous pipework in which this style is still apparent:

Left Hand: *Right Hand:*
Flautado (4′) Flautado I (4′)
Quincena (2′) Flautado II (4′)
Octava (1′) Octava (2′)

Docena (⅔')	Docena (1⅓')
Tapadillo (4' Stopped Flute)	Tapadillo (4' Stopped Flute)
	Tambor

Another surprise in Tlacochahuaya, where the façade pipework is so pristine that the underside of the cut-ups still carry the decorative paint of 1735, is that at the time it ceased to function around 1913, it was still pitched at A392 and had never been raised to modern pitch. During the rebuilding of the organ in the Cathedral of Oaxaca in 1997, the tuning slots which had been cut into the backs of the old open 8-foot façade pipes (to bring the pitch of the organ to A440 in the 1911 rebuild) were closed by in-soldering pieces of similar metal composition. Once restored, this stop tuned perfectly at A392. The organ in Zautla had suffered a crude raising of pitch in the 1930s, which included cutting the bass notes C, D, and E of each rank to correspond to E, F-sharp, and G-sharp. In other words, the classic mistake of the inexperienced modern organbuilder who has never seen a short octave before and assumes that the original organbuilder must have made a hideous mistake in making pipes that appear to correspond to the keys E, F-sharp and G-sharp, actually play the pitches of C, D and E. Lacking the funds to restore each pipe to its original pitch, we left the organ at A415 pitch during the restoration of 1997.

My personal theory as to why organs in Oaxaca remained at A392 for such a long time relates to the aforementioned band tradition – in other parts of Mexico, and in most of the European Catholic world, band instruments and the village band, while a welcome accoutrement to outdoor processions, are considered "profane" and remain outside the church building. I have seen many feast days in Tlaxcala, where the band players park their instruments in the graveyard in front of the church when they enter to take communion – they consider it impolite even to bring the instrument inside the church, much less *play* it inside the church.

In Oaxaca, this is somewhat different. The band tradition is alive and well and connected to the sacred. Tlacochahuaya (population *ca.* 7,000) has four village bands, and while they usually simply accompany processions to the front door of the church, they *do* play inside the church on special occasions. The din is unbelievable. With band instruments tuned in B-flat, and the organ tuned at A392, both organ and band can read from the same music. At times during the voicing and tuning process, when the band approached the church, we would accompany them on the organ which, even though tuned in mean-tone, did quite well.

One such occasion occurred when a man in the village committed sui-cide, and we were told to cease our racket when we heard the band approach the church for the funeral Mass. Though the deceased and his "wife" had nev-er formally married, they had spent their adult lives together and raised several children. At around 3 P.M. we heard the band – it was playing a lively, dance-like piece. Puzzled, we asked the *campanero* (bell-ringer) what all the frivolity was about. He replied that the village tradition commanded that when a sin-gle person died, happy music be played in the procession, but when a married person died, dirges were played. During the sermon, the priest regaled the au-dience with tales of the tortures of Hell the deceased was going to endure, as he had not only committed the sin of suicide, but also never formally married his mate. As if to soften the harangue, most of the attendees in the back rows were passing around bottles of mescal, and enjoying generous swigs. We were complimented later on the organ music we provided for the service.

During our work in Tlacochahuaya, we knew almost nothing about other organs in the state of Oaxaca. Visitors often came up to the loft and said things like, "in my uncle's village, there's an organ just like this one," or "my father used to talk about the organ in his village, and the description is similar to this one." Given how often one stumbles into a church asking about a rumored organ only to find that the church has nothing more than an old harmonium, I dismissed most of these reports as wishful thinking. Yet recent research by the IOHIO and others has begun to make inroads into the history of these instruments.

Taking the group of organs whose decorative elements put them in a class with that of Tlacochahuaya, we now know that the organ of San Andrés Zautla dates from 1726, that of Quiatoni from 1729, Ixtaltepec, 1730, and Tlazoyaltepec, 1724. This would suggest that the Tlacochahuaya organ's 1735

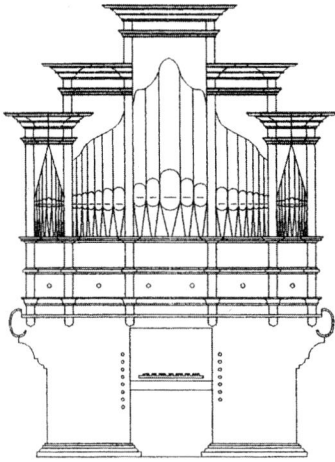

ASUNCION TLACOLULA   SAN DIONISIO OCOTEPEC

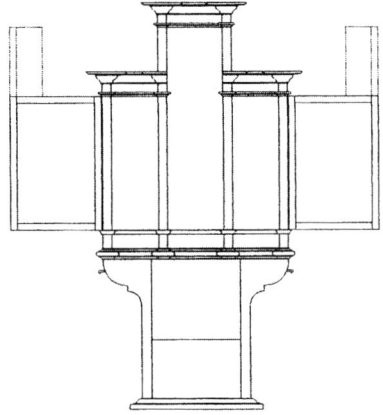

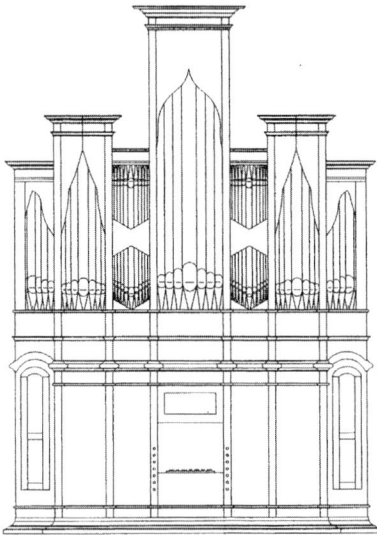

CATEDRAL   SANTO DOMINGO YANHUITLAN

Drawings by Arquitecto José-Luis Acevedo

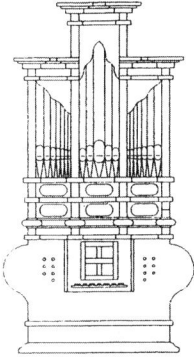

SAN JERONIMO
TLACOCHAHUAYA

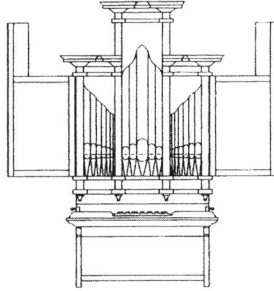

SAN ANDRES ZAUTLA

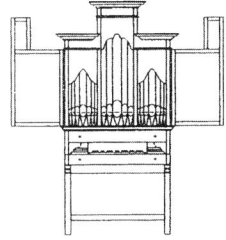

SAN ANDRES HUAYAPAN

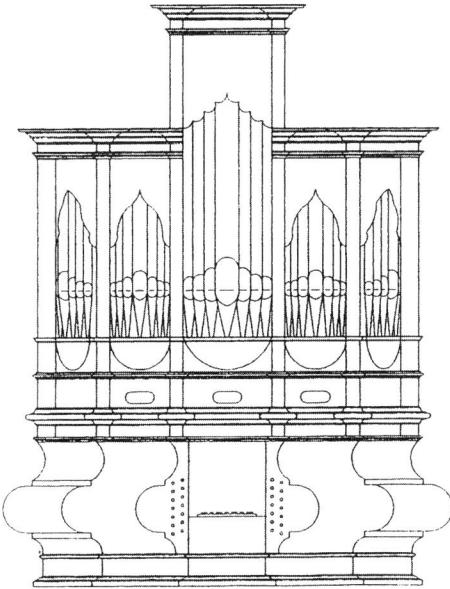

LA SOLEDAD

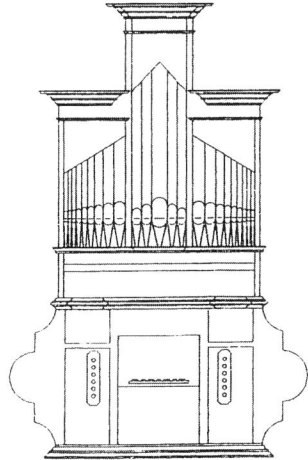

SAN MATIAS JALATLACO

changes were made shortly after the organ was first built, sometime in the 1720's. In 1990, when it was the only organ in Oaxaca to have been dismantled and documented, its disposition appeared to date from the mid-seventeenth century, and it was surprising to discover, through the IOHIO's efforts, that the Tlacochahuaya organ is about 70 years younger than I'd surmised. Jacques Oortmerssen, the well-known Dutch organist, made an interesting observation recently, after playing concerts in Tlacochahuaya and Zautla. He believes they are not Spanish organs at all, but pertain to a type that might be called the "pan-European" organ, the sort of instrument built all over Europe before the emergence of national styles of organ design. Their lack of cornetas, large external reed divisions, and nasardos speak to an earlier style.

Mechanically and stylistically, some general statements can be made about the Oaxacan organs. First, like their Iberian ancestors, all Oaxacan organs have divided stops, with the division at $c^1/c\#^1$. No two-manual organs appear to exist, and the few organs that have small pedal boards are from the late-nineteenth century. The standard key compass of the eighteenth century organs is $C - c^1$, or 45 notes. Organs were built right into the late-eighteenth century with short octaves, though later organs developed full bass octaves, and a typical organ from the 1870s (Jalatlaco) is likely to have a complete bottom octave, and a treble compass up to g^3, or 56 notes. In these ways, the Oaxacan organ is very much like its counterpart in the rest of Mexico.

Much study needs to be done concerning the disposition of Oaxaca's early organs, and luckily there are several organs which retain more than 50% of their original pipes: Tlacochahuaya, San Andrés Zautla, San Pedro Yucuxaco, Santa María Tinú, Santa María Xalatlaco, Asunción de María Tehuantepec, and San Mateo Yucucuí. There are several others whose pipework has been altered, but which retain enough old material to merit close scrutiny and eventual incorporation into the big picture: San Andrés Huayapan, Tlacolula (large organ), San Pedro Quiatoni, Santiago Comaltepec, Santa María Tiltepec, San Andrés Sinaxtla, Santa Mariasun Tlaxiaco, and Santiago Ixtaltepec. Unfortunately, two of the largest and oldest organs in the state – the large organ in the church of La Soledad (Oaxaca City: case 1686, organ late-eighteenth, intervention in the 1950s) and the gorgeous old organ in Yanhuitlan (mid-eighteenth century) – suffered careless "restorations" recently which not only altered their tonal character, but left little documentation on the pre-intervention state of the organ. The La Soledad organ retains enough of its old pipework to merit careful documentation and study; the Yanhuitlan organ's pipework was a mish-mash of styles and was categorically replaced by new pipes, save a dozen or so. The old pipes were thrown helter-skelter in a large carton, but at least, were not destroyed.

Only a few of these organs were known to us in 1991, as we began the second stage of the work, and none was capable of making so much as a peep. We were eager to reassemble the organ, and half-crazy to know what it sounded like.

- The chest table, toeboards and channel-board elements had been re-lined with sheepskin and their holes cut open and burned in the Mexican/Spanish tradition. Burning the holes raises the rims around the holes, creating a natural slider-seal. Not possessing the specially-made iron pokers nor a safe place to heat them red-hot, we used an electrician's soldering iron.

- The channel boards and toeboards which feed the façade pipes, the *batalla* and the *Bajoncillo* were assembled. I confess I am a sinner when it comes to pieces that are impossible to access without taking every pipe out of the organ, and I assembled them with wood screws, not the original nails, for security.

- The toeboards were nailed back into place with the original nails. We cleaned the old nails with a metal brush, and then ingratiated ourselves with Doña Licha, the lady who fed us each day at noon. She allowed us to slip our frying pan full of oiled nails onto her tamale-cooking fire until they turned a nice oily black color, and turned her courtyard into an acrid-smelling environment.

❊   The sliders were adjusted, and the stop action, a crude affair, was reassembled using its original nails as pins.

❊   The old stone weights, nicely cut to size with beveled edges, had been left in the bellows' lids even after their ribs had been converted to cowskin bags 100 years ago. Once the restored bellows were finished, they gave an astonishing 84 mm of wind pressure.

❊   The façade pipes had not been transported to Mexico City because they were in excellent condition, and because their decoration would have made them vulnerable to damage during transport. One was missing, and its measurements were sent to Wesslowski, who made a replacement. Upon my arrival in the Oaxaca airport for the second stage of the restoration, I fell into a conversation with a priest who reported that many years ago a man had come to his door and tried to sell him a painted organ pipe purportedly from the organ in Tlacochahuaya. The priest didn't believe him, and refused to buy the pipe. How unfortunate, as we might have been able to recuperate the original pipe! Mireya painted the new pipe, which is nearly indistinguishable from the older pipes.

Just as we began to hear the first sounds from the organ, a howling puppy appeared at the church door. This frustration was ameliorated by adopting the pup and bringing it up to the loft with us.[3] The next frustration was a bit more complicated. I became ill, and after several rounds of antibiotics, fasting, and two doctors' visits, I was too weak to work through the day without resting periodically. The village authorities caught me lying down on the job one day and became alarmed, as they would have been criticized mercilessly by their fellow villagers for letting a sub-contractor sleep during working hours. They questioned me pointedly about my condition, and huddled in Zapotec at length. They became more formal than usual in presenting their diagnosis – evil eye. Someone had given me the "eye," probably while I was dancing at their annual fiesta a couple of weeks previously. I was escorted to the house of the village *curandera*, Katy and seated on a chrome and plastic chair in Katy's open patio. Soon dense clouds of incense smoke surrounded me. Katy took an egg out of the refrigerator, poured rubbing alcohol over it, put the egg on the top of my head, made a sign of the cross with it, and began rubbing it vigorously on my head. The shell was hard and hurt my scalp. The egg made its way all over my body, right down to my feet, Katy's whispered prayers intermittently broken with exclamations of "ay Dios!" She then cracked it open into a tall glass of water and inspected it gravely. Gathering up an armload of basil, rosemary and rue, she waved them in the incense smoke, dripped alcohol over them and as I floated in the soothing smells and her whispered prayers – *whack!* – she began to beat me hard with them as leaves flew, smoke billowed, and every part of my body stung as I tried to sort out which was worse, evil eye or this beating, and trying to imagine what went horribly wrong in Zapotec childhoods that healers beat up their healees. The massacre finished, Katy told me to return the next day for Round Two. The next morning, to my astonishment, my illness was gone.[4]

At this point, the organ began to reveal itself to us on an almost daily basis. We repaired the façade pipes (4-foot open principal, left hand) in the *coro* and with very little encouragement, they spoke cleanly on their wind. Installing their right-hand counterpart inside the case came next. This rank was nearly complete and untouched, and with the small rips at the tops of the pipes repaired, it was clear that not only was the organ tuned to A392, it was in a mean-tone temperament, and sang out beautifully on 84 mm of wind pressure. With each new addition, half-stop by half-stop, the organ gained more volume and brilliance. However, the *Bajoncillo* proved to be a challenge. Since this addition originated with the 1735 rebuild and was installed on the small *Tambor* slider, it consequently had very little room. The channel board that transmits the wind to the pipes from the slider is an exercise in latin virtuosity to be sure, yet the pipes received very little wind. The stop was original, except for one resonator, two shallots, and a few reed tongues. As this was the first restoration in Oaxaca, of a type of organ that had never been studied, it was imperative to retain all the available old material. While the result was disappointing musically, the educational and historical value of retaining the old material until more was known about the Oaxacan organ tradition, was infinitely more valuable.[5]

The only lighting in the *coro* (excepting the two light-bulbs we had rigged to a pirated electric line that came through one of the bell-tower windows) came from an arched opening in the front *coro* wall, some six feet wide and fourteen feet high. A huge rough wooden frame to which chicken wire had been nailed, provided the only barrier between the outside flora and fauna, and the inside of the church. Unfortunately, the birds had long ago figured out how to perch on the barricade, dip under the arch, and fly into the church. No sooner had Mireya finished restoring the lovely oval oil portrait of Saint Jerome (patron of the church) which perches atop the organ, than a bird alighted upon it and relieved itself copiously all over the unfortunate saint. The sound of the organ attracted the birds, and simply holding a note for tuning provoked an animated chorus of bird cheeps and whistles. Discouragement was only heightened as discussion after discussion with the villagers proved useless; they found the birds' singing delightful, and could not conceive of any way possible of keeping them out as they had never known the church to be without birds, ever, period. The opening also allowed in every noise created within a two-block radius, so the blast of the horn of the hourly bus to Oaxaca City, the donkeys braying, and the turkeys gobbling were added to the cheeping, and the patter of the tour guides' voices inside the church. The lack of light and of peace and quiet was overcome only by the excitement of hearing layer upon layer of the organ – which, fortunately, is quite loud.

The sound of the organ, of course, carried out of the church through the same opening, and people began to be curious. Several villagers appeared in the loft, panting and clutching their chests, declaring it to be the first time in their lives they'd ever come up the tortuous stairway. One was a man who declared himself to be the current organist (of the Hammond below) and the grandson of the church's last organist who played upon the pipe organ. He brought with him a book of music left him by his grandfather – an organ method written by a student of Hilarion Eslava, the famous Romantic Spanish organist. He asked permission to try the organ, and acquitted himself beautifully, playing only in keys that work in meantone, and negotiating the short octave like a pro. Another visitor was an octogenarian who remembered hearing the organ as a five-year-old, going to Mass with his grandmother. He stated emotionally that he could die now, having heard the organ again.

Finishing the organ was anticlimactic. No inauguration festivities were held. No concert took place. So little was known about organ building in Oaxaca at that point, there was no means by which to judge the organ, its restoration, or to assess its place in the larger context of the tradition. It would be another six years before a second organ in Oaxaca was restored, allowing a heightened level of investigation and study to shed some light on the broad patterns emerging in the history of the organ in Oaxaca.

Musically, Oaxaca's classic organ dispositions may have followed two parallel developments. First, we have the style exemplified by the Tlacochahuaya and Zautla organs, which appear to have the earliest homogeneous, consistent, and original pipework in the state. These present a fascinating musical conception, as discussed above: dividing at $c^1/c^{\#1}$, consistent with Iberian practice, the disposition of stops in the left hand follows the *ripieno* principle, i.e. the pitch of the *Flautado Mayor* is followed by its octave, its fifteenth, its nineteenth and its twenty-second. In the right hand, however, the *Flautado Mayor* is doubled by a separate, independent stop, whose scale shows no differentiation from the *Flautado Mayor*. These are followed by the octave, and it, too, is doubled in the same fashion. A twelfth follows, and, depending on the size of the organ, a fifteenth. As both of these instruments are small, it is difficult to predict how this style would elaborate in an organ of larger proportions.

A second style is represented by the dispositions of the La Soledad organ and the Yanhuitlan organ (this analysis is based on having studied these organs before their "restorations"), which also date from the eighteenth century, and which are larger than the previous two. This style incorporates the use of 8-foot and 4-foot flutes, which a larger organ in the first style may also have included. More importantly, not only do the left-hand stops proceed in *ripieno* fashion, as in the first style, but the right hand stops do so as well – there is no doubling of pitches in the right hand. Additionally, the horizontally-placed reeds (the *batalla* or *trompetería*) appear to be more narrowly scaled than the reeds in Tlacochahuaya, although this could be an error made in the recent work on those organs (their sound, frankly, is not congruent with the style). The organ in La Soledad has a three-rank mixture, which is unusual. Additionally, organs of this group or style often contain an interior *Trompeta Real* (interior 8-foot full-length reed, *real* = 'real' not 'royal') in the left hand only, as a complement to the 8′ *Trompeta de batalla* in the façade.

Generalizations can also be made about the Oaxacan organ, including Oaxacan organs from the mid- to late-nineteenth century, in comparison to other organbuilding styles in Mexico:

The Oaxacan organ sound rests squarely on the *Flautado* (principals) and lacks mutation stops or compound stops. Even large organs have no *cornetas*, third-sounding individual ranks, or wide-scaled quints. If there is a flute stop, it is a work-horse flute: a *Bardón*, meant either to double the lowest pitched *Flautado*, or, as in Tlacochahuaya, serve as the lowest pitch in the organ, while conserving space. The 4-foot flutes in La Soledad and Yanhuitlan may be considered luxuries. Organs in the Poblano tradition, on the other hand (i.e. those extant in the states of Tlaxcala and Puebla), exploit the *Corneta* abundantly: the organ in El Señor del Despojo, Huamantla includes a *Corneta* as one of only five half-stops in the right hand. The organ in San Pablo Apetatitlan, has among the twelve stops in the right hand: two *cornetas*, a 3⅕-foot rank, but is missing its 1⅗-foot rank.

Spicing up the *Flautado* sound are reed stops, which, again, are not found in nearly the abundance as they are in Tlaxcala, Puebla, Mexico State or Guanajuato, where a medium-sized organ is likely to have a horizontally-placed reeds of 4-foot and 2-foot in the left hand, and 16-foot and 8-foot in the right. In Oaxaca, the *batalla* consists only of one half-stop, or occasionally two half-stops. On the other hand, there is the aforementioned left-hand *Trompeta Real* that is found in one set of Oaxacan organs; it is generally *not* the case that there are interior reed stops in the rest of Mexico.

An unofficial moratorium on organ restorations is now in place in Oaxaca, to prevent any more damage to the instruments by poorly conceived projects or untrained "restorers," and to allow time for thorough documentation of extant instruments. More importantly, the IOHIO maintains close communication with the communities that possess old pipe organs (in whatever state they may be!) in a continuous propaganda campaign aimed at encouraging the communities' efforts to protect the organs they have, and to "keep the faith" making the effort to conserve material in communities where the organ is restorable. Villages change municipal authorities every year or every few years, and the constant contact and constant exhortation to respect what is, after all, their own history, is crucial to protecting the material information necessary to forming a complete history of the organ in Oaxaca. Now, fifteen years after being questioned constantly as to the German origin of the organ in Tlacochahuaya, communities know that their own ancestors were the builders of these gems, and their pride is palpable.

: : N O T E S : :

[1] Titled *Órganos Históricos de Oaxaca, estudio y catalogación,* it contains good photographs, but the written information it contains – stoplists, historical commentary, descriptions – is fatally flawed. Buy it for the beautiful pictures, but beware of the text!

[2] Photos and information about many of the organs mentioned in this essay are available on the website of the IOHIO. Go to <www.iohio.org>.

[3] Named "Lupita," she returned to New York with me where she became famous locally for escaping the confines of the yard and raiding the bagel shop's dumpster. When I received the first recording of the Tlacochahuaya organ (by Dominique Ferran) and played it, Lupita jumped up on the sofa, perked her ears, put muzzle skyward and howled for the duration. Though deaf and arthritic now, she can still steal a bagel from five paces, in the blink of an eye.

[4] Katy and I became very good friends, and for years, when I brought groups to Tlacochahuaya to play the organ, her house was our rest stop. I have seen her cure migraines, diagnose autoimmune illnesses, heal pulmonary and digestive woes and there was even an exorcism in Detroit I won't go into. I have no more understanding how she does this now than I did then.

[5] To make matters worse, the *Bajoncillo* never had a rack, and several years later, the resonators began to fall over and their basses to collapse under their own weight. In the summer of 2004, after years of revisiting the problem of the *Bajoncillo,* the decision was reached, with the collaboration of the IOHIO, to replace the crushed basses of the four largest resonators with antimonial lead pieces, and to disassemble the channel boards and open the channels to allow more air to pass to the reeds. The result, done in the fall of 2004, is a reliable *Bajoncillo* that keeps its tuning and lends the color and brilliance to the ensemble and to solo work that it should.

MANUAL DESIGNATIONS AS
REGISTRATION INDICATORS
IN THE ORGAN CHORALES OF J.S. BACH

Lynn Edwards Butler

FOR MUCH OF THE LAST TWO CENTURIES, discussion about the designation *à 2 Clav. et Ped.* has focused on its use in specifying the instrument intended for the performance of a given work. Johann Nikolaus Forkel's claim that Johann Sebastian Bach's *Passacaglia* BWV 582 "is more for two clavichords and pedal (*zwey Claviere und Pedal*) than for the organ," and his reference to the six *Sonatas* BWV 525–530 as trios "for two claviers and obbligato pedal" (*für zwey Claviere mit dem obligaten Pedal*) led some nineteenth-century scholars to conclude that these works were written for an instrument other than the organ.[1] Friederich Conrad Griepenkerl, editor of the mid-nineteenth-century Peters edition of the Bach organ works, viewed both the *Passacaglia* and the six trio sonatas as works "really written for the Clavichord with two Manuals and the Pedal."[2] Wilhelm Rust thought the *Passacaglia* was for a "harpsichord with pedal."[3] Philipp Spitta saw the trio sonatas as lying somewhere between "organ-style" and "chamber-style" and therefore best performed on a "pedal Clavier with two manuals" (*Pedal Clavier mit zwei Manualen*).[4] Georg Kinsky argued (and others have agreed) that because *à 2 Clav. et Pedal* was applied by Bach to pieces that were "indisputably for the organ" (chorale preludes in the *Orgelbüchlein,* for example), it could not have meant pedal clavichord or harpsichord.[5] For Kinsky, Peter Williams, and Robert Marshall, the designation "2 Clav. e(t) Ped(al)" is synonymous with the organ. Most recently, Joel Speerstra argues convincingly that the term can be applied to any keyboard instrument with two manuals and pedal, whether organ, pedal clavichord, or pedal harpsichord, but that it was often used to refer specifically to the pedal clavichord.[6]

In this paper I will argue that when Bach employs *à 2 Clav. et Pedal* in the title heading of a work, he is not designating an instrument; rather, he is giving registrational information to the performer. He is specifying that two manuals (or keyboards) are required for the piece's performance, that there is an obbligato pedal part, and that each manual part requires its own distinct registration. Furthermore, such pieces allow – indeed, require – the performer to demonstrate the "art of using the stops," matching the character of the music with the character of the registration. As such, these works stand in marked contrast to those designated *Organo pleno*, pieces that require only one manual and pedal for their performance, and that are registered with a "full organ" sound, that is, a combination of primarily principal-scaled stops at a wide range of pitches.[7]

The following discussion will deal first with contemporary late Baroque views of organ registrations – in particular, with the opposition between music for *à 2 Clav. et Pedal* and music for *Organo pleno* registrations. The second part of the paper will address Bach's use of the *à 2 Clav. et Pedal* designation in autographs and printed sources of his organ chorales.[8]

TWO CATEGORIES OF REGISTRATIONS

Contemporary late Baroque German theorists divide organ registrations into two basic and over-arching categories. This division can be inferred from Jacob Adlung's *Musica mechanica organoedi*. In the two chapters that he devotes to the art of organ registration, Adlung first provides detailed descriptions of all of the organ's stops – at ninety pages, easily the longest chapter in his monumental study. Then, in the chapter entitled "On the Use of the Registers," he sets out the fundamental precept of organ registration: each register is to be used "according to its character." Devoted "solely to organists," this chapter deals first with combining stops of various pitches, and then with registering in two basic ways: either with two manuals and pedal (he recommends use of a wide variety of registrations) or with full organ sound in both the manual(s) and the pedal.[9]

Johann Mattheson puts it succinctly:

Generally speaking, organ registrations can be divided into two classes. To the first belongs the full organ [registration]; to the second belong all the other diverse variations [registrations] that can be made, especially by using different manuals, and [playing] with weaker, yet well-chosen registers.[10]

Forkel's now famous description of how Bach registered the organ is revealing as well:

When Joh. Seb. Bach seated himself at the organ when there was no divine service … he used to choose some subject and to execute it in all the various forms of organ composition so that the subject constantly remained his material … First, he used this theme for a prelude and a fugue, *with the full organ*… . Then he showed his *art of using the stops* for a trio, a quartet, etc. … Afterwards followed a chorale, the melody of which was playfully surrounded in the most diversified manner by the original subject, in three or four parts. Finally, the conclusion was made by a fugue, with the full organ (emphasis added).[11]

Bach employed "full organ" registrations at the beginning of the "concert" when he improvised a free prelude and fugue, and again at the conclusion. For the rest of the concert, he "showed his art of using the stops." Improvising preludes, Adlung tells us, "can be done with both soft and strong stops" – that is, with the strong, loud stops that comprise the *Organo pleno* or with the softer stops one employs to make diverse variations or registrations:

It [improvisation] can be done with both soft and strong stops, depending on what ideas one has, or on whether one is improvising a prelude to a sad or a happy piece or chorale. Improvisations at the beginning and conclusion of the church service are best played with the full organ. But when one is improvising before something, it can either be a free improvisation (*eine gemeine Fantasie*), in which case one would use the full organ but also provide variety by changing once in a while to soft sounding stops, or one can play on two manuals that are specially registered, not too loudly, but with one more dominant than the other, and the dominant voice would play the chorale melody, or a least some part of it, if one is improvising on a chorale.[12]

Which registration one chooses depends (1) on the nature of the musical ideas one has, (2) on the affect of the chorale or cantata that follows the prelude (whether it is "sad or happy"), (3) on whether one is improvising a prelude to a chorale or a cantata (which can be improvised using "full organ" or "two manuals and pedal"), or (4) on whether one is improvising a prelude before or after a church service ("best played with the full organ"). It is important that the prelude express the feeling or *Affekt* of the chorale, hymn, or concerted music that is to follow. "There are occasions," according to C.P.E. Bach, "when an accompanist must extemporize before the beginning of a piece. Because such an improvisation is to be regarded as a prelude which prepares the listener for the content of the piece that follows ... the construction ... is determined by the nature of the piece which it prefaces; and the content of this piece becomes the material out of which the prelude is fashioned."[13] Daniel Gottlob Türk warns: "If [the organist] is negligent in this regard, and preludes on a chorale about human suffering, e.g., with the full organ ... or if he pulls on a soft stop and the tremulant to play a prelude to a lively chorale, to a wedding, or before the *Te Deum* ... then he handles himself very thoughtlessly (*unbesonnen*)."[14] Türk lavished particular praise on Gottfried August Homilius (a student of Bach, and, according to Forkel, an "excellent organist"[15]), who "preluded so masterfully, and performed the chorale with such excellence that even the best connoisseurs wondered at his insight and listened with enchantment."[16] That Bach's chorale preludes were viewed by his contemporaries as models in this regard is clear, as can be seen in this comment by Bach's pupil Johann Friedrich Agricola: " ... the rule expressed already by many writers and, fortunately, observed by many important composers – for example, Joh. Seb. Bach – namely, that the expression in a musical prelude must reflect the content of the song [it preceeds], is very reasonable and legitimate *(vernünftig und rechtmäßig)."* [17]

Circumstances, or the occasion, also were important. "One of course plays with louder *(schärfer)* stops at Easter than at a funeral or on Good Friday, when it is customary to play far more quietly. One must also take the space into consideration. For example, in small churches the *Gedackt* alone may sometimes be used for a chorale; this would be ridiculous in a large principal church where one can barely perceive even the full organ over the singing of the congregation."[18]

Importantly, contemporary late Baroque descriptions do not relate particular organ registrations to particular genres. Rather, an organist chooses whether to play *Organo pleno* or to register with a "variety of registrations" depending on his or her ideas, on the *Affect* sought, on the occasion, and on the circumstances. *Organo pleno* and "variety" registrations were used in all spheres of an organist's activity – whether playing continuo, improvising a prelude, or accompanying congregational singing.[19]

BACH'S REGISTRATIONAL DESIGNATIONS

Not surprisingly for a composer who carefully marked articulation and ornamentation, Bach also indicated the mode of registration appropriate for the pieces he composed. In the autographs and printed sources for Bach's organ chorales we find only six designations: *à 2 Clav. et Pedal, manualiter, Organo pleno, à 3, Duetto,* or nothing. The designation *à 2 Clav. et Pedal* is reserved for works that are conceived for – that require – two manuals and pedal for performance (trios, for example). Pieces that can be played on one manual and pedal are either given no designation at all or are designated as *Organo pleno* pieces. The *manualiter* designation is reserved for pieces that can be played on one manual without obbligato pedal. (The rarely used designations *à 3* and *Duetto* are discussed below.)

These designations suggest that organists expected to be told if a piece was to be played in some way other than on one manual with obbligato pedal; their meanings are obvious. Importantly, however, they also imply particular methods of registration. Pieces to be registered according to the first class of registration, "full organ," are marked with the *Organo pleno* designation. Pieces to be registered employing "the other diverse registrations" available, carry other designations.

Bach used the designation *à 2 Clav. et Pedal* throughout his career. It appears in the earliest extant manuscript in Bach's hand – the chorale *Wie schön leuchtet der Morgenstern à 2 Clav. Ped.* BWV 739, written in Arnstadt around 1705 – and also in the last collections prepared by Bach in Leipzig in the years *ca.* 1745-49 – the *Sechs Choräle* BWV 645-50, and the canonic variations on *Vom Himmel hoch da komm ich her* BWV 769. The designation appears in the headings of the six trio sonatas BWV 525-30, in the *Orgelbüchlein,* the "Great Eighteen" chorales, and in *Clavier-Übung III.* (It is also found in the d-minor concerto BWV 596; however, the designation *à 2 Clav. et Pedal* is notably absent from autographs of Bach's preludes and fugues.)

The *à 2 Clav. et Pedal* designation speaks for itself: the work is to be played on two manuals or keyboards and pedal. The pieces so designated are 1) trios where each voice is played on a separate keyboard, 2) chorales where one voice, often an ornamented cantus firmus, is to be played on a stronger registration, and 3) concerto arrangements where parts played by solo instrument(s) are contrasted with parts played by the entire ensemble.

Importantly, Bach *always* indicates when two manuals are required. Most often he does this by means of the *à 2 Clav. et Pedal* designation, but there are some exceptions. Two chorales from the *Orgelbüchlein* clearly written for two manuals lack the *à 2 Clav. et Pedal* designation (see Table 1).[20] In *Herr Gott, nun schleuss den Himmel auf* BWV 617, Bach brackets the soprano and alto parts together to indicate that they are to be played on a separate manual from the "dramatic, sweeping contours"[21] of the left-hand tenor part.[22] The designation is also missing from Bach's revision of *Liebster Jesu, wir sind hier* BWV 633, but here Bach indicates performance on two manuals by marking the upper manual part "Forte," the lower manual part "Pia[no]," and the lowest stave "Ped." There is also an exception in the "Great Eighteen" chorales, where the *à 2 Clav. et Pedal* designation is missing from *Nun komm, der heiden Heiland* BWV 660 (see Table 2). However, the heading "*a due Bassi è canto fermo*" calls for a performance on two manuals and pedal, and the early version of the piece, BWV 660a, whose autograph, Staatsbibliothek zu Berlin Mus. ms. Bach P 271 (hereafter P 271), also survives, does include the expected designation *à 2 Clav. et Pedal*.

Although it may seem obvious, it is nevertheless necessary to state that pieces to be played on one manual do not include the *à 2 Clav. et Pedal* designation. Conversely, the absence of *à 2 Clav. et Pedal* indicates performance on one manual. This is clear from a survey of Bach's *Sechs Choräle*. The title page reads: "Six Chorales of various kinds to be performed on an organ with two manuals and pedal." In the title headings themselves, however, three chorales include the *à 2 Clav. et Pedal* designation and three do not (see Table 3). Two of the chorales with the designation, *Wachet auf, ruft uns die Stimme* BWV 645 and *Meine Seele erhebet den Herren* BWV 648, have manual cantus firmus melodies that are best played using a registration different from and louder than the other parts. Indeed, Bach's *Handexemplar* of the original edition includes the notation "*dextra forte*" over the melody of BWV 648. On the other hand, *Wo soll ich fliehen hin* BWV 646, which also carries the designation *à 2 Clav. et Pedal,* does not necessarily require performance on two manuals: the voices never cross and performance on one manual is possible. With *à 2 Clav. et Pedal* Bach indicates that the two upper parts, similar to the two upper parts in a trio sonata, be played with separate registrations. He reinforces his intention by specifying that one manual (the left hand) be at 16-foot, the other manual (right hand) at 8-foot, and that the chorale melody (originally for alto solo) be played by the pedal at 4-foot (alto) pitch.

Three of the *Sechs Choräle* do not include the designation "*à 2 Clav. et Pedal*" in the title headings. *Wer nur den lieben Gott läßt walten* BWV 647 is a four-part setting in which the right hand plays the original soprano and alto duet, the left hand plays the bass line, and the pedal plays the chorale melody. Many organists have noted that the piece is much easier to play with the left and right hands on one manual, and Bach seems to be indicating this mode of performance by omitting any designation to the contrary in the title. *Kommst du nun, Jesu, vom Himmel herunter auf Erden* BWV 650 is often played with the original violin solo part from cantata BWV 137/2 on one manual, the bass line on a second manual (sometimes at 16-foot pitch), and the alto in the pedal. But both manual parts were played by strings in the original version and, in spite of crossing of the parts now and again, performance on one manual is possible. (Indeed, having the thumb of the left hand free to take some of the low notes of the transcribed violin solo part can be quite helpful.) Because the third voice, which is played in the pedal, does not enter until m. 13, Bach indicates right- and left-hand parts with "*dextra*" and "*sinistra*" (in the *Handexemplar*), but without specifying performance on separate manuals. Finally, the chorale *Ach bleib bei uns Herr Jesu Christ* BWV 649 also carries no designation – indeed, no instruction of any kind from the composer. The left-hand obbligato melody is a transcription of the original violoncello piccolo part from BWV 6/3; the right-hand chorale is a transcription of the soprano solo. Clearly it is possible, perhaps even preferable, to register these two parts on separate manuals. But they *are* playable on one manual and Bach seems to have intentionally omitted the designation *à 2 Clav. et Pedal* which would have indicated that two manuals were *required*. In fact, the opposite seems to be the case. By not indicating that the piece is for two manuals and pedal, Bach is indicating that it is a one-manual and pedal piece.[23] No manual designation of any kind, then, indicates performance on one manual and pedal. In the absence of an *Organo pleno* designation, the pieces would be registered using "diverse registrations."[24]

The six trio sonatas BWV 525-30, the "Great Eighteen" chorales, and the canonic variations on *Vom Himmel hoch, da komm' ich her* BWV 769a are gathered together in P 271.[25] The title heading of each trio sonata includes the designation *à 2 Clav: et Pedal* as do the trio settings in the "Great Eighteen" chorales, BWV 655 and 664. (In this collection, *à 2 Clav. et Pedal* is the most frequent designation, appearing in ten of fifteen autograph chorales.[26]) One of the "Great Eighteen" chorales has no designation: *Von Gott will ich nicht lassen* BWV 658 (with its cantus firmus in the pedal) is written for performance on one manual (and pedal).

Bach's canonic variations, according to the title page, are for an "organ with two manuals and pedal." Only three of the five variations include the designation *à 2 Clav. et Pedal* in the title headings, however. While *Variatio 3* and 5 (autograph version) lack the designation in the work heading, Bach does indicate a two-manual performance. In the latter, the *forte* marking(s) suggest that at least a section of the variation is to be played on two manuals. The former is simply marked *Cantabile*, a term used for a composition with "a fine melody."[27] In this variation, an accompaniment in canon is played by the pedal and left hand while the right hand, on another manual, plays both the free *cantabile* alto melody and the soprano cantus firmus. The marking *Cantabile*, then, indicates the presence of an ornamented solo melody that would be played on a separate registration from the accompanying parts.[28] (In this variation both the ornamented alto melody and the simple *cantus firmus* are played by the dominant right hand.)[29]

The title page to Bach's *Dritter Theil der Clavier-Übung* (CUIII) states that the collection comprises "various preludes on the Catechism and other hymns for the organ".[30] Published under Bach's supervision in 1739, the CUIII pieces are replete with performance instructions from Bach (only Bach's early setting of *Wie schön leuchtet der Morgenstern* BWV 739 contains a similar abundance of detail).[31] Bach marks pedal entrances with *Ped.*[32] and informs the player in what voice the cantus firmus appears, where there are echoes, that the second of two settings is an *alio modo* setting,[33] and, if a work is not voiced *a 4*, how many voices there are. In other words, this is a collection where Bach seems to leave nothing unmarked, which is not so surprising, perhaps, in a collection whose title, "keyboard practice," is so patently pedagogical in its thrust. Notably, Bach meticulously provides a performance indication for every piece in the collection (see Table 4).[34]

The designation *à 3* appears only once in CUIII, in *Allein Gott in der höh sei Ehr* BWV 675. While playable entirely on one manual, the piece carries no *manualiter* designation. Furthermore, even though it is possible to play the alto cantus firmus in the pedal at 4-foot pitch[35] (the challenging footwork in m. 28 notwithstanding) and to play the two other parts either on different manuals (or together on one manual for that matter), there is no *à 2 Clav. et Pedal* designation. Bach's rather enigmatic "*à 3*", suggests, unusually, that it is at the discretion of the organist how this piece is to be registered.

That *manualiter* is the most frequent designation in CUIII is surprising, for it is found in only one other primary source – the autograph of the three-verse chorale *O Lamm Gottes unschuldig* BWV 656 from the "Great Eighteen" chorales where the first of three verses is marked *manualiter*. The *manualiter* designation indicates two essential pieces of information – that there is no obbligato pedal part and that the piece requires only one manual.[36] By extension then, a *manualiter* designation is not appropriate for a duo setting played on two keyboards. The difference between an obbligato pedal part and a discretionary pedal part should be emphasized, for the designation *manualiter* allows for a part, at the organist's discretion, to be played in the pedal. In the *manualiter* setting of *Aus tiefer Not* BWV 687, for example, which carries the designation *a 4 alio modo manualiter*, it is possible to play the soprano cantus firmus in the pedal at 2-foot pitch.

The *Organo pleno* designation is the only registrational designation that is applied by Bach to both chorale-based works and to free works, and it appears in both the "Great Eighteen" chorales and in CUIII. In the latter, of course, *Organo pleno* is indicated for the free prelude and the fugue that frame the collection, and also for five of the chorale-based preludes. While not specifically stated, *Organo pleno* indicates that a work be played with both hands on one manual (at a time), and that there is always an obbligato pedal part, so that both the manual(s) and pedal are registered with a "full organ" sound. As pointed out earlier, this registration stands in contrast to "all the other diverse registrations that can be made."[37]

Finally, it should be noted here that there are chorales which carry absolutely no registrational designation (*Ach bleib bei uns Herr Jesu Christ* in the *Sechs Choräle*, for example, as well as a considerable number of the *Orgelbüchlein* chorales). Importantly, lack of any registrational indication is itself a registrational indication. That is, when there is no designation to the contrary, a piece will require one manual and obbligato pedal for its performance. In the *Orgelbüchlein,* for example, where all pieces include an obbligato pedal part, there are only two kinds of pieces – those for two manuals and pedal (designated *à 2 Clav. et Pedal*) and those for a single manual and pedal (without designation). Lack of any registrational indicator, can be seen as a sort of "base-line", as an expression of "basic," "regular," or "normal" practice. For any registration that deviates from "basic" practice, however, Bach provides a specific designation.[38]

To summarize, Bach is characteristically meticulous in providing registrational indications for the performer. He uses four basic designations, each with a specific meaning – *à 2 Clav. et Pedal*, *manualiter*, *Organo pleno*, and no designation. The *a 2 clav. et pedal* designation is reserved for pieces in which two manual parts are to be contrasted either by timbre – as in trio sonatas (where each part is equally "important" but benefits from having a different, but equal sound), and/or by loudness – as in a chorale prelude (where the solo part needs to be more dominant than the accompanying parts), or in a concerto (where parts played by solo instrument(s) are contrasted with parts played by the entire ensemble). Bach seems to reserve the designation for those pieces that *must* be played using two manuals and pedal. The *manualiter* designation indicates the absence of an obbligato pedal part in a piece that can be played on one manual. The *Organo pleno* designation indicates performance on one manual and pedal (at a time) with a "full organ" sound. Finally, the absence of any designation in chorales is itself a designation indicating "basic" or "normal practice" – that is, performance on one manual and pedal. Only the *Organo pleno* designation calls for "full organ" sound, Mattheson's first class of organ stops. The other designations call for registration using Mattheson's second class of organ stops – that is, "all the other diverse registrations" – with each stop being used "according to its character." The following chart sets out these divisions:

FULL ORGAN REGISTRATION

Organo pleno	1 manual (at a time)	Pedal	(chorales, free works)

VARIETY OR "DIVERSE" -REGISTRATIONS

à 2 Clav. et Pedal	2 manuals	Pedal	(chorales)
manualiter	1 manual	no obbligato pedal	(chorales)
"no designation"	1 manual	Pedal	(chorales only)
pedaliter or			
pro Organo	1 manual	Pedal	(free works only)

In light of this discussion, Forkel's celebrated description of Bach's "mode of registration" as being "peculiar" and "uncommon," but nevertheless successful, so that listeners were surprised that "the organ sounded best just so," is especially interesting. As Forkel tells us, Bach early on adopted the habit of giving "to each and every stop a melody suited to its qualities," which led him to new registrations he might otherwise not have thought of. The ability to match music with the appropriate sound, to provide as much variety as possible, to display the "art of registration," is linked with the second category of registrations – that is, with "variety registrations." More than most, it seems, Bach knew how to improvise and compose music for the organ that gave "to each and every stop a melody suited to its qualities."[39]

:: N O T E S ::

[1]   Johann Nikolaus Forkel, *Über Johann Sebastian Bachs Leben, Kunst und Kunstwerke* (1802), edited and with an afterword by Walther Vetter (Kassel: Bärenreiter, 1970), 112-13. See Hans T. David and Arthur Mendel, ed., *The New Bach Reader: A Life of Johann Sebastian Bach in Letters and Documents (NBR)*, rev. and enlarged by Christoph Wolff (New York and London: Norton, 1998), 471.

[2]   F.C. Griepenkerl, foreword to *J.S. Bach Organ Works*, vol. 1, Preface and English translation by Albert Riemenschneider (New York: C.F. Peters, 1950), 3.

[3]   Wilhelm Rust, ed., *Organ works: BWV 525-30, 531-48, 564-66, 582*, vol. 15, *Johann Sebastian Bachs Werke* (Leipzig: Bach-Gesellschaft, 1867), xiii.

[4]   Philipp Spitta, *Johann Sebastian Bach*, 3 vols., trans. Clara Bell and J.A. Fuller-Maitland (New York: Dover Publications, 1951), 3:211.

[5]   Georg Kinsky, "Pedalklavier oder Orgel bei Bach?", *Acta Musicologica* 8 (1936): 158–61.

[6]   These views are discussed in detail in the chapter entitled "J.S. Bach's Trio Sonatas: A Reception History of a Rumor," in Joel Speerstra, *Bach and the Pedal Clavichord: An Organist's Guide* (Rochester: University of Rochester Press, 2004), 32-51.

[7]   I use the terms *Organo pleno* and "full organ" interchangeably. For a discussion of full organ (*das volle Werk, die volle Orgel, Organo pleno*, full organ), see George Stauffer, "Bach's Organ Registration Reconsidered," in *J.S. Bach as Organist: His Instruments, Music and Performance Practices*, ed. G. Stauffer and Ernest May (Bloomington: Indiana University Press, 1986), 195–200. Stauffer cites descriptions by Johann Mattheson and Jacob Adlung of how to register "full organ." Bach's student Johann Friedrich Agricola also provides instruction for how to "draw full organ." See the Quentin Faulkner, "Information on Organ Registration from a Student of J.S. Bach," *The American Organist* 27 (June 1993): 58-63. German registration practices at the time of Bach (including *Organo pleno*) are discussed in detail by Thomas Harmon, *The Registration of J.S. Bach's Organ Works: A Study of German Organ-Building and Registration Practices of the Late Baroque Era* (Buren: Frits Knuf, 1981), 137–223. (Stauffer points out some errors in Harmon in a review published in *NOTES* 36 (1979): 360–62.)

[8] Autograph titles specifying *à 2 Clav. et Pedal* exist for some thirty-five chorales, the six trio sonatas BWV 525-30, and for the Concerto in d minor BWV 596. (The remaining concertos, BWV 592-595, in copies by Bach sons or pupils, also contain the designation *à 2 Clav. et Pedal.*) The designation *à 2 Clav. & Pedal* is entirely absent from autographs of Bach's preludes and fugues; however, secondary sources for the 'Dorian' toccata BWV 538 indicate a two-manual performance. Because there is no autograph or print of this work, we do not know whether Bach provided the manual change indications that appear in copies or how he might have titled the work. The two copies that give all the manual changes – Staatsbibliothek zu Berlin Mus. ms. Bach P 416 (copied by an anonymous scribe) and Staatsbibliothek zu Berlin Mus. ms. Bach P 803 (in the hand of J.G. Walther) – are both entitled "Toccata con Fuga ex D.♯", but the more common title, in four of the sixteen sources, is "Toccata per l'Organo, D. moll à due Clav: è Pedale col la Fuga." There are remarkably varied titles for this work in its sixteen sources. Several include the designation *â due Clavier e Pedal* (or something very similar), while others give it an *Organo pleno* designation. The Lowell Mason manuscript conflates the two with the title "Praeludio in Organo Pleno à 2 Clav: con Fuga". BWV 538 may be the only example of a free work by Bach with a title heading that indicates performance *both* with two manuals and *Organo plena* registrations.

[9] Jacob Adlung, *Musica mechanica organoedi (Mmo),* 1768. Facsimile reprint with afterword by Christhard Mahrenholz (Kassel: Bärenreiter, 1931 and 1961), § 228 – § 238, 167-73.

[10] Johann Mattheson, *Der Vollkommene Capellmeister,* 1739. Facsimile reprint with an afterword by Margaret Reimann (Kassel: Bärenreiter, 1954), 467: "Überhaupt theilen sich die Orgel=Züge in zwo Gattungen. Zur ersten gehört das volle Werck; zur andern zehlt man alle übrige vielfältige Veränderungen, die sich mit verschiedenen Clavieren besonders, und mit schwächern, jedoch ausgesuchten Stimmen machen lassen."

[11] Forkel, *NBR,* 440.

[12] Adlung, *Mmo,* § 236, 172 (my translation): "Im Fantasiren ist man noch weniger gebunden: denn es kann mit schwachen und starken Registern geschehen, nachdem die Einfälle sind, oder nachdem man auf ein trauriges oder

lustiges Stück oder Choral zu präludiren hat. Beym Anfange und Beschluß des Gottesdienstes läßt es besser mit dem vollen Werke zu spielen. Präambuliret man aber auf etwas; so kann es entweder durch eine gemeine Fantasie geschehen, und da kann man das volle Werk nehmen; aber auch zur Abwechselung zuweilen stille klingende Register ziehen; oder man spielt mit 2 Clavieren, die beyde besondere Register haben, nicht allzustark, eines aber pflegt zu prädominiren, und diese prädominirende Stimme läßt den Choral hören, oder doch etwas davon, wenn man auf den Choral präambuliret."

[13] Carl Philipp Emanuel Bach, *Essay on the True Art of Playing Keyboard Instruments,* translated by William J. Mitchell (New York: Norton, 1949), 431.

[14] Daniel Gottlob Türk, *Von den wichtigsten Pflichten eines Organisten,* 1787. Facsimile reprint with an afterword by Bernhard Billeter (Hilversum: Frits Knuf, 1966), 118–19: "Ist er hierin nachlässig, und präludirt auf ein Lied vom menschlichen Elende u. mit dem vollen Werke…oder zieht bey dem Vorspiele zu einem muntern Gesange, bey einer Trauung, vor dem *Te Deum* etc. einige schwache Stimmen, nebst dem Tremulanten: so handelt er sehr unbesonnen."

[15] Forkel, *NBR,* 457.

[16] Türk, *Pflichten eines Organisten,* 127–28: "Der Erste [Homilius] präludirte so meisterhaft, und führte den Choral so vortreflich aus, daß selbst die größten Musikkenner seine Einsichten bewunderten, und ihn oft mit Entzücken hörten."

[17] Werner Neumann and Hans-Joachim Schulze, eds. *Bach-Dokumente.* Vol. III (Kassel: Bärenreiter, 1972), 212: "… die Regel, die schon von manchen Schriftstellern gedruckt gesagt, und von manchen großen Componisten, z.E. Joh.Seb.Bach glücklich beobachtet worden, nemlich, daß der Ausdruck der Musik im Vorspiele, dem Inhalte des Liedes gemäß seyn müsse, sehr vernünftig und rechtmäßig ist."

[18] Adlung, *Mmo,* § 228 (unpublished translation by Quentin Faulkner).

[19] For example, the practice of playing chorales on two manuals and pedal is described by J.F. Agricola in his review of Birnstiel's publication in 1765 of J.S. Bach's four-part chorales: "It is my belief that these chorales [published in open score], in addition to other uses, are especially useful to beginning organists as a beginning practice in the art, now disappearing, of playing ob-

bligato pedal. The upper voice must be played on one manual, the two middle [voices] on another [manual], and the bass in the Pedal." *BDok* III, 187: "Wir glauben daß diese Choräle ausser andern Verdiensten, sonderlich angehenden Orgelspielern, nützlich seyn können, um sich anfänglich in der fast vorlohren gehen wollenden Kunst, das Pedal obligat zu spielen, zu üben. Sie müssen die Oberstimme auf dem einen Claviere, die zwey mittelsten auf dem andern, und den Paß auf dem Pedale spielen."

[20]   There is no designation indicating performance on two manuals in the chorale BWV 600, *Gott, durch deine Güte* or *Gottes Sohn ist kommen*. On the contrary, Bach's registrations – 'Man. Princip. 8 F.' and 'Ped. Tromp. 8 F.' – and the absence of the 'à 2 Clav. et Ped.' designation indicate performance of both hands on one manual.

[21]   Russell Stinson, *Bach: The Orgelbüchlein* (New York: Schirmer Books, 1996), 126.

[22]   The brackets are not included in the *Neue Bach-Ausgabe*. Bach used brackets for the same purpose in other *Orgelbüchlein* pieces as well – in *Christe, du Lamm Gottes* BWV 619; *Hilf Gott, dass mir's gelinge* BWV 624; and *Liebster Jesu, wir sind hier* BWV 634. In these three pieces, however, the designation *à 2 Clav. et Pedal* is provided.

[23]   Certainly a performer can choose to register a piece differently from the way Bach has designated it, but if we accept that the *Organo pleno* designation is a prescription – and it is rare when an organist chooses to ignore an *Organo pleno* designation – then we also need to accept that the other designations are prescriptive. In his *Tabulatura nova* (1624), Samuel Scheidt gives instructions for various ways to distribute the parts, but leaves it up to the organist to decide on a case by case basis. A hundred years later (or so), Bach seems to be determining the distribution of parts himself.

[24]   As the example from the *Sechs Choräle* demonstrates, there seems to be a difference between the directive Bach regularly gives on title pages and what he provides in work headings. Title-page titles give the genre ("chorales") and the instrument ("an organ with two manuals and pedal"). In work headings, on the other hand, Bach gives registrational information (*à 2 Clav. et Pedal, manualiter, Organo pleno*). This practice is also observable in autographs

of the free organ works. The title-page title for the C Major praeludium BWV 545, for example, reads "Praeludium pro Organo cum Pedale obligato" whereas the work heading reads "Praeludium in Organo pleno pedaliter." The essential information that there is an obligato pedal part is thus notated in two places.

[25] Is it possible that these three collections were gathered together because most of the pieces in them require performance on two manuals and pedal?

[26] Non-autograph pieces from this collection – BWV 666, 667, and 668 – are not considered in this discussion.

[27] Walther defines *cantabile* as a composition in which "a fine melody is employed or used [… *eine feine Melodie in solchen führet*]." See Johann Gottfried Walther, *Musikalisches Lexikon,* 1732. Facsimile reprint (Kassel and Basel, Bärenreiter, 1953), 134.

[28] This florid alto melody has been compared by Peter Williams to an aria or another highly embellished piece. See Peter Williams, *The Organ Music of J.S. Bach,* 2nd ed. (Cambridge: Cambridge University Press, 2003), 520.

[29] Bach applies the *cantabile* designation to *Allein Gott in der Höh sei Her,* BWV 663 from the "Great Eighteen" chorales, as well, and it can also be found in works by Bach's students – for example, in works by Johann Ludwig Krebs.

[30] One wonders whether there is significance in Bach's use of "organ with two manuals and pedal" for the *Sechs Choräle* and the canonic variations, and simply "the organ" for CUIII.

[31] See Russell Stinson, "Bach's Earliest Autograph [Bach P 488]," in *Musical Quarterly* 71 (1985): 235-63.

[32] This practice is common, especially in works written on only two staves.

[33] The term *alio modo* can be literally translated as "in another time." Interestingly, all of the *alio modo* pieces in CUIII carry a different time signature than the preceeding setting of the same chorale melody.

[34] The *Duetti 1-4* BWV 802-805 have no performance designation other than the title itself. All are playable on one manual and while they clearly require no pedal, they are not designated *manualiter*. Indeed, the title *Duetto* sug-

gests performance on two manuals. Like trios, here each of the two voices is to be rendered using a distinct keyboard (sound) of its own. That Bach expected a duet to be played on two separate keyboards is clear from *Nun komm, der Heiden Heiland* BWV 660, which carries the designation *a due Bassi è canto fermo* in the later version, but *à 2 Clav. et Pedal* in the earlier (Weimar) version. Also, although not in autograph, the designation for *Allein Gott in der Höh sei Ehr* BWV 711 is *Bicinium,* a term which, like *Duetto,* suggests performance on two manuals.

[35] It was common for Baroque organists to "solo out" a chorale melody from a three- or four-voiced texture, as we know from Samuel Scheidt's description of the practice. That performers continued to do this well into the eighteenth century – at least with a soprano melody – is clear from Agricola's comments about Bach's four-part chorales (see note 19 above).

[36] Robert Marshall has pointed out that the term *manualiter* appears in a few early, non-autograph Bach sources for the keyboard toccatas BWV 910-16. (See Robert L. Marshall, "Organ or 'Klavier'", in *J.S. Bach as Organist,* edited by George Stauffer and Ernest May (Bloomington: Indiana University Press, 1986), 212-39.) For Marshall, *manualiter* is an instrumental designation that makes sense only when applied to the organ, and the designation implies that these toccatas "must have been intended by Bach for the organ." It seems to me, however, that Bach provided the *manualiter* designation in order to alert the performer to the fact that these pieces do not have an obbligato pedal part, which many toccatas did. At first glance a performer might not realize that the toccatas BWV 910-16 are not large-scale works that include a pedal part. The designation *manualiter* makes this clear. The toccata titles passed down in early sources (see Marshall's Table 3, 226), while not totally consistent, do often include either a *pedaliter* or *manualiter* designation (For example: *Toccata col pedale obligato,* BWV 540; *Toccata ex C. pedaliter,* BWV 564.) The *manualiter* designation, then, does not designate a particular instrument, such as the organ, but rather indicates that there is no pedal part. Such *manualiter* toccatas could be played on any keyboard instrument, whether organ, harpsichord, or clavichord.

[37] Free works and Bach's use of 'Organo pleno' designations are discussed by the author in a related, forthcoming article.

[38] Bach's free works for a keyboard instrument (whether organ or stringed instrument) seem to operate with a different "base-line" or "basic" practice. In the free works for which we have autograph scores – a telling, although admittedly small sample – Bach specifies whether the piece has a pedal part and whether it requires more than one manual. Preludes that require pedal are titled "Praeludium pedaliter" or "Praeludium pro Organo cum Pedale obligato", for example, while the trio sonatas have the designation 'à 2 Clav. et Pedal.' In the free works, no designation indicates that the piece can be played on one manual and that there is no obbligato pedal part. (There may be a pedal part, such as a concluding pedal point, but there is no obbligato pedal part.) These pieces are simply titled "Praeambulum" (BWV 772-86) or "Fuga ex Gis dur" (BWV 886 in P274). Similarly, the partitas in *Clavier-Übung I,* which have no designation, only require a single manual or keyboard for performance, whereas in parts II and IV Bach indicates that these works require an instrument with two manuals.

[39] Forkel, *NBR,* 439-40.

TABLE 1

Chorales for Two Manuals and Pedal from the *Orgelbüchlein*

BWV	Title	Designation	Other information
604	Gelobet seist du, Jesu Christ	à 2 Clav. & Ped.	
605	Der Tag, der ist so freudenreich	à 2 Clav. & Ped.	
614	Das alte Jahr vergangen ist	à 2 Clav. & Ped.	
617	Herr Gott, nun schleuss den Himmel auf	Bracket around upper two voices	
619	Christe, du Lamm Gottes	à 2 Clav. & Ped.	in Canone alla duodecima
622	O Mensch, bewein dein Sünde groß	*Adagio assai* à 2 Clav. & Ped.	
624	Hilf, Gott, dass mir's gelinge	à 2 Clav. & Ped.	
629	Erschienen ist der herrliche Tag	à 2 Clav. & Ped.	in Canone
633	Liebster Jesu, wir sind hier *distinctus*	*Forte* over top two voices (canon); *Pia[no]* between staves (over two lower voices); lowest voice on its own stave and marked *Ped.*	
634	Liebster Jesu, wir sind hier	à 2 Clav. & Ped. Also, two brackets pairing off four upper voices	in Canone alla Quinta
639	Ich ruf zu dir, Herr Jesu Christ	à 2 Clav. & Ped.	
641	Wenn wir in höchsten Nöten sein	à 2 Clav. & Ped.	

Source: Johann Sebastian Bach, *Orgelbüchlein,* facsimile of the autograph [Staatsbibliothek zu Berlin, Mus. ms. Bach P 283] edited by Heinz-Harald Löhlein (Kassel: Bärenreiter, 1981).

TABLE 2
"Great Eighteen" or Leipzig Chorales

BWV	Title	Designation	Other information
651	Komm, Heiliger Geist, Herre Gott	Fantasia super… in organo pleno	*c.f.* in Pedal
652	Komm, Heiliger Geist, Herre Gott	alio modo à 2 Clav. et Ped.	
653	An Wasserflüssen Babylon	à 2 Clav. et Ped.	
654	Schmücke dich, O liebe Seele	à 2 Clav. et Pedal	
655	Herr Jesu Christ, dich zu uns wend	Trio super… à 2 Clav. et Pedal	
656	O Lamm Gottes, un-schuldig	3 versus 1 Versus. manualiter [Verse 3:] Ped.	
657	Nun danket alle Gott	à 2 Clav. et Ped.	*c.f.* in soprano
658	Von Gott will ich nicht lassen	[lowest stave:] Ped.	
659	Nun komm, der Heiden Heiland	à 2 Clav. et Ped.	
660	Nun komm, der Heiden Heiland	a due Bassi è canto fermo	
660a	Nun komm, der Heiden Heiland	à 2 Clav. & Pedal	
661	Nun komm, der Heiden Heiland	in Organo pleno	*c.f.* in Pedal
662	Allein Gott in der Höh sei Ehr	a 2 Clav. et Ped. 'adagio' below opening tenor	*c.f.* in Sopr.
663	Allein Gott in der Höh	a 2 Clav. et Ped. below right hand, 'cantabile'	*c.f.* in Tenore
664	Allein Gott in der Höh	Trio super… à 2 Clav. et Ped.	
665	Jesus Christus, unser Heiland	'sub communione' 'pedaliter'	

Source: Information in this table is taken from Russell Stinson, *J. S. Bach's Great Eighteen Organ Chorales* (Oxford: Oxford University Press, 2001).

Note: BWV 666-68 are excluded because they are not autograph.

TABLE 3
Sechs Choräle, BWV 645-50

BWV	Title	Designation	Other Information
645	Wachet auf, ruft uns die Stimme	à 2 Clav. et Pedal	Canto fermo in Tenore; 'Dextra 8 Fuss', 'Sinistra 8 Fuss', 'Pedal 16 Fuss' (in composer's copy)
646	Wo soll ich fliehen hin *or* Auf meinem lieben Gott	à 2 Clav. et Pedal	'1 Clav. 8 Fuss', '2 Clav. 16 Fuss', 'Ped. 4 Fuss'
647	Wer nur den lieben Gott läßt walten		'Pedal 4 Fuss'
648	Meine Seele er-hebt den Herren	a 2 Clav. et Pedal	'sinistra', 'dextra forte', 'Pedale' (in composer's copy)
649	Ach bleib bei uns, Herr Jesu Christ		
650	Kommst du nun, Jesu, vom Himmel herunter		'Dextra', 'Sinistra', 'Pedal 4 Fuss und eine 8tav tiefer' (in the composer's copy)

Source: Johann Sebastian Bach, *Sechs Choräle von verschiedener Art,* facsimile of the original print, ed. Hans Schmidt-Mannheim (Innsbruck: Musikverlag Helbling, 1985).

Note: "Composer's copy" refers to Bach's *Handexemplar.* See Christoph Wolff, "Bach's Personal Copy of the Schübler Chorales," in *Bach: Essays on His Life and Music* (Cambridge: Harvard University Press, 1991), 178-186.

TABLE 4
Clavier-Übung III

BWV	Title	Designation	Other Information
552.1	Praeludium	pro Organo pleno	
669	Kyrie, Gott Vater	a 2 Clav. et Ped.	*c.f.* in soprano
670	Christie, aller Welt Trost	a 2 Clav. et Ped.	*c.f.* in tenor
671	Kyrie, Gott heiliger Geist a 5	cum Organo pleno	*c.f.* in bass
672	Kyrie, Gott Vater	*alio modo [in 3]* manualiter	
673	Christie aller Welt Trost	[manualiter][a]	
674	Kyrie Gott heiliger Geist	[manualiter][a]	
675	Allein Gott in der Höh	à 3	*c.f.* in Alto
676	Allein Gott in der Höh	a 2 Clav. et Pedal	
677	Fugetta super Allein Gott	manualiter	
678	Dies sind die heilgen zehen Geboth	a 2 Clav. et Ped:	*c.f.* in canone
679	Fugetta super Dies sind die heiligen zehen Geboth	manualiter	
680	Wir glauben all	in Organo pleno con Pedale ["Ped."]	
681	Fugetta super Wir glauben all an einen Gott	manualit:	
682	Vater unser im Himmelreich	à 2 Clav. et Pedal	*c.f.* in canone
683	Vater unser im Himmelreich	*alio modo [in 4, not 3]* manualiter	
684	Christ unser Herr zum Jordan kam	a. 2. Clav.	*c.f.* in Pedal
685	Christ unser Herr zum Jordan kam	*alio modo [in 3, not 4]* manualiter	
686	Aus tieffer Noth schrey ich zu dir a 6	in Organo pleno	*con Pedale doppio*
687	Aus tieffer Noth schrey ich zu dir a 4	*alio modo [¾, not ¢]* manualiter	

688	Jesus Christus unser Heyland, der von uns den Zorn Gottes wand	a 2 Clav	*e Canto fermo in Pedal*
689	Fuga super Jesus Christus unser Heyland a 4	manualiter	
802	Duetto I	[duetto]	
803	Duetto II	[duetto]	
804	Duetto III	[duetto]	
805	Duetto IV	[duetto]	
552.ii	Fuga a 5	pro Organo pleno	*con pedale*

[a] Gregory Butler has pointed out that BWV 672-674 were originally conceived as one work in three movements. This may account for the absence of the *manualiter* designation in the CUIII print, where it is left out. See Gregory Butler, *Bach's Clavier-Übung III: the making of a print, with a companion study of the Canonic Variations on "Vom Himmel hoch" BWV 769* (Durham, NC: Duke University Press, 1990), 54-55.

RESTORATION OF TUBULAR-PNEUMATIC ORGANS IN NORTHERN GERMANY

THREE EXAMPLES OF DEALING WITH 'OUT-OF-DATE' INSTRUMENTS[1]

Uwe Pape

DEALING WITH 'OUT-OF-DATE' ORGANS of another era is always a hot topic. In the nineteenth century, and above all, in the period of the *Orgelbewegung* (tracker organ revival), organists and organ builders were tempted to rebuild or revise 50 to 80-year-old instruments, or to do away with them altogether. Today, the instruments of the earlier *Orgelbewegung* are in danger of extinction,[2] and post-World-War II organs are next in line if they are even now still standing.[3] One has the impression that the time gap between the building of new organs and of tearing them down, is becoming ever shorter.

In the case of instruments from the 1950s and '60s one might understand the inclination to build new instruments in light of the economic boom after 1950. But this argument does not hold true for pre-World-War I instruments. These instruments are excellent in quality, but they do not reflect current taste with respect to tonal ideal.[4] Very few of these instruments in Western Germany have survived the deep freeze organs fell into in the first half of the twentieth century. But in Eastern Germany, the contrary is true – the majority have survived, although they are in poor condition.

Throughout the campaign of destruction from 1930 to the present, instruments from the *Kaiserzeit* (*ca.* 1871-1919) were among its principal victims – instruments with a rich 8-foot spectrum in the manuals, pneumatic action, and ventil chests. Threadbare arguments had to be used in order to make the specifications more "presentable", i.e. suitable for the music of Buxtehude and Bach. If the mechanical design of the organs couldn't support these changes, then demolition seemed to be the only alternative. If the cost of repairs was simply too high, then this reasoning was used to justify liquidation. After all, the leather of the pneumatic chests is only expected to last for a few decades.

The bag of tricks was a large one. There was a colorful array of methods used to transform and re-voice, ranging from small changes in the scaling of the pipes, to shortening string pipes to make higher pitches, to lowering the upper lips in the case of reduced wind pressure. Once the work had been done however, no one was truly pleased with the results. Nevertheless, this was rarely acknowledged. Judgments and opinions about reconstructions, either planned or carried out between 1950-1980, speak volumes.

The era of *Wiedergutmachung* (reclamation) followed closely behind. Today one might indeed ask when the next pneumatic organ with cone valve chests (*Kegelladen*) will be built.

1 | THE BERLIN CATHEDRAL

The *Berlin Cathedral* is truly the most frequently-visited church by tourists in the German capital. The plan to build this splendid new structure dates back to the time of King Friedrich Wilhelm IV. JULIUS and OTTO RASCHDORFF designed a magnificent central dome structure in the style of the Italian High Renaissance. The festive dedication took place on February 27, 1905[5].

The building, with its excessive adornment and uneasy form, was controversial from the very start. Its vast bulk not only sets the tone for the nearby neighborhood, it also strongly influences the character of central Berlin, and not in an entirely positive way.

World War II caused severe damage inside and out to the Cathedral in 1944-45. The cupola had to be closed off on an emergency basis by means of a temporary roof construction. Further deterioration on the inside was prevented by the installation of glass. During the reconstruction of the 1970s and '80s the decision was made to restore the façade, the main cupola, and the cupola tower in simplified fashion.

The organ is the work of the "royal Prussian master organ builder and artist scholar," WILHELM SAUER, an especially prestigious organ builder at the turn

Berlin Cathedral, organ

Berlin Cathedral, console

of the century.[6] With 113 stops spread over four manuals and pedal, it was the largest cathedral organ of its time in Germany. With respect to the historicized architecture of the church, Raschdorff designed an organ front with Renaissance elements – anything but a Classical disposition. Indeed, the *Rückpositiv* was incorporated as a stylistic element, something that Sauer had not employed since 1869. Despite this fact, historical considerations apply only to the organ case, not to the function – the *Rückpositiv* is not a foil to the *Hauptwerk*, but rather its five foundation stops mainly serve to accompany. Or was this stipulation of purpose merely an attempt to justify an architectural idea?

Wilhelm Sauer built cone valve chests.[7] The *Rückpositiv*, however, had a chest with pouches. The reason for the building of a pouch chest must surely have been the limited space at the railing. The distance must have been *ca.* 8 meters from the organ console to the *Rückpositiv* and *ca.* 14 meters from the console to the pipes of Manual IV.

Berlin Cathedral, organ

Moving forward from the freestanding console, four double-fold bellows measuring 3.20 x 2.00 meters are located in the lower section of the main case. The organ was provided with wind as follows: 115 mm for the action and *forte* voices, 85 mm for the *piano* stops. The wind was produced by a ten-horsepower blower and the wind volume was declared to be fifty cubic meters per minute.

The divisions are distributed within the organ case as follows:

◆ Manual I: In the lower section of the case on the left side are found the front and rear chests, with the upper chest above them.

◆ Manual II: In the lower section of the case on the right side are three chests, similarly arranged as for Manual I.

  Manual III: Along the back wall behind the middle flat of façade pipes, two chests enclosed in a swell box. The Glockenspiel is located on the roof of the Swell division.

  Manual IV: Above the Swell division, on two chests. The enclosure for the Vox humana 8′ is located on the roof of the swell box.

  Pedal: In the lower section of the case along the back wall, are the C and C♯ chests of the *Haupt* pedal; between them in the center are two chests for the *Kleine* pedal. Above and behind the center front section is the chest for the pedal façade pipes.

N.B. unless otherwise specified, the pipes of the following specification are of 75% tin.

I. Manual, C–a³

Principal	16′	C–F wood, rest metal (85%)
Majorbaß	16′	C–f¹ wood
Principal	8′	C–E wood, rest metal (85%)
Doppelflöte	8′	C–b° wood
Principal amabile	8′	C–B wood
Flûte harmonique	8′	C–b° wood
Viola di Gamba	8′	metal (87.5%)
Bordun	8′	C– f¹ wood
Gemshorn	8′	C–B wood
Quintatön	8′	
Harmonica	8′	C–B wood
Gedacktquinte	5⅓′	
Octave	4′	
Flûte octaviante	4′	C–B wood
Fugara	4′	
Rohrflöte	4′	
Octave	2′	

Rauschquinte 2 ranks	2⅔'	
Große Cymbel 3 ranks	3⅕'	
Scharf 3–5 ranks	2'	
Cornett 3–4 ranks	2⅔'	
Bombarde	16'	C–B wood
Trompete	8'	
Clairon	4'	

II. Manual, C–a³

Principal	16'	C–E wood, rest metal (85%)
Quintatön	16'	C–B wood
Principal	8'	C–D♯ wood, rest metal (85%)
Doppelflöte	8'	C–b⁰ wood
Geigenprincipal	8'	C–B wood
Spitzflöte	8'	C–B wood
Salicional	8'	C–B wood
Soloflöte	8'	c⁰–b¹ wood
Dulciana	8'	C–B wood
Rohrflöte	8'	C–B wood
Octave	4'	
Spitzflöte	4'	
Salicional	4'	
Flauto dolce	4'	
Quinte	2⅔'	
Piccolo	2'	
Mixtur 4 ranks	2'	
Cymbel 3 ranks	2'	
Cornett 3 ranks	2⅔'	
Tuba	8'	
Clarinette	8'	

III. Manual, Swell, C–a³

Salicional	16'	C–b⁰ wood

Bordun	16′	C-f¹ wood
Principal	8′	C-B wood
Hohlflöte	8′	c⁰-b¹ wood
Gemshorn	8′	C-B wood
Schalmei	8′	C-B wood
Concertflöte	8′	C-b¹ wood
Dolce	8′	
Gedackt	8′	C-f⁰ wood
Unda maris	8′	
Octave	4′	
Gemshorn	4′	
Quintatön	4′	
Traversflöte	4′	C-B wood
Nasard	2⅔′	
Waldflöte	2′	
Terz	1⅗′	
Mixtur 3 ranks	2′	
Trompete	8′	
Cor anglais	8′	
Glockenspiel		

Rückpositiv, played from III. Manual

Flötenprincipal	8′	C-B wood, rest metal (85%)
Flöte	8′	C-B wood
Gedackt	8′	C-B wood
Dulciana	8′	C-B wood
Zartflöte	4′	C-B wood

IV. Manual, Swell, C-a³

Lieblich Gedackt	16′	C-f¹ wood
Principal	8′	C-B wood
Traversflöte	8′	c⁰-b⁰ wood
Spitzflöte	8′	C-B wood

Lieblich Gedackt	8′	C-f° wood
Quintatön	8′	
Aeoline	8′	
Voix céleste	8′	
Prästant	4′	
Fernflöte	4′	c°-b° wood
Violini	4′	
Gemshornquinte	2⅔′	
Flautino	2′	
Harmonia aeth. 3 ranks	2′	
Trompete	8′	
Oboe	8′	
Vox humana	8′	

Pedal: C-f¹

Principal	32′	wood
Untersatz	32′	wood
Principal	16′	C-A wood, rest metal (85%)
Offenbaß	16′	wood
Violon	16′	wood
Subbaß	16′	wood
Gemshorn	16′	wood
Lieblich Gedackt	16′	wood
Quintbaß	10⅔′	wood
Principal	8′	C-D wood, rest metal (85%)
Flötenbaß	8′	wood
Violoncello	8′	C-B wood, rest metal (85%)
Gedackt	8′	wood
Dulciana	8′	C-B wood, rest metal (85%)
Quinte	5⅓′	
Octave	4′	
Terz	3⅕′	
Quinte	2⅔′	

Septime	2⅔′	
Octave	2′	
Contraposaune	32′	wooden resonators
Posaune	16′	C-f° wooden resonators
Fagott	16′	C-f° wooden resonators
Trompete	8′	
Clairon	4′	

Cone valve chests (except *Rückpositiv*)

Tubular-pneumatic action

Six manual couplers: II-I, III-I, IV-I, III-II, IV-II, IV-III

Three pedal couplers: I-P, II-P, III-P

Three free combinations (blind general pistons settable by organist)

Forte, Tutti (fixed combinations)

Rohrwerke an (reeds on)

Registerschweller [Walze] (crescendo roller pedal)

Absteller für Handregistrierung (disables stops drawn by hand)

Absteller für Rohrwerke (disables reed stops)

Absteller für Registerschweller (disables the crescendo)

Piano-Pedal, Mezzoforte-Pedal (fixed combinations)

Jalousieschweller III. Manual (Manual III swell-pedal)

Jalousieschweller IV. Manual (Manual IV swell-pedal)

Tremolo Vox humana

Windanzeiger (wind indicator).[8]

The swell-shutters of Manuals III and IV are mechanically controlled from the freestanding console. A crescendo roller-pedal (*Walze*) strengthens the expressiveness of the instrument.

In the archives, three free combinations are mentioned, but upon closer examination of Manual IV, it actually has only one free combination. On the whole, Manual IV seems to depart from Wilhelm Sauer's original cost estimate, dated 14 November 1899. Either during the building process, or right before it, it was enlarged and brought to its present state.

With the notable exception of a few historic organs built before 1750, all tin façade pipes in Germany were sacrificed to the war effort in 1917. In 1928, a new façade of an 85% tin-lead alloy was installed. In 1934, the *Orgelbewegung*, so gung-ho for alterations, fortunately halted before it got to the main cathedral organ. The value and the artistic integrity of the work were recognized, and surely also defended by the cathedral organist at that time, Prof. FRITZ HEITMANN. There were only small encroachments: the *Rückpositiv* with its five registers was altered with the cooperation of the consultant HANS HENNY JAHNN. The following disposition shows this quite clearly.

RÜCKPOSITIV 1905		*RÜCKPOSITIV 1934*	
Flötenprincipal	8′	Gedackt	8′
Flöte	8′	Terzian	2f
Gedackt	8′	Sifflöte	1′
Dulciana	8′	Cymbel	3f
Zartflöte	4′	Krummhorn	8′

In addition, a four-rank Pedal *Mixtur* was built on a spare channel of the Pedal façade chest, and the stop control of the *Violon* 16-foot was used as its "on" switch. The *Violon* was not usable but remained in place on top of the chest. As a result, the linkage of the crescendo roller was altered, and the *Mixture* was logically incorporated into the crescendo sequence at a later point.

Further, there was now a tremolo for Manuals III and IV and for the *Rückpositiv;* also, a IV-Pedal Coupler, a Collektiv Pedal and a Manual 16′ cancel. At this time, there was a Manual II super coupler whose origin has never really been completely explained. However, the wind chests of Manual II were never extended in the treble to accommodate the extended range of the Super II coupler.

In 1944, the cupola of the cathedral was destroyed by an Allied bomb. The blast tore the swell boxes of Manuals III and IV from their anchorages on the back wall of the side aisle. Likewise, one wind chest of Manual IV was torn from its support posts. The façade pipes were riddled with holes from shell fragments, and the interior pipes behind them were also damaged.

The organ now remained exposed to the elements for ten years. In 1954, the cupola was once again enclosed. The organ was relatively well protected in the aisle. Even so, a gradual deterioration of the instrument took place. During this period, pipes were stolen, some registers disappeared entirely, and in other instances, complete octaves had been removed. At the same time, there was senseless destruction; e.g., the *Vox humana* 8′ pipes were removed from the Manual IV swell box and strewn about the organ.

In 1952, HANS-JOACHIM SCHUKE and Prof. FRITZ HEITMANN successfully completed the reconstruction plans. In conformity to the goals of the *Orgelbewegung* the placement of 94 registers on slider chests was provided for in these plans. Due to the lack of available materials in the postwar years, however, the plans fortunately could not be carried out. This saved the instrument.

In October 1971, the firm of WILHELM SAUER in Frankfurt/Oder received the commission to undertake a comprehensive restoration of the organ. With this goal in mind, it was established, that as a result of this work, "the organ, by means of a thorough restoration", could be preserved for future generations. Among the subjects that were subsequently discussed were: whether or not the original specifications should be preserved, whether the original action could be kept, whether the number of stops should be reduced, and how high the cost would be.

In 1982, after another inspection of the organ, the firm of Sauer submitted another cost estimate for the reconstruction of the organ. The following assumptions were included in that estimate:

1. The pneumatic action would not be restored or rebuilt; instead, an electric key and stop action with adjustable pistons would be installed.
2. The restoration and reconstruction of all ranks of pipes was possible, with the goal of preserving the original disposition. As a result, the voicing and original tuning would be retained.
3. To restore the original disposition of the *Rückpositiv.*
4. The still extant *Violon* 16′ would be reactivated, and the four-rank Pedal *Mixtur* would remain the same. This would increase the total number of stops to 114.

The reconstruction was to be carried out in conjunction with the rebuilding of the cathedral (1986-1993). The organ building contract was signed in 1985.

Even before the pipes were removed and before the planned dismantling of the console and pneumatic relay, a vigorous discussion took place in 1987 about whether the earlier decision to not restore the pneumatic action had been the right one. As the result of an investigation of the console, it was ascertained that twenty missing, celluloid stop labels, the broken-off combination pins and the broken steel stop control springs, etc., were capable of being rebuilt, and the console and the pneumatic action could also be repaired, as well.

This ushered in a whole new round in the restoration of the cathedral organ. Many questions and concerns were raised regarding the sound of the organ. Not a single person charged with the restoration had ever heard the instrument. What tonal concept prevailed in 1905? What were the people of that time listening for in terms of sound? The organ favored finely-graded intensities, a full and powerful Tutti, and with characteristic color stops, it reflected a now barely-recognizable tonal picture of the Late Romantic.

In addition to the opinion that the organ may have been too weak, there was great concern about the liveness of the acoustic in the domed church. Continually at the crux of the debate, was the question as to whether it was advisable to preserve the pneumatic action. Assessing pneumatic action on the basis of the criteria of mechanical action seemed prejudicial, since pneumatic action has by its very nature a built-in delay. But no one could predict how long that delay might be.

The length of the lead pneumatic tubes fueled the argument against the restoration of the pneumatic action. But questions concerning how to deal with pneumatic action, and the possible advantages of a short delay in the articulation among the stops themselves, shed new light on the entire issue. A parallel action (tubular-pneumatic and electro-pneumatic) was also submitted for consideration.

On 11 April, 1991 the committee in charge of the restoration of the Sauer organ made the decision to furnish the instrument with a pneumatic action, and to make the console playable in its original configuration. The cost estimate from 23 May, 1991 laid down these plans, which included:

🎔 Reconstruction of the pneumatic action.

🎔 Restoration of the 1905 disposition.

🎔 Reactivation of the *Violon 16'*, with the resultant omission of the four-rank Pedal *Mixtur.*

🎔 No changes in the placement of the wind chests of Manuals I and II.

The restoration was carried out between 1991 and 1993. Peter Dohne reported extensively about this work at a Symposium on the restoration of pneumatic organs, sponsored by the International Association for Organ Documentation IAOD).[9]

2 | LÜNEBURG, ST. NICOLAI

The gothic brick Basilica of *St. Nicolai* in *Lüneburg* is among the most important historic buildings in Northern Germany. Of particular interest are the unusual proportions of the church: the choir is directly connected to the four-bay nave, without a transept. This space is visually increased by the extreme height of the vault, at nearly 30 meters. The clearly separated aisles hardly matter either visually or acoustically. With its upward-reaching architecture *St. Nicolai* clearly differentiates itself from the other two major churches in *Lüneburg, St. Johannis* and *St. Michaelis*, which, as hall churches appear much more compact.

St. Nicolai, at that time in dilapidated condition, was substantially remodeled in the nineteenth century, and the preponderantly brick interior was preserved. In connection with the rebuilding of the organ in 1899 by the firm of FURTWÄNGLER & HAMMER, the organ loft was newly arranged: the organ is positioned at a height of a good 15 meters in the separate west tower space above the entrance hall.[10] The organ loft was visually extended downward to the apex of the passageway arch by means of ornamentation. Apparently, in order to fill in the extreme height, the lower section of the neo-gothic organ

Lüneburg, St. Nicolai, organ

Lüneburg, St. Nicolai, interior of the new tubular-pneumatic console

case was artificially stretched, so that the dummy façade pipes stood more than two meters above the level of the wind chests. In a newspaper article of the period, the oak façade with its two towers was called, "a true ornament of the church."[11]

Only during the first third of its well-nigh 100-year history, did the pneumatic organ remain in its original configuration (except for the sacrifice of the façade pipes in 1917). Even before 1930, the first stoplist changes in the spirit of the *Orgelbewegung* began. Further alterations ensued in 1946, 1954, and, finally, in 1978-1980. Even with all of these desired changes (a brighter sound, electro-pneumatic action, installation of schwimmer bellows in the wind system), which from today's perspective are hard to comprehend, it is to be noted that already in 1975 the organ consultant, HANS HEINRICH STEL-LJES, had suggested that the organ, even though considerably changed from its original condition – both technically and tonally – be placed under state historical monument protection. The resulting decision of the church board to authorize a repair instead of a new construction, against the will of the organ consultant, was in no way obvious.

And so, in 1978-1980 it came to the "mere" electrification of the action, alteration of the wind system with schwimmer bellows, and repairs by the firm of E.F. WALCKER & CIE., Murrhardt. Although in those years interest in nineteenth-century organ building was awakened, (in 1976 the first specialty Conference, "Early Romantic Organ Building in Lower Saxony",[12] took place in Hildesheim at the suggestion of the organizers), the complete reconstruction of a pneumatic organ was unthinkable due to a lack of experience.

For the first time, in 1993, the Lüneburg organist-choir director, PAULA HYSON, called for the complete restoration and a return to the original disposition of 1899. That was easier said than done because large portions of the pipe work had either been exchanged, cut up, or moved to other locations within the organ. Meanwhile, the control of the pneumatic cone valve chests continued to operate electrically, but from a new console. The wind supply was also altered requiring that the large reservoirs and their wind trunks be reestablished. Bids for the restoration of the organ were submitted in 1998-99 by the firms of SCHEFFLER, VLEUGELS, RIETZSCH, WALCKER and LENTER. The firm

Lüneburg, St. Nicolai, old console

of GERHARD LENTER from Löchgau, now in Sachsenheim, was awarded the contract in 1999, and carried out the restoration in 2002. TOBIAS GRAVENHORST, organist-choir director of the *Lüneburg Michaeliskirche*, acted as consultant.

In spite of all the changes, the intentions of the original organ building firm were easily discernible in the instrument itself. The wind chests remained in their original positions, and stood next to one another about one meter below the impost. Parts of the original reservoirs were still to be found utilized as walk boards in the organ, so the bellows could again be reconstructed in the lower section of the organ. Luckily, the visible portions of the attached pneumatic console with its keys and drawknobs had also been preserved. However, all of the interior mechanical equipment had been removed.

The reinstallation of the pneumatic control from the keys to the wind chest presented a big challenge for the Lenter firm, because this exact method of console construction was not available for study, anywhere. Oddly, the touch boxes of Manuals I and II do not sit directly behind the keys, but rather are placed further away, and are operated by means of long trackers. It is also no secret that, for lack of ability to compare many details, new methods had to be found in order to guarantee a lasting and reliable operation. For the first time, the desire to install a *prolongement* [13] for the stop action was now realized in fully pneumatic form with this instrument. The result of the restoration is an astonishingly precise attack, involving a thoroughly pleasant touch, with a light toggle resistance that reminds one of a pianoforte action. It must be emphasized that neither the key nor the stop action create disturbing, extraneous noises.

No other organs of comparable size from this period by this organ building firm have been preserved in their original form. To be sure, instruments such as the *Stiftskirche* in *Königslutter* (1892) and the *Verden Cathedral* (1916) could have been examined for comparison. However, enough documentation was available so that recourse to other instruments as references was not necessary. Therefore it was possible for the FURTWÄNGLER & HAMMER organ in Lüneburg to be technically restored in its original form.

I. Manual, Hauptwerk, C-f³

Principal	16′	1899, C-a♯° wood, from b° metal
Bourdon	16′	C-e² wood, from f² metal, C-e¹ reconstructed 2002; from f¹ 1899
Major-Principal	8′	1899, C-a♯° wood, metal from b°
Gamba	8′	1899 metal, pipes lengthened 2002
Gemshorn	8′	C-B wood, 2002 using historical parts;[14] from c° metal, 1899
Hohlflöte	8′	1899, wood
Groß-Gedackt	8′	C-b¹ wood, 2002 using historical parts, from c² metal, 1899

Octave	$4'$	2002 metal, reconstructed
Rohrflöte	$4'$	1899, metal
Quinte	$2\frac{2}{3}'$	2002 metal, reconstructed
Mixtur 3-5 ranks	$2'$	1899, some pipes lengthened, 92 pipes reconstructed 2002 C: $2'$, $1\frac{1}{3}'$, $1'$, c^0: $2\frac{2}{3}'$, $2'$, $1\frac{1}{3}'$, $1'$, c^1: $4'$, $2\frac{2}{3}'$, $2'$, $1\frac{1}{3}'$, $1'$
Cornett 3-4 ranks	$2'$	1899, some pipes lengthened, 126 pipes reconstructed 2002
Tuba	$16'$	2002 reconstructed, boots and resonators tin, beating tongues
Trompete	$8'$	$C-f^2$ 1899, $f\sharp^2-f^3$ 2002 reconstructed, boots and resonators tin, beating tongues

II. Manual, $C-f^3$

Lieblich Gedeckt	$16'$	2002 $C-b^1$ wood, renewed with historical parts; c^2-f^3 metal, reconstructed
Minor-Principal	$8'$	$C-b^0$ wood, 2002 using historical parts; c^1-f^3 metal, 1899
Viola	$8'$	1899, metal
Dolce	$8'$	2002, $C-b^0$ wood; from c^1 metal, reconstructed
Gedecktflöte	$8'$	2002, $C-b^0$ wood, using historical parts; from c^1 metal, reconstructed
Quintatön	$8'$	1899, metal
Principal	$4'$	1899, metal
Harmonieflöte	$4'$	2002, metal, reconstructed
Progressivharmonica 2-3 ranks	$4'$	1899, some pipes lengthened; 55 pipes reconstructed 2002 C: $2\frac{2}{3}'$, $2'$; c^0: $4'$, $2\frac{2}{3}'$, $2'$

| Oboe | 8′ | 1899, boots and resonators tin, beating tongues |

III. Manual, Swell, C-f³

Salicet	16′	2002, C-b¹ wood, from c² metal; reconstructed
Geigen-Principal	8′	1899, C-B wood, c⁰-f² metal; f♯²-f³ metal, reconstructed 2002
Salicional	8′	2002, metal; reconstructed
Aeoline	8′	2002, metal; reconstructed
Vox celestis	8′	2002, from c⁰, metal; reconstructed
Concertflöte	8′	2002, wood, using historical parts
Harmonieflöte	8′	2002, C-b⁰ wood, using historical parts; from c¹ metal
Liebl. Gedackt	8′	1899, C-b⁰ wood, from c¹ metal
Fugara	4′	2002, metal; reconstructed
Zartflöte	4′	1899, wood
Harmonika aetherea 3-4 ranks	2′	2002, metal; reconstructed, C: 2⅔′, 2′, 1⅓′; c⁰: 4′, 2⅔′, 2′, 1⅓′
Clarinette	8′	2002, reconstructed using parts of a Walcker stop from *ca.* 1900 (boots and resonators tin, free reeds, wooden blocks); resonators reconstructed

Pedal, C-f¹

Principalbass	32′	1899, wood, open
Contrabass	16′	1899, wood
Violon	16′	2002, historic wooden pipes, lengthened

Subbass	16′	1899
Gedecktbass	16′	2002, wood, using historical parts; in Manual III swell box
Quintbass	10⅔′	2002, stopped wood; reconstructed
Octavbass	8′	1899, wood
Cello	8′	2002, C-b° wood using historical parts; from c¹ metal; reconstructed
Bassflöte	8′	1899, wood, open
Octave	4′	1899, tin
Posaune	16′	1899, boots wood, resonators zinc, beating reeds
Trompete	8′	2002; Transmission from Manual I; substitution for the unrealized Fagott 8′, planned for in 1898

Couplers: Normal couplers, Melody coupler, Sub-octave II-I, Pedal Super coupler, General coupler (all couplers together).

Accessories: Reed Cancel, Bellows Signal (since 2002: blower switch), Prolongement (new 2002)

Pistons: Fixed combinations: Tutti, Forte, Mezzoforte, Piano, Pianissimo, hand registration, Pedal I, Pedal II, Pedal III, Crescendo.

Registerschweller [*Walze*] (crescendo roller pedal with indicator)

Jalousieschweller III. Manual (Manual III swell pedal)

Jalousieschweller (Schwellwerk).

The importance of this restoration lies in the recreation of a palette of sound to which interpreters and listeners must, first of all, become newly reaccustomed, because until now reliable examples for comparison have also been missing. Instruments by other organ builders show clearly divergent characteristics in sound structure from those of the Hannover builders.

Fortunately the proposal from FURTWÄNGLER & HAMMER for the 1898

Lüneburg Nicolai organ was available, which gives not only the scaling speci-fications for every individual register, but also contains short descriptions of the tone quality. Thus it was possible to reliably verify the number of pipes, and to replace the missing pipework. Of special help were rich discoveries in the organ storehouse of the Landeskirche of Hannover, and in the pipe ware-house of the Hammer firm. Admittedly, a subjective risk with regard to voic-ing always remains with such delicate undertakings; how are the very subjec-tive statements in the cost estimate to be interpreted, and how are they to be carried out in practice? Are the repeated indications regarding wide and very wide scaling to be interpreted as the desire for loudness at any cost? How did the organ builders define a vigorous sound?

On the basis of original pipes that had been preserved, it was possible to reconstruct the original sound palette which led to the flabbergasting result of a Romantic organ with low wind pressure. The sound does not emanate directly from the organ case because of the restrictively enclosed lower sec-tion. Rather, it mixes in the spacious tower area above the pipe work, and then, reflected from the vault, spreads out into the sanctuary. The sound that reaches the listener is a dense yet richly differentiated one, and on the whole, astonishingly light.

Interestingly, even chamber and solo registrations are subjectively experi-enced as barely softer in the church. In particular, the strings with their deli-cate overtone structures come through and blend excellently, especially with the "soft" reeds, *Clarinet* and *Oboe*. Here the frequently encountered gap in the area of the 4-foot 'Principal' register has been avoided, so that finely graded crescendi and decrescendi can be applied in all divisions.

Extensive experiments in listening and registration only gradually reveal the individual but many-sided (with regard to the spectrum of repertory) conception of this organ. Namely, it is not a matter of the building of terraced dynamics in the manuals – which in the case of instruments of this size, was often done at that time. On the contrary, a principle that binds together the Baroque and late Romantic seems to have been realized here: in particular, Manual II, with its 16-foot basis, a 'Principal' 8′ (indeed designated as "minor", but according to the cost estimate, "powerful, somewhat more lively [than in the Hauptwerk]"), the *Principal 4'*, and with the revealing mixture; seems to be, in fact, the tighter and more transparent 'Hauptwerk' for polyphonic music.

It is important to realize that no attempt was made to create a large and dominating sound where such was possible. Rather, the desire which remained above all, was to allow the instrument to "speak" insofar as possible in all its individuality. Consequently, an organ was restored whose sound spectrum gives plenty of room for the development of the alto and tenor ranges, and by means of the discreetly maintained but thoroughly present extreme ranges, it has a smoothness of effect. These qualities are especially suited to literature of the early Romantic period.

For organ concerts held in the main churches of Lüneburg this instrument, as a consequence of the reconstruction of an 1899 work, represents a convincing counterpoint. In the *Michaeliskirche,* a likewise late Romantic organ was preserved in a state of several alterations. And, in *St. Johannis,* the 1954 BECKERATH organ contains a register inventory that harkens back to the seventeenth century.

3 | BAD HARZBURG

A generous donation gave the *Martin Luther Congregation* in *Bad Harzburg* the opportunity to contract the firm of WILHELM SAUER for an organ for their newly built church (1901-1903).[15] The organ builder's cost estimate of June 2, 1902, with 29 sounding registers, was accepted without discussion by the congregation, and the contract was finalized between July 1-8, 1902. Only a 2-3 rank *Progressio* (progressive mixture) was later eliminated by Sauer, and replaced with a *Piccolo 2'*, a voice that, "is especially suited for ensemble purposes, the more so because the organ is sufficiently strong for this, after all, rather small church". The pipe façade, in contrast, had to be built larger than had been planned, but Sauer made no additional demands other than to suggest that he hopefully, "due to a longer sojourn in delightful Harzburg, could be compensated."

The organ, Opus 891, was built in 1903. On November 25, 1903 delivery was taken by the organist of the *Church of the Blessed Virgin Mary* in *Wolfenbüt-*

Bad Harzburg, organ

Bad Harzburg, new console

tel, FERDINAND SAFFE. The Certificates of Delivery state that "The organ is an exemplary work with regard to its musical effect. With respect to its technical features, which in every way represent the present standard of organ building, it belongs to the series of the finest, new works that the Duchy of Braunschweig has produced." This conclusion was certainly no exaggeration.

The organ contains the following specifications:

I. Manual, C-f³

Principal	8′	tin, partly in the façade
Bordun	16′	C-f¹ fir, rest 75% tin
Flûte harmonique	8′	C-b° fir, rest 75% tin
Viola di Gamba	8′	C-F♯ fir, rest 75% tin, with brass beards
Gemshorn	8′	C-B fir, rest 75% tin
Liebl. Gedackt	8′	C-f¹ fir, rest 75% tin
Trompete	8′	"of brass and spotted tin", beating reeds
Octave	4′	tin, partly in the façade
Rohrflöte	4′	75% tin
Rauschquinte 2 ranks		2⅔′, 2′; 75% tin
Cornett 3-4 ranks		4′, 2⅔′, 2′, 1⅗′; 75% tin

II. Manual (Schwellwerk), C-f³

Geigenprincipal	8′	C-B fir, rest 75% tin
Liebl. Gedackt	16′	C-f¹ fir, rest 75% tin
Schalmei	8′	labial, C-B fir, rest 75% tin
Concertfloete	8′	C-B from Gedackt 8′, c°-b° fir open, rest 75% tin
Aeoline	8′	75% tin, with brass beards
Voix céleste	8′	75% tin, with brass beards
Rohrfloete	8′	C-f° fir, rest 75% tin
Fugara	4′	75% tin
Traversfloete	4′	C-B fir, rest 75% tin

Piccolo	2′	replaced orig. Progressio harm. 2-3 ranks, 4′, 2⅔′, 2′; 75% tin

Pedal, C-d¹

Principalbass	16′	fir
Violon	16′	fir
Subbass	16′	fir
Posaune	16′	resonators fir, blocks metal
Octavbass	8′	fir
Gedacktfloete	8′	fir
Violoncello	8′	C-B fir, rest 75% tin
Octave	4′	75% tin

Manualcoupler, Pedalcoupler I, Pedalcoupler II, Piano, Mezzoforte, Forte, Tutti, combination cancel, swell pedal for Manual II, Bellows Signal. Reservoir with normal and inverted folds. Four feeder-bellows. Wind ducts with two small concussion bellows.[16]

Shortly after World War II, in 1951, the responsible consultant WILHELM DRÖMANN from Holle submitted a disposition proposal, to which the Braunschweig organ builders FRANZ DUTKOWSKI, OTTO DUTKOWSKI and FRIEDRICH WEISSENBORN responded with bids. Seven new registers were to be delivered, nine registers altered, and seven registers revoiced and, in part, transposed. Only six pedal registers remained unchanged and in their original positions. FRIEDRICH WEISSENBORN carried out the alterations. The result was a neo-baroque medley of 16′ Quintade through 3-rank Cymbal with the old mechanism.

Eleven years later (1963), the congregation allowed the organ to be electrified and to be furnished with a new console. The pedal was extended from low C to f¹. The work was carried out by HANS-HEINZ BLÖSS from Oker. The cone valve chests were preserved, and the disposition was altered no further.

In 1970-71 Blöß finally carried out a drastic rebuild. Slider chests with new supporting structures replaced both the cone valve chests and the 1903 framework, as well as the wind supply that had been preserved until that time.

The specifications were lightly modified, and the pipe work was completely revoiced. Finally, the manuals were expanded from 54 to 56 notes in 1974.

Frivolous meddling with historical materials gives pause for thought. What does the altered instrument have to do with Sauer's original organ, of which just the organ case and 14 registers (most of which were greatly altered) still remained?

A few years ago a new construction with a reconstruction of Sauer's sound palette, with cone valve chests and pneumatic action was decided upon. CHRISTIAN SCHEFFLER from Frankfurt/Oder was awarded the contract for a new construction with 39 stops on three manuals. The new construction sought to recreate the specifications of 1903 for Manual I and the Pedal and used all of the historic materials in these divisions. The second and third manuals were constructed from the repository of stops from the former Manual II, and were completed in a style leaning toward Sauer's instruments dating from the turn of the century.[17] The new, free-standing pneumatic console faces the organ in order to make more room for the wind-chests, and to make direction of the choir possible from the console.

N.B. the numbering in the following specification indicates placement on the chest, front to back.

I. Manual C-a³

Upper chest, left front

1 Principal	8′	façade 1917, zinc, inner pipes old
2 Bordun	16′	originally *Liebl. Gedackt* 16′, old, wood, completed with new pipes
3 Gamba	8′	new
4 Gemshorn	8′	old
5 Flûte harmonique	8′	new; many trebles, old
6 Trompete	8′	new

Lower chest, left front

1 Gedackt	8′	old

2 Octave	4′	old
3 Rohrflöte	4′	old
4 Octave	2′	old
5 Cornett 3-4 ranks		mostly old
6 Mixtur 4 ranks		new

II. Manual C-a³

Upper chest, right front

1 Principal	8′	new
2 Quintatön	16′	new
3 Salicional	8′	new
4 Rohrfloete	8′	new
5 Clarinette	8′	new

Lower chest, right front

1 Octave	4′	new
2 Flauto dolce	4′	new
3 Nasard	2⅔′	new
4 Piccolo	2′	new
5 Progressio 2-4 ranks		new

III. Manual, Swell, C-a³

Upper chest, right rear

5 Liebl. Gedackt	16′	new
4 Geigenprincipal	8′	new
3 Aeoline	8′	new
2 Voix céleste	8′	new
1 Oboe	8′	new

Lower chest, right rear

5 Koncertfloete	8′	new
4 Gedackt	8′	new
3 Fugara	4′	new
2 Traversfloete	4′	new
1 Harm. aeth. 2-3 ranks		new

Pedal C-d¹

Back chest, center, along the wall

3 Principalbass	16′	old, wood, d#¹-f¹ new
2 Violon	16′	new, wood
1 Posaune	16′	old, wooden resonators, d#¹-f¹ new

Front chest, upper left, behind the Hauptwerk (I)

5 Subbass	16′	old, wood, d#¹-f¹ new
4 Octavbass	8′	old, wood, d#¹-f¹ new
3 Cello	8′	new, wood
2 Bassflöte	8′	old, wood, d#¹-f¹ new
1 Octave	4′	old, metal, d#¹-f¹ new

Manual couplers II-I, III-I, III-II, Pedal couplers I, II, III; tutti coupler; crescendo pedal (*Walze*), swell pedal for III; non-adjustable combinations for Piano, Mezzoforte and Tutti; three free combinations, Reed Tutti, Reeds Off, Crescendo Off, manually-controlled stop selection off.[18]

Is it a new organ or a reconstruction? Outwardly the organ is a reconstruction, because even the console is entirely modeled on Sauer's style of construction. The interior structure is essentially based upon the layout of the chests in the *Leipzig Thomaskirche*.[19] The disposition, as well as the chests and action, are also a reconstruction of an imagined prototype. The idea and concept, two manual divisions, and two-thirds of the pipe materials are new. Daring to build an almost entirely new organ with pneumatic action and cone valve chests is a sign of a new understanding of dealing with Romantic organs. Hopefully, it is also an example for future encounters with organs from another era.

4 | EVALUATION

What criteria must a pneumatic organ meet in order to be capable of preservation, worthy of restoration, or that even permit it to be reconstructed? The three, previously-mentioned organs may serve as representative examples in answer to these questions.

From 1950-1990, when pneumatic organs were being pushed aside or altered, organ builders and organists put forward the following arguments against preservation:

Susceptibility to disturbances caused by fluctuations in weather, imprecise playing response, delay in attack and cutoff, quicker decay of leather components, costly and expensive maintenance.

These reservations are still valid today, but a change in the evaluation of these arguments has come about because the above-mentioned disadvantages do not apply to every pneumatic organ. Here one must differentiate more precisely. The result of this has been that no general criteria can be applied to all instruments.

The most important criterion is certainly the quality of the pneumatic action. Pneumatic actions are not the same in all cases. The advantages and disadvantages of particular systems are well known. Thus one would surely make different decisions in the case of SAUER, RÖVER, and FURTWÄNGLER & HAMMER, as compared with other organ builders whose instruments are more experimental in nature.

However, even when an organ demonstrably possesses an outstanding pneumatic action, this is no absolute criterion for its worthiness to be preserved. Surely one must include whether the instrument is well-voiced and has, in its totality, a character worth modeling. If the organ were placed within a Baroque case its preservation value would certainly be diminished. The same would apply if the instrument is perceived as a foreign object within it, for example, if it noticeably disturbs the historic character of the church. If, however, the sanctuary and organ appear homogeneous, one could be well-disposed toward a restoration or a return to the original form.

No less important, is the exercise of objectivity regarding the decision to either restore or eliminate. Excessive idealism that overlooks deficiencies and ignores disadvantages is uncalled for. To be sure, pneumatic instruments require more care than slider chest organs. If, during a thirty-year period, only the most urgent repairs were made to an organ, it would certainly present a different picture than if it had been regularly serviced. Here, a judicious decision must be made.

The generation of fifty years ago that altered pneumatic organs, must also now learn that organs from 1890-1930 are historical instruments and that one needs to accept them as such. Historical instruments must not be sacrificed to personal preferences.

Restorations of this order of magnitude are, however, a large financial undertaking. Pneumatic organs originated in times of inexpensive labor. Today, reconstruction is considerably more expensive and often not affordable. Even so, many of the pneumatic organs in Eastern Germany could be restored.

If pneumatic organs are to be restored, two conditions must be met:

- The technical requirements are: good quality of mechanical systems and materials, good workmanship, good condition of the physical instrument, originality of the work, and good accessibility for future maintenance.

- A positive initial viewpoint regarding pneumatic organs: tolerance for specific deficiencies, acceptance of the limitations that historical organs demand, letting go of the desire to make improvements, and the readiness to acknowledge the higher costs of maintenance.

The organs that have already been preserved to date will be useful, if we are to refute prejudices against future restorations of pneumatic organs.

: : N O T E S : :

[1]   Translation into English from the original German by Linda Mariani-
ello

[2]   Rudolf Meyer, *Umgang mit unzeitgemäßen Orgeln* [Consorting with Organs from Another Era] (Berlin: 1999).

[3]   Martin Balz, "Was wird aus den Orgeln der Nachkriegszeit?" [What
Will Become of the Organs of the Postwar Period?], *Ars Organi* 47, no. 1
(1999): 17-19.

[4]   Christian Scheffler, "Restaurierung pneumatischer Instrumente – Prob-
leme und Erfahrungen" [Restoration of Pneumatic Instruments – Problems
and Experiences] in ed. Uwe Pape, *Restoration of Pneumatic Organs* (Berlin:
1995), 37-42.

[5]   Berthold Schwarz, *500 Jahre Orgeln in Berliner Evangelischen Kirchen* [500
Years of Organs in Berlin's Protestant Churches] (Berlin: 1991), 251.

[6]   Peter Dohne, "Die Restaurierung der Berliner Domorgel und Fragen
der Instandsetzung pneumatischer Instrumente" [The Restoration of the Organ of the Berlin Cathedral and Questions Concerning Restoration of Pneumatic Instruments] in ed. Uwe Pape, *Restoration of Pneumatic Organs* (Berlin:
1995), 43-52. The text of chapter 1 agrees in part with this publication. The
author thanks Peter Dohne of the W. Sauer Company, Müllrose, for his permission to use the text of his publication.

[7] The *Kegellade* (cone valve chest) used cone-shaped valves for each pipe
because this shape reduced the pluck felt upon opening the valve. But Wilhelm Sauer reversed the cone so that the surface covering the hole was flat
instead of cone-shaped. Of course this made no difference because the key
action was pneumatic rather than mechanical.

[8]   Berthold Schwarz, *500 Jahre Orgeln in Berliner Evangelischen Kirchen* [500
Years of Organs in Berlin's Protestant Churches] (Berlin: 1991), 255.

[9]   See the report of Peter Dohne, "Die Restaurierung der Berliner
Domorgel und Fragen der Instandsetzung pneumatischer Instrumente" in ed.
Uwe Pape, *Restoration of Pneumatic Organs* (Berlin: 1995), 43-52.

[10]   Markus Zimmermann, "Alte neue Klänge: Die Furtwängler-&-Ham-

mer-Orgel der Nicolaikirche in Lüneburg" [Old New Sounds: The Furtwängler & Hammer Organ of the Lüneburg Nicolaikirche], *Ars Organi* 51, no. 3
(2003): 178-181. The text of chapter 2 agrees in part with this publication. The
author thanks Markus Zimmermann from March-Hugstetten, for his permission to use the text of his publication.

[11] In the *Lüneburg'sche Anzeigen*, October 9, 1899.

[12] Edited by Uwe Pape, *Bericht über die Fachtagung Frühromantischer Orgelbau in Niedersachsen (1976)* [Report on the Professional Conference on Early
Romantic Organ Building in Lower Saxony (1976)] (Berlin: 1977).

[13] A device which prolonged the present registration while the stops were
changed for the next registration.

[14] "Historical parts" means stops manufactured by the firm Furtwängler &
Hammer *ca.* 1899, stops from the warehouse of the firm Emil Hammer, Hannover, and stops from the organ storehouse in Wittenburg.

[15] A description of this organ, including generous source materials can be
found in: Uwe Pape, "Neubau und Rekonstruction der Sauer-Orgel in Bad
Harzburg" [New Construction and Reconstruction of the Sauer Organ in
Bad Harzburg], *Ars Organi* 47, no. 3 (1999): 150-153.

[16] The *Landeskirchliches Archiv Braunschweig*, Bad Harzburg 23 (6/2/1902
and 7/9/1902). Material specifications from the cost estimate of 6/2/1902.

[17] The *Pfarrarchiv Bad Harzburg*, organ dossier (8/6/1997, 8/19/1997,
8/21/1997).

[18] The Christian Scheffler Archive, work documentation at Bad Harzburg;
personal documentation by U. Pape, November 1998.

[19] Christian Scheffler, *Die Restaurierung der Sauer-Orgel in der Thomaskirche
zu Leipzig* [The Restoration of the Sauer Organ in the Thomaskirche in
Leipzig], (Wiesbaden: 1989), 40-44.

THE BAD TEMPERED ORGAN

Stephen Bicknell

Small old-fashioned organs, in mean-tone temperament, are still to be found in some country churches; and the sweetness of their tone, and the smoothness of the chords and progressions played in the practicable keys upon them, will make many a church-goer grieve when they are replaced by modern equally-tempered instruments, with all the jangling abominations that represent power, and all the theatrical prettinesses that represent pathos to the XIX century organ builders.

— GEORGE BERNARD SHAW[1]

DURING THE 1970s the organ-building world was gradually made aware of the interesting possibilities offered by the exploration of unequal temperaments. Harpsichord makers led the way: the ease with which a harpsichord can be tuned and retuned by one pair of hands in half an hour or so meant that successive experiments were both easy and instructive.

The chances of unequal temperaments filtering out into the wider musical world might at that time have seemed slight. To be a good keyboard player requires no understanding of the Pythagorean or syntonic commas and there was, indeed still is, a widely-held belief that Bach's exploration of all the major and minor keys in *das Wohltemperirte Klavier* was a promotional exercise for the newly discovered equal temperament. The misconceptions extend not just to the misinterpretation of Bach's intention and method but also to the idea that equal temperament was 'new' in Bach's time, and reflect as much as anything a post-industrial view of scientific 'progress'.

Meanwhile, back in the field, there were relatively few opportunities to put theory into practice since organists were usually eclectically trained church musicians who thought in terms of their 'job': historical enquiry was left to amateurs and enthusiasts!

In Great Britain, despite the characteristic insularity that brought us a classical revival in organ building a whole generation later than the rest of the western world, there were one or two individuals in organ building who kept up with the latest developments. John Norman, rather ahead of the field, devised as early as 1961 an unequal temperament for the 1790 Samuel Green organ from Sandbeck Park, then being restored for the Queen's Private Chapel in Buckingham Palace.[2] This was an isolated example – setting aside for now the possibility that there may have been some 'survivors' from earlier periods awaiting discovery – until in 1973 the Steketee-designed Flentrop was installed at Eton College, in a case of 1773 by Johannes Mittenreiter. This instrument was tuned to one of the Werckmeister temperaments. Then in the late 1970s John Mander began applying unequal temperament to a number of small new organs, rather bravely concluding with ⅙ comma meantone *à la* Silbermann at St. Anne Kingston Hill in 1978, before settling on Vallotti as his favourite when the customer could be persuaded (the Kingston organ has since been retuned to something more 'acceptable')

The Mander company was exposed to influence in another unexpected way. As the last large organ workshop in central London the firm was much in demand for supplying continuo organs on the very active London concert scene. Noel Mander, connected with the Britten circle and later a friend of David Munrow, had foreseen the demand in the 1950s and had built a number of highly portable two- or three-rank unit organs. In the 1970s these began to be replaced with mechanical-action continuo organs, at first with three ranks and no case and then later by properly encased box and chamber organs, some with four ranks.

The activity generated by this small fleet of hire organs was prodigious, especially during the BBC Promenade Concerts and shortly before Christmas.

The organs were also in regular demand throughout the year for the growing number of specialist early music groups – requiring that the newer model hire organs had to be fitted with transposing devices so that they could be used at A415 as well A440 – and there was also regular involvement with recordings. By 1980 the hire organ diary would be filled with several events every week, requiring attendance to deliver and tune organs all round the capital and often to stand by for concerts or recordings. The van would sometimes leave in the early hours of the morning with three organs on board and a mixed crew of strong lads and a tuner, coming back late in the day, only to go out again the following morning to sweep up the bits and bring them back again.

Demands on staff properly engaged in designing and making organs were considerable. When the orders started coming in for continuo organs tuned in unequal temperaments, John Mander was for a time the only member of the team with the knowledge required and this took him away from the drawing board far too much. So, in the early 1980s shortly after joining the firm from University, I started to follow in his footsteps and relieve him of some of the load. Using at first the guide to harpsichord tuning by Klop,[3] I soon graduated to the rather more elegant circular tuning 'compass' – a kind of circular plastic slide rule – devised and circulated by the harpsichord makers Richard Clayson and Andrew Garret. With this I was armed with enough information to tune all the circulating temperaments then in demand and some others that were not.

Nobody wanted us to tune in meantone until in 1982, the Mander company was asked to provide an organ to accompany Andrew Parrott and the Taverner Choir and Consort on a tour in France where they were performing the Monteverdi *Vespers* of 1610. I was awarded the prize of going on the expedition with them and driving the van with the organ in it – live concerts in Nantes, Angoulême, Bordeaux and Pau.

At the rehearsals in London before we left, Andrew Parrott told me what he wanted. He quickly explained that he didn't think his team of singers and players, despite their experience, would cope well with being dumped into ¼ comma meantone straight off. We had Oxbridge choral scholars with 'perfect' pitch on the one hand, and then string players on the other hand, half of whom were playing fretless instruments and had one set of views on how to achieve good intonation and the other half were playing fretted lutes and theorbos and had quite a different outlook. So the plan was that we would start in Vallotti but as soon as we landed in France I would open the circle of fifths out to ⅙th comma meantone and see what happened. This I duly did, and as the tour went on, with Parrott's encouragement I pushed the tuning further, so that by the time the band returned to London to put their performances on disc[4] they were singing and playing in ¼ comma meantone.

In Monteverdi's music the results were stunningly beautiful. Written entirely in the friendly keys and inhabiting a harmonic world where there is little modulation as such, the listener was greeted with a ravishing succession of nearly pure chords. The singers and players adapted with great success and quickly realised the difference between performing in circular tuning and this 'new' open-ended meantone world. The tenor Charles Daniels (we had sung together at school and he had a remarkably accurate sense of pitch) explained to me how it worked from his viewpoint. Singing in equal temperament or a circulating temperament (to him much the same thing but for detail) he would consciously pitch intervals of a fifth, fourth, third or whatever, from the previous note sung. In meantone the intervals varied conspicuously from each other, so it was necessary instead to develop a sense of absolute pitch, particularly when it came to the two commonly used notes that define the wolf, E-flat and G-sharp.

A further excitement came in discovering Monteverdi's other harmonic world, for as well as the passages of conventional polyphony and solid harmonic progression, there are also moments of poignant chromaticism. The skilled performers of the Taverner band, singers and instrumentalists alike, soon realised that the unequal steps of the chromatic scale – especially bumpy as you pass through that familiar 'dying' fall of d, c-sharp, c – have to be pitched with absolute accuracy for the effect to be right. Far from being the oily enharmonic sliding about that characterises chromaticism in the nineteenth century, these passages prove to have a strongly lurching quality, each step in the chromatic scale seemingly pointing to a specific new tonality before the view dissolves and is replaced by a new one.

This valuable experience gave me a lasting interest in the importance of meantone temperament and its musical qualities. Returning to the world of organ building I kept up to date with current thinking as it appeared in English publications, while pondering all the while the alleged history of temperament in the British Isles: briefly, that Britain had remained unequal, possibly even meantone, until the mid-nineteenth century, with some organs not being retuned until much later (Wells Cathedral supposedly in 1893).[5]

What we read in the 1980s was coloured by the work of those who were enthusiasts for theoretical and circulating temperaments. So Alexander Mackenzie[6] gave us a very useful insight, reminding us quite forcibly that not all of our immediate predecessors had been so enamoured of equal temperament as we liked to imagine. There was S.S. Wesley of course, but Mackenzie also found the reference to the Willis voicer John Potter who "couldn't bear equal temperament tuning" and the letter written by Dr. William Pole to the organ builder Thomas Hill in 1879:

> For my own part I have ceased to take any interest in organs since the introduction of the detestable equal-temperament tuning. Under Handel's system an organ was a charming sweet harmonious instrument, that it was a real pleasure to listen to. Now, no matter how much skill and pains are bestowed on the voicing, the temperament converts it into an offensive harsh cacophony that drives people away. I never will go to any organ performances, & it is a penance to attend any church service... .

It is Mackenzie's conclusion in the same article that should alert us to his underlying motive: "There is no lack of choice of good Unequal Temperaments to suit differing situations; there is therefore no defence for the ubiquitous and continued indiscriminate use of Equal Temperament". Well! This had all the character of pamphleteering! And, indeed, in the following article[7] we were invited to put ourselves in the shoes of a randomly chosen panel of listeners who had been exposed to the same pieces played in ¼ comma meantone, ⅕ comma meantone, Werkmeister III, Mackenzie's '18th-Century English', and Equal Temperament. How were we readers to disagree with the conclusions drawn from a test so scientific?

Figure 1 – The anonymous late-seventeenth-century organ in Wollaton Hall, Nottingham, seen here in the 1980s before restoration. – *Mander Organs*

The overall order places 18th-century English temperament firmly in the lead, with Werckmeister 3 second and perhaps surprisingly equal temperament following closely but in third place. Except in the early examples [sc 'early music'], ⅕ comma and ¼ comma mean tone occupy fairly consistently the 4th and 5th positions respectively. It appears therefore that the mean tone temperaments are not acceptable to modern ears. In general it seems that temperaments with large 'wolves' are unacceptable.

Perhaps I should add that the Mackenzie temperament described as '18th-century English temperament' is not one derived from surviving instruments or from primary sources, but was a theoretical position developed *in vacuo* by Mackenzie based on a subjective desire to find a middle ground between meantone and equal temperament,

By the time of Charles Padgham's book 'The Well-Tempered Organ'[8] we had had the opportunity to explore further. John Mander and I had worked closely together on two restorations where we could be fairly sure that we had recovered details of an old tuning. At Wollaton Hall the chamber organ,

Figure 2 – Wollaton Hall: the front pipes, rich in tin, overlaid with painted decoration.
– *Mander Organs*

probably undisturbed since Alexander Buckingham's visit in 1826 (Figures 1 & 2), seemed to retain the tuning applied by Henry Holland when he rebuilt the organ in 1799. We scrupulously preserved the condition and voicing of the pipes as found, and made a detailed map showing which way every pipe in the organ faced when we started dismantling. On reassembly we found a convincing temperament survived and did little re-tuning.[9] We did not try and guess what type of temperament was employed; it was Charles Padgham who later told us that we had a modified meantone tuning similar to Silbermann's ⅙ Pythagorean comma or to ⅕ syntonic comma meantone.[10]

A later experience led us to a more unexpected result. In November 1982, the Mander company bought at auction a Snetzler bureau organ signed and dated 1763, on behalf of Dr. Barabara Schnetzler, a descendant of the builder (Figure 3). The instrument was not quite in original condition, but was very well preserved with some original leather surviving. The pipes had not been fitted with tuning slides, but many had been retuned by being slit with a pair of shears near the top so that they could be sharpened. We soldered up the slits and with the pipes back in the reassembled organ listened for groups of pipes that were still nearly in tune with each other in case an old tempera-ment survived. The surprise was that several pure thirds emerged at once. In consultation with Dr. Schnetzler we explored the possibility that the organ was meant to be in ¼ comma meantone and quickly found that this could be achieved without the slightest injury or inconvenience to the pipes. A modi-fied meantone was a far less likely solution.[11]

These two experiences led me to ask questions about other organs in Britain that were alleged to survive with an early temperament. It seemed to me that in the case of the organs at Oakes Park[12] and Finchcocks[13] it was not sufficiently evident that there had been no previous attempt to tune the

Figure 3 – The Snetzler bureau organ resting temporarily in Schaffhausen Cathedral before going to its present home in the town Museum. – *Barbara Schnetzler*

organs to equal temperament, whereas at Wollaton Hall we knew that the organ had been unplayable all through modern times and in the case of the Snetzler bureau organ, the later intervention was obvious. In the case of both the Oakes Park and Finchcocks organs an irregular temperament was claimed, hovering between modified meantone and a circulating temperament.[14] I believe this is exactly what would be found in an organ once in meantone that had been roughly cut down to equal temperament. The pipes too long for equal temperament would have been cut shorter; those that could be retuned by coning alone would be left. The result would be that the pipes for some notes would be cut shorter, others would be left as found, according to a tuning-related consistent pattern. This could easily be misinterpreted as a 'surviving' circulating temperament.

With these and other thoughts I came to distrust the 'movement' for unequal temperaments (with its Orwellian sloganeering of 'circulating good, equal bad, wolf intolerable') and wonder afresh where the historical truth lay. In this I have been anticipated by Ibo Ortgies, whose doctoral thesis presently being submitted at Göteborg covers some similar ground from a North European perspective. Ibo has been kind enough to share his thoughts with me from time to time over the last few years.

First, I would like there to be a distinction made between theoreticians' writings and what was actually practiced or practicable in historical organ building. We know Vallotti's temperament, but we cannot show that it was ever applied to an organ until modern times. We know the writings of Werckmeister and Kirnberger, but we do not know to which organs their temperaments were applied, if any. We might even be suspicious of those temperaments that are, after all, modern fabrications (Kellner, Barnes, Mackenzie *et al.*).

Secondly, we should examine carefully how long meantone tunings survived and why. In English organ history we can see the quarter-notes of Father Smith as an attempt to extend the keys available in quarter-comma meantone, not as a move away from meantone. Likewise the Parker organ of 1768 for the Foundling Hospital, with its levers for changing tonality and its many extra slides and pipes, is surely an example of an experiment made in a world which is simply not aware of the possibility of applying circulating temperaments to the organ. If it had been possible to imagine tuning the Foundling Hospital organ to, say Werckmeister III, surely nobody would have countenanced the fabulous extra expense occasioned by the system eventually employed? In wider European organ history we have misjudged the pace of events: Ortgies's work will show that the F.C. Schnitger at Alkmaar was not in equal temperemant when it was finished in 1725, but in meantone. The retuning came in the 1760s. He will also point out that none of the Arp Schnitger organs in the Netherlands have been tuned in a manner that reflects history: they should all be in some kind of meantone; most are now in Vallotti.

Thirdly, we should consider how many organs ever were originally tuned in circulating temperaments. We may expect there to be some significant examples in areas where the influence of theoreticians such as Werckmeister, Neidhart and Kirnberger is felt, but we would surely be surprised to find any universal movement until late in the eighteenth century and then in certain areas only, the vast majority of organs still being built in meantone or modified meantone, especially in Britain, France, Iberia and Italy.

Fourthly, we should consider whether many organs were ever retuned from their original meantone tunings into circulating temperaments. We know a little bit about what happened in modern times: Mackenzie[15] has noted the pattern in the records of English organ builders and estimated that the peak year for retuning to equal temperament was 1875. Even in Northern Europe, where circulating temperaments might have filtered through to the organ-building community, there would not have been the desire or money to retune smaller organs. Larger organs would have required a major intervention. To retune a three-manual sixteen-foot organ is not a matter of a few day's effort. If it is cut to length, then every pipe has to be handled, including the largest ones. All will warm up in the hand while being cut and will have to be left to cool before the tuning can recommence. Bear in mind also, that we are considering a period when the tuner was accompanied not only by an assistant at the keys but also by others at the bellows and, in addition, the team could only hope to work during hours of daylight. As Ibo Ortgies is now asking, *pace* Kerala Snyder,[16] could Buxtehude really have had his organ at Lübeck retuned to a new temperament in eighteen days, or was this just a touch-up?

Fifthly, we should guard against the spurious argument that an analysis of musical sources can show what temperament the composer in question preferred. There have been many attempts to do this and they have no validity. The processes of composition are far too variable for this kind of thinking to be valuable. To take Bach alone: how do we assess the *48* on the one hand (circulating or equal?) against the organ music on the other (using the meantone keys but with enharmonic excursions into 'difficult' territory)? And what about the *Art of Fugue,* in d minor throughout but with an enharmonic language that looks back to Froberger? When Peter Williams wrote his introduction to some of the fugues (1728, 1750) of Thomas Roseingrave[17] he said, "Roseingrave liked the key of f minor, but this was intolerably discordant in mean-tone temperament. Since there is no evidence that the keyboards of the organ at St. George's [Hanover Square] possessed divided sharps it is reasonable to assume that Roseingrave had modified the organ's tuning in some way, perhaps to something approaching equal temperament." Another explanation, perhaps more plausible, is that though Roseingrave may have recognised f minor as discordant, he did not necessarily find it intolerably so, and may have used it to express, say, anguish or sorrow.

Sixthly, and following from the above, we should distinguish between what theoreticians described in writing as being the bad or even 'intolerable' intervals in meantone tuning (the wolf, the 'bad' third B – D-sharp) and what composers and musicians might actually have wished to inflict on their listeners. Composers may use harsh sounds for deliberate effect. Cabanilles may write a single A-sharp in his *Tiento lleno de Pange Lingua de Quinto Tono*, or Roseingrave a whole string of wolves in his fugue in f minor, not because these effects are 'intolerable' and will therefore drive the audience from the building, but because they have a specific degree of harshness which is desired at that point in the composition.

After many years living with different temperaments and with music of different periods, I have come to a set of personal conclusions, which though they have changed over time and may yet change again, currently stand approximately thus:

The movement to apply circulating temperaments to the organ was one of the last manifestations of neo-classical organ reform, where a subjective judgment (circulating 'good', equal 'bad', wolf 'intolerable') was applied regardless of historical accuracy. Many new organs were built in temperaments such as Vallotti which were unsettling enough to ruin the process of enharmonic modulation in the music of Vierne while on the other hand being completely insufficient to give real beauty to, say, a toccata by Frescobaldi. I cannot help feeling that circulating temperaments have all the defects of equal temperament with few of the benefits.

Regardless of the position of historical theorists, the difficulties presented by meantone tuning, and the *oeuvre* of J.S. Bach, the organ world remained largely meantone until the early-nineteenth century. That is simply how most of the organs were, and we will not get very far with some of the greatest repertoire left to us – Muffat, Froberger, the Couperins, Buxtehude, the English voluntary – until we have the opportunity to listen to it in a tuning that closely approximates what was meant. In the case of some of this repertoire – say the English trumpet voluntaries – nothing happens at all (in a purely musical sense) until the thirds and sixths are very nearly in tune.

The meantone world as it applies to organs is gradually being revealed to us, whether in some of the finest French restorations or, in Britain at Lulworth Castle Chapel (Seede 1786, restored Drake 1990) and St. James Bermondsey (Bishop 1829, restored Goetze & Gwynn 2003). This is a musical world full of surprise and beauty; we know that it also houses the wolf in his awful lair. We should not be too fastidious either to look on him, as our ancestors were obliged to for so many generations, or to acquiesce to his horrid growl and feel afraid – as is only natural.

: : N O T E S : :

[1]   From Shaw's review of the Musical Instruments at the Inventions Exhibition in *The Magazine of Music*, August 1885, quoted in *Shaw's Music: The Complete Musical Criticism of Bernard Shaw*, ed. Dan Laurence (London 1989), 1:321.

[2]   Cecil Clutton, "The Samuel Green Organ in the Private Chapel at Buckingham Palace", *The Organ*, (October 1963), 43:170:57-60; John Norman

"The Musical Effects of Tempering the Scale", *Musical Instrument Technology*, (Spring 1980), 3:4:143-146.

3   G.C. Klop, *Harpsichord Tuning – Course Outline*, Werkplaats voor Clavicim-belouw (1974).

4   *Monteverdi – Vespro della Beata Virgine,* Taverner Consort, Choir and Players, EMI-Reflèxe EX.157 27 0129 3.

5   L.S. Colchester, R. Bowers, A. Crossland: *The Organs and Organists of Wells Cathedral* (Wells 1974).

6   Alexander Mackenzie of Ord, "The Well-tuned Organ. An introduction to keyboard temperaments in 18th and 19th century England", *BIOS Journal* 3 (1979) 56-72.

7   C.A. Padgham, P.D. Collins and G.K. Parker, "A Trial of Unequal Temperaments on the Organ", *BIOS Journal* 3 (1979), 73-91.

8   C.A. Padgham, *The Well-tempered Organ* (Oxford 1986).

9   S. Bicknell, "The Organ in Wollaton Hall" *BIOS Journal* 6 (1982) 43-57.

10   C.A. Padgham, *The Well-tempered Organ*, 34, 101.

11   M. Renshaw and A. Barnes, *The Life and Work of John Snetzler* (Aldershot 1994) 124-5.

12   C. Stevens, "An Interesting English Chamber Organ", *The Organ*, (October 1973), 53:210:13-16.

13   N.M. Plumley, "The Harris/Byfield Connection: some recent findings", *BIOS Journal* 3 (1979) 108-134.

14   C.A. Padgham, *The Well-tempered Organ,* 33, 86-89.

15   Alexander Mackenzie of Ord, "The Well-tuned Organ. An introduction to keyboard temperaments in 18th and 19th century England", *BIOS Journal* 3 (1979) 56-72.

16   K.J. Snyder, "Buxtehude's Organs: Helsingør, Helsingborg, Lübeck." *The Musical Times,* (1985) CXXVI:365-369, 427-434.

17   P.F. Williams (ed.), *Ten Organ Pieces by Thomas Roseingrave,* (London 1961, 1970).

THE QUESTION OF EUGENE THAYER

John Ogasapian

SOME SIXTY YEARS after Eugene Thayer shot himself to death in a Burlington, Vermont, hotel room, the pioneer historian of American music, John Tasker Howard penned an entry on him for the *Dictionary of American Biography*. Very much the tactful gentleman of his time, Howard delicately omitted the details of Thayer's death; however when he came to append the bibliography to his article, Howard admitted to being puzzled. "In view of his contemporary prominence," he wrote, "Thayer is surprisingly neglected by writers on American music." He went on to list standards in the literature of his time on American music that made little or no mention of Thayer, among them his own monumental history.[1]

The situation also troubled the late Elfrieda Kraege thirty years ago. Indefatigable researcher that she was, Kraege published an article on Thayer in *The Bicentennial Tracker* in 1976 that is still the best study of the man and his career, in the course of which she reiterated Howard's question and her own puzzlement.[2] And indeed, Thayer's renown hasn't fared any better in the later histories of our own time. Standard works, like Crawford, Hamm, and Hitchcock ignore him just as those of a generation ago did.

I would argue that Howard, and by extension Kraege, asked the wrong question and begged the right one. Howard assumed that Thayer had a sufficient degree of "contemporary prominence" to make his neglect by later writers "surprising." Yet the weight of evidence suggests that Thayer in fact had no such degree of "contemporary prominence," at least not among the significant musical figures and trendsetters of his era. Moreover, many if not most serious writers on music all but ignored him during his life and in the years immediately after his death. Accordingly, the right question would appear to be why he was disregarded in his own time.

Perhaps the place to begin is a book that constituted something like a musical Who's Who in America during Thayer's most active period, Mathews and Howe's *A Hundred Years of Music in America*, published Chicago in 1889, the year Thayer took his life.[3] A virtual register of professional musicians, it makes only six passing references to Thayer, for the most part in the context of students of his who are more fully profiled. Moreover, although Thayer regularly accompanied the great Norwegian violinist, Ole Bull, during American concert tours, the section on Bull omits mention of him. Nor is there even a brief entry on Thayer in the section headed "Supplemental Dictionary of American Musicians" with which the volume closes. Yet Mathews and Howe devote space to numerous other organists, some of them with reputations seemingly less deserving of attention than Thayer.

Interestingly, the editors specifically mention having drawn on F.O. Jones's slender though evidently not very selective *American Musicians*,[4] which contains a lengthy entry on Thayer. Thus, they cannot have been ignorant of whatever "contemporary prominence" he had. Perhaps it is that Jones apparently solicited his biographical entries directly from subjects where possible. As Jones himself put it, "Much of the information has been derived from first sources by correspondence." In any case, the tone of his entry on Thayer is fulsome enough to make one suspect that it was written by Thayer himself, and Mathews and Howe may accordingly have discounted it.

Be that as it may, we cannot know for sure why – or even if – Mathews and Howe purposely neglected Thayer. Whatever they might have thought of him as a composer or even a performer, Thayer had taught enough prominent musicians, from George Whitefield Chadwick to Gerrit Smith, that a degree of note might reasonably have been taken of him as a pedagogue. Needless to say, there is also and always the suspicion to be had that politics played some part. Nineteenth-century musicians – and organists in particular – were no less apt than those of the twenty-first century to play professional hardball with one another as a blood sport.

Whatever the reason, one can easily imagine Thayer, like anyone who passes the half-century mark, taking stock of his life's work. A proud man, he may well have been aware of his virtual banishment from the pages of Mathews and Howe's volume, and even been moved to cast a sober look at what the future might hold for his musical legacy. We cannot know if at least a part of the depression Thayer is said to have suffered in his last years may have been rooted in despair about his place in American musical history; or if at some level that despair seized his final thoughts in that lonely Vermont hotel room. But one thing we can know is that Matthews and Howe's silence resonated in the literature of subsequent decades.

Accordingly, this essay is a sort of meditation on the question Howard ought to have asked: how came it to pass that Thayer, prolific of publications, acclaimed by his audiences, and respected–even beloved – by his students, never quite managed to achieve the kind of professional recognition he might have expected and deserved? The answer may well lie with the cultural and musical contexts in which Thayer's professional life unfolded: a period during which American attitudes toward its own art music underwent a change, and a place – that is, Boston – that during that period – the years immediately after the Civil War – became America's capital of high art and culture, in the sense that New York became the nation's entertainment and financial capital and Washington its political capital.

More to the point, Boston became the nation's musical center, with its two concert halls and its highly influential *Dwight's Journal of Music*, published bi-weekly from 1852 to 1881. In a sense, the *Journal* had a synergism with the city's other musical institutions that gave it – or more accurately, its editor, John Sullivan Dwight (1813-1893) – significantly more influence than even New York's Richard Storrs Willis and the periodical he edited over many of the same years, variously titled *Message Bird*, *Musical World*, and *Musical Times.* Dwight and his *Journal* were never especially supportive of Thayer, even as an organist or teacher, the two things he seems to have been quite good at.

There is both symmetry and irony in the coincidence that *Dwight's Journal* discontinued publication the very year the Boston Symphony Orchestra was founded, bringing to at least one aspect of Dwight's advocacy to fruition. For Thayer, the events of that year signaled the end of the sort of musical world for which he had trained himself: one in which music was not so much a professionally-cultivated High Art in the European manner, as Dwight perceived it, but rather a primarily amateur activity whose highest endeavor was in the service of religion, much as Lowell Mason had preached and practiced in Boston fifty years earlier.

Mason saw music on one hand as an amateur and democratic activity in which all could take part, especially in the framework of worship; and on the other as a morally edifying, socially commendable endeavor that – though not especially valuable as a commodity in and of itself – could serve to heighten and improve more utilitarian skills (a position, in passing, that still crops up regularly, especially in music education literature). Such was the prevailing view in America before the Civil War, and Thayer shared it for the most part. Dwight, by contrast, espoused the idea of music as a formal Art in the restrictive and self-referential sense of the word, and American music at its best as a tributary of European art music in the tradition of Mozart and Beethoven.[5]

In the twilight years of his *Journal*, Dwight's purpose began to be realized in the circle of composers who gathered around Professor John Knowles Paine of Harvard during the late 1870s and 1880s. Paine was born in 1839, studied as a youth with Hermann Kotzschmar in Portland, Maine, and then traveled to Germany to work with Haupt and the theorist Friedrich Wilhelm Wieprecht. He may have been encouraged to study in Europe by the great Beethoven scholar, Alexander Wheelock Thayer (1817-1897); for Paine sailed from New York in 1858 along with A.W. Thayer, and the older man's company was doubtless an education in and of itself. Paine remained in Europe for three years, making the acquaintance, among others, of Clara Schumann, doyenne of German musical romanticism, and internalizing the musical culture.

By the time he returned in 1861, Paine's professional focus had moved from a youthful enthusiasm for playing the organ to a broader and more mature sense of music as Art and himself as an American exponent of that Art as manifested in the European Romantic tradition. Dwight, who considered Paine a superb organist, encouraged and supported him in this broadened view and in Paine's subsequent promotion of it among his students at Harvard.

It is at this point that Eugene Thayer entered Paine's life. A month older than Paine, Thayer emerged from relatively provincial Worcester County where he had gained somewhat of a reputation as an organist, to study with Paine, shortly after the latter's return from Europe. Thayer was a good enough player to share the spotlight with Paine and other prominent Boston organists at the opening of the Music Hall's E.F. Walcker organ in 1863, as well as the inauguration of the E. and G.G. Hook organ at Mechanics Hall in Worcester a year later. Paine was enough of an influence on Thayer so that Thayer followed in his footsteps, journeying to Berlin in 1865 to study with Haupt and Wieprecht. But here the two men's footsteps diverge.

In addition to his evidently superior creative talent, Paine had also had A.W. Thayer to open doors for him, and to share musical insights and experience. Probably more to the point, Paine had no personal responsibilities back home, and was thus able to take his leisure and imbibe deeply of German musical romanticism in all its breadth. Eugene Thayer, by contrast, had gone abroad leaving behind a wife who was expecting their first child; and indeed, during his absence she had to suffer alone the bereavement of losing that child. Unlike Paine, Thayer's time in Europe had to be brief and focused. He took a bit of time after his formal studies to tour Europe, gave a few recitals, made a few contacts (among them Bull and the pianist Moscheles), and then returned to Boston in 1866 to resume his family responsibilities and his career as a church organist, performer and private teacher.

By coincidence, Paine sailed again for Europe the very year Thayer returned. But this time he was a Harvard instructor on leave and an established, European-trained musician. In February of 1867, he led a performance of his *Mass in D* before a distinguished audience in Berlin. The performance earned mixed reviews, with some critics taking note of its patches of academic aridness; however the *Leipziger Allgemeine Musikalische Zeitung* characterized the work as a "delightful sign of beginning artistic development across the sea," burnishing Paine's musical reputation with the glitter of international recognition.[6]

Back at Harvard and supported by Dwight, Paine secured ever more firmly his place in Boston's musical life. Harvard bestowed an honorary M.A. on him in 1869, making him an alumnus and therefore eligible for a professorship there. In the early 1870s, he was made professor at Boston University, along with his Harvard instructorship; and in 1875 Harvard designated him its first professor of music, over the protests of some of the other professors, among them the historian Francis Parkman.

The 1870s and early 1880s were the high point of Paine's career. His student Henry Lee Higginson, drawing on his advice and assistance, founded the Boston Symphony Orchestra in 1881. But most importantly, Paine became the focus for a Boston school of European-oriented American composers, each of whom would achieve distinction in the wider world of music. The main members of the group were Arthur Foote (1853-1937), Horatio Parker (1861-1919), George Whitefield Chadwick (1854-1931), Edward MacDowell (1860-1908), and later Amy Beach (1867-1944).

Foote grew up in nearby Salem and was the only one of the group to work with Paine at Harvard, as well as the only one without formal European study. Parker, born in the Boston suburb of Auburndale, eventually became professor of music at Yale. Chadwick, a Lowell native who studied the organ with Thayer for a time, would achieve the most celebrity of the group as a composer and as director of the New England Conservatory. MacDowell, back in Boston in 1888 after a number of years in Europe, would write some of his best music there before departing in 1896 for a professorship at Columbia. Beach was a brilliant pianist and arguably the most gifted composer of all.

These men (as a woman Beach was limited in her contact with the others by the custom of the day) were more than casually acquainted with one another, both personally and professionally. They dined together regularly in Boston, discussing their own music and the music of other composers. Some, like Paine, spent all or part of each summer at the poet Celia Thaxter's artists' colony on Appledore in the Isles of Shoals, off the New Hampshire seacoast. Chadwick and Parker were such close friends that as young marrieds, they vacationed in Europe together, even though they were all too aware that their wives cordially disliked each other.[7]

Parker, MacDowell and Beach, of course, arrived too late to be a part of the musical scene during Thayer's time in Boston.[8] But that is really beside the point. By the mid-1870s, even as he was engaged in editing his *Organist's Jour-*

nal and Review, Thayer was well out of the musical mainstream, as the earlier Boston romantics were defining it; in fact, in a sense the *Journal and Review* can be seen as his declaration – or at least acceptance – of the separate road he had taken. Unlike them, he had systematically focused his career and activities on the organ and church music, fields that had been central in the American musical scene during his youth, but were now decentered by the cult of German romanticism that bestrode the Boston scene. It was not solely because of his pronounced deficiencies in formal compositional technique that Thayer stood outside the charmed circle. In a sense, he had embraced the reality of his vocation and positioned himself accordingly.

To be sure, several in the Paine circle held church positions. Chadwick had been organist at Park Street Church, Parker would serve Trinity Church, and Foote spent well over thirty years as organist of First Church. But for each of them church work, though it might be a welcome source of income to support their composing and even a rewarding activity, was not central to their artistic identity. They all composed organ pieces and church music; but except for Parker, such work rarely if ever exemplified their best endeavors. For Thayer however, both as a musician and professional, the organ and church music were central and primary.

An article Thayer wrote in late-1880 for *Scribner's Magazine* reveals much about the man and musician.[9] Over four pages of text and charts, and based on his "life-long familiarity with the king of instruments," Thayer portrays Niagara Falls as a mighty musical instrument, a "great diapason … in praise of Him who first gave it voice… ." and "a chronometer which shall last as long as man shall walk on earth. It is the clock of God." One can scarcely imagine Dwight, or Paine, or anyone else in their circle, penning a purportedly serious musical article on such a subject, attempting a theological interpretation, or adopting such a prose style. Thayer's choice of subject and mode of rhetoric alike are far closer to American musical thinking the 1830s or '40s than to the era of William Henry Fry and John Sullivan Dwight in the 1850s and early '60s, let alone the urbane 1880s readership of *Scribner's*.[10] In any event, the physics in the article, though not Thayer's musical or theological assertions, provoked a few letters, to which he duly replied.[11]

By mid-1881, Thayer was ready to leave Boston. The *Journal and Review* had reached its end in 1877; by 1880, the Music Hall organ, scene of many of his triumphs, was deteriorating. Always sluggish of action and impossible to keep in tune, it was finally put up for sale in 1883 to make room for the two-year-old Boston Symphony Orchestra, and consigned to storage the next year.[12] Under the circumstances, Thayer, as an organist and teacher of the organ, may have felt out of place himself, as far as Boston was concerned.

Consequently, the opportunity at Fifth Avenue Presbyterian Church in New York might have seemed like a heaven-sent chance to do the work to which he felt called, and to do it in one of the most prestigious and visible church situations in America's foremost city. He remained at Fifth Avenue Presbyterian Church for only four years and then apparently retired from church work, though he may have served Holy Trinity in Harlem during that period. According to his daughter, he spent much of this time composing.[13] And indeed, he wrote his posthumously published fifth organ sonata, one of his best works and the only one of the sonatas that has a formal and structured sonata form, during this period.[14]

He also sought and gained by Oxford examination, through the Wooster University in Ohio, a Doctor of Music degree in 1885 or 1886 (the sources differ). Thayer's 1850s predecessor as music director at Fifth Avenue Presbyterian Church, Lowell Mason, had been awarded an honorary Doctor of Music degree by New York University, and Paine would be similarly honored by Yale in 1890; however earned music doctorates – even those gained by examination rather than prescribed program – were virtually unknown in America at the time. Examinations for the Cambridge MusD or the Oxford DMus invariably consisted of a pedantic "exercise" or two demonstrating a measure of mastery in formal counterpoint followed by a larger-scale and often equally pedantic work for chorus and orchestra, usually climaxing with a performance of that work for the university community. Thayer's degree piece was a "Festival Cantata" for soloists, double chorus and orchestra; however, there is no record that it was performed.

Why Thayer should have sought a degree at this point in his life is somewhat puzzling. He might have been contemplating a career move into academe; however, possession of a doctorate was by no means the necessity for a college or university appointment in Thayer's time that it is now. In fact, the only requirement for a Harvard professorship, for example, was that the candidate hold a Harvard degree. Paine's honorary M.A. from Harvard was clearly given by the Corporation to satisfy that requirement. A more likely possibility is that Thayer was either attempting to validate himself as a composer alongside the Boston group or to regain some of the prestige he may have felt was slipping away from him. Not to put too fine a point on what is, after all, only a hypothesis, he may even have envisioned the doctorate as a means of positioning himself as Paine's counterpart in New York

Whatever the story is behind the timing of Thayer's doctoral efforts, he and his family remained in New York, in their Park Avenue apartment, until May of 1889, when they moved to Connecticut. A month later, in Burlington, Vermont, to recoup his health and take part in one of William Sherwood's summer music schools, Thayer took his life.

Ironically, Paine's creative prime had passed, even though he was not yet fifty. Evidently the labor of teaching and administrative duties at Harvard had sapped his inspiration. Lacking the benefit of our hindsight, Thayer could not have known this of course. Nor for that matter could anyone else save for Paine himself and possibly those closest to him, primarily his fiercely protective wife. In any case, the 1890s, the years after he was honored with a Yale music doctorate, would leave Paine frustrated and discouraged at his inability to have a staged performance of his one opera, *Azara*, the labor of decade or more.[15]

In the end, of course, it is always a dicey business to attempt an interpretation of attitudes a century or more in the past. One easily risks perceiving situations through the omniscient lens of subsequent events that the protagonists in those situations could not have anticipated. After all, what is history to us was the present to those who made that history. Still, certain elements emerge with enough clarity to suggest a reason why Thayer's reputation seemed to languish in his own time and after.

To be sure, Thayer enjoyed a considerable amount of professional and financial success during the late 1860s and 1870s. His public recitals at his Hollis Street Church and subsequent Boston churches he served gained him recognition and pupils; he produced his *Organ School*; he launched the *Journal and*

Review in 1874 to provide usable teaching and service music, and a year later he opened his own private studio, equipping it with a two-manual Hutchings, Plaisted & Co. organ.[16]

But in the scheme of things, Thayer had become an anachronism, even as a relatively young man. He wrote and thought a generation behind his Boston contemporaries. He had little real aptitude for formal composition; or maybe it was that he had no aptitude for the sort of composition in European forms that was being practiced by his Boston contemporaries. He had spent his youth tooling himself to perform on an instrument that had fallen out of favor with the leading composers and musical trend setters in German musical fashion, and to provide training in specialties – organ playing and church music – that fewer and fewer of Boston's most prominent musicians were much interested in, except as a sideline.

Ultimately, the most difficult question to be pondered, both from an historical and humanitarian perspective, is the extent to which Thayer himself came to this recognition, and the extent to which it haunted him in his latter years. We can never know for sure, of course; but perhaps the real answer to that question was played out at its most basic level in his Burlington, Vermont hotel room sometime around 11 o'clock the morning of June 27, 1889.

: : N O T E S : :

[1] *DAB* 18:412. John Tasker Howard, *Our American Music* (New York: Crowell, 1929 and subsequent editions to 1965).

[2] Elfrieda Kraege, "Eugene Thayer," *The Tracker* 21 (1976), 172.

[3] W.S.B. Mathews [and Glanville Howe], *A Hundred Years of Music in America* (Chicago: n.p., 1889; repr. New York: AMS Press, 1970).

[4] F.O. Jones, *A Handbook of American Music and Musicians* (Canaseraga, NY: n.p., 1886; repr. New York: Da Capo Press, 1971), 165. In his Preface, Jones claims to have begun gathering his material as early as 1878.

[5] On Dwight, see, among numerous other items, Mark N. Grant, *Maestros of the Pen: A History of Classical Music Criticism in America* (Boston: Northeastern University Press, 1998), 35-52. Apart from the reprint of *Dwight's Journal*

itself, the major modern resource is Irving Sablosky, *What They Heard: Music in America 1852-1881 from the Pages of* Dwight's Journal of Music (Baton Rouge: L.S.U. Press, 1986).

[6] John C. Schmidt, *The Life and Works of John Knowles Paine* (Ann Arbor: UMI Research Press, 1990), 104.

[7] One of the best studies of this group, unfortunately out of print and hard to find, is Nicolas Tawa, *The Coming of Age of American Art Music: New England's Classical Romanticists* (Westport, CT: Greenwood Press, 1991).

[8] Boston was home to a number of other composers during those years and shortly after, among them Charles Martin Loeffler, Arthur Farwell, Arthur Battell Whiting, and in the earlier generation that included Paine and Thayer, Samuel Brenton Whitney and even for a brief time Dudley Buck. In a sense the group only came to an end in 1972 with the death at age 104 of Margaret Ruthven Lang (daughter of B.J. Lang) and Mabel Daniels, who lived into her nineties. The group is often referred to by music historians as the Second Boston Classicist School, though Boston Romantics, or Post-Romantics, would be a more appropriate way of characterizing them.

[9] Eugene Thayer, "Music of Niagara," *Scribner's Magazine,* February 1881, 583–586.

[10] For an especially illuminating perspective, see Denise Von Glahn, *The Sounds of Place: Music and the American Cultural Landscape* (Boston: Northeastern University Press, 2003), 21–23.

[11] *Scribner's Magazine* (June 1881), 307–308.

[12] Barbara J. Owen, *The Organ in New England* (Raleigh: Sunbury, 1978), 244–245.

[13] Louise Friedel Thayer, "Eugene Thayer," *The American Organist* 16:8 (August 1933), 403–406.

[14] See John Ogasapian, "The Sonatas of W. Eugene Thayer: A Critical Appraisal," *The Tracker* 34:4 (1990), 18–22.

[15] During his lifetime, he had to be satisfied with a single concert performance, given on May 7, 1903.

[16] The instrument is now in the North Chapel Universalist Church, Woodstock, Vermont.

DUDLEY BUCK AND THE COMING
OF AGE OF THE AMERICAN ORGAN

❧

N. Lee Orr

THE 1929 EDITION of the *Dictionary of American Biography* stated that "American organ music practically begins" with Dudley Buck. Published under the auspices of the American Council of Learned Societies twenty years after Buck's death, the dictionary arguably had enough historical perspective to sum up Buck's importance. Indeed, a close look at the historical record offers solid support for the statement.

The twenty-three-year-old Buck returned from Europe in 1862 just as the American organ was experiencing new growth and potential. Larger instruments capable of playing a wide repertoire were being built, original organ literature was gradually supplanting orchestral transcriptions and improvisations, high-quality performance was increasingly held up as the model for organ recitals, and thorough organ instruction was becoming more widely available. Buck was to have a major role in influencing and strengthening these developments, which transformed the organ in the United States.

The American organ before the middle of the nineteenth century had changed little from the modest English chamber instruments of the previous century. In fact, prior to the nineteenth century, few American churches were of a sufficient size to warrant having an organ.[1] Towns such as Boston, Philadelphia, New York, and Charleston were little more than large villages, boasting few congregations of any size. Furthermore, Calvinistic prescriptions against instrumental music in worship discouraged even the larger Puritan worship houses in New England from installing organs. By the beginning of

the nineteenth century Boston had eight organs, while New York and Philadelphia each had five or six. The remaining few organs were to be found in
other important colonial cities, such as Charleston and Williamsburg, which
generally possessed one or two instruments. The German immigrants who
settled in Pennsylvania brought their musical heritage with them, installing a
surprising number of instruments in towns such as York, Lancaster, and Bethlehem. By the turn of the century, settlements along the Hudson and Connecticut Rivers also began installing organs in their churches, including Hartford, Connecticut, whose Christ Church obtained an organ by local craftsman
George Catlin in 1801. As the nineteenth century unfolded, organs became
more common, and by the 1830s many churches in Eastern cities possessed
organs of twenty or thirty stops.[2]

This increase in the prevalence of larger organs in the first decades of the
nineteenth century, however, did not bring with it a budding repertoire of independent literature for the instrument. Organs served mainly to accompany
the congregation and the choir; even anthems, which were not allowed in
the service itself, were sung before worship, thus eliminating the need for an
organ prelude. Most organists were immigrants who continued the European
practice of improvising any solo organ music required for the service. In addition, most organists were required to be proficient at a number of musical
skills, including teaching, singing, and the composition of keyboard, chamber,
and vocal music. Keyboard proficiency meant being able to play not only the
organ, but the harpsichord, spinet, clavichord, and, eventually, the pianoforte
as well. Little distinction was made between the individual idioms of each of
these instruments, and a career or a repertoire devoted solely to the organ
simply was not a practical consideration. For example, nearly all of the Moravian churches in Pennsylvania possessed organs by 1800, yet almost no solo
organ music is found in their impressive archives of anthems, songs, and string
and brass music. Anglican churches supported music just as enthusiastically as
the Moravians, yet only two of their organists – English-born William Selby
(1738–1798), and German immigrant Charles Zeuner (1795–1857) – left any
organ music of note. New concert halls built in New York and Boston also
sometimes contained organs, although these were usually small instruments

used mainly for accompaniment. The rare voluntary generally consisted of popular tunes, or a transcription of an overture or chorus from an oratorio by Handel. Other congregations that had resisted allowing organs in worship gradually joined the Anglicans and Moravians and purchased organs, but not for any newly discovered passion for music; the quality of the singing had deteriorated to the point that many congregations felt they had little recourse but to give in.

With the debate over the suitability of organs in worship largely over by the 1820s, a new body of writings on organ instruction began to appear. Some of the first published organ music in America appeared in instruction books, which contained voluntaries and variations intended more for practice than for public performance. Philadelphia became the first center of organ instruction; it was there that the first organ instruction book published in America (Andrew Law's *The Art of Playing the Organ*) appeared in 1809. Subsequent authors of organ instruction books also worked in Philadelphia, including Benjamin Carr (1769–1831), who wrote organ tutors for playing the Catholic mass, and Thomas Loud (d. 1834), who published an instruction book for the Episcopal liturgy. Later James Cox Beckel (1811–?) issued a similar volume, but not until 1830 did a volume of organ music intended for performance (by Charles Zeuner) appear. Even then, the pieces were "composed [for] and dedicated to the Handel and Haydn Society, Boston," a secular musical society. Not until a decade later, with his *Organ Voluntaries*, did Zeuner write a volume clearly intended for the church organist. Artemas Nixon Johnson (1817–92) became the earliest American to publish an anthology of organ music, with his *American Church Organ Voluntaries* of 1852, a collection of opening and closing voluntaries for service use. This publication is also important because it is the first book of American organ repertoire with instructions for the organist, rather than a vocal collection or accompaniment manual. One of the most successful organ method books was Johann Christian Rinck's (1770–1846) *Practische Orgelschule* (1819–1821), which was translated into French, English, and Italian during his lifetime. The English version, known as *Practical Organ School,* appeared in London in 1820, New York in the 1830s and 1840s, and in Boston by 1851. The work immediately set itself apart with its extensive etudes with obbligato pedal, as well as preludes, postludes, and voluntaries. As a student of J.C. Kittel, the last pupil of J.S. Bach, Rinck also provided a direct link to the revered German organist.[3]

The 1840s saw the first real development of a native organ style in the United States. Population increases resulted in larger congregations and churches, which soon began to require louder organs. This drew the ire of traditionalists like Nathaniel Gould (1781–1864), who decried the move away from the gentle, singing tone of the early nineteenth-century instruments. His 1853 book on church music idealized the "small organs, and those played lightly, just to accompany the voices, never to be made conspicuous, but moving gently along, bearing up and sustaining the vocal parts." The new tonal styles appalled him:

> But this manner of suppressing, or keeping back, the tones and power of the organ, could not long satisfy the taste and ambition of organists; and those who had advocated the doctrine of soft playing were observed, either by accident or design, gradually to mark their performance with crescendo, from Sabbath to Sabbath. By and by all restraint was thrown aside, and the struggle was for the organ of the greatest power. The small organs were set aside to make room for thunder tones, still more and more powerful, till an organ was *worthless* that would not make the granite walls of a church tremble, at times, when used in full strength. And many times now, when the doxology is sung, at the close of worship, we hear such a crash of sound on the organ, that, the choir and the whole congregation joining, could not more make words intelligible, than would be the words of a public speaker in the midst of a roaring artillery.[4]

Even with the increase in power and versatility, the organ at mid-century still generally had short-compass pedalboards, and the Swell, which was regarded as a solo division, generally had a short compass from tenor c or f.

By the 1840s things began changing. The centers of organ construction shifted from Pennsylvania to Boston and New York. While Boston's leading builder of the first part of the century, William Goodrich (1777–1833), spent his lifetime making a total of forty-nine organs (eleven of them chamber organs), by the 1850s brothers George and Elias Hook (doing business as E. & G.G. Hook) were producing that number of organs in three years' time. By the 1870s larger factories could produce between twenty-four and fifty organs per year. At the same time, builders began moving away from the English-oriented tonal design and incorporating the tonal ideals demanded by organists who had heard the magnificent instruments in France and Germany.[5] In 1873 Buck commented upon this trend:

> In America, of late years, we have followed suit, copying Germany in the voicing of most of our open and stopped pipes, both metal and wood; copying France in the main characteristics of their reed voicing (in which they were long preeminent), and copying England in the general plan of our organs, together with the conveniences of mechanism and effects of combination.[6]

As the playing of transcriptions of orchestral works on the organ grew in popularity in the 1850s, many organ builders responded with large, mechanically complex instruments tuned in equal temperament, and equipped with increased tonal resources and greater volume, all in an effort to emulate orchestral effects.[7] Transcriptions had been the mainstay of organ music all along, of course, but the traditional organ renditions of English anthems or Handel oratorios gave way to symphonic movements and orchestral overtures. Improvisations often became orchestral in scope as well, such as the irrepressible storm scenes that evoked ebullient responses from naive listeners. Henry Lahee relates that one storm scene was "so vivid that people involuntarily reached for their umbrellas. On one occasion an old woman rushed out of the church with great excitement, saying she had left the front door open, and she was afraid her best carpet would get wet."[8] For the organ to be taken seriously as a concert instrument, however, original organ music was required. It was not until after the Civil War that organ composition in America attained the stature of a professional repertoire.

The first true organ recitals were performed in the 1860s, sparked in part by the arrival of the Boston Music Hall organ. Built in Germany by the firm of E.F. Walcker of Ludwigsburg, the *Great Organ* arrived in Boston in February 1863 after a stormy three-month crossing. The concert hall series featured preludes and fugues of J.S. Bach and organ sonatas of Felix Mendelssohn, along with contemporary works by the French composer Louis J.-A. Lefébure-Wély (1817–70) and the German composer Ludwig Thiele (1816–1848). The programs generally consisted of equal parts of older organ music, orchestral transcriptions from various periods, as well as contemporary works, often performed by the composer.[9]

Buck addressed the issue of original organ literature versus transcriptions in an essay titled "On the Legitimate in Organ Playing," which he published in *The Musical Independent* in October 1871.[15] Consistent with his gracious personality, Buck sought a balance between artistic excellence and common taste. He addressed the whole contentious issue, but "without giving a dogmatic opinion." He quickly made it clear "that Bach was the greatest composer for his instrument that the world has ever known." After all, no one had been more zealous in presenting the Leipzig master's works in America than he. But why did Buck's critics insist that organists play only Bach's music and "turn with a sneer from nearly everything else of a dissimilar style?" They perhaps forgot that legitimacy in art results partly from its relevancy to the audience to whom the music is being presented. Buck points out how things had been improving: "Within the last eight years [since Buck's return from Europe], so far as this country is concerned, what wonderful improvements in organ building!" And these improvements will lead "to a new plane of the legitimate in organ-playing." Just in the last five years progress has been made, "and the comparative interest felt in organ performances, abundantly prove that this indispensable foundation-school of sound organ playing is attracting more and more attention." No doubt, it would be ideal to play only serious organ music, for "from a true art standpoint an organist should throw his influence toward works originally composed for his instrument." But this would most likely turn listeners away from all organ music, including Bach and orchestral music. He lauded "the great improvements and mechanical facilities ... [that] make it possible to treat our modern organs in many more ways than simply in contrapuntal style." Buck understood that "this matter of overture playing not infrequently serves as a stepping-stone to better things." For this reason, "even the playing of light overtures may find a certain justification in this land, where so much missionary work has yet to be done... ."

The challenge remained great, as John Sullivan Dwight, editor of *Dwight's Journal of Music*, reminded his readers.[16] Dwight well understood the problem of balance, and, like Buck, remained open to compromise between the serious and the light. He had little patience, however, with those who chose only the low ground. His vexation comes through in his review of a new E. and G.G. Hook organ at the Arlington Street Church in Boston. Barbara Owen has suggested that the performer (who remained unnamed) was probably John H. Wilcox. Dwight fumed:

> ...but why shall an "organ exhibition" always consist of making the organ do all sorts of things except just that which it is designed to do? These end-less, aimless wanderings among solo stops, these *potpourris* of operas, popular airs, bits of secular and bits of sacred, strung together upon idle fancies of the moment, may be very well to show the fine qualitites of all the stops as well as the skill of the exhibitor, – neither of which do we call in question – but they fatigue and dissipate the mind just when it seeks to be edified and strengthened by the grandest of all instruments voicing the great thoughts of Eternity. If you would show the virtues of an organ, why not play organ music? Give these exceptional things their place, but do not let them usurp all. We do not object to the queer scrolls and monsters carved here and there about a Gothic cathedral; but not to show them, nor to give them shelter, except incidentally, were the sublime proportions of the cathedral reared.[17]

This passage articulates the place organ music played in the larger move-ment to increase cultural awareness, and encourage development in paint-ing, music, literature, and other arts after mid-century.[18] Leading thinkers and writers advocated finer organ music and better music in general as a means to strengthen cultural unity and provide moral leadership during a period of intense social change and disruption. As a result of the difficult social transfor-mations that accompanied widespread industrialization in *ante-bellum* America, the idea of culture increasingly came to be seen as a redeeming, moralizing force. In addition, organized religion more and more seemed incapable of stemming the tide of what was perceived as social decay and aberrant behav-ior. With the weakening influence of firm Calvinistic theology in a growing period of secularization, the organized church saw its influence on American moral and social life recede. As Victorian theology supplanted Calvinism and accommodated itself to bourgeois culture, it lost its supernatural framework, which undermined the sense of an ordered universe. Reality itself seemed uncertain. Cultural historian T. Jackson Lears aptly sums it up: "A weightless culture of material comfort and spiritual blandness was breeding weightless persons who longed for intense experience to give some definition, some distinct outline for substance to their vaporous lives."[19] The confident Victorian alliance of society and heaven, wedded by Christian assumptions of love and charity, had little power to address the daunting social problems of a competitive market economy and the bureaucratic rationalization of the inner life. High culture increasingly supplanted traditional religion as the primary bulwark against declining morals and social decay in *post-bellum* America.

The secularization of the organ, its literature, and the spaces where organs were to be found, occurred as a part of this larger cultural development, and gave added impetus to the call for more professional organ playing, as well as better church music in general. Even before 1850, quartet singers had brought a new level of musical performance to church galleries. Latin Masses by Mozart and Haydn were sung to insipid English texts, and operatic styles began to infiltrate the choir loft. Larger churches increased music budgets, asking for double quartets. Dr. Tuckerman of St. Paul's Church in Boston pleaded with his vestry to increase the budget so as to add a double quartet to compete with the more prestigious Trinity Church, which had recently done the same. As the organ assumed a central place in American musical life, churches repositioned the organ (and the choir) from the rear gallery to the front, where it could function as a concert instrument as well. Henry Ward Beecher's Plymouth Church in Brooklyn intentionally installed the new Hook organ at the front of the church's sanctuary in 1864 so that it could be used as a concert instrument. For years the church functioned as Brooklyn's main performance venue, and the weekly public organ recitals given there sought to imitate the programs one might have heard in a typical concert hall.[20]

Buck's ideas on the performance of organ music had, of course, been informed by his years of study in Europe. After showing great promise as a child, his father sent him in 1858 to complete his musical education at the Leipzig Conservatory, where he spent eighteen months, studying harmony and composition with Moritz Hauptmann (1792–1868), piano with Louis Plaidy (1810–74) and Ignaz Moscheles (1794–1870), and orchestration with Julius Rietz (1812–1877). When Rietz moved to Dresden in 1860 as the city's musical director, Buck followed him, continuing his organ lessons with Johann Gottlob Schneider (1789–1863). Born in 1789, Schneider had been good friends with Mendelssohn, and, like Mendelssohn, was one of the first organists since the Baroque era to have developed the technical ability to play the difficult pedal parts in Bach's organ works. During the first decades of the nineteenth century Schneider's performances in Germany and England did much to encourage the renewal of interest in the Leipzig master's organ music. It was this tradition that Schneider passed on to his young protégé from Connecticut. Buck must have been an exceptional student, for he later explained to W.S.B. Mathews that he spent all week composing and practiced his organ music only on Sunday in preparation for his Monday morning lessons with Herr Schneider, including the demanding Bach preludes and fugues. He claimed to be able to "play any good Bach fugue through fairly well after going through it half a dozen times."[10]

After returning from Europe in 1862, Buck became organist at North Congregational Church in Hartford, Connecticut, and began a series of organ recitals there, playing the three-manual 1850 E. & G.G. Hook, Op. 110. With these concerts Buck earned a reputation as an outstanding organist. He made his position on organ literature clear from the outset by opening the first recital with the E-flat Major Fugue ("St. Anne") by Bach. In total he performed nine major Bach works; nearly every program he performed included one work by Bach, or another serious organ piece, such as a Mendelssohn sonata. Buck presented a second series in September 1866 at the Second Congregational Church while the North Church was being demolished to make way for a replacement. The success of these recitals, played on the three-manual 1854 Johnson organ (Op. 35), prompted Buck to give a third series of recitals.

Following the success of the Hartford programs, Buck took his professional organ performances on the road. In the small towns and middle-sized cities that constituted the majority of American population centers, the organ played a prominent role in the musical life of the community, since there were few established orchestras outside of the very largest cities. Opera found wide audiences, but again one could only see regular performances in places like New York, or, more typically, at performances given by the numerous traveling opera companies. In most cities the organ's tonal diversity, performance flexibility, and dynamic range eclipsed the other available instruments, and organ recitals became major musical events. W.S.B. Mathews, in his important book *One Hundred Years of Music in America*, points out that "It was not until Dudley Buck came back from Germany and began to be sent out by [organ builder William A.] Johnson to show off his organs, that legitimate organ playing began to have a run outside very limited circles in large cities."[11]

Technically, Buck and John Knowles Paine stood alone in their mastery of the organ, most importantly with their virtuosic pedal proficiency; no American organist had ever dazzled audiences with such facility of the feet. Mathews points out that Buck's "pedal playing was far ahead of anything then existing in America, saving possibly that of Prof. John K. Paine, who, on the other hand, lacked Buck's knack with a popular audience. In fact, Mr. Buck's organ playing has rarely or never been duplicated, for while greater virtuosi may have appeared in America since, there has been no other concert organist with so much natural gift for music, combined with orchestral experience and a practical knowledge of the mechanism of the organ."[12] Buck's impressive skills as a concert organist did much to acquaint American listeners with serious organ and orchestral music. Buck spent fifteen years concertizing throughout the Northeast and Midwest, playing in towns that had probably never before heard a professional player. He led the way to establishing the organ as a major instrument in the cultural life of the United States. No unfavorable reviews of Buck's programs have come to light, and virtually all of the critics praised both his playing and his compositions.

Given that the United States possessed very few individuals or institutions capable of offering first-rate training to organists, Buck well understood that for the level of playing to improve, he would have to pass along the technical skills he had acquired in Germany. He was among the most influential organ teachers in the country, and his students included major figures of the next generation of American musicians, including George Chadwick (1854–1931), Charles Ives (1874–1954), Clarence Eddy (1851–1937), Frederick Grant Gleason (1848–1903), Harry Rowe Shelley (1858–1947) and many others. He taught at the New England Conservatory in Boston from 1871 to 1874. In 1884 Yale University offered him a position as organ instructor, but he declined to move to New Haven. Comments about Buck's teaching consistently depict him as a thorough, patient, but demanding teacher who brought out the best in his students, earning their lasting affection and respect in the process. In addition to his private teaching, Buck wrote a number of pedagogical works that were among the first intended for the serious, professional organist. His *Eighteen Studies in Pedal Phrasing for the Organ* (Op. 28) saw new editions in 1895, 1917, and 1922, and reveals Buck's thorough experience as a performer and teacher. This manual differs from most other American organ tutors, which are aimed for the pianist or amateur organist. Buck published his work for the increasing number of moderate to advanced students interested in performing serious organ music and accompanying major choral works. Unlike so many organ tutors, this work eschews pedal-only etudes in favor of a series of concise pieces for two manuals and pedal that concentrate on a specific technical difficulty that the player was likely to encounter in other organ literature.

Buck's most complete instructional manual was the *Illustrations in Choir Accompaniment, with Hints in Registration* of 1877, the most valuable treatise on the subject written in Victorian America. The work proved enormously successful, and was reprinted in 1880, 1888, 1892, 1901, 1905, and 1992. Buck wrote the work owing to "the fact that no previous attempt has been made to put in print a certain amount of what may be termed 'traditional' matter bearing upon accompaniment" (p. 173). The work addresses in a professional manner two large issues: accompaniment and registration, topics only incidentally covered in the numerous other organ methods. In twenty-five modest chapters covering nearly 180 pages, Buck patiently instructs the reader in various issues, illustrating his text with copious, clearly referenced musical examples.

Buck also advocated standardizing the manual and pedal compasses of American organs, calling for fifty-eight notes for the manuals and thirty for the pedals, as well as the inclusion of mechanical devices that would greatly facilitate the organist's ease in performance. This standardization would enable organists to play nearly all of the instrument's literature, both original and transcriptions.

Shortly after his return from Europe, Buck joined forces with the organ builder William A. Johnson (1816–1901) and recommended Johnson's instruments as models for the modern American organ. He encouraged Johnson to adopt some foreign stop names and pipe voicing approaches, a departure from the heavily English style of earlier organs. Buck's positive influence shows in Johnson's organ construction from around 1866, as Barbara Owen has pointed out.[13] Buck had commissioned a two-manual, eleven-stop Johnson organ for a room in his home in Hartford which was "fitted up in his house for the use of his pupils and private musical parties," as the *Hartford Courant* of July 18, 1867, observed. Buck's European experience showed in his design of the organ, which included a manual compass of fifty-eight notes (previously used by Johnson only on his largest instruments), and a pedal compass of thirty notes – the largest pedalboard the builder had constructed to that time. Despite its small size, Buck's house organ contained an uncommon variety and tonal balance. What strikes one immediately about Buck's keen insight into organ construction is the inclusion of all families of organ timbre, which included both a solo and a chorus reed. Though the Swell *Open Diapason* stops at tenor c, the manual includes a full-compass *Principal* (probably at four-foot pitch), which the Great lacks, though it had a three-rank *Mixture*. The organ also included some of the most recent mechanical aids to playing: a Great to Swell coupler (which is probably a typographical word transposition), three combination pedals, a "ratchet swell pedal," and a Stiles water motor, which supplied steady wind.[14] From 1869 on, Johnson began employing European terms such as *Harmonic Flute, Hohl Flöte, Doppel Flöte, Rohrflöte, Gamba,* and *Geigen Principal.* While these names had been known in Boston earlier, it is quite likely that Buck influenced Johnson to begin building these stops. Buck's influence also shows in the decrease in the number of divided stops, and the replacement of the old hook-down swell control by a balanced swell pedal. He possibly composed his variations on *Home Sweet Home* for this instrument around 1868, and he dedicated the work to William A. Johnson's son, who became a full partner in his father's firm in 1871. Since the Johnson firm would become one of the most important American organ builders of the last three decades of the century, Buck's influence on the development of the organ in the United States was significant.

Buck's activity as a recitalist, teacher, and composer of organ music in the 1860s and 1870s did much to professionalize the organ as an important part of American musical culture. His move to Chicago in 1869 to become organist at the prestigious St. James Church placed him in a position of national prominence. The organs he caused to be built there and the concerts he presented there proved that the organ could be a legitimate performing instrument, not just a supporter of choral music. Upon his arrival, he persuaded the vestry that the old organ would not do, and they agreed to purchase a new instrument from William A. Johnson. When the new church had been built in 1857, the old Hall & Labagh organ – once considered a grand instrument – had been moved to the new building. The Johnson three-manual, thirty-eight stop organ (Op. 334) was valued at $12,000, for which the parish supposedly paid only $7,000, probably as a result of Buck's friendship with Johnson. Again, the manual compass was fifty-eight notes and the pedal compass was thirty notes. The instrument was designed according to Buck's specifications, with the newly patented pneumatic attachment on the Great and Pedal, which made the action as "easy as a piano." The elegant black walnut case matched the church's interior, and enclosed over 2,500 pipes. Notable is the 16-foot *Euphone* on the Solo and the large, seven-stop Pedal division.

In Chicago, he built a house with a music room seating about 200, and for this new studio he purchased a three-manual Johnson organ, again with a thirty-note pedal. The stop names for his Chicago organ were quite uncommon, especially for organs built in New England and New York. Like his mechanical specifications, this nomenclature reflects his German study on classic instruments. He was probably the first organist in Chicago to introduce the term *Principal* for the sixteen- and eight-foot diapason stops in the Swell and Great and sixteen-foot open wood in the Pedal, as well as the terms *Flöte* and *Rohrflöte*. This change in terminology visibly marked the shift in how the American organ was conceptualized. The new terms of *Principal* and *Rohrflöte* demonstrate that the organ was now oriented towards classical literature, with appropriate tonal design for that literature.

Buck's tenure in Chicago ended abruptly with the Great Fire of 1871, which wiped him out – to the estimated amount of $20,000. Within a month he had reestablished himself in Boston, where he joined the faculty of The New England Conservatory of Music, as well as the staff of St. Paul's Church. The next year, Buck was chosen by the Boston Music Hall Association to preside over the magnificent new Walcker Organ. He was soon presenting three hour-long concerts a week.

In Boston, Buck gradually turned his professional activity towards composing choral music. His first works had been written for his choir in Hartford, and by 1873 he had more than eighty pieces published. His *First Motette Collection* in 1864 found immediate success; the *Second Motette Collection* (1871) firmly established his reputation. Both works enjoyed a "popularity which is still unabated," as noted in the *National Cyclopaedia* in 1897. Mathews argues that the *First Motette Collection* "marked a new epoch in American church music." Mathews had become an influential music critic by the 1880s, which lends strong weight to his claim that Buck's book was "notable because it was the first collection published in America in which modern styles of German musical composition were freely used, with unlimited freedom of modulation and addition of an organ accompaniment, after the best traditions of the German school. In the latter respect the book had a vast influence, for to many organists, it was the first authentic information they had received concerning the proper manner of using the organ effectively for accompanying and heightening the effect of the choir singing."[21]

While in Boston, Buck began working with Theodore Thomas (1835–1905), whom he possibly met when Thomas's orchestra played in Hartford in the 1860s. When Thomas helped establish the Cincinnati May Festival in 1875, he invited Buck to become its organist, after which Buck followed Thomas to New York, where he served as assistant conductor for Thomas's summer garden concerts in Central Park. The concerts unfortunately failed to draw large audiences, and Thomas was forced to cancel them. Buck decided to remain in New York, becoming in 1877 the organist and music director at the influential Church of the Holy Trinity in Brooklyn, a position he would hold until 1900.

Buck's move to Holy Trinity added considerably to his growing reputation as one of the country's leading organ composers. Completed in 1847, the Brooklyn Heights church stood as one of the finest examples of the decorated English Gothic style. The magnificent tower with its spire reaching 275 feet high, was completed in December 1867. While Holy Trinity is one of the most distinguished examples of gothic revival architecture, it is probably the stained glass windows that caused the Department of the Interior to designate the church as a National Historic Landmark in 1987. The original organ was constructed by Henry Crabb in 1845 as an instrument of three manuals, forty stops, and two octaves of pedals; later Johnson added some new stops. In 1873, Hilborne Roosevelt built his first three-manual instrument for the church, Op. 3. In 1899 the church purchased a three-manual, forty-four-stop organ by Geo. S. Hutchings.

Buck's finer organ works display a contrapuntal sophistication, lyrical beauty, and artistic substance never heard before in organ music composed by an American. He skillfully introduced expressive Baroque and Romantic elements into a native organ tradition that had been virtually devoid of either, all the while maintaining the direct emotional appeal sought by Victorian Americans. He was among the first American composers to indicate registrations, which perfectly suited the three-manual Johnson and the E. & G.G. Hook organs that were among the finest organs of the day. He often included footnotes assisting performers in adapting his scores for organs with only two manuals. Like most of his contemporaries who had also studied at German conservatories, Buck learned to write large abstract works in traditional eighteenth-century European genres: preludes, fugues, canons, trios, and sonatas. Back home, these composers discovered that these early works proved too elitist for American audiences. They then wrote preludes, postludes, impromptus, and character pieces, which included delightful canons and trios often built on hymn tunes and displaying skillful counterpoint, which often served as teaching pieces for gaining independence in the hands and feet. They also produced grand works such as "Grand Sonatas" or "Grand Concert Fantasias" to show off their technical expertise and to appeal to the musical cognoscenti. These generally fit the Mendelssohnian model, with multiple movements in traditional forms, the outer movements often displaying flamboyant virtuosity, while the inner ones could possess a naively touching charm. One movement generally involved an extended passage in the fugal, so-called learned style.

Buck's organ compositions, like the organ music of Bach, fall into three major categories: pieces for the concert hall, church voluntaries, and pedagogical works.[22] Like Bach's *Orgelbüchlein*, his didactic pieces, such as the *Eighteen Studies in Pedal Phrasing*, are also suitable for church.[23] Like Handel, he was a populist, who had little use for esoteric instrumental pieces that appealed to a limited audience of connoisseurs. He certainly realized that the difficulty of his early organ sonata and variations, written for his own virtuoso technique, would be performed by only the most talented players. Thus, about the time he ceased actively performing in the early 1870s, he moved away from organ composing as well. It was at that time that he turned to the cantata genre that was so rapidly growing in popularity.

Buck's two solo sonatas stand as milestones of their genre in American organ music. They are not only the first two professional sonatas composed and published by an American for the organ, but they are also two of the finest works in the genre before Horatio Parker's sonata, which was published in 1908. Buck wrote the *Grand Sonata in E-flat*, Op. 22, after his first series of organ recitals in 1865 and early 1866 met with such an enthusiastic reception. Published the year of its premier (1866) by Beer and Schirmer, the work found immediate success, and continued to appear on organ programs through the end of the century. Buck waited until 1877 to compose and publish his second sonata, Op. 77 in G Minor, which was probably commissioned by his former pupil, Clarence Eddy (1851–1937), to whom Buck dedicated the work. Eddy was opening a concert series on March 3, 1879, in Chicago on the large Johnson & Son organ that Eddy designed for Hershey Music Hall. This sonata illustrates Buck's stylistic development, from Mendelssohn and early German Romanticism to the more brilliant symphonic style emerging in France, largely inspired by the Romantic organs of Aristide Cavaillé-Coll. Buck's highly idiomatic, orchestral writing exploits the increased manual and pedal ranges available in the symphonic organ that had developed since the writing of his first sonata. There is also a marked shift from the German Romantic model, with its emphasis on formal schemes and motivic development, in favor of the French Romantic passion for creating a stirring, dramatic effect. The writing is leaner, more resourceful, and more symphonic, while the texture is thinner at places, giving more prominence to individual musical lines. Buck's melodic writing is more concise and emphatic, as well, and the rhythm is more supple and irregular, displaying a general loosening of the squareness of the four- and eight-measure phrasing. Finally, the harmonic progressions and overall tonal schemes show increased purpose and variety.

Buck's most enduring works for the organ are his four concert variations on popular songs, which represent his creative life between 1868 and 1888. They were reprinted at least once, and with the resurgence of interest in American music around the Bicentennial in 1976 they have enjoyed a new performance life in concerts and on recordings. Buck's counterpoint in these works displays some of the most sophisticated writing found in nineteenth-century American organ music. He magnificently synthesized this most esoteric, abstract musical process with its aesthetic opposite – common popular song – striking exactly the right artistic balance. Buck has convincingly assimilated the various contrapuntal structures and made them an intrinsic, unforced part of his own musical voice. The contrast of different variations makes rich use of the various stops and colors available on the Victorian American organ. Buck's first three variations sets (*The Star-Spangled Banner*, Op. 23, 1868; *Variations on a Scotch Air: Annie Laurie*, Op. 51, 1871; and *The Last Rose of Summer*, Op. 59, 1877) are technical showcases with daunting, pianistic scales and arabesques in the manuals over some notoriously difficult pedal writing, including passages in sixteenth- and thirty-second notes. The final set, which is based on Stephen Foster's melody *The Old Folks at Home*, is considerably less difficult, generally following an elaborated hymn style. Buck also wrote one short work for the organ builder William H. Johnson on one of the century's most popular tunes, *Home, Sweet Home*.

Buck retired from active musical work in 1903. His work as a recitalist had accelerated the popularity of the organ recital and helped to establish a new level of excellence in playing. He also exerted a wide and enduring influence on organ building, and helped to standardize the American instrument, with full-compass manuals, thirty-note pedalboards, and numerous mechanical devices that made performance easier and more flexible. His compositions likewise provided a new model of idiomatic, professional organ literature that held a central place in the repertoire well into the twentieth century. Critics soon noted the results of his work, along the work of his colleagues, like Thayer and Paine. After about 1875 the organ recital had become a serious artistic event, in which the great music composed for the instrument by Bach, Mendelssohn, and others found a forum. Churches and concert halls instituted organ recital series, and recitals were often played to full houses. Trinity Church on Wall Street began an organ series performed by Henry Carter, Samuel P. Warren, George F. Bristow and others. In 1875 the reviewer for the *New York Daily Tribune* commended the players for performing primarily legitimate organ music with a minimum of transcriptions "inserted judiciously" for balance. He continued:

> It really seems as though all that wretched class of organ music, which seems to have been written solely with a view to showing off the solo stops of the organ, was at last to be driven from our concerts, to be replaced by what is good and pure and thoroughly sound.[24]

:: N O T E S ::

[1] For general background on the American organ and its music see Curtis B. Prudence, "American Organ Music North of Philadelphia before 1860: Selected Problems and An Annotated Bibliography" (DMA. diss., Manhattan School of Music, 1981); Barbara Owen, *The Organ in New England: An Account of its Use and Manufacture to the End of the Nineteenth Century* (Raleigh: Sunbury Press, 1979); Orpha Ochse, *The History of the Organ in the United States* (Bloomington, IN: Indiana University Press, 1975); Margaret Anderson Sihler, "The Organ Without a Master: a Survey of Nineteenth Century Organ Instruction Books in the United States" (Ph.D. diss., University of Minnesota, 1977); Howard Norman Bakken, "The Development of Organ Playing in Boston and New York, 1700-1900" (DMA diss., University of Illinois, 1975); William Joseph Beasley, "The Organ in America, as Portrayed in Dwight's Journal of Music" (Ph.D. diss., University of Southern California, 1971); Lanson Frederick Demming, "History of the Organ Recital in the United States of America" (Master's thesis, University of Illinois, 1943).

[2] Barbara Owen, liner notes for New World Records, *Fugues, Fantasia, and Variations.* See also: Nicholas Temperly, *Bound for America: Three British Composers* (Urbana: University of Illinois Press, 2003), 12-51; and *Charles Zeuner. Organ Music,* in Recent Researches in American Music (Madison, WN: A.R. Editions, forthcoming).

[3] See also Orr and Mark Stevens, "Bach in America. The Reception of His Organ Music in the United States," *The Tracker* 46, No. 4 (October 2002): 5-13.

[4] *Church Music in America, Comprising Its History and Its Peculiarities at Different Periods …* (1853; reprint, New York, AMS Press, 1972), 179.

[5] Ochse, *The History of the Organ in the United States,* (Bloomington, IN: Indiana University Press, 1975), 101-07.

[6] *Vox Humana,* Sept. 1, 1873.

[7] American builders lagged behind their European counterparts by a generation when it came to introducing new mechanical devices, however. The pneumatic lever had been invented by Charles S. Barker in England in 1832 and had been incorporated by Cavaillé-Coll in Paris in his larger organs in the early 1840s. It did not appear in North America, however, until the late 1850s. See Barbara Owen, "Technology and the Organ in the Nineteenth Century," in *The Organ As Mirror of Its Time* (Oxford: Oxford University Press, 2002), 213-29.

[8] Henry Lahee, *The Organ and Its Masters* (Boston: L.C. Page & Co., 1902), 279.

[9] Owen, *The Organ in New England,* 255.

[10] W.S.B. Mathews, "German Influence upon American Music," *The Musician* (July 1900): 160.

[11] W.S.B. Mathews, assoc. ed., *One Hundred Years of Music in America* (Chicago: Howe, 1889; Repr. New York: AMS Press, 1970), 240.

[12] Mathews, *One Hundred Years of Music in America,* 681-82.

[13] Owen, *The Organ in New England,* 285.

[14] William J. Beasley, "The Organ in America, As Portrayed in Dwight's *Journal of Music* (Ph.D. diss., University of Southern California, 1971): 380–83.

[15] 146–47.

[16] For more on Dwight see Mark N. Grant, *Maestros of the Pen: A History of Classical Music Criticism in America* (Boston: Northeastern University Press, 1998), 35-52; Ora Frishberg Saloman, *Beethoven's Symphonies and J.S. Dwight: the Birth of American Music Critcism* (Boston: Northeastern University Press, 1995); Irving Sablosky, *What They Heard: Music in America 1852-1881 from the Pages of* Dwight's Journal of Music (Baton Rouge: Louisiana State University Press, 1986); Marcia Wilson Lebow, "A Systematic Examination of the Journal of Music and Art Edited by John Sullivan Dwight, 1852-1881" (Ph.D. diss., University of California at Los Angeles, 1969).

[17] "Organ concerts," February 1875: 8.

[18] Steven Baur, "Music, Morals, and Social Management: Mendelssohn in Post-Civil War America," *American Music* 19, no. 1 (2001): 65-84.

[19] T. J. Jackson Lears, *No Place of Grace* (Chicago, 1994), 32.

[20] Owen, *The Organ in New England*, 258-59.

[21] Mathews, *One Hundred Years of Music in America*, 679-80.

[22] My thanks to Barbara Owen for pointing this out to me.

[23] Nearly all of his organ works were published soon after composition by G. Schirmer, and most stayed in print into the twentieth century. By the end of the same century, the sonatas and variations had again appeared, some in more than one edition. In 2006 my edition of the two sonatas and four variations cycles was published in *Dudley Buck: Selected Organ Works* (Madison, WN: A.R. Editions), Recent Researches in American Music.

[24] Dec. 16, 1875. George W. Morgan played a series of concerts in Chickering Hall in 1875-76 which included Bach preludes and fugues, Mendelssohn sonatas, as well as the popular transcriptions and lighter works. Student recitals at the New England Conservatory show a greater amount of Bach's works. In 1877, Clarence Eddy began presenting his one hundred recitals in a two year series, each concert anchored by a Bach work. By 1880 the organ recital had moved into a professional phase.

EARLY AMERICAN
ORGAN RECORDINGS

Rollin Smith

THE ADVENT OF RECORDING was the most significant musical event in the twentieth century. Performances no longer vanished as soon as they were heard, but could be preserved and repeated at any time.

For over twenty-five years, what could be recorded was what could be focused into an acoustic horn. The human voice fared best since it projected forward and was strong enough to rise above the rushing surface noise of shellac discs. Brass instruments were also ideal, and for some twenty years brass bands and jazz groups shared space in record catalogues with singers. Instruments that played "outside" the horn fared less well: stringed instruments had less carrying power and required more room to play; the piano often sounded like a banjo or guitar. Loud pieces could be recorded but soft slow movements were less successful. The acoustic process captured a limited frequency range. The human ear can hear frequencies between 20 and 20,000 cycles per second; the acoustic gramophone could only reproduce a range of between 168 and 2,000 cycles. Those overtones that give instruments their particular timbre could not be reproduced faithfully. Thus the notes below tenor e and any pitches above an 8-foot stop on the manuals top C were distorted.

Organists on early acoustic recordings, with few exceptions, played reed organs. In fact, when Sir Edward Elgar recorded his *Dream of Gerontius,* a bass concertina was used as a "convincing substitute" for the grand organ.[1] Since the performance was recorded through a horn, it was a simple matter to aim the horn into the back of a reed organ where the tone was but inches from the recording device, rather than try to capture the sound of an organ, with the pipes many feet away. It was thus possible to record a two-manual and pedal reed organ playing real organ literature and the results, at least in capturing the organist's style, were often satisfactory.

Perhaps the first musician to record on an organ (one who was probably not an organist) was Albert Benzler who, in 1897, recorded "Abide With Me" on a seven-inch disc for Émile Berliner's U.S. Gramophone Company.[2] Benzler (who lived in East Orange, New Jersey) later played bells, organ, piano, and xylophone on Edison cylinders.[3] He recorded "Abide With Me" again in August 1909 on a two-minute Edison wax cylinder (10180).[4] In all probability Benzler played a reed organ.

Actual pipe organ recording in America began impressively in September 1910 with performances of Bach's *Toccata and Fugue in D Minor* and the *Toccata* from Widor's Fifth Symphony played by the organist of the Mormon Tabernacle, John J. McClellan (1874–1925), on the Salt Lake City Tabernacle's 1901 Kimball organ.

A Utah native, McClellan earned a Bachelor of Music degree from the University of Michigan in 1896, and in 1899 went to Europe to study with Xaver Scharwenka and others. He was appointed Tabernacle organist on October 1, 1900, the first organist to have been actually trained in music and to have studied abroad, his predecessors having studied locally and most having been engaged in other professions. McClellan was responsible for the installation of the new Kimball organ and began playing semi-weekly organ recitals, which, by 1908, were given every day except Sunday between April and October. He founded the Salt Lake Symphony Orchestra in 1908 and the Utah Conservatory in 1911, where he taught organ, theory and piano, and directed the Salt Lake Opera Company. McClellan was best known for his *National Ode to Irrigation,* which *Musical America* assured its readers "has received recognition at a number of irrigation exhibitions."[5] In 1923 McClellan suffered a nervous breakdown,[6] and on July 3, 1925, he suffered a stroke while playing Handel's *Largo,* the last number on his noonday recital. He recovered quickly and resumed teaching, but a second stroke occurred a few weeks later during a lesson and proved fatal.[7]

A 1911 postcard from the Mormon Tabernacle

The Columbia Company had gone to Utah to record the famous Mormon Tabernacle Choir and while there experimented with recording the organ. The enormity of the task was described in the local newspaper:

> Thursday evening, September 1, 1910, recordings were made of the Tabernacle Choir and organ by the Columbia Phonograph Company of New York City, with Mr. Housman of that company in charge ... To make the recordings, horns were suspended from a rope stretched from gallery to gallery, the flaring bells of the two horns covering, one the sopranos and altos, the other the tenors and basses, the small ends connecting directly with the machine where the choir leader stands at the east of the organ console. The singers were massed together in the shape of a wedge, with the sidelines leading directly into the bells of the two large horns connected with the machine, the voices of the 300 singers focusing directly into the bells.
>
> Operations began at eight o'clock. At the experts' request, the ladies removed their hats (hats absorb sound) and the entire aggregation of singers was packed in together as close as possible, all facing the horns. Owing to the distance from the organ, Professor John J. McClellan had to play all of his accompaniments fortissimo, and the two soloists ... were placed with their faces inside of one of the horns. Of course, fine shading was out of the question; massive effects were the principal thing.[8]

It was not mentioned if the position of the recording horns was changed for the organ solos or if they were perhaps aimed directly at only one division, but the sound is clear and the style of the player can be observed, if not the entire effect of the 62-rank instrument.

In all, McClellan recorded seven solo pieces. All were released in England – four 10-inch discs with two different takes of the *Gondoliers* backing two separate discs. The catalogue numbers precede the selections:

C-R1704	Rubinstein, *Melody in F;*
	Bach, *Fugue in D Minor – Toccata and Finale*
C-R1926	Mascagni, *Cavalleria Rusticana;* Nevin, *Gondoliers*
C-R2232	Donizetti, Sextet from *Lucia di Lammermoor;*
	Wagner, *Tannhäuser* Overture
C-R2399	Widor, *Toccata;* Nevin, *Gondoliers*

It was still fairly common in England to refer to any organ work by Bach as a "fugue;" it is only strange in this instance as there is so much toccata and finale and so little fugue. There is no mention on the label of the Mormon

Tabernacle, only the ubiquitous "Grand Organ Solo," a term applied by early recording companies to instruments from harmoniums to theater and studio organs.

Only one disc was released in the United States: a second take of the Bach (although it bears the same matrix number as the Cigale) and the take of the *Gondoliers* that backed the Mascagni. The instrument is identified only as "Tabernacle Organ" and sold for 75 cents (in today's currency, $14.66).

The Bach record is the earliest live recording of a Bach organ work. Since a ten-inch disc can comfortably contain 3½ minutes of music, McClellan plays the complete Toccata and then begins the fugue at measure 120 (seven measures before the Recitativo). The label, in fact, reads "Toccata and Finale." The first take issued in England is timed at three minutes, 16 seconds; the second American take was longer, three minutes, 24½ seconds. Perhaps McClellan felt more comfortable the second time and realized he was able to use up another ten seconds.

Label of John McClellan's Bach recording

John. J. McClellan at the Kimball Organ console

McClellan interprets the mordent as A–B-flat–A rather than the now-ac-
cepted A–G–A. This was common. Karl Tausig's (1841–71) piano transcription
of the piece realizes it thus (actually giving each mordent an extra A–B-flat)
as did Louis Niedermeyer in an 1857 publication of the Fugue in E minor,
BWV 533. Such misinterpretation was *so* common that, when Louis Vierne
published his edition of Bach organ works in 1924, he called attention to the
mordent in the fugue of BWV 533, noting that it was a *pincé,* not an upper
mordent (*mordant*), and should alternate with the note below, not above.[9]

A few unconventional details noted in McClellan's playing are: the four
notes after the second mordent are played very slowly; the chord in m. 2 is
not rolled but played on the held sixteenth note D of the second beat; the
chord in m. 10 is not rolled; his erratically fast playing of 32nd-note passages
bears no relation to the tempo established with eighth and sixteenth notes; the
hands never play chords together (i.e. mm. 27–29); at the Vivace (m. 137) he
plays only an A[7] chord, no arpeggio, and a d minor chord, going right into the

penultimate measure. It remains to be said that, in spite of speed and lack of recording experience, McClellan plays practically a note-perfect performance.

Not only was the incumbent recorded, but his predecessor as well: the British-born Joseph J. Daynes (1851–1920) who had been appointed first organist of the Mormon Tabernacle at the age of 16 in 1867 and retired in 1900. He was the composer of the popular hymn "As the dew from heaven distilling." Daynes was recorded playing Mendelssohn's *War March of the Priests* but the disc was never released.[10]

A second recording session was held later in September – and it was apparently so successful that three other sides were also released: Ethelbert Nevin's *Gondoliers,* from his piano suite, *A Day in Venice,* Op. 25, Rubinstein's *Melody in F,* and another disc accompanying violinist Willard E. Weihe in Émile Sauret's *Cradle Song.* The Widor *Toccata* was only released in England on Columbia's Cigale label.[11] When test pressings from this session were auditioned at the Daynes-Beebe Music Company warehouse, they included "*The Pilgrim's Song of Hope* as played by Professor Daynes on the organ, and the first section of the overture to *Tannhäuser* as played on the organ by John J. McClellan."[12] Neither of these tests were issued.

A news item, "Records Prove A Success," dated October 20 appeared in the November 1910 issue of *The Diapason:*

> Those who have watched with interest the making of records of the Tabernacle choir and organ which were taken recently by the Columbia Phonograph Company of New York, were given an opportunity of hearing the proofs this week, when the Daynes-Beebe Music company gave a recital.
>
> Fifteen new proofs, making nineteen in all, were received, and after a trial were pronounced a success, many of the proofs exceeding even the most hopeful expectations. The other six were unsatisfactory and no proofs were sent, the trouble being an unevenness in the records, being good in places but blurred or too faint in others. Of the records received all were good, every note and sound being clearly recorded.

The article from which the above extract is taken continued:

> The organ numbers give satisfaction in everything but the absence of the heavy pedal tones, which under the circumstances was an acoustic impossibility, as it is now seen that separate receiving trumpet arrangements must be made to record the heavy pipes of the Pedal organ. However, con-

sidering that this is the first time anything of this kind has been attempted, the results may be considered marvelous and such criticism as is offered is only to point out ways for improvement on these initial experiments, in looking for more effective results.[13]

Another early acoustic recording, made on March 25, 1916, featured Richard Keys Biggs (1886–1962) playing the Chopin *Funeral March* on an organ at the Estey factory in Brattleboro, Vermont. The reverse side has the *Hallelujah Chorus* from *Messiah* identified as "Played on the / Estey Automatic Pipe Organ / by Reginald L. McAll." This was recorded on June 18, 1916, probably at the Estey New York Studio, since McAll[14] was the company's New York representative.

By 1925, recording engineers were successfully adapting for recording purposes microphones and amplifiers recently developed for radio broadcasting and the first electrical recordings were issued. By using microphones any instrument could be recorded; indeed, whole orchestras could be picked up in their traditional seating arrangement. Fidelity was better, too, with a wider range of sound frequencies and dynamics, especially the bass, which, with its fullness, matched the cleaner treble sound.

A Chicagoan named Orlando March was one of the earliest successful electrical recording engineers. In 1924 he interested theater organist Jesse Crawford in his projects and, welcoming the opportunity to invest in what appeared to be the wave of the future, Crawford raised several thousand dollars for Marsh. Not only did Crawford record on the organ in the Chicago Theatre, but Pietro Yon (1886–1943) recorded his own works[15] and Hugh Porter (1897-1960)[16] recorded in Chicago's Kimball Hall. These were released on the Marsh Laboratories label and when the business failed, the master discs were sold and appeared on the Autograph label. It was on Autograph that Arthur Dunham's (1875–1938) four sides appeared, recorded on E.M. Skinner's new four-manual, 64-rank organ in the First Methodist Church of Chicago, known as the Chicago Temple.[17]

In June 1924, Thomas Edison's company entered the organ recording field. The performer was the classically-trained Frederick Kinsley (1886–1960), then in his third year as organist of New York's Hippodrome Theatre.[18] On

June 14, 1924, Frederick Kinsley recorded on the three-manual, seven-rank Midmer-Losh organ of the Hippodrome Theatre. In addition to two popular selections, he played Rachmaninoff's *Prelude in C-sharp minor* and Liszt's *Liebesträum*. Both discs were released and the classical one was reviewed in the British record journal, *The Gramophone:*

> Mr. Kinsley is (to quote a quotation from an earlier number of *The Gramophone*) "rash man enough" to play the *C sharp Minor Prelude* on a Midmer-Losh organ, not to mention the – you can guess what is on the other side. The fidelity of the recording is beyond question; it is uncanny, and like most uncanny things more enjoyable in retrospect than at the moment of encounter. But this is a direction in which we would urge Mr. Edison to proceed. Many people are clamouring for good organ records and will be grateful for them, though it is unlikely that we shall get the real thing till recording "rooms" [i.e. studios] are a memory of the past.[19]

The Hippodrome organ was installed under the stage and because of its lack of presence and the inevitable scheduling constraints of finding time to record when the theater was not in use, it was necessary to find other instruments. The solution was for the Edison Company to acquire its own organ. In November 1926 a "specially built" three-manual, seven-rank Midmer-Losh organ was installed in Edison's Columbia Street Studios in West Orange, New Jersey. A conservatively voiced theater organ, it could also be used to play "classical" and religious music. Kinsley recorded on this instrument the next year.

The other notable classical organist to record on the Edison studio organ was Philadelphia-based Rollo Maitland (1884–1953). Two popular songs were recorded on April 18, 1927, and the next year on April 23, 1928, he returned to record electrically Braga's *Angel's Serenade,* the *Largo* from Dvořák's "New World" Symphony, Schubert's *Ave Maria* and d'Hardelot's "Because."

On September 24, 1925, the third organist of the Mormon Tabernacle, Edward Kimball (1882–1937), recorded an organ solo version of Sullivan's *The Lost Chord* on the reverse side of the Mormon Tabernacle Choir's performance of Schubert's "Great is Jehovah." This was on the 73-rank 1916 Austin organ. Two years later Victor issued his performance of Mendelssohn's *War March of the Priests.*[20]

It quickly became apparent to the recording industry that American record buyers had a particular fondness for hymns and the market was flooded with them in diverse forms from soloists accompanied by orchestra or organ, to choirs, quartets, and organ solos. While Albert Benzler was the first to record "Abide With Me" in 1897 others were more prolific, none more so than Mark Andrews (1875–1939),[21] who between 1925 and 1928 recorded fourteen discs of hymns for Victor – sometimes with four hymns per disc.[22] During the Second World War hymn records were in demand by armed forces chaplains to accompany group singing and to supply appropriate organ music for religious services. Through the years many organists recorded hymns, among them Clarence Snyder, C.A.J. Parmentier, Charles Raymond Cronham, Charles O'Connell, and an album of Catholic hymns recorded in 1945 by Charles Courboin (1886–1973) on the Kilgen organ in St. Patrick's Cathedral.

On January 11, 1926, Charles O'Connell (1900–62) recorded the *Angélus*, from Massenet's *Scènes pittoresque*[23] on the three-manual Estey organ, Opus 2529, (Swell duplexed from the Great) of 33 ranks with percussion stops and a toy counter, installed in Trinity Baptist Church in Camden, New Jersey, which had been converted into the Victor recording studio. He later regarded this as "the first successful electrically recorded" organ disc.[24] O'Connell was an amateur organist who had studied with Widor in Paris and who, from 1930 to 1944 was head of the artist and repertory department of the RCA Victor Company. Over the years he was responsible for producing the Victor recordings made by Charles Courboin, E. Power Biggs, Joseph Bonnet, and Virgil Fox.

The only recordings of the much-broadcast Skinner Studio organ were made by John D.M. Priest (1887–1926),[25] a classically-trained English organist, playing four popular songs.[26] One disc uses the *Vox Humana* liberally, the other not at all. Priest was organist of New York's Colony Theatre where he played a 32-rank Skinner organ. His associate there was Miss Ruth Barrett, a pupil of Lynnwood Farnam, who later, as Mrs. Arno, was organist of the Mother Church in Boston. He made the first organ records for Brunswick in April 1926, just one month before he died.

On record, Priest, as well as Kingsley and Maitland, played in an uninteresting, not to say turgid, style. Hearing their literal melody-and-accompaniment more than points up the reason for the popularity of such "theater organists" as Jesse Crawford who used a varied registration and had a personal "style." In addition, their registrations are stark; one or two stops for the solo and a couple softer stops for the accompaniment, whereas Crawford would have utilized select groups of stops with light percussion (primarily the harp). This comes through in the description of Priest's playing by T. Scott Buhrman, editor and publisher of *The American Organist:*

> Mr. Priest is an experienced player of many years active theater work; his playing tends toward the classic, with everything that is likely to be scholarly and musical. From frequent hearings his work is presumably from score and memory, with improvisation restricted to a minimum. Fortissimos never offend, though they may be used when the screen demands them; the background Mr. Priest furnishes is a pianissimo background, just as it should be.[27]

There was no serious attempt to produce recordings of classical organ music in America. There was in Europe, however, and these were all imported to the United States to sate the appetites of organ discophiles. In 1926 England

Label of John Priest's recording on the Skinner Studio organ

had Marcel Dupré recording, a magnificent series of discs on the organs of Queen's Hall and the Alexandra Palace. Attempts were made to record many cathedral organists as well as those of major London churches. In France, Édouard Commette recorded for Columbia throughout the 78 RPM era and well into LP years. In Germany, many classical (as well as popular) organ recordings were also issued; however, few by comparison were made in the United States.

The first phonograph recording of an American organ work was *The Bells of St. Anne de Beaupré* from Alexander Russell's *St. Lawrence Sketches.* Charles Raymond Cronham (1896–1969), at the time municipal organist at Portland, Maine, was later organist of New York's Marble Collegiate Church. The recording was made on January 31, 1927, on the Estey organ in the Victor Studio (Trinity Baptist Church) in Camden, New Jersey.

One of the great "missed opportunities" of organ recording came later that year when the famous English organist, Edwin H. Lemare (1865–1934), made five visits to Camden between March and August. Lemare was then in the middle of his four-year tenure as municipal organist of Chattanooga, Tennessee, one of the greatest organists in the world, and the highest paid. As a recording artist Lemare had made eighty-nine player organ rolls for Welte in Freiburg, Germany, sixteen rolls for Aeolian, and six for Möller. This was the first time in America a world-famous organist was before the recording microphone – one who had major works of Bach as well as many Wagner transcriptions in his repertoire – and all we are left with is his own *Chant de Bonheur,* his transcription of Schumann's *Träumerei,* and Queen Liliuokalani's *Aloha Oe,* Hawaii's traditional song of farewell. Lemare returned on July 31 and after twelve unsuccessful tries, managed a usable recording of his famous *Andantino in D-flat.*[28] It had been arranged as a song, "Moonlight and Roses," in 1925 (though not by the composer) and its popularity, then at its height, may have been the reason for the recording rather than the opportunity to have the composer's interpretation recorded. Reviews were not encouraging. *The Gramophone* noted that the "composer's own authentic dragging of it, and his performance of Schumann's *Träumerei* makes one wonder whether it really was meant as a case of sleepy-sickness."[29] A.C.D. de Brisay the ever hard-to-please critic for the British journal *The Organ* wrote:

It frequently happens that, when we hear world-famous pieces played by their own composers, a feeling of disappointment is experienced. This was the case when Rachmaninoff first played his C-sharp minor Prelude in England. Mr. Lemare here indulges in an excess of sentimentality which we frankly confess we do not like. He exploits the special tones of the (unnamed) cinema organ to the full. On the other side is Schumann's Träumerei, in which sentimentality is also pushed to the extreme limit.[30]

Between Lemare's two recording sessions, the dean of Philadelphia's choral conductors, Henry Gordon Thunder (1865–1954), recorded Édouard Batiste's *Communion in G,* popularly known, and identified on the label, as "The Pilgrim's Song of Hope," and Liszt's *Liebesträum.*[31]

The first electrical organ recordings on an equal footing with those of other instrumentalists were those made on January 18, 1929, by the brilliant Italian virtuoso, Fernando Germani, on the organ of the New York Wanamaker Department Store. The first, Franz Liszt's *Introduction and Fugue on "Ad nos, ad salutarem undam,"* was released around the same time as Alfred Sittard's recording on the organ of St. Michael's Church, Hamburg. George William Volkel, writing in *The Diapason,* found that Germani's "rendition throughout is brilliant, such as we would expect from such an artist, but unfortunately the recording itself becomes muffled shortly after the tremendous chords in the introduction. Perhaps the volume was greater than the delicate recording instruments could stand, and the operator forthwith turned a dial lessening the effect of a sforzando, both literally and musically."[32] This, in marked contrast to Sittard's disc in which the "recorders did not deem it expedient to cut down on the volume."

Germani's second recording was the *Final* from Vierne's First Symphony. Volkel noted that "The instrument is not particularly felicitous for recording, the tone being somewhat 'wooden' on records. This is due in part to the acoustics of the small auditorium. However, Germani's playing more than covers this deficiency."[33]

An even more unusual venue than a department store was the largest private residence in Manhattan, a French château-styled mansion, "Riverside," covering an entire city block on Riverside Drive – the home of Charles

Schwab, the highest-salaried executive in America. By 1919, his Aeolian organ had been expanded to 74 ranks and he retained Archer Gibson (1875–1952) for an annual fee of $10,000. At his Sunday afternoon musicales, the organist often accompanied Kreisler, Caruso, Schumann-Heink, and other great musicians of the era. The console was in a small chapel at the head of the main stairway and controlled the various parts of the instrument, some of them 150 feet away, and all concealed behind tapestries and paintings, under the floor, or embedded in the ceiling.

Archer Gibson was a graduate of the Peabody Conservatory in Baltimore (and later a Fellow of the American Guild of Organists) and had been on the organ faculty for three years, organist of Old First Presbyterian Church, and from 1901 of New York City's Brick Presbyterian Church. A few days before Easter 1909 he resigned, as reported in *The New York Times,* because of "unfriendly gossip" concerning himself and the soprano soloist," and for the rest of his life, devoted himself to what he called "housework," playing Aeolian organs in the homes of the wealthy. Among his "patrons" were Henry Clay Frick, Charles M. Schwab, and William D. Sloane, John D. Rockefeller, Louis Comfort Tiffany, and many others. His challenge was unique: a mildly voiced organ buried in chambers distributed throughout a house – sometimes with three floors separating one division from another – and an intensely dead acoustic of carpeted and draped rooms. Delicate, subtle tone coloring was out of the question. Gibson arrived at a registration formula based on a massed tonal palette and a style of playing that made Marcel Dupré's concept of legato primitive in comparison. Gibson's fingers never left the keys – not even for repeated notes. The organ, the ambience, and the interpretation made for a unique sound: one that not only did not sound like an organ, but resembled nothing else in the world of music. Nevertheless, with the residence organ as his medium, Archer Gibson enjoyed a career that brought him the loyal friendship of his patrons and a fortune of well over a million dollars.

Gibson's specialty was playing on three manuals at the same time as most of his photographs illustrate. His long fingers could reach from the third manual to the first. The theme was thumbed on one manual, harmonized on the one above, while the right hand flew up and down the third playing arpeg-

Archer Gibson at the console of his Aeolian organ

gios and chromatic scales, as he said, to "supply a background" to the themes. At other times, the melody was played to a strummed accompaniment, usually with harp.

The Edison Company attempted to record Schwab's organ acoustically as early as August 1921. Archer Gibson played the Chopin *Prelude in c minor* and three other numbers, but they were never released. Then, with the advent of electrical recording the Victor Company recorded Gibson on three double-sided black-label discs in June and July 1929.[34] Three years later, Gibson began broadcasting half-hour radio programs from the Schwab residence that gained such an audience that Victor contracted Gibson for another set of recordings, twelve sides made on the 26-rank Aeolian installed in Gibson's duplex apartment in 1918, many taking advantage of Deagan's new 49-note Vibra-Harp added in 1929. The discs were listed in the Victor catalogue under "Funeral Parlor Records" and some of the titles indicate their appropriateness for such use: *Consolation* (Mendelssohn), *Beautiful Dreamer* (Foster), *At Rest* (Nevin), and *Abide With Me* (Monk).[35] But in addition to these selections were the first two Bach choral preludes recorded on the organ in America: *Aus der Tiefe rufe ich,* BWV 745, a spurious work in the appendix of Peters Volume IX, and *I Cry to Thee, Lord Jesus,* BWV 639, from the *Orgelbüchlein.* The fact that Leopold Stokowski had transcribed and recorded them with the Philadelphia Orchestra was the reason for Gibson's choice; there certainly could be no other explanation for a recording of BWV 745.

Reviews of Gibson's recordings were not bad, one noting:

> Don't let the thought that these records were very likely made with the Funeral Parlor trade in mind, deter you from investigating them. They are really excellent examples of fine pipe organ reproduction. The choice of the selections is very good and Mr. Gibson plays them in a most refined and artistic manner. [36]

The Bach *Aus der Tiefe rufe ich* was issued as a special complimentary pressing; the reverse side featured Lily Pons singing "Lo, here the gentle lark."

> As everyone knows, organ recordings in the past have seldom been technically successful, and except for occasional ballads on studio or movie organs have been scarce in the American record catalogues. Victor has done us a good turn in releasing these two discs, which faithfully reproduce the organ tone, and which we hope are but the first issues in a series of organ records. The price is moderate [$1.25], and the artist is the well-liked Archer Gibson, who has long been the private organist in the home of Charles M. Schwab.
>
> The chorale is not one of Bach's best known works. As a matter of fact in the Bach Gesellschaft edition it is listed among the doubtful compositions; however, it is probably a genuine and early example of Bach's chorale prelude ... Mr. Gibson plays this reflective music simply. In one verse he uses the Vox Humana stop judiciously; in another, the Cornopean sounds a bit wheezy.[37]

On the other hand, one reviewer wrote of *I Cry to Thee, Lord Jesus Christ,*

> This might be a very attractive little disc were it not for Mr. Gibson's choice of stops. Throughout both selections he uses what we believe to be a Chime stop, but which sounds as though someone were accompanying him by playing chromatic chords upon a piano.[38]

With Archer Gibson the early years of American organ recording came to a close. Two years later Victor would begin issuing records made by Charles Courboin on the great organ of the Philadelphia Wanamaker department store, closely followed by the first Baroque organ recordings featuring Carl Weinrich and E. Power Biggs. Americans no longer had to import their classical organ music and the freshness of the sounds produced by the new exponents of the organ reform movement fulfilled the demand for recordings of great organ music and served to perpetuate the careers of many splendid organists.

In addition to documenting the playing of a number of classically-trained organists, recordings from these twenty-five years preserve, the sounds of some fine instruments: the Kimball organs in the Mormon Tabernacle and Chicago's Kimball Hall, the Skinners in the Chicago Temple and the New York Studio, the Aeolian organs in the Schwab residence and Archer Gibson's studio, the Austin in the Mormon Tabernacle, several Estey organs, and numerous theater organs, and the organ of the New York Wanamaker store. It hardly needs to be added that none of these has survived.

What is to be most regretted is the uncaptured performances by some of America's greatest organists: Clarence Eddy, Clarence Dickinson, Samuel Baldwin, Edwin Arthur Kraft, Charles Heinroth, Albert Riemenschneider, Wilhelm Middelschulte, the list is endless. Many of those who never recorded for the phonograph did make player organ rolls but the difficulty of finding a player organ to reproduce rolls is more than compensated for by the instant gratification of putting a disc on a turntable and hearing a performance not recreated, but live, from almost a century ago.

: : N O T E S : :

[1]   Joe Batten, *Joe Batten's Book: The Story of Sound Recording – Being the Memoirs of Joe Batten* [1885–1955], *Recording Manager* (London: Rockcliff Publishing Corporation, 1956), 58.

[2]   No. 097.

[3]   Benzler and other musicians and engineers left Edison to form their own companies, one of which was the U.S. Everlasting Cylinder Company. In

ROLLIN SMITH

1910, one of Benzler's xylophone solos, *Peter Piper*, a celluloid cylinder record-ed for U.S. Everlasting, was played for seven months on a machine in a penny arcade in Cleveland, Ohio, and, by automatic count, had been heard 40,444 times! Jim Walsh,writing in *Variety* on October 11, 1952, considered this to have been probably the long-play champion of all time.

⁴   This was the only solo organ cylinder listed in Edison catalogues up to 1928. Before this entry, only "Hymns, with organ accompaniment" were listed.

⁵   *Musical America* (October 12, 1912), 93.

⁶   *The American Organist* (January 1924), 56.

⁷   "John J. McClellan Dies of Paralytic Stroke," *The Diapason* (September 1925) 1.

⁸   *Deseret News* (September 2, 1910), quoted in J. Spencer Cornwall, *A Century of Singing* (Salt Lake City: Deseret Book Co., 1958), 198.

⁹   Louis Vierne, *Œuvres pour Orgue de J.-S. Bach* (Paris: Éditions Maurice Senart, 1924), 114.

¹⁰   Columbia 4889.

¹¹   Columbia R2399

¹²   *Deseret News* (September 29, 1910); quoted in Cornwall, *A Century of Singing,* 199.

¹³   *Deseret News* (October 11, 1910); quoted Cornwall, *A Century of Singing,* 200.

¹⁴   Reginald L. McAll (d. 1954) was born in Bocking, Essex County, Eng-land, came to the United States in 1897, graduated from Johns Hopkins in 1900, and then attended the Peabody Conservatory in Baltimore. In 1926 he was president of the National Association of Organists and later of the Hymn Society of America. He was organist of Church of the Covenant, New York City (1902–50). McAll died suddenly of a heart attack while in a canoe near Meredith, New Hampshire on July 9, 1954. ("Reginald Ley McAll Meets Sudden Death," *The Diapason, (*August 1954), 1.

¹⁵   Including *Christmas in Sicily, Gesù Bambino,* and *L'Organo Primitivo.* The March 1923 issue of *The American Organist* (p.326) noted that "Pietro Yon was the first to make organ records for the phonograph by the new process de-veloped by Marsh Laboratories, Chicago; the Kimball Hall organ was used

for the records and it is claimed that the new process makes organ records as satisfactory in results as records of other instruments."

[16] Lemare, *Andantino in D-flat.*

[17] Nevin's *The Rosary,* Liszt's *Liebesträum,* J.-B. Faure's *The Palms,* and Henry Parker's *Jerusalem.* A letter of May 25, 1926, from Dunham to Ernest Skinner saying the organ has worked perfectly for two years was reprinted in the July 1926 issue of *The Diapason.*

[18] Kinsley was a graduate of Yale University, licentiate of Trinity College, London, and student of Charles-Marie Widor. He had been organist and choirmaster of St. Paul's Church, New Haven, and when he returned from World War I to find his church position filled, he moved to New York and played on the theater circuit.

[19] Peppering, *The Gramophone* (October 1924), 181.

[20] Recorded June 8, 1927, at the Mormon Tabernacle.

[21] Andrews was an English organist who emigrated to the United States in 1902 to become organist of St. Luke's Episcopal church in Montclair, New Jersey. In 1912 he became organist and choirmaster of the First Baptist Church, and in 1917 of the First Congregational Church where he remained for the rest of his life. A Fellow of the American Guild of Organists and, at the time of his death, a member of its examination committee, Andrews composed more than three hundred organ works, songs, anthems, and secular choruses. He numbered among his organ students Carl Weinrich and Clarence Watters. His obituary appeared in *The Diapason,* (January 1940), 1.

[22] His other recordings were wedding and funeral marches and a few popular transcriptions. The two original organ works he recorded were Lemare's *Andantino in D-flat* and Easthope Martin's *Evensong.*

[23] The reverse featured Mark Andrews playing the Hallelujah Chorus from Handel's *Messiah.*

[24] *The Other Side of the Record* (New York: Alfred A. Knopf, 1947), 315.

[25] John D.M. Priest emigrated to America in 1914 and worked in theaters. In 1921–22 he opened the Skinner organ in the Cameo Theatre and three years later moved to the new Colony. He died after a brief illness on May 10, 1926. See his obituary in *The Diapason,* (June 1926), 1.

[26] O'Hara-King, "Tell Me You Love Me" and Davis-Greer, "Reaching for the Moon;" Donaldson-Lyman, "After I Say I'm Sorry," and Van Alstyne, "Drifting and Dreaming."

[27] "New York Invites You," *The American Organist* (May 1925), 202.

[28] Hugh Porter and Mark Andrews had already recorded the *Andantino* in 1924; three English recordings were also available.

[29] C.J., *The Gramophone* (May 1928), 500.

[30] *The Organ* (July 1928), 62.

[31] Victor 35832 recorded on July 12, 1927.

[32] George William Volkel, "Liszt's 'Ad Nos' Is Recorded for Organ by Two Men of Note," *The Diapason* (August 1932), 28.

[33] *Ibid.*

[34] On June 25, 1929, he recorded the Chopin *Prelude in c minor,* Op. 28, No. 20, and the Handel *Largo.* He returned on July 1 and recorded three more sides: the *Londonderry Air,* Kreisler's *The Old Refrain,* and Adams's *The Bells of St. Mary's.* The next day he recorded Bond's *A Perfect Day.*

[35] Other selections include Sammartini's, *Canto amoroso* (Andante from Sonata in a minor, Op. 1), the Minuet from Handel's *Bernice,* Franck's *Panis angelicus,* Wagner's *Träume,* and Schumann's, *Nachtstück,* Op. 23, No. 4.

[36] *The New Records* (June 1935), 4.

[37] A.P. DeWesse, *The American Music Lover* (June 1935), 57.

[38] *The New Records* (October 1935), 3.

GILES BEACH AND THE AMERICAN CHURCH ORGAN WORKS

Stephen L. Pinel

ON JULY 14, 1968, Barbara Owen (b. 1933), a well-known author, scholar, organ builder, organist, and church musician – and the founding president of the Organ Historical Society – played the dedicatory recital on a newly restored organ at the United Presbyterian Church in Schaghticoke, N.Y.[1] Originally built in 1865 by Giles Beach (1826-1906), the organ was thoughtfully restored by Richard Hamar (b. 1938) of New Hartford, Conn., who had studied organ building in Hamburg with Rudolf Von Beckerath (1907-76). What made the restoration significant was that for almost the first time in American organ history, the refurbishing was undertaken with the premise that nothing of the original fabric of the instrument should be altered. This allowed Beach's organ to speak to listeners today as it did when it was first installed, without a layer of additions, stop changes and re-voicing, all of which were common in rebuilds of the time. During the intervening thirty-seven years, Hamar's then germinal approach to restoration – "First, do no harm"[2] – is gradually becoming a standard adhered to by enlightened restorers, and insisted upon by progressive consultants.

Who was Giles Beach? He was a rural, Upstate-New-York maker, whose documented new instruments spanned twenty-seven years from 1849 to 1876. Much of his work was located within 50 miles of Kingsborough, N.Y. (later Gloversville, and originally a section of Johnstown), but a few instruments were ordered by congregations in New Jersey, on Staten Island, and as far away as Minnesota. One organ was actually built about 1862 for the Forty-Third Street Baptist Church in New York City, right in the backyard of Henry Er-

The façade of the 1865 Giles Beach organ in the United Presbyterian Church of
Schaghticoke, New York. The case is fashioned of solid, American black walnut,
and represents the best of American organ building of the time.
– *All photographs in this essay by Stephen L. Pinel unless otherwise noted.*

The keydesk of the 1865 Giles Beach organ at the
United Presbyterian Church of Schaghticoke, New York.

ben (1800-84) and George Jardine (1801-82). Tables I and II outline the known and suspected work of Beach, although this roster certainly represents less than half of his total output. Beach is most often remembered today for relocating the 1847 Davis & Ferris organ from Calvary Episcopal Church in New York City to the Round Lake Auditorium, Round Lake, N.Y., in July, 1888.[3]

Little has been written about Beach. A feature by Dr. Robert M. Palmer, the Fulton County (N.Y.) Historian, appeared in the Gloversville *Leader-Herald* during 1961.[4] Compiled largely from local sources, it was slanted more toward genealogy and property transfers than organs. The late Thomas L. Finch (1926-2003),[5] a university professor and a former vice president of the Organ Historical Society, also wrote a brief account of Beach in his "Organ building in Upstate New York,"[6] but as a survey it lacked detail. One reason the secondary literature on Beach is so meager is that none of the standard sources historians use to tell his story has survived. His business records burned in 1876;[7] he is not known to have published a trade catalog, list of instruments, or any promotional materials, and the bulk of the Johnstown and Gloversville newspapers of the mid- to late-nineteenth century are lost. The one weekly that does – the *Gloversville Intelligencer* (1867-89) – was not particularly generous in publishing organ news. Thus, this chronology has been reconstructed from dozens of minor and previously untapped sources.

Nearly a century after Beach's death in 1906, the time has come to publish a more complete version of his life, to identify and list as many of his instruments as possible from the sources available, and to assess his contribution to the larger scene of nineteenth-century organ building in Upstate New York. And what better opportunity is there than in honor of Barbara Owen, who has spent the greater part of her own professional life informing the rest of us about the remarkable old organs of New England.

BEACH'S FAMILY AND APPRENTICESHIP

Giles Beach was born on the family farm in Kingsborough, N.Y., just outside Gloversville on May 29, 1826.[8] After emigrating from Wallingford, Conn., his paternal grandfather, Amos Beach, Sr. (1751-1831), bought a farm of 54¼ acres for £270 on the Kingsborough Patent on Mar. 1, 1794.[9] Called by Beers a Revolutionary War hero,[10] Amos and his wife Olive Carrington (d. 1846) had ten children.[11] Giles' father, Amos Beach, Jr. (1793-1861), later bought 27 acres of the same farm for $700.[12] He was married twice: first to Huldah Gillet (d. December 20, 1821) on October 31, 1818, but her premature death left him two children, and again on April 5, 1825. With his second wife, Sarah Giles (1792-1876), they had one son, the organ builder, who was named after his mother.[13]

While little is known of Giles' upbringing, we can assume he did the expected chores of any healthy farm boy, including tending livestock, gardening, and hauling produce to the markets in both Johnstown and Gloversville.[14] On Sundays, the family attended the Congregational (after 1853, Presbyterian) Church in Kingsborough.[15] Their pastor, the Rev. Elisha Yale, D.D. (1780-1853),[16] writes this about Giles as a youth:

> ...after the new house of worship was occupied in 1838, some improvements were made... . Organs began to be more generally used in country congregations. This congregation was imposed upon by a poor one. An organist was wanted.
>
> Various opinions were entertained as to music and the style of performance. Sometimes the organ was used and sometimes not. At length, a youth, born among the people, very fond of music, became an organ builder. His taste was very correct and delicate and his skill in both building and performing very well. He built the organ anew and gave a new impulse to the music... .
>
> He used the organ to sustain and aid the voice, not to drown it. He played interludes sufficient only to keep the choir in the right tone, not to show his skill and fancy. And the music used was generally good, and well adapted to the words, suited to impress them upon the mind with power.[17]

So in addition to playing the organ, Giles kept it in repair. There are later accounts of him playing the public exhibitions on his own organs,[18] singing as a tenor soloist in concert,[19] and both playing and making violins.[20] We can also surmise from Pastor Yale's account that Giles was sensitive and artistic.

At age 18 in 1844,[21] Giles began his organ-building apprenticeship with Augustus Backus (1802-66) in Troy, N.Y. Backus, a native of nearby Coeymans, first appears in the Troy directory in 1835 as a "music teacher" at 54 State St.[22] By the mid-1840s, he was selling organs, pianos, æolines, and other musical merchan-

The *ca.* 1847 organ built by Augustus Backus in Christ Church, Episcopal, Duanesburg, New York, was likely worked on by Giles Beach during his apprenticeship. Opposite – Detail of the organ.

dise. An advertisement in the Troy *Budget* during May, 1845, announces that a four-stop church organ was finished.[23] Backus then took regular advertisements through 1847, when it appears that he joined forces with another Trojan, John C. Andrews (d. 1858). Perhaps they became partners, for Andrews replaces Backus as the solicitor in the advertisements.[24] In 1851, Andrews' name disappears from the ads, but Backus reappears. By 1852, Backus left Troy altogether, and later turns up in Michigan, where he died in Detroit on January 10, 1866.[25] What is pertinent about Backus' establishment is that it became the prototype for Beach's own musical warehouse in Gloversville during the 1870s. In addition to learning organ building under Backus, Beach became an entrepreneur.

Backus' advertisement of April 22, 1847, assesses the scope of his establishment, and provides details about the background of his workforce:

> The organs made at this establishment are considered by competent judges, to be equal to any made in the country, both in power and in quality of tone, and at the same time the prices are fully 15 per cent lower than in New York and Boston for the same work. The most accomplished mechanics from Germany and from the celebrated manufactories of Appleton and [the] Hooks, Boston, are now employed, who in skill and experience are unsurpassed. Forty organs have during the past few years been erected, which in all cases have given the most perfect satisfaction. A Premium and Diploma was awarded for one presented at the last Annual Fair of Rensselaer County.[26]

The fact that Backus had former Appleton and Hook employees explains in part why Beach's later organs show Boston characteristics in their construction, including bung-board straps rather than screws, which were not used in New-York-built organs. Further, Troy had some particularly notable instruments installed during the latter 1840s, including a large, three-manual organ of Erben's manufacture at St. Peter's R.C. Church.[27] Beach's Troy years provided him the opportunity to observe seasoned organ builders at work, to make important contacts that would serve him later in life, and to become acquainted with the best of concurrent American organ building. Under Backus, Beach learned one other critical axiom of working in a market economy: the Troy shop was successful largely because Backus could build a comparable organ in Troy fifteen percent cheaper than his Boston or New York competition. Beach offered his own clientele the same incentive after he set up shop in Gloversville.[28]

How long Beach remained in Troy, and under what circumstances is difficult to determine. Between 1845 and 1856, we can document his presence in three places – Gloversville, Troy, and Westfield, Massachusetts – and on one occasion in two places at once. In 1850, he appears in the *Population Schedules* of the federal census in both Troy[29] and Gloversville.[30] In 1855, he is found in the *Massachusetts State Census* in Westfield,[31] probably working for William A. Johnson (1816-1901). Even more telling is the fact that he appears in the *Products of Industry Schedules* of the decennial census on June 1, 1850, in Johnstown, New York, as an independent organ builder with two employees, having built four organs during the enumeration year worth $1,000, quite apart from either his Troy or Westfield associations.

Barbara Owen states that "kindred spirits" find each other, so it is not hard to imagine how Johnson became entwined in the Backus circle. In 1852, he sold an instrument to the Second Baptist Church of Troy – his Opus 28 (1853), a two-manual organ. It was installed during June, 1853,[32] and it may be that Johnson hired Beach (or another Backus journeymen) to help set the instrument up. A general advertisement by Johnson in the Troy papers during Jan., 1853, relates that "The subscriber is constantly manufacturing church organs, of every style and size, ranging in price from Four Hundred Dollars, upward... . Further information may be obtained by enquiring of Mr. James W. Andrews, Troy, or by addressing the subscriber at his manufactory, in Westfield, Massachusetts." How John C. and James W. Andrews were related has not been determined with certainty, but they were likely father and son.[33] While the specifics are left to conjecture, all of these men not only knew each other, but were working together as colleagues. Table III outlines the locations of Backus and the Andrews in Troy city directories between 1835 and 1852, and illustrates many common addresses.

What conclusions can we draw about Beach's apprenticeship? While he served his indenture under Backus, he often relocated back and forth between Troy and Gloversville, and the Erie Canal made that an easy trip in the 1840s. By 1855, he was likely working with Johnson, but exactly when he started there or how long he remained is unclear. During the latter 1840s, he was already building organs under his own name on the Kingsborough farm, and at least three instruments of the period are documented.[34] The first was a rebuild of the four-stop organ in the Kingsborough Church, the second was for a Presbyterian congregation in Laurens, N.Y.,[35] and the third is currently located at the Corwallville Methodist Episcopal Church on the grounds of the Farmer's Museum in Cooperstown, N.Y. This last instrument was likely Beach's first effort as an independent organ builder, and as such is worth considering in greater detail.

THE ORGAN OF THE FARMER'S MUSEUM

The instrument was built in 1849 for Grace Church, Episcopal, Cherry Valley, N.Y. The organ has no nameplate; the attribution is based on two inscriptions found on the interior of the instrument by Sidney R. Chase (b. 1940), the first of which reads

G. Beach

Guilford Centre Chenango Co NY

Feb 4th 184?

Lamentably, the final digit of the date was cut off when the board was trimmed before its original installation. A second inscription states

Very { *Windy* *Blustering* *Stormy* }

& also the last day of March

packing the organ

The edifice of Grace Church was finished in the latter part of 1847,[36] so it is hard to escape the conclusion that the vestry ordered the organ during the fall of 1848. Beach finished it in Mar., 1849, and on the last day of the month, packed it to move it to Cherry Valley. A newspaper shim found inside the instrument contains advertisements from Westford and Cherry Valley, and is dated 1847. The manuscript records of the Grace Church, examined by Edward L. Partridge in 1964, indicate that an Apr., 1849 insurance policy on the organ set its value at $250.[37] Thus, the instrument certainly dates from the spring of 1849, and this chronology is consistent with its stylistic characteristics, including its G-compass keyboard, which went out of fashion in most places during 1850.

Why the first inscription included "Guilford Centre Chenango County" is open to discussion. A 1960's supposition – no longer endorsed – suggested that the organ was originally built for an undetermined patron in Guilford, and was moved to Cherry Valley second-hand in 1863. The Episcopal and Presbyterian Churches as well as the local Guilford Academy were posited as potential first locations for the organ. Guilford, however, was the home of another rural, New-York organ maker named Ellsworth Phelps (b. 1803). Could Beach have visited Guilford, and could the two men have worked on the organ together? Unfortunately, almost nothing is known about Phelps.[38] He made a few organs in the Southern part of New York State, and at one point was working collaboratively with Chauncey Pease in Cooperstown, N.Y.[39] Additional research is needed on these makers and their business relationships.

The more recent history of the Grace Church organ is well documented. By 1858, the seating capacity of Grace Church was inadequate, so the building was enlarged; this made the organ too gentle. During the summer of 1863, the church women raised funds to add a pedal bass to the instrument. The 1864 *Proceedings...of the Protestant Episcopal Church* relate: "A portion of the funds included under the head of 'Parish Purposes' were the proceeds of sales by the ladies of the parish, and appropriated to the finishing of the chancel ceiling with tracery, and adding a pedal base to the organ."[40] Who did the work is not certain. The organ served the congregation of Grace Church in that state until 1904, when a new organ was installed down front. Providentially, the gallery of Grace Church was too small to house Hook & Hastings, Opus 1997 (1903), a two-manual organ with thirteen registers,[41] so the Beach remained in the rear gallery of the church mute, unused, and unplayable until 1963.

That fall, the New York State Historical Association purchased the organ, and on Jan. 6, 1964, it was moved to the shop of organ builder Sidney Chase in Worcester, N.Y. Chase reversed alterations to the instrument, including removing the added pedal keyboard and pipes, and replaced a missing stop with a rank closer in pitch and scale to the original. The action was renewed,

The 1849 organ built by Giles Beach for Grace Church, Episcopal, Cherry Valley, New York; later relocated to the Cornwallville Methodist Episcopal Church at the Farmer's Museum, New York State Historical Association, in Cooperstown, New York. Published with permission of the Association.

A *ca.* 1850 organ attributed to Giles Beach in the
First Presbyterian Church, Laurens, New York.

and the wind system, including the original feeders, was re-leathered. When completed in June, 1964, the organ was installed in the Corwallville Methodist Church, recently relocated to the grounds of the Farmer's Museum in Cooperstown, N.Y.[42] The instrument was re-dedicated at a service on July 12, 1964,[43] and remains an appropriate and salient part of the museum's holdings.

Inspecting the organ shows some telling features. It was clearly the product of a precocious yet unsophisticated artisan, who creatively used the meager resources available to him to complete an instrument for an equally modest client. The case is fashioned of Butternut, a wood local to Upstate New York, and frequently found in organs of the region. Some attributes of its construction – the use of nails, for instance, to hold the case together – suggest a lack of experience or resources. As a package, however, this charming little organ transcends any limitations of its place or construction. It shows the promise of a young builder who was just about to fill a niche in the rural organ business of Upstate New York.

ESTABLISHING THE BUSINESS

According to Pastor Yale, Beach's indenture ended in 1849, and he returned to Kingsborough: "Completing his apprenticeship, he returned to his father's home, the old farm on the Mayfield Road. Here he had a small shop where he did his first work, repairing and rebuilding the … organ in the Congregational (now Presbyterian) church in Kingsborough in 1849. This organ had four stops and a single foot pedal, with a hand lever for blowing."[44] On June 24, 1851, Beach married Charlotte C. Smith (1826-1913),[45] daughter of Samuel Smith and Mary E. Baird, with Pastor Yale performing the ceremony at the local church.

Initially, Beach used a shed on the family property, but it was almost immediately found to be too small. In 1853, he purchased ¼ acre of land from James H. Burr for $1,050 on the south side of Vine between Main and Cayadutta Sts. in the center of Gloversville.[46] There was already a dwelling on the property, so Beach built a shop at the back of the lot fronting on Cayadutta.[47] Here he did the initial work in Gloversville, although only one organ from the early 1850s has been positively identified. It was a one-manual instrument costing $500 built in 1853 for St. John's Reformed Church in Saint Johnsville, N.Y.[48] Business was apparently not good; by 1855, Beach is found in Westfield, Mass., probably working for Johnson. As expected, he does not have an entry in the *Products of Industry Schedules* of the New York State Census for 1855.

He didn't wait long for a contract; or, perhaps it was the award of the contract that brought him back to Gloversville. In 1856, his own congregation – the Kingsborough Presbyterian Church, where he grew up as a congregant and was later married – turned to him to replace their *ca.* 1838 organ with a larger instrument. Referencing minutes of the congregation, Pastor Edward W. Miller (1865-1939) in the early twentieth century, writes:

> The present organ – and there was at least one earlier one – was built by Giles Beach, who then had an organ factory on East State Street [*sic,* Vine St.], later moved to South Main Street. The only clue to its date is the minute of a meeting of the congregation held in October, 1856, which appointed a committee of which G.G.W. Green was chairman "to consider the subject of purchasing an organ." [49]

Alan M. Laufman (1935-2001) examined this organ during the spring of 1960, and writes:

> This charming little organ stands completely free in the rear gallery of the pleasing frame [*sic,* i.e. brick] church, and was probably made by Giles Beach [it was!]… . He is known to have worked on the instrument, and he may have added the 27-note pedalboard. The case is 3-sectional, with pipes arranged 3 | 5 | 3, and the central flat projects and is taller than the side two. It shows Boston influence; the console is recessed, there is a complete foundation board, and the console is supported by brackets. 2-piece folding doors cover the console, which has square-shanked knobs in vertical jambs. The bench has been altered to fit the pedals; a balanced swell pedal replaced the earlier h.d. [i.e. hitch down], and there are horizontal shades. "July 21 1857" is written on CC of the 15th. The instrument was overhauled by Frank Weston of Utica… .[50]

Barbara Owen played the re-dedicatory recital on Apr. 16, 1961.[51] Unfortunately, the church closed *ca.* 1980, but the building was purchased and has since been splendidly maintained by an Assembly of God congregation; the intact Beach organ remains in the rear gallery.

The Kingsborough Presbyterian Church, erected in 1838, is located on
North Kingsborough Avenue in Gloversville, New York. Giles Beach was baptized
in the edifice on July 30, 1826, and married there on June 24, 1851. During the nineteenth
century, generations of the Beach family considered this their home church.

The organ in the rear gallery of the Kingsborough Presbyterian Church.
Built by Giles Beach in 1857, this instrument was likely his first two-manual organ.
— Photographs courtesy of the Kingsborough Assembly of God

The year 1857 was happy for Beach personally. His first son, Charles Sumner Beach (1857-1947) – who also became an organ builder – was born Dec. 15, 1857, just in time for Christmas. Of his four other children, Bertie Beach (1864-64) and Lottie Giles Beach (1868-75) died as youngsters, Arthur D. Beach (1869-1936), also an organ builder, was born Aug. 13, 1869, and a daughter, Estelle C. Beach, became a medical doctor.[52]

BUILDING A REPUTATION
AND EXPANDING THE BUSINESS

Beach's reputation was spreading: for the first time he was included in the 1857 *Business Directory* of Gloversville (actually a map) as "Giles Beach, organ manufacturer."[53] By June, 1860, the *Products of Industry* schedule of the federal census indicates that Beach had invested $1,500 in real estate, employed four people, used 4,000 board feet of lumber, and with hand labor produced three organs worth $3,000.[54] Regrettably, none of these instruments has been identified, but we can assume they were small and probably intended for rural congregations along the Mohawk Valley Region of New York State.

The following year, one known instrument was erected in the Brick Presbyterian Church, Salem, N.Y., during Mar., 1861. Said the *Press:*

> Mr. Giles Beach of Gloversville, Fulton Co., is now setting up an organ in the Presbyterian Church in this village. It is 11 feet wide, 5½ feet deep, and 15 feet high. The case is plain, but in good taste; special pains, as we learn, have been taken, by the committee having the thing in charge, to secure a superior instrument for one of its size and cost.
>
> An exhibition of the organ, with a concert by the choir of the church is to be given on Friday eve. of this week.[55]

In 1862, Beach built an organ for the Forty-Third Street Baptist Church in New York City,[56] and in 1863, for the Second Presbyterian Church of Newark, N. J.[57]

Perhaps anticipating that the Cayadutta-St. shop would be too small, Beach purchased new property on South School St. (later Arlington Ave.) in 1861,[58] and erected a two-story frame structure to continue his business. In 1864, he sold the previous property,[59] and moved his family and shop to the

Giles Beach, 1826–1906
Organ Builder of Gloversville, New York
— *Photograph courtesy of the Rev. Matthew B. Splittgerber, the Church Council,
and the congregation of the Kingsborough Assembly of God*

new location. This space served temporarily until business increased dramatically after the Civil War.

In Dec., 1864, he built a substantial two-manual organ for the Unitarian Church of Troy, N.Y. His earlier connections in the area had begun to pay off. Noting the installation, the *Times* remarks:

> The number of stops is twenty-two, of which sixteen are speaking stops. The schedule presents, in the swell organ, Open Diapason, Stopped Diapason, Principal, Viol de Gamba, Kalaphone, and Hautboy; in the pedal organ, the Double Stopped Diapason; and in the great organ, the Open and Stop Diapasons, Principal, Dulciana, Clarabella, Wald Flute, Twelfth, and Fifteenth. A tremulant is added to the swell, and there are three couplers, Pedal to Great Organ, Swell to Great, and Pedal to Swell. The Kalaphone is, we understand, a new stop of the invention of the builder, voiced a little differently from the Viol de Gamba and the Dulciana, being made a little more clear, and adapted especially for solo use.
>
> In respect to the character of the tones of the organ, each stop, from the softest to the loudest, is perfect in its kind, and is so delicately voiced as to be capable of use in solo passages, while all together are made to blend with excellent consistency. The diapasons are very rich and full in tone, while fully free from any extraneous noise. The flutes are silvery and clear. The hautboy is especially to be commended for its purity of tone and freedom from the usual unpleasant quality of reed stops. The pedal sub bass is deep and pervading, and distinct without being ponderous and overpowering.[60]

The Kalaphone (variously spelled Kalophone) is a two-rank stop playing at 4′ and 2′ pitch, and is described by the Rev. E.A. Boadway (b. 1936) as of "pleasing Gemshorn quality."[61] The *Times* article goes on to praise the mechanism, and ends with the statement: "Several organs of his construction are known also in the large villages and country towns within a few miles of this city." Regrettably, none of the locations of these instruments has been discovered. In Feb., 1865, he installed a two-manual organ in the Reformed Protestant Dutch Church in Tompkinsville, Staten Island, N.Y.,[62] and in Sept., 1865, a large, two-manual organ in the Presbyterian Church, Schaghticoke, N.Y.[63] The 1865 *Industry other than Agriculture Schedules* of the New York State Census relates that Beach had invested $3,000 in real estate, had six employees making $45 in monthly wages, used $2,000 of lumber, and made four organs during the year worth a value of $6,400.[64]

Business increased dramatically after the Civil War. In 1866, Beach built two three-manual organs, one for the Fifth Street Presbyterian Church in Troy – the largest organ the firm ever made – and for the Dutch Reformed Church in Cohoes,[65] and another large, two-manual organ for the Presbyterian Church of Waterford, all in New York State.[66]

The Troy instrument had unique features, including pneumatic action, differing wind pressures, unusual stops, and other novel construction details. The *Times* reports:

> The organ is one of Beach's first-class instruments – the largest ever produced by him. Its superiority consists of simplicity and economy of space in the arrangement of its parts, the great variety and selection and quality of its stops, the peculiar fullness and power of its diapasons in both manual and pedal organs. Also [in] the excellence of its imitation stops, and an improved application of the "pneumatic lever," by which the performer may, by employing the usual couplings, play the three manuals at once with as little effort as on the ordinary piano forte. The wind is supplied by two bellows of about one hundred and thirty feet superficial capacity, of different pressures, the lighter using the surplus wind of the heavier one. The swell organ is contained in a triple box. The scales of the pipes are chosen with care, and their great variety of tone is the result of a long experience and careful study of the art of voicing. The whole number of pipes is 1938.[67]

The exhibition, played on Mar. 26, 1866, by Geo. W. Morgan (1822-92), was successful: "Mr. Beach, of Gloversville, the builder of the organ, has accomplished a great triumph. His work is a masterpiece. The critics all paid it the highest compliment, and Mr. Morgan, who never flatters anybody's work, was highly pleased."[68] The organ was used until 1907, when it was replaced with a larger organ built by the Hutchings-Votey Organ Co., of Boston, Mass.[69] The Beach was relocated second-hand to the Congregational Church of Whitman, Mass., and E.A. Boadway, who examined it, described it as a "remarkable" instrument. It was unfortunately destroyed about 1980. What a shame that such a large and important example of Upstate-New-York organ building came so close to our own day.[70] Had it survived just a little longer, it would surely today be cherished and eventually restored.

After the newsworthy opening of the Troy organ, it must have been apparent to Beach that the business was taking off. Once again, the two-story shop

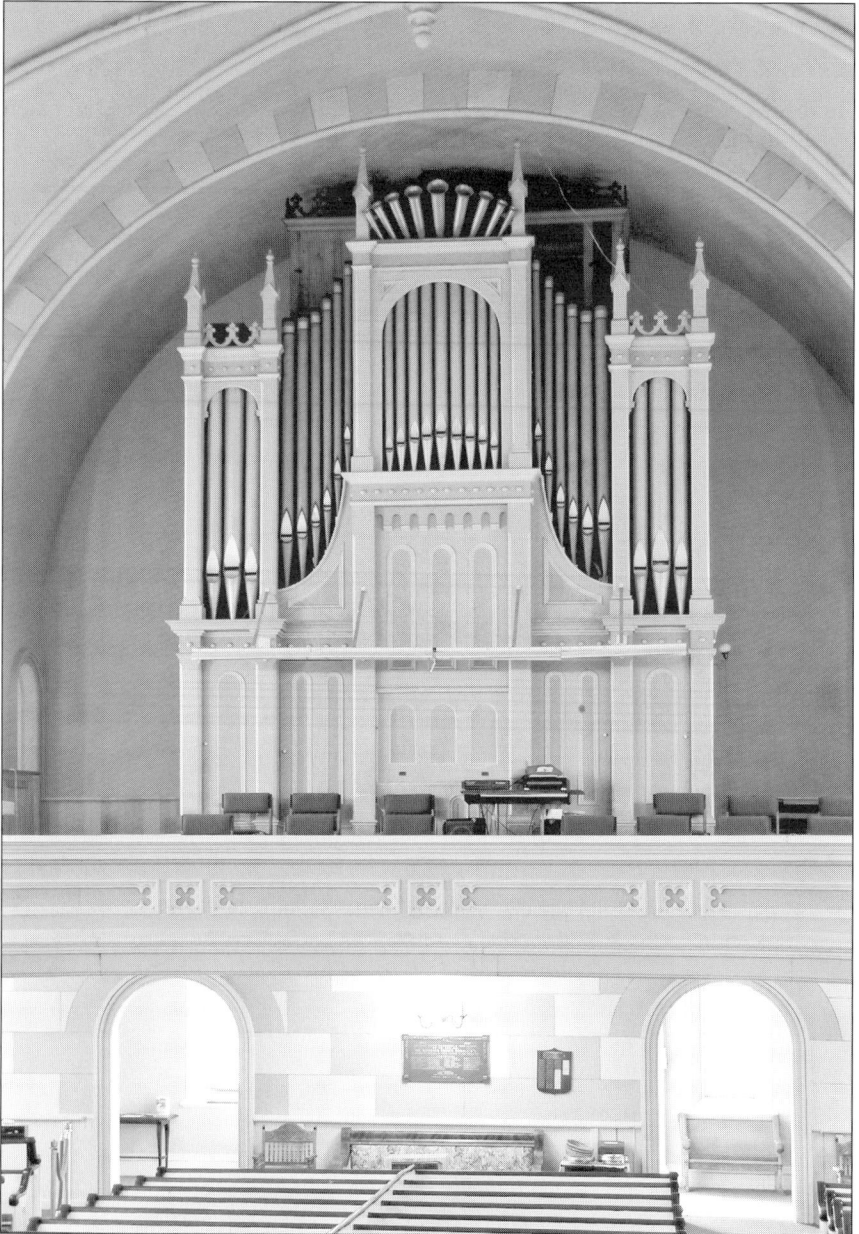

The façade of the 1866 three–manual organ built by Giles Beach for the
Protestant Dutch Reformed Church of Cohoes, New York.

space was inadequate to manufacture an increasing number of larger organs, and as the City of Gloversville grew in size and sophistication, there was an increasing demand for musical merchandise of all kinds. By 1868, he had taken Stephen Moore into partnership. The third directory of Johnstown and Gloversville (also a map) identifies them as "Beach & Moore – dealers in pianos, organs, and musical merchandise. Books, stationary, picture frames [undoubtedly made in the wood shop], mirrors, etc."[71] A notice in the *Intelligencer* announces: "Musical Instruments. Messrs. Beach & Moore wish to notify the musical public that they have opened rooms at their Organ Factory, corner Main & Spring Streets, where they will keep for sale Pianos, Melodeons, &c., &c., at low fair prices."[72] Moore was an Englishman, and in 1870 was thirty-four years old.[73]

The production of new organs continued apace, but most of the instruments of the latter 1860s are unidentified. One known client was the Presbyterian Church on Green Island, just outside of Troy. This one-manual organ was relocated to the Dyer-Phelps A.M.E. Church in Saratoga Springs, N.Y., by M.P. Möller in Oct., 1910 as their opus 1176. This instrument was reputedly given as a gift for their role in the Underground Railroad. After passing through private hands, it is owned by S.L. Huntington & Co., of Stonington, Conn. It is currently undergoing restoration, and is for sale.

Two two-manual organs were built in 1870. The first was completed in Mar., 1870, for the new Methodist Episcopal Church in Gloversville. With obvious pride, the local paper recounts:

> The organ is one in which not only the church, but also our whole community, may well take pride, inasmuch as it is one of our own production, having been built at the establishment of Messrs. Beach and Moore in this village. We are sure that all who have seen or heard it will agree it is a "thing of beauty," both in the richness and appropriateness of its external finish and in the fullness, harmony and perfection of the sweet sounds which issue from it, when touched by skillful hands. The makers of this really superior instrument will need no further recommendation to their customers than to introduce them to this, one of the choicest results of their skill and fidelity in the production of church organs.[74]

Another was built for the Second Presbyterian Church in Amsterdam, N.Y. The latter organ was opened at a concert June 7, 1870, and was reported by the press to be a decided success.[75]

By the late 1860s, the shop was again inadequate, so Beach looked toward moving to a larger space. On May 6, 1870, he bought lots at the corner of South Main and Burr Sts. in Gloversville, and later that year, erected a four-story brick building to use as a factory.[76]

THE AMERICAN CHURCH ORGAN WORKS

When the American Church Organ Works opened, Beach & Moore arrived at the summit of their careers. While Beach owned the property, he did not own the structure. A later account relates that the building was owned by Charles Roberts of Poughkeepsie, with John L. Getman acting as the local agent, ostensibly to collect rent and make repairs. Nor was Beach & Moore's firm the sole occupant. While the upper floors were relegated to organ building, there were a number of other individuals on the ground floor and in the basement. These included John C. Anthony (a machinist), Geo. W. Hildreth (a steam-operated 'laying-off' shop, i.e. a fancy glove cutter), and Mrs. Elizabeth Taylor, who lived in the rear of the building as a dwelling house.[77] Beach had a business card printed, and a fuzzy image of it is published with Palmer's 1961 article. In the center of the card is an engraving of the factory. Typically, the building is rectangular in shape, has a flat (or slightly sloping) roof with four windows in front and six or seven along the sides on each of the four stories. The text on the card reads "G. Beach & Co. – American Church Organ Works – Gloversville, N.Y."[78] Beach & Moore's retail shop was on the first floor.

Somewhat naïvely, Palmer wrote:

> Mr. Beach employed 10 to 15 men and it took more than a year to complete the one organ of the newer type with pneumatic key action. An organ maker in those days [had] not only…to build the case for the instrument, but construct and voice the pipes and manufacture the other parts.[79]

The *Industry other than Agricultural* schedule of the 1875 census indicates that Palmer was exaggerating. Beach had 9 employees (8 men and 1 boy under age 18) earning monthly wages of $75 and $50 respectively. He had invested $12,500 in real estate, and $3,000 in tools and machinery. During the enumeration year, the firm made 3 organs worth $5,000. For the first time the firm used steam machinery (the equivalency of 10 horse power), and billed $600 for organ repairs[80] Table IV outlines the known employees of Beach over a twenty-six-year period from 1850 to 1876.

More new organs followed. In Feb., 1871, a small two-manual organ was installed in the Presbyterian Church, Havana (later Montour Falls), N.Y.,[81] and in Jan., 1872, a similarly-sized instrument was sent to the Market St. Methodist Church in Paterson, N.J.[82] Two large organs were completed in March. The first was installed in the new Masonic Hall in Troy, N.Y., and was first heard about the 29th of the month. The *Times* said only that "The new organ, although it still lacked a good deal of being finished, was tested by Prof. Andrews [likely the same James W. Andrews as discussed above]. The universal verdict of satisfaction and pleasure was not departed from in this instance."[83] The organ was apparently late: the *Intelligencer* notes that "The ceremonies were of the most beautiful and impressive character, the interest of which were heightened by the beautiful music from the new and splendid organ, manufactured by Giles Beach & Co., of Gloversville, and which, after much severe night work, Mr. Beach had set up for the dedication services."[84]

The largest instrument of the early 1870s was a three-manual organ built for the new Methodist Episcopal Church in Saratoga Springs, N.Y.[85] The building, still standing in Saratoga today, is a colossal Victorian, English-Gothic structure of brick, designed by architect E. Boyden & Son, of Worcester, Mass. The magnificent edifice measures 166 by 84 feet, and the tower is 193 feet high. The Beach was equally grand: it had three manuals and 43 registers behind a three-sectional, prickly-Gothic case fashioned of American black walnut. The organ was described at length in the *Saratogian*.[86]

By June, 1872, the firm was installing another two-manual organ in St. Paul's Lutheran Church in Johnstown, N.Y.[87] If the first half of 1872 represents the firm's on-going work during the early 1870s, then the factory in full operation had the capacity to manufacture a number of sizeable organs in quick succession. A short notice in the *Intelligencer* on Feb. 8, 1872, relates that "Their business has largely increased during the past season, and they are constantly receiving orders in their line."[88] Unfortunately, we know nothing of the organs built during the remainder of 1872, and almost nothing about those built

A *ca.* 1880 photograph of the Methodist Episcopal Church of Saratoga Springs, New York, is a splendid Victorian edifice designed by architect E. Boydon & Son of Worcester, Massachusetts. It was dedicated in March, 1872.

A *ca.* 1890 photograph of the 1872 organ by Giles Beach in the
Methodist Episcopal Church of Saratoga Springs, New York. This three-manual
instrument was one of the largest contracts the American Church Organ Works completed.
— *Photographs from the George S. Bolster Collection, Historical Society of
Saratoga Springs, N.Y. Used with permission.*

between 1873 and 1876. A $2,000 organ was installed in the Reformed Dutch Church of Caughnawaga (later Fonda), N.Y., in Dec., 1873,[89] and an organ of slightly larger size in the Methodist Church of Herkimer, N.Y., in Mar., 1874.[90] Said the *Intelligencer* on Christmas Day, 1873:

> The elegant Church Organ just completed by Messrs. G. Beach & Co., for the new M.E. Church, at Herkimer, is now on exhibition at the American Church Organ Works, Gloversville. On Tuesday afternoon and evening, the establishment was thronged with visitors, when Messrs. Pettee and Henry Giles presided at the entertainment, and delighted the guests with inspiring and most eloquent music… . The Organ has twenty-eight stops – the case is of black ash and black walnut – the entire cost being $3,000. By competent judges it is considered fully equal, if not superior, in style, quality, execution and finish, to anything of its kind manufactured in this country, and while Messrs. Beach & Co. may congratulate themselves on their success, our citizens have reason to be proud that their establishment is located in Gloversville. The Organ will continue on exhibition [for] the remainder of the week; Mr. Henry Giles will be in attendance; and we are requested to add that Messrs. Beach & Co. extend a cordial invitation to all who may desire to visit their establishment, and inspect the new Organ.[91]

Most other new organs of the period 1874 to 1876 have escaped detection.

On Sept. 29th, 1876, Beach suffered the same fate as many other nineteenth-century American organ builders. Like Erben, Johnson, the Hooks, Steer & Turner, Richard M. Ferris, Marklove, and others, the factory was destroyed by fire. Lamenting, the *Intelligencer* reports on the following Thursday:

> LARGE FIRE. – At about half past 3 o'clock, last Friday morning, the residents of Main street were startled by the cry of fire. In a few minutes flames were seen bursting from the windows of the American Church Organ Works, and soon the whole structure, owing to the combustible nature of the material within, and the imperfect construction of the building, was a mass of ruins. There was no wind at the time, and never has been when conflagrations occur in this village; that is one reason why we have no fire apparatus. The fire was first discovered by the family of Mr. J.L. Burr, and they gave the first alarm. Their wonderful brick residence, adjacent, was badly scorched and barely escaped the devouring flames. – The frame dwelling of Mrs. French, on Burr street, escaped destruction owing to the rear wall of the factory having no openings.
>
> Mr. Beach, the proprietor of the Organ Works, lost heavily. Among the property destroyed was a finished organ, also, one partly completed, a piano-cased melodeon, a parlor pipe organ, and all his implements and tools used

in the business. – Henry Fosmire and Stephen Moore, workers at the factory, lost all their tools… . There was no insurance on any of the property, as far as known.[92]

With the conflagration came the end of the American Church Organ Works, and as it turned out, the end of Beach's career as a builder of new organs. His hefty financial loss made it impossible to recover. Following the disaster, Beach concentrated on rebuilds, relocations, and service work, and a number of references to him have surfaced in church records of Eastern New York, and Southern Vermont.[93]

One bit of personal gratification came on Mar. 25, 1879, when he was awarded a United States Patent for an "improvement in paper organ-pipes." A specification from the Patent Office relates:

> The invention has principally for its objects the construction of the pipes and wind-conductors of organs free from liability to change from alterations in the hygrometric state of the atmosphere, and also far less liable to change in length and diameter through changes in temperature; but other advantages secured are cheapness, durability, and an improvement in the quality of the tone in the speaking or the sonorous pipes.
> The invention consists in the manufacture of such pipes and conductors of paper, as hereinafter described… .[94]

There is no indication that any builder took the invention seriously.

Beach continued service and repair work well into his seventies. During the latter part of the nineteenth century, he serviced many organs in Troy, including the three-manual, J.H. & C.S. Odell organ, Opus 190 (1882), at the Troy Music Hall. Some of his last known work was repairing the organ of First Presbyterian Church in 1902,[95] and enlarging the organ of Fifth Ave. Baptist Church in 1903,[96] both in Troy. He spent the latter part of his life living at 61 Woodside Ave. in Gloversville, where he died on Sept 6, 1906, just a few months after his 55th wedding anniversary. His widow, Charlotte C. Beach, lived until July 30, 1913. Both sons, Charles Sumner and Arthur D. Beach worked with organs. Charles became a representative of M.P. Möller, and Arthur was briefly involved in an organ-building partnership in Troy known as Beach & Freitag (1906-09).[97] One instrument of the partnership still exists at the Evangelical Lutheran Church, Raymertown, N.Y., where it was restored by William Baker & Co. in 1980.[98] The entire family is buried in Prospect Hill Cemetery in Gloversville.

SOME CLOSING REMARKS

Giles Beach was not a major producer of organs compared to Erben, Jardine or the Hooks. He did not influence buying trends, or set standards. For the most part, his instruments were never even considered by the more affluent congregations of nineteenth-century America. His career, however, is fairly representative of a number of organ builders plying their trade along the Mohawk Valley Region of New York State. His story is similar to that of Alvinza Andrews (1799-1862) and John Gale Marklove (1827-91) in Utica, Garret House (1810-1900) in Buffalo, William J. Stuart (1828-1904) in Albany, and Thomas H. Knollin in Syracuse. Each of these firms (and their successors) produced four or five competently-built organs yearly for a generation or more. They competed with better-established firms by keeping their overhead costs in check, and by using local talent and materials.

Throughout his life, Beach was highly respected. The *Round Lake Journal* calls him a "master of organ work." After his death, his obituary appeared in the expected newspapers in Johnstown and Gloversville,[99] but also as far away as Albany and Troy. The Johnstown *Herald* says "Mr. Beach was scrupulously honest in his work and upright in all his dealings, and was a compassionate man from his geniality and his extensive fund of information."[100] The *Leader* declares "Mr. Beach was a man of sturdy, upright character, scrupulous in business relations and by his integrity won many sincere friends. In religious matters he was inclined towards Unitarianism, attending service at that church."[101] The *Albany Argus* continues "Mr. Beach was in the truest sense one of nature's noblemen. Liberal in religious views, and not strictly in accord with some of the teachings of the churches, he yet exemplified in his life the spirit of the Christian religion. Those so fortunate to possess his friendship were fully cognizant of his nobility of character, and no one could know him well without loving him and being better for knowing him. He was an ardent lover of music and an appreciative admirer of the best in art."[102]

On Aug. 4, 1997, Barbara Owen and I sat together at a recital at the United Presbyterian Church in Schaghticoke, N.Y. The program, played by Philip Majkrzak, was part of the Upper Hudson Valley Mini-Convention of the Organ Historical Society.[103] By the concert's end, it was plainly apparent that the organ was unusually good. Its tall and handsome black-walnut case, satisfying ensemble, elegant keydesk, and general quality left a marked impression on the audience.[104] Barbara and I collectively bemoaned the lack of even basic information on Beach, who was obviously a competent organ builder. Barbara encouraged and challenged me to investigate Beach's life and work. I now have the pleasure to offer the fruits of that research in her honor.

SOURCES (SELECT LIST)

Boadway, E.A. [compiler]. *Twelfth annual convention of the Organ Historical Society, Incorporated. Capital District Region, New York, June 20-22, 1967.*

Census documents. Federal Census: *1850, 1860, 1870, 1880, and 1900.* New York State Census: *1845, 1855, 1865, and 1875.* Massachusetts State Census: *1855.*

"Church organ," *Gloversville Intelligencer* 7:52 (Dec. 25, 1873), 2.

City directories: Gloversville, Johnstown and Troy, N.Y.

"Concert," *Amsterdam Recorder* 20:36 (Dec. 17, 1873), 3.

Court records: Fulton County Courthouse, Johnstown, N.Y.

Deeds (and other property records): Fulton County Courthouse, Johnstown, N.Y.

Finch, T.L. "Organ building in Upstate New York in the nineteenth century," *Bicentennial Tracker* (1976), 63-80.

"Grand organ exhibition," *Richmond County Gazette* 6:52 (Feb. 1, 1865), 3.

History of Montgomery and Fulton Counties, N.Y., with illustrations descriptive of scenery, private residences, public buildings, fine blocks, and important manufactories... . New York: F.W. Beers & Co., 1878.

Hollister, William H. *Second Presbyterian Church of Troy, N.Y.: historical sketch prepared and read at the reopening of the auditorium, October 3, 1915. Revised and extended to April, 1916.* Troy, N.Y.: [Published by direction of the Session], 1917.

Kingsborough Presbyterian Church: Baptismal, Marriage and Death Records. Presbyterian Historical Society, Philadelphia.

Miller, Edward Waite. *Historical manual of the Kingsborough Ave. Presbyterian Church, Gloversville, N.Y.* Gloversville: [published by the church], *ca.* 1932.

Mortgages: Fulton County Courthouse, Johnstown, N.Y.

Newspapers: *Albany Argus; Amsterdam Recorder; Cohoes Cataract;* [Cooperstown] *Watch-tower; Fulton County Republican; Gloversville Intelligencer; Herkimer Democrat; Leader-Herald; New York Times; Richmond County Gazette; Salem Press; Saratogian; Troy Daily Times;* [Troy] *Northern Budget.*

"New M.E. Church," *Saratogian* 3:154 (Mar. 19, 1872), 3.

"New organ in Troy," *Troy Daily Times* 13:135 (Dec. 1, 1864), 3.

One hundred years : 1838-1938. First Methodist Episcopal Church, Gloversville, N.Y.

"Organ exhibition," *Troy Daily Times* 14:227 (Mar. 23, 1866), 3.

Palmer, R[obert]. M[orris]. "Church organs once manufactured in Gloversville – historian gathers data about life, work of Beach, native of area," [Gloversville] *Leader-Herald* 7:68 (Apr. 12, 1961), 7.

Partridge, Edward L. *Dismantling and restoration of the Grace Church organ, Cherry Valley, New York, January 6, 1964.* An unpublished paper provided by the courtesy of Kathryn Boardman, Associate Director of Programs, the New York State Historical Association, Cooperstown, N.Y., August 25, 1997.

Pinel, Stephen L. "A documented history of the Round Lake Auditorium organ," *Tracker* 30:1 (1986), 44-55.

_____ [compiler]. *The Organ Historical Society in conjunction with the Round Lake Historical Society presents the Upper Hudson Valley Mini-Convention, August 3-6, 1997.* Round Lake, New York: Round Lake Historical Society, 1997.

Sprague, Horace. *Gloversville: or, the model village.* Gloversville, N.Y.: William H. Case, 1859.

Two hundredth anniversary : Reformed Church of Fonda : 1758-1958 : Reformed Dutch Church of Caughnawaga, Fonda, New York.

United States Patent Office. *Specifications forming part of Letters Patent No. 212,612, dated March 25, 1879; application filed April 5, 1878.*

Yale, Elisha: Papers. Presbyterian Historical Society, Philadelphia.

ACKNOWLEDGEMENTS

Many colleagues assisted in gathering the information for this article. Foremost was the invaluable aid of the Rev. Edgar A. Boadway, whose generosity in sharing his own research on Beach with the author is gratefully acknowledged. Other details and materials were provided by Peter T. Cameron, Sidney Chase, Mary Danyew, Michael D. Friesen, Scot L. Huntington, Alan M. Laufman, Barbara Owen, Robert Reich, Stephen J. Schnurr, Jr., Matthew B. Splittgerber, William T. Van Pelt III, Martin R. Walsh, Robert N. Waters, and Keith B. Williams. The staff at the Johnstown and Gloversville Public Libraries, the Fulton County Hall of Records, Fulton County Historical Society, the New York State Library in Albany, all in N.Y., and the Presbyterian Historical Society in Philadelphia, provided ready access to church records, city directories, parish and county histories, census documents, court records, deeds, mortgages, and old newspaper files. The librarians at these institutions, often with heavy workloads and inadequate support staff, were always willing to help. Finally, I would like to thank Prof. Dr. John K. Ogasapian and the Governing Board of Publications of the Organ Historical Society for sponsoring this publication.

: : N O T E S : :

[1]   The extant program is found among the collections of the American Organ Archives of the Organ Historical Society, Westminster Choir College of Rider University, Princeton, N.J.; hereinafter AOA.

[2]   This was the title of a panel discussion at the 31st Annual Convention of the American Institute of Organbuilders, New York, N.Y., Sept. 28 to Oct. 1, 2004; Laurence Libin moderated the discussion with panelists Joseph Dzeda, Richard Hamar, and Scot L. Huntington.

[3]   *A history of the Round Lake Association with special related articles compiled by Woman's Round Lake Improvement Society for the centennial celebration, Aug. 11-17, 1968,* 13, quoting the *Round Lake Journal* of July, 1888. The best source of information on the Round Lake organ is the author's "A documented history of the Round Lake Auditorium organ," *Tracker* 30:1 (1986), 44-55; hereinafter *T.*

⁴   R[obert]. M[orris]. Palmer, "Church organs once manufactured in Gloversville – historian gathers data about life, work of Beach, native of area," [Glov-
ersville] *Leader-Herald* 7:68 (Apr. 12, 1961), 7; hereinafter Palmer.

⁵   See "Obituaries – Thomas Lassfolk Finch," *T* 48:2 (Spring, 2004), 19.

⁶   Thomas Finch, "Organ building in Upstate New York in the nineteenth
century," *Bicentennial Tracker* (1976), 73-74.

⁷   See "Large fire," *Fulton County Republican*, Oct. 5, 1876, 2; hereinafter
FCR.

⁸   Horace Sprague, *Gloversville: or, the model village*. Gloversville, N.Y.: Printed by William H. Case, 1859, 111-12; hereinafter Sprague; the date is also found
on his tombstone in Prospect Hill Cemetery, Gloversville. Giles was baptized
on July 30, 1826 by Dr. Yale; see MS, Baptismal Records, Kingsborough Presbyterian Church, Presbyterian Historical Society, Philadelphia.

⁹   Deed [first series]: book 1, pp. 276-77, Mar. 1, 1794 [recorded July 22,
1796], between Amos Beach [Sr.] & Enos Seymour. Readers can presume that
all deeds cited in this paper are located at the Hall of Records, Fulton County
Courthouse, Johnstown, N.Y. Amos Beach, Sr., who died Feb. 1, 1831, is buried
in Kingsborough Cemetery; see Lewis G. Decker, *Cemetery recording, 1992, City
of Gloversville, Kingsborough Cemetery*, book 1.

¹⁰ *History of Montgomery and Fulton Counties, N.Y., with illustrations descriptive of scenery, private residences, public buildings, fine blocks, and important manufactories...* . New York: F.W. Beers & Co., 1878, 209.

¹¹ Sprague: Huldah, Sally, Clarinda, Philinda, Diadema, Olive, Amos, Elizabeth, Allen and Ebenezer C. The genealogical website – <www.familysearch.
org> – maintained by the Church of Jesus Christ of Latter Day Saints in Salt
Lake City, Utah, is a goldmine of information. Their database already has records on six generations of the Beach family, beginning with Giles Beach's
great-grandfather, Amos Beach (1723-1790?). The site is freely available for research.

¹² Deed [first series]: book 6, pp. 185-86, June 1, 1825 [recorded Jan. 23,
1826], between Amos Beach [Sr.] and Olive his wife & Amos Beach [Jr.]; and
deed: book 6, p. 186-87, Nov. 30, 1815 [recorded Jan. 23, 1826], between Ar-
chibald McLaren and Mary his wife & Amos Beach [Jr.].

[13] Sprague, 112.

[14] The 1845 census provides a good image of what the Beach family farm was like: among the livestock Giles tended were 5 cattle, 3 of which provided milk, 200 lbs. of butter, and 200 lbs. of cheese; 15 sheep, providing 36 lbs. of wool, and two hogs. See 1845 New York State Census: Fulton County; Town of Johnstown; dwelling house 54; Amos Beach, head of household.

[15] A plaque over the main portico of the edifice at 255 N. Kingsboro Ave. states: "This church was organized in 1793 as the Congregational Society of Kingsborough and became Presbyterian in 1853. The original church stood in the park until 1838 when this building was erected."

[16] For more information on Yale see William B. Sprague, *Annals of the American pulpit; or commemorative notices of distinguished American clergymen of various denominations… .* Vol. IV, Presbyterian. New York: Robert Carter & Brothers, 1859, 348-53. His pastorate in Kingsborough lasted 49 years, from 1804 to 1853.

[17] Elisha Yale, *Review of a pastorate,* 171, as cited by Palmer; a typescript of this MS is located in the collections of the Presbyterian Historical Society in Philadelphia: record group 141, box 1, folder 16.

[18] "The concert," *Salem* [N.Y.] *Press* 11:47 (Mar. 26, 1861), 2; hereinafter *SP.*

[19] "Concert for the benefit of Trinity Church," 8:4 *Gloversville Intelligencer,* 8:4 (Jan. 29, 1874), 2; hereinafter *GI.*

[20] Palmer.

[21] According to Yale.

[22] *Troy directory for the year 1835-6; containing the names of residents within the first four wards of the city, their professions and occupations; and a list of city and bank officers, etc.* Troy: Published by N. Tuttle, 1835, 5. By 1839, his entry states "piano forte room," and from 1846 to 1850 as "factory" or "organ factory," and in 1851 as "professor of music." A complete list of Backus' Troy directory entries are provided in Table III. Beach does not appear by name in any Troy directory of the period.

[23] "Conservatory of music," [Troy] *Daily Budget* 51:268 (May 10, 1845), 2.

[24] There is no question that these men were collaborating. A Backus advertisement of Oct. 31, 1845, in the [Troy] *Daily Budget* relates: "One [organ] recently set up weights two tons. The North Adams Transcript notices it: 'The Congregational Society in this village have procured a new and valuable Organ.

It is of the manufacture of A. Backus, of Troy, and is rich and powerful enough for a Cathedral. It is a fine piece of workmanship, and reflects credit on the establishment which furnishes such auxiliaries to church music.'" A church history notes that it was purchased of a "Messrs. Andrews of Troy, N.Y.;" see *First Congregational Church, North Adams, Massachusetts. Addresses and papers presented at the Diamond Jubilee 1827-1902, May 11-14.*

[25] Michael D. Friesen, *A survey of Michigan organ builders: from the earliest times to about 1920.* A handout given with his lecture on Aug. 7, 1995, at the 1995 National Convention of the Organ Historical Society, in Ann Arbor, Michigan. By 1860, Backus was located in Grand Rapids, Michigan, where he is listed as being 67, married with six children, and a stove manufacturer by profession. See 1860 Michigan census; Grand Rapids; 3rd ward; dwelling house 930, family 819. He also appears the year before in the 1859 city directory; see C.S. Williams, *Williams' Grand Rapids directory, city guide, and business mirror.* Grand Rapids: P.G. Hodenpyl, 1859, 35, where he is listed as a "stave and shingle manuf. e[ast of] s[outh] Almy b[elow] Island and Oaks, h[ome] c[orner] Fulton and Ransom."

[26] "Organs. A. Backus, Manufacturer of Church and Chamber Organs, Troy, N.Y.," *Troy Daily Whig* 14:4919 (Apr. 22, 1847), 4; hereinafter *TDW.*

[27] "New organ in St. Peter's Church," *TDW* 16:5728 (Dec. 17, 1849), 2.

[28] The congregational minutes of the Reformed Protestant Dutch Church (later the Brighton Heights Reformed), Tompkinsville, S.I., N.Y., note that Beach was "Highly recommended as the best and cheapest organ builder." See also Una Ratmeyer, *A history of the Brighton Heights Reformed Church, formerly the Reformed Dutch Church in Tompkinsville.* Staten Island, N.Y.: [Published by the church], 1978, 52.

[29] 1850 Federal Census: *Schedule 1. – Population.* State of New York, Rensselaer County, City of Troy, 2nd Ward, dwelling house 671, family 1064; he is indexed as Giles Beach, 21 years of age, male, white, an 'organ maker' by profession, born in N.Y. Living in the same household was Anson Beal, aged 17, male, white, an 'organ maker,' born in N.Y., and also a likely Backus apprentice.

[30] 1850 Federal Census: *Schedule 1. – Population.* State of New York, Fulton County, City of Johnstown, dwelling house 950, family 994, Amos Beach, head of household.

[31] *1855 Massachusetts State Census,* Westfield, Mass.; this information was supplied by Martin R. Walsh.

[32] "Organ of the Fifth Street Baptist Church," *Troy Daily Times* 2:649 (June 17, 1853), 2; hereinafter *TDT.*

[33] Between 1839 and 1845, John C. and James W. Andrews appear in Troy city directories both working at the same address, variously 307½ or 186 River St., and living together at 49 Seventh St. It seems hard to escape the conclusion that they were blood relatives, probably father and son. In 1847, the Troy directory has James C. Andrews and Augustus Backus both working in the "boardman buildings." While John C. Andrews died on Aug. 16, 1858, James W. Andrews is later listed in Troy directories as a "teacher of music" until 1905. Presumably, he either retired or died about that time.

[34] A *ca.* 1850 instrument built for the Methodist Church, Rockwood, N.Y., may also be from this period, but the date has not been determined with certainty.

[35] "Organ returned to use – Laurens," [Oneonta, N.Y.] *Daily Star* 94:84 (Sept. 25, 1984), 6. The organ is extant.

[36] The completed building was consecrated Aug. 21, 1849, by Bishop William R. Whittingham (1805-79) of Maryland; see the *Journal of the proceedings of the sixty-fifth convention of the Protestant Episcopal Church in the Diocese of New-York... .* New-York: Daniel Dana, Jr., 1849, 63.

[37] MS, Edward L. Partridge, *Dismantling and restoration of the Grace Church organ, Cherry Valley, New York, January 6, 1964.* An unpublished paper quoted through the courtesy of Kathryn Boardman, Associate Director of Programs, the New York State Historical Association, Farmer's Museum, Cooperstown, N.Y., 17.

[38] For more information on Phelps, see Finch, 77-78, and Leona R. Weir, *History of Christ Church, Guilford, New York, 1830-1955: in commemoration of its 125th anniversary.* Guilford: [published by the church], 1955.

[39] "Dissolution," [Cooperstown, N.Y.] *Watch-Tower* 15:749 (Aug. 4, 1828), 2.

[40] *Journal of the proceedings of the eighty-first convention of the Protestant Episcopal Church in the Diocese of New York, which assembled in St. John's Chapel in the City of New York, on Wednesday, September 28, A.D. 1864.* New York: James Potts, 1864, 207-208.

[41] William T. Van Pelt [compiler], *Hook opus list, 1829-1916 in facsimile... .* Richmond, Virginia: Organ Historical Society, 1991, 84.

[42] "Notes, quotes and comments," *T* 8:4 (Summer, 1964), 14.

[43] The dedication of the building inspired a detailed report in the *New York Times.* The organ, however, was only mentioned in passing: "The organ, built in the 1840s, came from Grace Episcopal Church in nearby Cherry Valley... ." See "Restored church joins scene at Cooperstown," *New York Times,* July 19, 1964, 3.

[44] Yale, *Review of a pastorate,* 171, as cited by Palmer.

[45] Sprague, 112.

[46] Palmer; and deed [second series]: liber 20, pp. 67-68, Apr. 28, 1853 [recorded Mar. 20, 1855], between Giles Beach & James H. Burr and Azubah his wife.

[47] Yale.

[48] *The 150ᵗʰ anniversary of the organization of Saint John's Reformed Church, Saint Johnsville, N.Y., November 7-11, 1920. Reprinted from newspaper articles from the Enterprise and News of November 10-17, 1920.* The organ is not extant.

[49] Edward Waite Miller, *Historical manual of the Kingsborough Ave. Presbyterian Church, Gloversville, N.Y.* [n.p.], *ca.* 1932.

[50] MS, Alan M. Laufman, *Stoplist collection,* AOA.

[51] "Notes, quotes and comments," *T* 5:3 (Apr., 1961), 6.

[52] Three generations of the Beach family are buried in Prospect Hill Cemetery, Gloversville, N.Y., Lot 35, Section H, just across from the intersection of Woodward and Kingsboro[ugh] Aves. The plot has a central granite monument surmounted by a finial flanked by smaller individual markers. Another plot in the cemetery contains the remains of Estelle C., Beach's daughter.

[53] 1857 Gloversville business directory – a map.

[54] 1860 Federal Census: *Schedule 5. – Products of Industry.* State of New York, Fulton County, City of Johnstown, Giles Beach, organ builder. Scot L. Huntington points out that this is an enormous amount of lumber. Could Beach also have included the lumber he used to build the shop?; or, did he include *all* the lumber used since he established his business?

[55] "Mr. Giles Beach," *SP* 11:46 (Mar. 19, 1861), 2.

[56] This instrument is mentioned in passing in "New organ for Troy," *TDT* 13:135 (Dec. 1, 1864), 3.

⁵⁷ "Second Presbyterian Church," *Newark* [N.J.] *Daily Advertiser* 32:189 (Sept. 7, 1862), 2.

⁵⁸ Deed [second series]: liber 29, pp. 448-49, Dec. 17, 1861 [recorded Jan. 21, 1864], between Giles Beach & Bostwick Hawley and Elizabeth R. his wife.

⁵⁹ Deed [second series]: liber 30, p. 83, Jan. 8, 1864 [recording date not indicated on the deed], between Giles Beach and Charlotte C. his wife & William F. Steele; liber 31, p. 389, May 2, 1865 [recorded May 27, 1865], between Giles Beach and Charlotte his wife & Solomon Jeffers; and liber 33, p. 151, May 2, 1865 [recorded May 14, 1866], between Giles Beach and Charlotte his wife & Michael Kennedy.

⁶⁰ "New organ in Troy," *TDT* 13:135 (Dec. 1, 1864), 3.

⁶¹ *Convention Handbook* (1967), 43-44; the organ, currently in Our Saviour's Lutheran Church, Troy, was visited by the Twelfth Annual Convention of the Organ Historical Society on June 22, 1967; the organ was demonstrated by Boadway.

⁶² "Organ exhibition," *Richmond County Gazette* 6:52 (Feb. 1, 1865), 3.

⁶³ "Congregation of the Schaghticoke Presbyterian Church," *TDT* 14:81 (Sept. 21, 1865), 3.

⁶⁴ 1865 New York State Census: *Industry other than Agriculture.* State of New York, Fulton County, City of Johnstown, 2ⁿᵈ election district, Giles Beach, Organs.

⁶⁵ "New organ," *Cohoes Cataract* 18:42 (Oct. 20, 1866), 3; and "Organ concert," *CC* 18:49 (Dec. 8, 1866), 3.

⁶⁶ "Waterford," *TDT* 14:266 (May 8, 1866), 3; and 14:268 (May 10, 1866), 3.

⁶⁷ "Organ exhibition," *TDT* 14:226 (Mar. 22, 1866), 3.

⁶⁸ *Ibid.*, *TDT* 14:227 (Mar. 23, 1866), 3.

⁶⁹ William H. Hollister, *Second Presbyterian Church of Troy, N.Y.: historical sketch prepared and read at the opening of the auditorium, October 3, 1915.* Troy: Published by direction of the Session, [1917], 52.

⁷⁰ MS, E.A. Boadway, *Stoplist collection;* used with permission of the author.

⁷¹ See also *Gazetteer and business directory of Montgomery and Fulton Counties, N.Y., for 1869-70. Compiled and published by Hamilton Child.* Syracuse: Printed at the Journal Office, 1870, 235, where the firm is listed as "Beach & Moore,

(Gloversville,) (Giles Beach and Stephen Moore,) dealers in musical instruments, books and stationary, 23 Bleeker."

[72] "Musical instruments," *GI* 4:3 (Jan. 26, 1870), 3.

[73] 1870 Federal Census – *Schedule 1: Population*. State of New York, County Fulton, City of Johnstown, dwelling house 816, family 1145, Stephen Moore, head of household.

[74] "Dedication," *GI* 4:10 (Mar. 16, 1870), 2.

[75] "Organ concert," *Amsterdam* [N.Y.] *Recorder* 17:9 (June 15, 1870), 3; hereinafter *AR*.

[76] Deeds [second series]: liber 37, p. 491, Oct. 9, 1869 [recorded Oct. 29, 1869], between Giles Beach & George A. Butler and Elizabeth; liber 40, pp. 244-45, May 6, 1870 [recorded, Aug. 18, 1870], between Giles Beach & Selina B. Churchill [et al.]; and liber 40, pp 245-46, May 6, 1870 [recorded Aug. 18, 1870], between Giles Beach & Henry Churchill and Ella his wife.

[77] "Large fire," *FCR*, Oct. 5, 1876, 2.

[78] Palmer.

[79] *Ibid.*

[80] 1875 New York State Census: *V. Industry other than Agricultural*. County Fulton, City Johnstown, 2nd election district, for the year 1874.

[81] "Handsome testimonial," *GI* 5:8 (Mar. 9, 1871), 2.

[82] "Grand concert and organ exhibition," *Paterson* [N.J.] *Daily Press* 17:2577 (Jan. 31, 1872), 3; "Entertainments," *PDP* 17:2579 (Feb. 2, 1872), 3; and "Organ concert," *PDP* 17:2580 (Feb. 3, 1872), 3.

[83] "Masonic assemblage in the new temple," *TDT* 21:235 (Mar. 30, 1872), 3.

[84] "Troy Masonic Hall Dedication," *GI* 6:15 (Apr. 11, 1872), 2.

[85] "Messrs. Beach & Co.," *Daily Saratogian* 3:137 (Feb. 28, 1872), 3; hereinafter *DS*.

[86] "New M.E. Church," *DS* 3:154 (Mar. 19, 1872), 3.

[87] "New Lutheran Church," *GI* 6:23 (June 6, 1872), 3.

[88] "Business men of Gloversville," *GI* 6:6 (Feb. 8, 1872), 2.

[89] "Fonda matters," *AR* 20:32 (Nov. 19, 1873), 3; *Ibid.*, 20:34 (Dec. 3, 1873), 3; *Ibid.*, 20:35 (Dec. 10, 1873), 3; and "The concert," *AR* 20:36 (Dec. 17, 1873), 3.

90 "The organ," *Herkimer* [N.Y.] *Democrat* 32:30 (Mar. 11, 1874), 3; and "Grand organ concert," *HD* 32:31 (Mar. 18, 1874), 3.

91 "Church organ," *GI* 7:52 (Dec. 25, 1873), 2.

92 "Large fire," *GI*, Oct. 6, 1876, 2.

93 Margaret Boulet, *St. Francis de Sales: a proud tradition, 1854-1992.* Bennington, Vermont: Published by St. Francis de Sales, 1992, 96.

94 United States Patent Office. *Improvement on paper organ-pipes.* Letters Patent No. 213,612, dated March 25, 1879; application filed April 5, 1878.

95 "Giles Beach," *Music Trades,* June 28, 1902.

96 "The contract to enlarge," *Music Trades,* Aug. 29, 1903.

97 "Evangelical Lutheran Church," *Boston Organ Club Newsletter* 16:2 (Fall-Winter, 1980), 11-12.

98 The rededication program is extant in the collections of the American Organ Archives of the Organ Historical Society. The organ was actually built for Trinity Evangelical Lutheran Church in Troy, N.Y., and was purchased by the Raymertown congregation second-hand in Nov., 1944.

99 "Giles Beach," *FCR,* Sept. 13, 1906, 7.

100 "Late Giles Beach," [Johnstown and Gloversville] *Morning Herald,* Sept. 13, 1906, 5.

101 "Obituary – Giles Beach," [Gloversville] *Daily Leader,* Sept. 10, 1906, 5.

102 "The late Giles Beach," *Albany Argus,* Sept. 14, 1906, 6.

103 Stephen L. Pinel [compiler]. *The Organ Historical Society in conjunction with the Round Lake Historical Society presents the Upper Hudson Valley Mini-Convention, August 3-6, 1997... .* Round Lake, N.Y.: Round Lake Historical Society, 1997, 30-32.

104 Paul R. Marchesano, "Notable birthday party and something more," *Northeast Organist* 7:6 (Nov.-Dec., 1997), 15.

The 1867 one-manual organ built by Giles Beach for the First Presbyterian Church, Green Island, New York, as shown in the Dyer-Phelps A.M.E. Church in Saratoga Springs, New York, about 1978.
– *Photograph by Robert C. Newton courtesy of S.L. Huntington & Co., Stonington, Conn.*

The *ca.* 1860 one-manual organ built by Giles Beach for St. Luke's Church,
Episcopal, in Cambridge, New York. It was moved second-hand to the
United Methodist Church of North Marion, Massachusetts, about 1910, when St. Luke's
bought a new organ built by the Austin Organ Company, their Opus 260 (1911).
– *Photograph courtesy of William T. Van Pelt and the Organ Historical Society.*

TABLE I:

KNOWN ORGANS BUILT BY
GILES BEACH, 1849-1876, ORIGINAL LOCATIONS.

STATE:					
LOCATION:	PATRON:		DATE:	SIZE:	PRICE:

MINNESOTA:

Minneapolis?	Unknown[1]				

NEW JERSEY:

Newark	Second Presbyterian (Dr. Smith's)		1863	2	
Paterson	Market St. Methodist Episcopal[2]		1872	2	$3,500

NEW YORK:

Amsterdam	Second Presbyterian[3]		1870	2	$3,500
Broadalbin	Presbyterian			1	
Cambridge	Baptist			1?	
Cambridge	St. Luke's, Episcopal[4]		1860?	1	
Canajoharie	Methodist Episcopal		1864	1?	
Cherry Valley	Grace Church, Episcopal[5]		1849	1	$250
Cohoes	Dutch Reformed		1866	3	
Fonda	Dutch Reformed of Caughnawaga		1873	2	$2,000
Gloversville	First Baptist		1865?	2	
Gloversville	First Congregational		1864	2	
Gloversville	First Methodist Episcopal		1870		
Gloversville	Freemont St. Methodist				
Gloversville	Kingsborough Presbyterian[6]		1857	2	
Gloversville	Masonic Lodge[7]		1875?	2	
Green Island	First Presbyterian[8]		1867	1	
Green Island	Hudson Ave. Methodist Episcopal		1875	1	
Herkimer	First Methodist Episcopal		1874	2	$3,000
Johnstown	First Methodist Episcopal		1871?	2	
Johnstown	St. Paul's Lutheran		1872	2	$3,000
Johnstown	Unknown				

Lake George	Methodist Episcopal	1860?	1	
Laurens	Presbyterian	1850?	1	
Montour Falls[9]	Presbyterian	1871	2?	
New York City	Forty-Third St. Baptist	1862?	2?	
Rockwood	Methodist Episcopal	1850?	1?	
Salem	First Presbyterian ("Brick")	1861	1?	
Saratoga Springs	First Methodist Episcopal[10]	1872	3	$5,000
Schaghticoke	First Presbyterian[11]	1865	2	
St. Johnsville	St. John's Reformed[12]	1853	1	$500
Tompkinville, S.I.	Reformed Protestant Dutch	1865	2	$2,000
Troy	Fifth St. Presbyterian[13]	1866	3	$6,000
Troy	Masonic Temple[14]	1872	2	
Troy	Unitarian[15]	1864	2	
Waterford	First Presbyterian	1866	2	

TABLE II:

SUSPECTED ORGANS BUILT BY
GILES BEACH, 1849-1876, ORIGINAL LOCATIONS.

STATE:				
LOCATION:	PATRON:	DATE:	SIZE:	PRICE:

NEW YORK:

Amsterdam	East Main St. Methodist[16]			
Amsterdam	First Baptist	1874?	1?	
Amsterdam	First Presbyterian	1867?	1?	
Fort Plain	Lutheran			
Frankfort	Baptist		1	
Hoosick Falls	First Presbyterian	1867?	1?	
Stillwater	Presbyterian	1870?	2	

:: N O T E S ::

[1] Palmer stated that Beach built an organ for Minnesota, but the location has not been identified.

[2] In 1914, this organ was sold second-hand to the Methodist Church, Butler, N.J., and was ultimately replaced in 1965 with a new organ built by the Peragallo Organ Company of Paterson, N.J., their Opus 426.

[3] This organ was replaced by Ernest M. Skinner, his Opus 483 (1924), a four-manual organ, retaining the 1870 Beach case in the rear gallery; the entire building was destroyed by fire *ca.* 1997.

[4] This instrument was later relocated to North Marion, Massachusetts, where it was examined by Peter T. Cameron about 1979. It has one manual and six ranks, and is slated to be visited at the Fiftieth Annual Convention of the Organ Historical Society during the summer of 2005.

[5] Replaced with a new organ built by Hook & Hastings, their Opus 1997 (1903), a two-manual organ, the Beach organ remained in the rear gallery unused. In 1964, it was moved to the Cornwallville Methodist Church on the grounds of the Farmer's Museum in Cooperstown, N.Y., where it was restored and installed by Sidney Chase; it remains there.

[6] The Kingsborough Presbyterian Church closed in 1980, and became the Kingsboro Assembly of God.

[7] Later, this organ was moved by Paul C. Buhl in 1921 to St. Patrick's R.C. Church in St. Johnsville, N.Y., where it was ultimately destroyed *ca.* 1970. The stoplist was recorded by E.A. Boadway.

[8] This organ was relocated to the Dyer-Phelps A.M.E. Church, Saratoga Springs, N.Y., by M.P. Möller, Opus 1176, a one-manual organ with eleven registers. When the Saratoga church closed about 1978, the organ went into private hands, and was ultimately purchased by S.L. Huntington & Co., of Stonington, Conn.; it is currently in storage, awaiting restoration.

[9] Originally, the community was known as Havana, N.Y.

[10] This organ was moved second-hand to the Methodist Episcopal Church, Mayfield, N.Y., about 1919 when the Saratoga Church acquired a new organ built by the Austin Organ Co., Opus 952 (1920), a four-manual organ. Robert

Rowland worked on the organ in 1929; the instrument is now gone.

¹¹ This is the largest and best remaining example of Beach's work.

¹² In 1871, this organ was moved to the rear gallery of St. Paul's Lutheran Church, St. Johnsville, N.Y., and in 1923, it was rebuilt by Robert Rowland. In 1947, it was moved to the Baptist Church, Schenevus, N.Y., where it disappeared about two years later. See: "Some Rowland Correspondence," *Tracker* 15:1 (Fall, 1970), 5.

¹³ This instrument was moved second-hand to the Congregational Church, Whitman, Mass. in 1906, and was ultimately destroyed there *ca.* 1980.

¹⁴ It later burned with the building.

¹⁵ The church became Our Saviour's Lutheran Church; the organ is extant, but in very poor condition. It was visited at the Twelfth Annual Convention of the Organ Historical Society on June 22, 1967.

¹⁶ This organ was not original to this location, as it was clearly second-hand in Amsterdam. It was later rebuilt by Robert Rowland in 1925, and sold to the Methodist Episcopal Church of Bloomville, N.Y.

TABLE III:

ENTRIES FOR JAMES W. ANDREWS, JOHN C. ANDREWS,
AND AUGUSTUS BACKUS IN TROY DIRECTORIES
BETWEEN 1835 AND 1852, SHOWING COMMON ADDRESSES.

YEARS: LOCATION:

1835-36:[1]

> Andrews John C., music store, 3 washington square
>
> Backus Augustus, music teacher, h. 54 state

1837-38:

> Andrews John C., music store, 7 cannon place, h. 49 7th
>
> Backus Augustus, music teacher, h. 129 second

1838-39:

> Andrews John C., prof. music, 7 cannon place, h 49 7th
>
> Backus Augustus, prof. music, h 129 second

1839-40:

> Andrews James W., piano for. tuner, 307½ riv., b. 49 7th
>
> Andrews John C., prof. music, music store 307½ river, h. 49 seventh
>
> Backus Augustus, piano forte room 48 congress, up stairs, h. 129 second

1840-41:

> Andrews James W., piano forte tuner, 186 riv., b. 32 7th
>
> Andrews John C., prof. music, music store 186 river, h. 32 seventh
>
> Backus Augustus, piano forte room 184 river, up stairs, h. 129 second

1841-42:

> Andrews James W., piano forte tuner, 186 riv., b 32 7th
>
> Andrews John C., prof. music, music store 186 river, h. 32 seventh
>
> Backus Augustus, prof. of music, piano forte room 184 river, h 129 second

1842-43:

> Andrews James W., piano forte tuner, 186 riv., b. 174 4th
>
> Andrews John C., prof. music, piano forte wareroom 186 river, h 32 seventh

Backus Augustus, chemical oil lamps, 293[# with no street], h. 108 river

1843-44:

Andrews James W., music store, 232 river, b 32 seventh

Andrews John C., prof. music, piano forte wareroom 232 river, h 32 seventh

Backus Augustus, prof. music, h 108 river

1844-45:[2]

Andrews James W., music store, 253 river, b 32 seventh

Andrews John C., prof. music, pianoforte wareroom 253 river, h 32 seventh

Backus Augustus, prof. music, h 19 river

1845-46:

Andrews James W., music store, 253 river, b 32 seventh

Andrews John C., prof. music, pianoforte wareroom 253 river, h 32 seventh

Backus Augustus, prof. music, h 19 river

1846-47:

Andrews James W., music store, 253 river

Andrews John C., prof. music, pianoforte wareroom 96½ second, h 32 seventh

Backus Augustus, prof. music, h corner grand division and eighth, factory south troy

1847-48: [3]

Andrews James W., music store 253 river, h 32 7th

Andrews John C., professor in music, pianoforte wareroom 9 boardman buildings, h 32 seventh

Backus Augustus, prof. music, h corner grand div. and eighth, factory boardman buildings

1847-48:[4]

Andrews James W., music store, 253 river, b 32 7th

Andrews John C., prof. music, pianoforte saloon, 9 boardman buildings

Backus Augustus, prof. music, h corner grand division and eighth, factory south troy

1848-49:

> Andrews James W., music store, 253 river, b 8 albany
>
> Andrews John C., professor music, pianoforte wareroom 9 boardman buildings, h 32 seventh
>
> Backus Augustus, prof. music, h corner grand division and eighth, organ factory rear boardman buildings

1849-50:

> Andrews James W., music store, 225 river, b 8 albany
>
> Andrews John C., professor music, music academy, 32 congress, h 32 7th
>
> Backus Augustus, prof. music, h 4 lafayette place, organ factory rear boardman's buildings

1850-51:[5]

> Andrews James W., music store, 218 river, h 6 clinton place
>
> Andrews John C., professor music, music academy, morris place, up stairs, h 32 seventh
>
> Backus Augustus, prof. music, h 4 lafayette place, organ factory 5 grand division

1851-52:[6]

> Andrews James W., sole agent for chickerings, hallet and allen's piano fortes, also dealer in music, violin strings, and musical instruments, music store 218 river, h 91 fifth
>
> Andrews John C., jr., b 32 seventh
>
> Backus Augustus, prof. music, h Lafayette place

1852:[7]

> Andrews James W., Music and Musical Instruments, W. 218 River

1852-53:[8]

> Andrews James W., sole agent for chickerings, hallet and allen's piano fortes, also dealer in music, violin strings, and musical instruments, music store 218 river, h 91 fifth
>
> [no entry for either John C. Andrews or Augustus Backus]

1852-53:[9]

> Andrews James W., music store 218 river, h 91 fifth
>
> [no entry for either John C. Andrews or Augustus Backus]

: : N O T E S : :

[1]   *The Troy directory, for the year 1835-6: containing the names of residents within the first four wards of the city, their professions and occupations; and a list of city and bank officers, &c.* Troy: Printed and published by N. Tuttle, 1835. The reader can assume the format of the directory is consistent for the entries following until a new footnote provides different authors and new publishing information.

[2]   *Tuttle's city directory for the year 1844-5, containing the names of residents, with their trades and occupations: and a list of city and bank officers, &c.* Troy: N. Tuttle, Printer and Publisher, 1844.

[3]   *Kneeland's Troy directory, 1847-8, containing the names of residents, with their occupations and professions, and a list of city and county officers, banks, and other public institutions.* Troy: J.C. Kneeland & Co., Printers and Publishers, 1847.

[4]   *Prescott & Wilson's Troy city directory, for 1847-48: containing the names of residents, with their occupations and professions; and a list of city and bank officers, &c., &c.* Troy: Prescott & Wilson, Printers and Publishers, 1847.

[5]   *John F. Prescott's city and business directory for 1850-1.* Troy: John F. Prescott, Printer and Publisher, 1850.

[6]   *C. L. Mac Arthur's reliable Troy directory, for the years 1851-52. Containing the names of residents, with their trades and places of business; together with a list of city officers, &c., &c.* Troy: Chas. L. Mac Arthur, Printer and Publisher, 1851.

[7]   *Troy and Albany County business directory containing the census for 1850 and of each city in the union.* Troy: Merriman Moore & Co., 1852.

[8]   *C. L. Mac Arthur's reliable Troy directory for the years 1852-3. Containing the names of residents, with their trades and places of business; together with a list of city officers, &c., &c.* Troy: Chas. L. Mac Arthur, Printer and Publisher, 1852.

[9]   *Wilson & Ryan's Troy directory, for 1852-3: containing the names of residents, with their occupations and professions: a list of city and county officers, &c., &c.* Troy: Wilson & Ryan, Printers and Publishers, 1852.

TABLE IV:

EMPLOYEES OF GILES BEACH, 1850-1876.

The following list of employees (and workers) has been reconstructed from city directories, state and federal census documents, and newspaper articles.

NAMES:	DATES:	TITLE:	DOCUMENTATION:
Beach, Charles S.	1871?-76+	Son	1873 directory,[1] and Palmer
Billingham, Myron W.	1865	Employee	1865 state census[2]
Billingham, Willis	1865	Employee	1865 state census[3]
Fosmire, Henry	1860-76+	Employee	1860 federal,[4] 1865 state,[5] 1870 federal census,[6] newspaper references,[7] and after 1876, Fosmire continues to be listed in city directories as a "carpenter."
Luederwald, Beno	1873-76+	Employee	1873 directory,[8] 1875 state census,[9] and after 1876, Leuderwald continues to be listed as an "organ builder."
Marriott, Charles	1873-75	Employee	1873 directory,[10] 1875 state census[11]
Mills, William	1850	Laborer	1850 federal census,[12] could he be the William Mills that later shows up in New York City working for Henry Erben?

Moore, Stephen	1865–76+	Partner	1865 state census,[13] 1870 federal census,[14] 1875 state census,[15] Gloversville directories,[16] newspaper references,[17] and after 1876, he continues to be listed in city directories as an "organ builder."
Morris, Jason E.	1860–65	Employee	1860 federal[18] and 1865 state census[19]
Pettee, William	1875	Employee	1875 state census,[20] also an organist.
Royckey, Otto	1873	Employee	1873 directory[21]

+ = *continues to be listed in Gloversville directories after 1876.*

:: N O T E S ::

[1] *The Gloversville and Johnstown directory, comprising a list of residents, churches and their officers, secret societies, miscellaneous organizations, and much other matter of local interest.* New Haven: Henry Bradley, 1873, 36.

[2] Johnstown, 2nd election district, dwelling house 197, family 226: Myron W. Billingham (Son of Willis Billingham), aged 19, single, listed his profession as "organ builder," works in Gloversville. The reader can assume that all references to the census that follow are from the State of New York and Fulton County.

[3] Johnstown, 2nd election district, dwelling house 197, family 226: Willis Billingham, aged 41, married, a native of Connecticut, owner of land, listed his profession as "organ builder," works in Gloversville. Sprague (p. 110) notes that he was born June 20, 1824, and married Martha Clark on Dec. 23, 1846.

[4] Johnstown, dwelling house 1340, family 1354: Fosmire, aged 37, married, a native of N.Y., listed his profession as "Organ Business."

⁵   Johnstown, 2ⁿᵈ election district, dwelling house 208, family 265: Fosmire, aged 42, married, owner of land, a native of N.Y., listed his profession as "organ builder."

⁶   Johnstown, dwelling house 735, family 976: Fosmire, aged 47, married, listed his profession as "carpenter."

⁷   When the factory burned in 1876, the local newspaper notes that Henry Fosmire "lost all his tools." See "Large fire," *Fulton County Republican*, Oct. 5, 1876, 2.

⁸   1873 directory, 66.

⁹   Johnstown, 2ⁿᵈ election district, dwelling house 311, family 441: B. Luederwald, aged 35, married, a native of Germany, listed his profession as "Organ Builder."

¹⁰   1873 directory, 69.

¹¹   Johnstown, 2ⁿᵈ election district, dwelling house 485, family 685: Charles Marriott, aged 46, married, a native of England, listed his profession as "organ builder."

¹²   Johnstown, dwelling house 950, family 994: Mills was living in the household of Amos Beach, Jr., aged 19, was a native of Scotland, listed his profession as "laborer."

¹³   Johnstown, 2ⁿᵈ election district, dwelling house 129, family 152: Stephen Moore, aged 28, married, a native of England, listed his profession as "Organ Builder."

¹⁴   Johnstown, dwelling house 816, family 1145: Moore, aged 34, married, a native of England, listed his profession as "Organ Manuf."

¹⁵   Johnstown, 4ᵗʰ election district, dwelling house 238, family 355: Moore, aged 40, married, a native of England, listed his profession as "Organ Maker."

¹⁶   1873 directory, 70.

¹⁷   When the factory burned in 1876, a reference in the newspaper notes that Stephen Moore "lost all his tools." See "Large fire," *Fulton County Republican*, Oct. 5, 1876, 2.

¹⁸   Johnstown, dwelling house 1339, family 1353: Morris was living in the household of Giles Beach, aged 19, a native of Connecticut, listed his profession as "organ business."

[19] Johnstown, 2nd election district, dwelling house 129, family 151: Morris, aged 24, married, a native of Connecticut, listed his profession as "Organ Builder."

[20] Johnstown, 4th election district, dwelling house 250, family 376: Wm. Pettee, aged 36, married, a native of Massachusetts, listed his profession as "Organ Maker."

[21] 1873 directory, 78.

TABLE V:
ORGANS BY GILES BEACH, 1849-1872,
SELECTED DESCRIPTIONS.

ORIGINAL LOCATION [★ = EXTANT] AND DATE:

DESCRIPTION AND/OR STOPLIST:

SOURCE(S):

★GILES BEACH (1849)
Grace Church, Episcopal
Cherry Valley, New York

Manual, GG, AA-f[3], 58 notes:

Open Diapason [Treble]	Principal
Stopped Diapason Treble	Fifteenth
Stopped Diapason [Bass]	

Source: Edward L. Partridge, *Dismantling and restoration of the Grace Church organ, Cherry Valley, New York, January 6, 1964.* An unpublished paper provided by the courtesy of Kathryn Boardman, Associate Director of Programs, New York State Historical Association, Cooperstown, N.Y., Aug. 25, 1997.

★ GILES BEACH (1857)

Kingsborough Presbyterian Church
Gloversville, New York

GREAT: C-g³, 56 notes:

Open Diapason: *C-A♯, zinc; B-G³, common metal, dubbed mouths. Façade pipes
  have Roman mouths, large half-round ears, new aluminum tuning inserts to
  replace broken-off zinc tuners, zinc tubing from chest to impost.*
Dulciana: *from tenor f; common metal.*
Clarabella: *pine to top, inverted mouths, low cut-ups; from tenor f long blocks, walnut
  caps and blocks, screwed-on caps to top.*
Std. Diapason Bass: *C-e°, stopped wood pipes; painted pine, screwed walnut caps.*
Principal: *C-B zinc bodies with soldered in spitzlabium, common metal feet (dubbed
  lower lips); c°-g³ common metal, dubbed mouths.*
Flute: *from tenor c; on rear-most slider; identical to Clarabella; open wood to g², 12
  open metal trebles.*
Twelfth: *from tenor c; common metal; ¼ mouths, narrower scale than 2'.*
Gt. Fifteenth: *common metal; dubbed mouths; C labeled "CC 15ᵗʰ July 21ˢᵗ 1857".*

SWELL: C-g³, 56 notes: *39 note chest, enclosed: f°-a♯° diatonic, "W" pipe layout;
  b°-g³, diatonic, "A" layout. Pine swell box, 5 horizontal shades. Swell Std. Diap.
  Bass chest located behind Great walkboard: C-e°, diatonic, "N" layout.*

Open Diapason: *common metal, dubbed mouths.*
Viol de Gamba: *common metal, narrow scale, dubbed mouths.*
Sw. Std. Diap. Treble: *f°-a♯° stopped wood; b°-g³ common metal chimney flutes,
  soldered caps, ear tuned, long, narrow chimneys.*
Std. Diap. Bass: *pine, screwed-on walnut caps.*
Principal: *missing original label, Dymo plastic insert labeled "Dulcet 4", pipes
  marked "Princ.", common metal, dubbed mouths.*
[empty slide]: *stop action installed (disconnected), but no shank, knob, or hole in jamb.*

PEDAL: C-c¹, 25 notes [original pedal board compass 17 notes].

Pedal Bourdon: *C-e°, 17 pipes; pine, screwed-on walnut caps; top 6 pipes tubed off
  on wooden conductor toeboard blocks.*

COUPLERS:

Swell to Great: *cam coupler between keyboards.*
Great to Pedal: *operates stickers from backfall to key tails.*

Source: Examination of extant organ by Scot L. Huntington and the author, Jan. 28, 2005.

GILES BEACH (1864)
Reformed Protestant Dutch Church
Tompkinsville, S.I., New York

The Organ, which is, beyond all comparison, the largest and finest instrument on the Island, was built by Mr. Giles Beach, of Gloversville, N.Y., and contains nearly 1,000 pipes, 2 sets of manuals, 25 pedals, and 28 registers, as follows:

GREAT ORGAN.

1. Open Diapason.
2. Principal.
3. Twelfth.
4. Fifteenth.
5. Wald Flute.
6. Dulciana.
7. Clarabella.
8. Stopped Diapason Bass.
9. Clarionet.
10. Trumpet.

SWELL ORGAN.

11. Open Diapason.
12. Principal.
13. Cornet (2 ranks).
14. Stopped Diapason Treble.
15. Stopped Diapason Bass.
16. Bourdon.
17. Keraulophon.
18. Viol de Gamba.
19. Hautboy.
20. Tremulant.
21. Violin.

PEDAL ORGAN.

22. Grand Open Diapason (16 feet).
23. Grand Stopped Diapason (8 feet).

COUPLERS, ETC.

24. Great to Swell (octaves).
25. Great to Swell (unison).
26. Bellows Signal.
26. Great to Pedals.
27. Swell to Pedals.

Source: "Grand Organ Exhibition," *Richmond County Gazette* 6:52 (Feb. 1, 1864), 3.

*GILES BEACH (1864)
Unitarian Church
Troy, New York

A NEW ORGAN IN TROY. – The organ just erected in the Unitarian church in this city deserves a more particular notice than we have given it. It is true, it is not of a large size compared with the first-class organs in our largest churches, but as far as the size allows, we believe it will bear comparison with them in regard to excellence. The external design was drawn by Mr. Cummings, of this city, an architect whose talents and taste are well known in some of the finest buildings which the city presents. The case of the organ is of black walnut, to correspond with the wood work of the interior of the church, and the front exhibits the Open Diapason pipes of the Great organ in three compartments, gilt.

The number of stops is twenty-two; of which sixteen are speaking stops. The schedule presents, in the Swell organ, Open Diapason, Stopped Diapasons, Principal, Viol de Gamba, Kalaphone, and Hautboy; in the Pedal organ, the Double Stop Diapason; and in the Great organ, the Open and Stopped Diapasons, Principal, Dulciana, Clarabella, Wald Flute, Twelfth and Fifteenth. A Tremulant is added to the Swell, and there are three couplers, Pedal to Great organ, Swell to Great, and Pedal to Swell. The Kalaphone is, we understand, a new stop of the invention of the builder, voiced a little differently from the Viol de Gamba and the Dulciana, being made a little more clear, and adapted especially for solo use.

In respect to the character of the tones of the organ, each stop from the softest to the loudest is perfect in its kind, and is so delicately voiced as to be capable of use in solo passages, while all together are made to blend with excellent consistency. The Diapasons are very rich and full in tone, while wholly free from any extraneous noise. The flutes are silvery and clear. The Hautboy is especially to be commended for its purity of tone and freedom from the usual unpleasant quality of reed stops. The pedal Sub-Bass is deep and pervading, and distinct without being ponderous and overpowering.

The Viol de Gamba and Kalaphone, in the Swell, and Dulciana, in the Great organ, are fine specimens of the string tone. As a whole, from the fundamental Diapasons to the lightest stops of the register, the tone and volume build up grandly; the noble mission of the service of the organ in church worship not being lost sight of or impaired. We regard this organ as excellently adapted to the church in which it is placed, and as a perfect instrument of its kind.

It is proper to speak of the mechanical work. Mechanics, skilled to judge who have examined it, approve most heartily the accuracy and fidelity of the workmanship, and those who are best acquainted with the builder, Mr. G. Beach, of Gloversville, Fulton County, in this State, say that he puts his conscience into his work. They aver that he is a man who never slights what he undertakes, and is as faithful in what is most removed from observation as in what is never likely to attract attention. He is comparatively a young man, and apparently more solicitous to do his work well than to secure a reputation or acquire money. He has lately erected large organs at Staten Island, in the Presbyterian church of Rev. Dr. Smith, Newark, N.J., and in the Forty-Third street Baptist church, New York. He is also erecting one in his own town, Gloversville. Several organs of his construction are known also in the large villages and county towns within a few miles of this city. Arrangements will be made in a few days to give the musical public of the city an opportunity to hear the new instrument.

Source: "New organ," *Troy Daily Times* 13:135 (Dec. 1, 1864), 3.

★GILES BEACH (1865)
First Presbyterian Church
Schaghticoke, New York

Great Organ: C-g³, 56 notes.

Open Diapason	8'	56	pipes.
Dulciana	8'	56	"
Clarabella [t.c.]	8'	44	"
Stop'd Diapason Bass	8'	12	"
Principal	4'	56	"
Twelfth	2⅔'	56	"
Fifteenth	2'	56	"
Trumpet Treble [t.f.]	8'	39	"
Trumpet Bass	8'	17	"
Clarionette [t.c.]	8'	44	"

Swell Organ: C-g³, 56 notes.

Bourdon [t.c.]	16'	44	"
Open Daipason [t.c.]	8'	44	"
Viola de Gamba [t.c.]	8'	44	"
Stop'd Diapason Treble [t.c.]	8'	44	"
Stop'd Diapason Bass	8'	12	"
Keraulophon [t.c.]	8'	44	"
Principal	4'	56	"
Flageolette [t.c.]	2'	44	"
Cornet	II	112	"
Hautboy [t.c.]	8'	44	"

Pedal Organ: C-c¹, 25 notes.

Double Open Diapason	16'	25	"
Double Stop'd Diapason	16'	25	"
Violoncello	8'	25	"

Couplers:

Swell to Great.
Swell to Great Octaves.
Great to Pedal.
Swell to Pedal.

Sources: *Convention Handbook: the Organ Historical Society in conjunction with the Round Lake Historical Society presents the Upper Hudson Valley Mini-Convention, August 3-6, 1997.* Round Lake, N.Y.: Round Lake Historical Society, 1997, 30-31; and Thomas L. Finch, "Organ building in Upstate New York in the nineteenth century," *The Bicentennial Tracker* (1976), 73-74.

GILES BEACH (1866)
Fifth Street (Second) Presbyterian Church
Troy, New York

GREAT, C-g³, 56 notes (knobs in upper right-hand jamb)

Open Diapason 16 ft.	60 pipes; C-D♯ large-scale 8′ open wood pipes with stopped "monkey-quint" helpers at 5⅓′ pitch, non-original stop label
1ˢᵗ. Open Diapason	56 pipes; non-original stop label
Döppel Flute.	56 pipes; stopped wood, double mouths from c°
Clarabella.	56 pipes; wood
Bell Gamba.	56 pipes
Principal.	56 pipes
Harmonic Flute.	56 pipes; tapered, open metal
Twelfth.	56 pipes
Fifteenth.	56 pipes
Sesquialtra [*sic*].	168 pipes; C: 17-19-22; c¹; 12-15-17 to top
Trumpet.	56 pipes; 7 open metal trebles

SWELL, C-g³, 56 notes (knobs in upper left-hand jamb)

Bourdon.	56 pipes; stopped wood, C-B unenclosed
Open Diapason.	[44 pipes?]; large scale
Stop. Diapason Treble.	44 pipes; from c°, capped metal with chimneys
Stop. Diapason Bass.	12 pipes; stopped wood
Melodia.	44 pipes; from c°, open wood
Viol D'Gamba.	44 pipes; from c°
Principal.	56 pipes
Piffaro.	112 pipes; 4′ open pipes + 2′ open wood Melodia with 20 open metal trebles
Cornett.	168 pipes; 12-15-17 throughout; principal scale
Cornopean.	56 pipes; 7 open metal trebles

Hautboy.   56 pipes; 7 open metal trebles
Tremulant.

CHOIR, C-g³, 56 notes (knobs in lower right-hand jamb)
Open Diapason.   [56 pipes?]
Stop Diapason.   56 pipes
Keraulophon.   56 pipes
Dulciana.   56 pipes
Violin.   56 pipes; 4′ open metal
Wald Flute.   56 pipes; 4′ open wood
Clarinette.   44 pipes; from c°, 7 open metal trebles
Unused stop-shank hole

PEDAL, C-d¹, 27 notes (knobs in lower left-hand jamb)
Double Open Diap.   27 pipes; large-scale open wood (19″ x 19 ½″)
Double Stop. Diap.   27 pipes; stopped wood
Double Dulciana.   27 pipes; en *façade*
Violoncello.   27 pipes; 8′ open metal

COUPLERS AND MECHANICALS (knobs in lower left-hand jamb)
Swell to Great. Un.
Swell to Great. 8ves.
Choir to Great.
Great to Pedals.
Swell to Pedals.
Choir to Pedals.
Swell to Choir. (right-hand jamb)
Bellows Signal. (right-hand jamb, Hook & Hastings stop knob and label)

The Great key action and couplers were aided by pneumatic assist (Barker lever) with a vertical stack located immediately behind the keydesk. The Great wind chest was divided, with the Choir chest situated between them and elevated slightly higher than the two Great chests. The Swell chest was at the top, with pipes in an "A" arrangement. The Choir eight-foot open basses were tubed off to stand along the rear of the Choir chest. The Swell reeds were located at the front of the chest, directly behind the shutters, at the opposite end from the pallet box. The Pedal stops were divided on C and C♯ chests at the sides of the organ.

The case was painted white with no woodwork above the impost; the front pipes played by pneumatic activation. The projecting keydesk had terraced, horizontal stop jambs, and the stopknobs had flat-fronts on round shanks. The Choir keys had flat fronts; The Great and Swell keys had overhanging fronts. Three combination pistons and a cancel piston were located over the Swell keys. There were four "blind" combination pedals: two each controlling the Great and Choir stops. A centrally located wooden Swell shoe controlled thick, vertical shutters, and a wooden crescendo pedal was positioned to the left of the Swell shoe. The Stop action was pneumatically operated.

This painted inscription was found inside the Swell box: "G.E.D. 5 Troy N.Y.". The oval-shaped, silver nameplate was located below the Great keyboard. The organ was relocated second-hand to the Congregational Church, Whitman, Mass. in 1907, likely by the Hutchings-Votey Organ Co., of Boston, which replaced the organ in Troy with a new instrument. About 1980, the organ incurred significant water damaged during a roofing project, and later junked.

Source: Reconstructed by Scot L. Huntington from notes by E.A. Boadway, who
       examined the extant instrument during the early 1960s, and Barbara Owen.

⋆GILES BEACH (1866)
Protestant Dutch Reformed Church
Cohoes, New York

The church merged in 1969 with the Presbyterian congregation to form the United Church of Cohoes. The organ was electrified with pneumatic pulldowns, new wind system, and several stop alterations *ca.* 1950. This stoplist is reconstructed from pipe markings, traditional Beach nomenclature and windchest information. The note names are letter-stamped on the pipework and stop name information is handwritten in script.

GREAT (two diatonic chests, C and C-sharp; double pallets C-f°)

Open Diapason   8'   56 pipes; C-d° façade, zinc; remainder on chest,
                                spotted metal; large scale; ears to c².

Viol d'Amour	8′	56 pipes; bell gamba construction, basses stand on chest; C-B painted zinc, remainder common metal; moveable bells and large tuning ears; arched cut-ups, ⅖ mouth.
Clarabella	8′	56 pipes; quarter-sawn pine; C-B stopped; remainder open wood to top; inverted mouths with low, slightly arched cut-ups; walnut caps screwed on in the bass, glued-on in the treble. Marked *"No. 2"*.
Dulciana	8′	56 pipes; C-B zinc, façade; $c°$, c-sharp° painted zinc, remainder low-tin spotted metal on common metal feet; similar to a small diapason in scale; slotted, ears to c^2; ¼ mouth.
Principal	4′	56 pipes; C and C-sharp painted zinc, remainder spotted metal on common; ears to b°.
Harmonic Flute	4′	56 pipes; quarter-sawn pine; C-b° like Clarabella, c^1- g^3 harmonic with small node holes; walnut caps; low, slightly arched cut-ups.
Twelfth	2⅔′	56 pipes; spotted metal on common metal; ears C-e°; longer feet than Fifteenth.
Fifteenth	2′	56 pipes; spotted metal on common; ears C-c°.
[Compound stop]	III	168 pipes; pipes missing, likely a *Sesquialtera*.
Trumpet	8′	56 pipes; pipes in a pile on the floor; spotted metal bells on zinc resonators with zinc boots in bass, spotted metal throughout in the treble, 7 flue trebles; tapered shallots with inverted bottom bevel; stamped "H.T. Levi". Tuned dead-length.

SWELL (two diatonic chests, C and C-sharp, pallet box at front of chest; double pallets C-f°)

Bourdon Treble	$16′^1$	44 pipes; from c°; quarter-sawn pine, walnut caps
Bourdon Bass	$16′^2$	12 pipes; red milk-paint finish, pine caps. Pyramidal stopper handles from f°.

Open Diapason	8′	56 pipes; C-B painted zinc and offset with four mitered pipes; remainder spotted on common; ears C-c²; large scale.
Std. Diap. Treble	8′	44 pipes; from c°; quarter-sawn pine, walnut caps; c¹- g³ pyramidal shaped stoppers bored halfway vertically and then through-bored longitudinally; slightly arched cut-ups. Marked "No. 2".
Std. Diap. Bass	8′	12 pipes; quartered pine.
Melodia	8′	44 pipes; from c°; inverted mouths; pine, red milk-paint finish; walnut caps, glued-on in the treble. Marked "No. 2".
German Gamba	8′	44 pipes; from c°; first two pipes painted zinc, remainder spotted on common; ears c° - b¹, slotted c° - d-sharp³; ¼ mouth. Marked "G Gamba".
Principal	4′	56 pipes; C-E painted zinc, remainder low-tin spotted; ears C-c¹.
[Missing stop(s)]³	II	112 pipes.
[Compound stop]⁴	II	112 pipes.
Hautboy	8′	56 pipes; C-B common metal bells on zinc stems with zinc boots, remainder spotted metal throughout; 7 flue trebles; tapered shallots with inverted bevel. Tuned dead-length.

Tremulant

CHOIR (single chest, C-b° diatonic, chromatic from c¹)

Open Diapason	8′	56 pipes; C-B painted zinc, offset; remainder spotted on common; ears C-c².
Stopped Diapason	8′	56 pipes; rift-sawn pine; walnut caps, glued-on in the treble; slightly arched cut-ups; trebles have pyramidal stopper handles.
Keraulophon	8′	56 pipes; C-B painted zinc, offset; remainder

spotted on common; slotted throughout; ears C-b°; relatively large scale; ¼ mouth.

Violin	4′	56 pipes; C and C-sharp painted zinc, remainder spotted on common; ears C-b°; slotted C-e³.
Wald Flute	4′	44 pipes; from c°; quarter-sawn pine, slightly arched cut-ups; walnut caps, glued-on in the treble; inverted mouths, open wood to top. Marked *"No. 2"*.
Clarinette	8′	44 pipes; from c°; 7 open metal trebles; common metal resonators and boots with short conical tips; narrow *Cremona* scale, tapered shallots with inverted bevel. Tuned dead-length with no moveable bells.

PEDAL (four chests: bass and treble for each stop, C and C-sharp division at the case sides)

| Double Open Diap. | 16′ | 25 pipes; very large-scale; pine bodies and caps, red milk-paint finish. |
| Double Stop. Diap. | 16′ | 25 pipes; pine bodies and caps, red milk-paint finish. |

COUPLERS

unknown

Compass: Manuals: C-g³, 56 notes. Pedals: C-c¹, 25 notes.
Pitch: A444 @ 70°
Windpressure: 65 mm (2½″)

The material for the pipe bodies is generally spotted metal, with a variety of tine contents ranging from common metal (approx. 28% tin), to the point where spots just begin to appear (approx. 38% tin), to normal 50% tin spotted metal, to tin-rich metal with small spots (approx. 68% tin). The pipe walls are on the thin side, perhaps due to the inherent strength of the tin-rich metal, although the common metal pipework has normal thickness pipe walls. The languids are on the thick side, with an approximate 65° bevel. The nicking is vertical, and only moderately deep. The nicks on the string stops are numerous and light. The nicking on the wooden stops is light and at an angle. The wooden stops all have flat-topped English-style blocks, with the windway formed in the cap. The caps are screwed on with flat-head screws, and glued on beginning usually at 2' c. The stops with inverted mouths do not have sunken blocks, but the leading edge at the mouth is raised slightly above the level of the block. The regulation of the wooden stops is with wedges inserted into the feet. The quarter-sawn pine used for the wooden stops is of exceptionally high quality, of slow growth, and quartered wood is used for all four sides of a pipe. The metal pipes have quarter width mouths unless noted, with moderate windways, relatively low cut-ups, and light skiving of the upper lip. The strings do not have voicing aids such as box beards or rollers. The reed stops have slightly tapered shallots, with closed openings in the bass and open faces in the treble. The bottom bevel is only a few degrees out of square, but beveled nonetheless. The bass resonators are not slotted but do have small regulating flaps and all resonators are cut dead to length. The fluework comes to speech quickly and easily. The tone is gentle and free but not soft, an attribute of the 2.5" wind pressure, which is low for the period.

The case is of pine, now painted gray with white trim. There exists trace evidence that it may once have been fake-grained to imitate oak.

The console was originally recessed into the case behind a large counterweighted panel that slid vertically.

The Choir chest is behind and below the Great, approximately six feet above the floor, with the pallet box at the rear, and the pipework is arranged with the *Open Diapason* at the front of the chest progressing through to the upperwork and reed at the rear. The Pedal *Diapason* bass chests are also found at this level. The Great chests are located three feet higher at the front of the case. The Pedal *Bourdon* chests and *Diapason* treble chests are located at this level. The Swell chests are directly above the Choir division, at an elevation approximately five feet above that of the Great chests. There is a walk board in front of the Swell shutters, as well as an internal walk board directly behind the shutters. The Swell pipework is arranged with the longest stop at the rear and upperwork and reed at the front, directly over the pallets. The top and front of the Swell box is painted and decorated. The dummy fan-trumpet

STEPHEN L. PINEL

resonators are made of metal and gilded. The pedal chests are finished in milk-paint, the manual chests and framing were left unfinished.

The large pine swell box has eight thick, vertical shutters with the contacting edges felted and covered with cotton ticking. Machine markings on the swell box woodwork indicate the use of a powered thickness planer.

There are front and rear floor frames are not inter-connected, and the case is not structural. The interior framing is original.

The original windsystem is gone, having been replaced with four moderate-sized supply-house regulators. There are two empty slots for pump handles and wind indicators for each. The wind pressure measured the same in all four divisions..

::NOTES::

[1] This toeboard is now occupied by a new *Viol d'Orchestre 8'*: spotted metal, slotted, and with rollers and 12 offset zinc basses. The original *Bourdon 16'* pipes are now placed on a new unit chest playing at 16', 4', 2⅔', and 2' pitches. The original stop has been extended with 36 treble pipes, most likely from the original swell 2' stop: 18 small-scale open wood diapason pipes of pine, glued-on walnut caps and exceptionally long blocks, labeled "Sw", delicately voiced with very low cut-ups, and 18 common metal trebles.

[2] These 12 pipes are now placed unenclosed on a pneumatic offset chest, on the floor. The two longest pipes are mitered. These pipes were originally offset from the main chests and located within the swell enclosure.

[3] These two stops have been replaced with string stops, although one of them uses pipes that match the stops in all details of construction. There are four rows of toe holes and four sliders, however the spacing of the holes and sliders into two groups of two, suggests that at least one, if not both were two rank compound stops. The Great three-rank mixture also has individual sliders for each rank. The manner in which the pneumatic stop action has been fitted to the sliders makes it impossible to determine the exactly how many stops controlled these four ranks of pipes. The size of the toe holes would indicate that the back set of toe holes controlled a four-foot and a two-foot respectively:

perhaps a compound stop named *Kalaphone* or *Piffaro*. The rear-most set of sliders could also have controlled two independent stops – perhaps a *Vienna Flute 4′* or *Violina 4′* and *Flageolette 2′*. The rear set of sliders are now ganged and control an *Aeoline 8′* comprised of 12 new zinc basses and what is obviously a set of original Beach pipes from c° to the top: c° - e° zinc, remainder spotted on common; slotted, ears to c², softly voiced. These pipes are marked both *"Vn"* and *"No. 2"*. The extension trebles of the 16′ Bourdon unit match in detail the *Flageolette 2′* at Whitman (sweetly voiced open wood pipes with metal trebles).

4   As described above, the size, location and spacing of this set of two rows of toe holes would indicate a mixture stop, perhaps a *Cornett* of 2⅔′ and 2′ throughout. These two sliders are also ganged and now control a new *Voix Celeste 8′* from c° of spotted metal, and identical in all respects to the *Viol d'Orchestre*.

Source: extant organ documented by Scot L. Huntington

★GILES BEACH (1867)
First Presbyterian Church
Green Island, New York

Manual compass: C–a³, 58 notes, enclosed

Open Diapason	8′	56 pipes; C–G façade (zinc); G♯–B zinc, remainder 50% tin
Melodia	8′	46 pipes; from c°, open wood, inverted mouths
Dulciana	8′	46 pipes; from c°, 50% tin
St. Diap. Bass	8′	12 pipes; C–B, stopped wood, milk-paint finish
Principal	4′	58 pipes; C–E painted zinc, remainder 50% tin
Flute	4′	46 pipes; from c°, like Melodia, metal trebles
Fifteenth	2′	58 pipes; 50% tin
Hautboy	8′	46 pipes; from c°, spotted metal bells on zinc stems, open metal trebles. Tuned dead-length.

Pedal compass: C–c¹, 25 notes

Ped. Dble. St. Diap.	16′	17 pipes; C–e°, stopped wood, milk-paint finish

Horizontal shades operated by balanced swell pedal, originally hitch-down
Manual to Pedal Coupler

Tremulant

Bellows Signal

Double-rise reservoir with twin feeders; turned oblique stopknobs of ebony, square shanks, with hand-engraved ivory inserts; projecting keydesk, with flat, vertical stop jambs; case of chestnut with black walnut trim; façade pipes of zinc, originally gilded, later stenciled in beige with accents of blue, maroon, gold, silver, dark green and black.

Source: S.L. Huntington & Co., 2005.

GILES BEACH (1872)
Methodist Episcopal Church
Saratoga Springs, New York

DESCRIPTION OF THE ORGAN.

The organ was built by Messrs. G. Beach & Co., at the American Church Organ Works, Gloversville, N.Y., from the following specification: three manuals compassing CC to a in alt, 58 notes, pedals compassing CCC to D, 27 notes.

GREAT ORGAN.

Open Diapason, metal,	8 feet,		58	pipes.
Dulciana,	"	"	58	"
Melodia, wood		"	58	"
Principal, metal	4 feet,		58	"
Twelfth, "	2⅔ feet,		58	"
Fifteenth, "	2 feet,		58	"
Mixture, "	3 ranks,		174	"
Trumpet, reed,	8 feet,		58	"

CHOIR ORGAN.

Open Diapason, metal,	8 feet,		58	pipes.
Keraulophon, "	8	"	58	"
Stopt Diapason, wood,	8	"	58	"
Violin, metal,	4	"	58	"
Wald Flute, wood,	4	"	46	"
Clarionette, reed,	8	"	46	"

SWELL ORGAN.

Bourdon Bass, wood,	16 feet	58	pipes.
Bourdon Treble, wood,			
Open Diapason, metal,	8 "	58	"
German Gamba, metal,	8 "	58	"
Stopt Diapason, wood,	8 "	58	"
Octave, metal,	4 "	58	"
Vienna Flute, wood,	4 "	58	"
Picolo, metal,	2 "	58	"
Cornette, metal,	2 ranks,	116	"
Bassoon Bass, reed,	8 feet,	12	"
Hautboy Treble, reed,	8 "	44	"
Cornopean, reed,	8 "	58	"

PEDAL ORGAN.

Double Open Diapason, wood,	16 feet,	27 pipes.
Double Stopt Diapason, "	16 "	27 "
Violoncello, metal,	8 "	27 "

COUPLERS, ETC.

Great to Pedals.
Choir to Pedals.
Swell to Pedals.
Choir to Great, super-octaves.
Choir to Great unisons.
Swell to Choir.
Swell to Great unisons.
Swell to Great super-octaves.
Tremulant.
Bellows Signal.
Reversible Pedal to operate the coupler Great to Pedals.
Two Composition Pedals, Forte and Piano.

The bellows has five feeders operated by shaft and pulley, the power being supplied by a small turbine engine in the cellar. The case of the organ is black walnut with gothic pinnacles, having in front 17 gilded display pipes.

Source: "New M.E. Church," *Daily Saratogian* 3:154 (Mar. 19, 1872), 3.

GILES BEACH (1875?)
Masonic Lodge
Gloversville, New York

Great Organ: C–a³, 58 notes:

Open Diapason	8′	58
"Melodia"	8′	58
Principal	4′	58
Fifteenth	2′	58

Swell Organ: C–a³, 58 notes:

Keraulophon	8′ TC	46
Aeoline	8′	58
Stp. Diapason Treble	8′ TC	46
Stp. Diapason Bass	8′	12
"Violin"	4′	58
Hautboy	8′	46
Bassoon	8′	12
Tremolo		

Pedal Organ: C–d¹, 27 notes:

Doub. Stp. Diap.	16′	27

Couplers:

Great to Pedals.
Swell to Great.
Bellows.

Source: E.A. Boadway, Stoplist Collection.

United States Patent Office

GILES BEACH, OF GLOVERSVILLE, NEW YORK.

IMPROVEMENT IN PAPER ORGAN-PIPES.

Specification forming part of Letters Patent No. **213,612,** dated March 25, 1879; application filed April 5, 1878.

To all whom it may concern:

Be it known that I, GILES BEACH, of Gloversville, in the county of Fulton and State of New York, have invented an Improvement in Pipes and Conductors of Organs; and I do hereby declare that the following is a full, clear, and exact description of the same, reference being had to the accompanying drawings, forming part of this specification.

The invention has principally for its objects the construction of the pipes and wind-conductors of organs free from liability to change from alterations in the hygrometric state of the atmosphere, and also far less liable to change in length and diameter through changes in temperature; but other advantages secured are cheapness, durability, and an improvement in the quality of the tone in the speaking or sonorous pipes.

The invention consists in the manufacture of such pipes and conductors of paper, as hereinafter described.

The invention will be sufficiently illustrated by a description of the same as applied to a chimney-top-stopped diapason pipe, although it is applicable to other organ-pipes and the conductors of wind employed in organs.

Figure 1 in the drawings represents a vertical central section of such an organ-pipe constructed in accordance with my invention. Fig. 2 is a front view of the same, and Fig. 3 a horizontal cross-section.

A is a pipe of paper, made by winding a sheet of paper on a mandrel, said paper being coated or saturated with a suitable cement, which binds the several layers of paper, and which, when dry, cements the said layers together into a rigid tube, impervious to air and moisture, and which has a very small coefficient of expansion by heat or of contraction by cold.

The cement which I have so far found preferable for this purpose is composed of about one part gum-shellac, dissolved to a thick varnish in alcohol, two parts bichromate of potash, in saturated aqueous solution, and seven parts of glue, dissolved in water, by the aid of heat, to about the consistency of ordinary glue for joining wood, the said parts or proportions of the materials being determined by weight; but other cements which are not affected by moisture and which are little affected by temperature, may be employed.

After the pipe thus made has dried and hardened, a portion is cut away from the side at the bottom, and a plate, B, of similar material, is cemented thereto, the lower edge of which plate forms the vibrating lip or wind-cutter of the pipe.

Within the bottom of the said pipe is cemented the block D, constructed in the usual manner, into which the hollow cylinder E is inserted for conveying air from the sound-board to the pipe. To the front of the lower part of the said block D, and also to the cut edges of the pipe, at the usual distance below the wind-cutter C, is attached the block F, of the usual form. Said block is cemented to the block D, and also to the cut edges of the pipe A, and is preferably further secured to the block D by screws G.

H represents a chimney-top inserted in the tampion I, in the usual manner, said tampion being fitted to the interior of the pipe A, as is ordinarily done.

Organ-pipes constructed of the materials and in the manner described are practically unalterable in diameter and length through thermometric or hygrometric influences, and consequently when tuned they remain in tune in either cold or damp or warm and dry rooms. The pipes may be made at much less cost than that of wood or metal pipes. They are far lighter than ordinary metal or wooden pipes, and are far stronger than pipes of wood or metal having the same weight. Said pipes also give a more refined tone than pipes of wood or metal.

Instead of making the pipes or conductors of paper wound on a mandrel and laid up with cement, I may employ paper material of any kind in the form of pulp or otherwise, and having first formed a pipe or conductor of the same, coat or saturate the same with a cement or varnish impervious to water or watery vapor. In forming these pipes or conductors I employ the known methods of working paper or paper-pulp in various forms.

2   **213,612**

I claim—

1. An organ-pipe constructed of paper or paper-pulp, as herein described.

2. An organ-pipe composed of a series of convolute layers of paper cemented together and coated with impervious cement, substantially as specified.

3. In combination with an organ-pipe con-structed of paper, as described, the vibrating lip or wind-cutter B, constructed of paper coated with cement and secured to the pipe, substantially as described.

GILES BEACH.

Witnesses:
HENRY T. BROWN,
VERNON H. HARRIS.

G. BEACH.
Paper Organ-Pipe.

No. 213,612.   Patented Mar. 25, 1879.

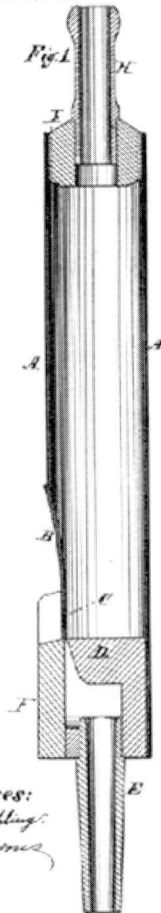

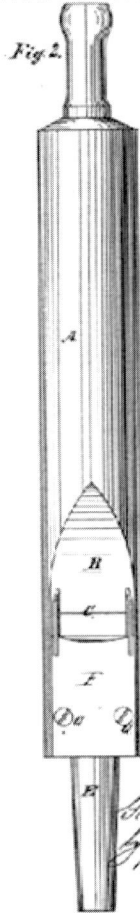

ORGAN RESTORATION ODYSSEY

※

Dana J. Hull

HOW DOES ONE DETERMINE the original provenance of an old pipe organ when a name plate does not exist, or even sometimes if one does? Clues often do not come to light until an organ is completely dismantled. Graffiti left behind by a bored long-ago pumper, or perhaps a voicer's mark on a pipe, or perhaps a shipping label still in evidence on an inner surface – all leave valuable clues.

Consider my first restoration in the Presbyterian Church in Cass City, Michigan. There was no name plate. The style of the case suggested perhaps, an instrument by E. & G.G. Hook. However, close examination of the pipes showed the names of D.A. Carnes and G.W. Osler, both of whom were voicers who worked exclusively for Henry Erben. Church records and artifacts in a glass top exhibit case at the rear of the sanctuary revealed that the organ had come to Cass City in 1908 – the gift of the Presbyterian Church in Pontiac, Michigan. A visit to the Pontiac church revealed nothing; parishioners were unaware that they ever had an old organ. A checklist of various attributes of the organ was compiled, with Erben and Hook receiving the most attributions. A study of the output of these two firms showed that in 1865 Henry Erben sold a one-manual organ to the Pontiac church. The dedication of the restored organ in 1978, was the catalyst for a twenty year Annual Village Bach Festival, which joined professional musicians from across the United States for a series of exciting Thanksgiving weekend concerts. To quote from the dedication program:

> Of the eleven Erben organs built for churches in Michigan, this is the only one known to survive. Paul Schneider (now deceased), member of the Organ Historical Society, visited the church some years earlier and declared

the organ to be: "one of the finest period instruments in our state." Alan Laufman (also deceased), a past president of the Organ Historical Society and director of the Organ Clearing House, wrote a fitting conclusion to this history: "When built in 1865, Abraham Lincoln was President of the United States. Through the years it has survived the vicissitudes of change, speaking out in times of sorrow, in times of joy, in times of thanksgiving, with clear quiet grace. Now that it has been carefully and lovingly restored, it will sing forth praise to God for another century and beyond." Another Erben organ, a little older (1857) was obtained through the Organ Clearing House from Steuart Goodwin, a builder in California. The 1857 date was uncertain; Erben records showed the date as 1859 but the 1857 date is clearly marked on one of the inside frame pieces, along with the Erben name. The organ was originally built for Christ Episcopal Church in Rouse's Point, New York, very near to both Vermont and Canada. This small Episcopal Church was so remote that for many years it was considered to be part of the Diocese of Montreal. Eventually that little church closed and was torn down, and the organ put in storage at the facility of A. David Moore, a Vermont organ builder. Steuart Goodwin moved it to his shop in California, intending to some day restore it. Through the good offices of the Organ Clearing House, the organ was purchased by St. James Episcopal Church in Dexter. Michigan for restoration by Dana Hull.

This organ, like the Cass City organ, has but a single manual. The keyboard was designed to slide into the case when not in use, with a fold-up panel to cover it. Of the four ranks of pipes, three 8-foot ranks share a common bass of seventeen stopped wood pipes. The 4-foot stop is full compass. The key action is not the usual pulldown mechanism, but a pin action which pushes the pallets open from above. Originally, the organ had no pedals; adding a pedal board made it necessary to remove (and store within the case) the mechanical parts such as the foot pump lever and the swell shoe for operating the shutters – which were left in an open position to obtain as much sound as possible for the small church. An old Hook pedal chest was donated by Barbara Owen, and a 16-foot *Bourdon* (Erben) came from Allen Kinzey. In order not to modify the organ case to add a stop knob, it was decided to keep the chest pressurized at all times. The pedal action was designed to run beneath the organ. A shallow twenty-seven note pedal board was built by Charles Ruggles.

The organ case was originally fake-grained, a process similar to painting that looks like fine grained wood which has been stained and varnished.

Graining had become almost a lost art, but a firm located in nearby Ann Arbor was found which grained the pine case to match the oak furnishings found elsewhere in the church. The result was amazingly convincing. This organ, as well as the Cass City organ, delighted Organ Historical Society convention goers in 1995.

Sometimes there are no identifying clues in an organ, or if there are they only confound the researcher/restorer. Such was the case with the old organ fondly called "Old Homer." This organ was built *ca.* 1830 by an as yet unidentified builder, probably from the Boston area. Its original home is unknown, but for many years (from about 1892 until 1977) it was in the Unitarian-Universalist Church in Oldtown, Maine. When the church was scheduled for demolition, the organ was rescued just ahead of the wrecking ball by Charles Ferguson of East Vassalboro, Maine and moved to storage in his barn. Three years later, through the help of Alan Laufman's Organ Clearing House, the organ was bought by St. Thomas à Becket Catholic Church of Canton, Michigan. Philip Laufman and I trucked it to Michigan, unloading it during a blizzard. The pipes were temporarily stored in my shop in Ann Arbor until they could be repaired. I was afraid to have the Canton church people see them in their present bad condition!

Certain factors about this organ pointed to its probable very early manufacture. The two manuals were GG compass, but included the bass GG♯, thus indicating that at some point in its past, someone had done extensive work on the organ. The three-rank *Mixture* had been replaced by an 8-foot *Gamba* on the old mixture toeboard. The *Twelfth* pipes were missing, but when it was found that the *Gamba* was the exact scale needed, these pipes were cut to tuning length and placed on the *Twelfth* toeboard. Winding to the façade pipes was fed through channels cut into the panel below them; these channels were then covered with leather.

The Swell stops began on tenor e. The so-called "Choir Bass" completed two Swell ranks (an 8-foot and a 4-foot) thorugh full compass on small "chestlets" outside the Swell box – an English practice.

Although the manual chests began on bass GG, the pedal *Sub Bass* began on C, with only thirteen pipes, but with twenty pedal keys. The pedal action was very curious, emanating from a sort of "squirrel cage" affair centered behind the knee panel.

No written clues had as yet been found, outside of a few names supposedly written by pumpers. These names led to Auburn, New York, but this was a dead end. I finally concluded that these names were of perhaps of high school boys on holiday, as they had been written upside-down.

Retabling of the manual chests was done in Detroit with the help of David Wigton in his shop. Beneath the toeboards were found shims of paper with handwriting on them. Prying the spacers off carefully, I took them home to steam off the slips of paper, and found they were cut-up letters written by one David Babcock to his father, dated 1824 through 1827. The content of the letters concerned various aspects of organ building. It was difficult to piece these pieces together – the slips of paper are still in a bag at my home!

When the bellows was taken apart, the first clue appeared. The name "Old Homer" was founded pencilled inside in two places. Whether this indicates that Homer built the bellows, or whether he later repaired and releathered it, I have been unable to ascertain.

Another "teaser" clue – the organ bench was padded, as was an early custom. When this deteriorated pad was removed, the initials "TCA" were found underneath. One would be tempted to surmise that this could be Thomas Appleton. When Barbara Owen learned of these initials, she declared that Thomas Appleton did not have a middle name. However, I later learned that his mother's maiden name was Clark. I am sure it is only a coincidence, but it does tease the imagination.

Regrettably, after ten years the priest at Canton, Michigan decided he wanted the organ removed, but did allow it to be stored in the basement of the church until a buyer could be found. At about the same time, the Congregational Church in Calais, Maine burned (and which contained an old George Stevens organ). The Calais church decided to rebuild on the same site, and desired another historic organ. So, Old Homer went back to Maine and now sits in a prominent place in the new building, having been installed by David Wallace and myself. Old Homer sounds much better in the Calais church because there is no carpet. Or wasn't, last time I looked!

This story is not quite finished. Prior to Old Homer coming to Calais, David Wallace restored an old one-manual tracker (builder unknown) in East Eddington Community Church in Maine. On our way to install the organ in Calais, we stopped to see it, and came to the following conclusions: C.P. Graves, an organ builder in Portland just before the turn of the century, installed this one-manual organ in East Eddington in 1892, having moved it from its former home in the Unitarian-Universalist Church in Oldtown, and consequently installed Old Homer in the Oldtown Church the same year. It seemed plausible to us that the present thirteen-note pedalboard may have originally been on Old Homer, because we surmised that the one-manual instrument did not have a pedalboard until it was installed at East Eddington. Since Old Homer has thirteen pedal notes, it seems reasonable that Graves may have done this work. It is only conjecture, but it all adds up.

One other "teaser" found in Old Homer: when the case was stripped (the fake grain was badly damaged) some undecipherable shorthand writing was found on the now bare wood on the C♯ side of the case. Above it was the caption: Exerpt from "The Course of Time." This seemed vaguely familiar, and upon arriving home that day, I went directly to my collection of miniature books and pulled out "The Course of Time" by Robert Pollock, *ca.* 1828, England. Attempts were made to try to discover what kind of shorthand this was. Experts were baffled. Before the case was refinished, the shorthand was faithfully copied, and is still awaiting conclusive identification.

As can be seen from the foregoing accounts, organs sometimes got moved, often more than once, which attests to their longevity.

The one-manual Thomas Hall organ (1823) in Trinity Church, Milton, Connecticut, was moved from St. Michael's Episcopal Church in nearby Litchfield. To quote from the 1985 rededication recital program at Milton: "It is the oldest organ in service in the state ... a national treasure."

The identity of the builder of this organ was unknown for some time. However, John Ogasapian noted that the decorative urn at the top of the case resembled an urn on another Thomas Hall organ. It seems that when Hall & Erben were working on an installation in Charleston, South Carolina, Hall suddenly to left for Litchfield to install an organ. An excerpt from the

Charleston City Gazette of June 15, 1824 lists various organs installed by Hall & Erben, one of them being the Hall at Litchfield.

The Milton organ boasts more than its share of graffiti, some of which is no more than names or initials, and some is in rhyme, such as:

Hickory, dickery dock
The mouse ran up the clock
The clock struck one
And down he run
Oh! How is that for _____

Good morning, Mr. Fisher
I hope I see you well
Have you got any seashells to sell?

Underneath the pedalboard was glued a paper (or piece of leather) on which was written:

Rev. Mr. Willey, Litchfield, Organ No. 1

Another organ for which there was no name plate was the organ which came to the University Lutheran Church, East Lansing, Michigan. It was obvious it originally had a name plate – evidence suggested where it had once been attached. It was originally supposed that the builder was W.B.D. Simmons & Company, of Boston. In fact, the East Lansing church bought it on just this premise. The organ was obtained from Hillside Universalist Church in Medford, Massachusetts. As the dismantling crew was taking it apart, it was decided to remove the toeboards to make the chests easier to carry. Along the side of one toeboard was found written: "Hurry. The church committee will be here by 9:00. (Signed) S.S. Hamill." Now we knew two things – the builder's name, and the fact that some things never change!

Although the builder's name plate was missing, Samuel S. Hamill's name was later found on various parts of the organ. According to Alan Laufman, Hamill was known to have built an organ for the Second Universalist Church in East Cambridge, Massachusetts. The church edifice was dedicated on September 26, 1866. In 1907, the East Cambridge church was closed and the building destroyed in the hurricane of 1938. In 1959, Robert J. Reich of the Organ Historical Society, found an organ in the Hillside Universalist Church in Medford, Massachusetts. The church told him at that time, that the organ had come from the Second Universalist Church in East Cambridge.

The organ had not been playable for a number of years and its interior had sustained water damage. Following the dismantling process, the Andover Organ Company, Inc. was engaged to rebuild the manual chests. The church people in East Lansing stripped and refinished the chestnut and walnut case. I releathered the large bellows and its feeders. A church member, Paul Schneider, donated a wagon part from his grandfather's carriage shop to replace the missing pump handle. A few alterations were made to the Hamill to make it more useful for a Lutheran service. A three-rank *Mixture*, made by Frank Gyuratz of Erie, Pennsylvania, replaced a nondescript *Keraulophon*. A pedal 16-foot *Trombone* (made by the Laukhuf firm of Germany to the exact measurements of a Hook pedal reed, from measurements provided by George Bozeman), and a pedal *Flute* 4-foot and *Gedackt* 8-foot were placed on a new three-rank pedal chest built by Andover. The chest was located directly behind the original pedal chest, both chests sharing the same action. The original pedalboard of twenty-five notes was replaced with a new clavier of twenty-seven notes built by Charles Ruggles. Naturally, two pallets needed to be added to the pedal chest.

After the restoration was complete, a name plate bearing the name of Samuel S. Hamill was donated by Alan Laufman. There is every reason to believe that it is probably the name plate belonging to this organ as it fit the silhouette perfectly.

The Organ Clearing House found another organ needing restoration, for me – this being a one-manual E. & G.G. Hook, Opus 226, 1857. This instrument was originally built for the First Congregational Church of Manchester, Connecticut, where it had served faithfully for many years. At some point, it was moved to the Bethlehem Lutheran Church in East Hampton, Connecticut, where it was in use until 1967. Charles Ferguson of East Vassalboro, Maine bought it and set it up at his residence there, and in 1981 he offered it for sale through the Organ Clearing House.

In the meantime, Covenant Orthodox Presbyterian Church of Rochester, New York had asked the Clearing House to find them a new instrument. The Clearing House recommended Hook Opus 226. Every part of the organ was cleaned – broken, worn, or missing parts were repaired or replaced. The bellows was reconstructed from the remains of the original – it and the feeder bellows were releathered. The original thirteen-note pedal clavier had been replaced by Charles Ferguson with an old twenty-seven note pedalboard. I reused the Fergusen pedalboard, utilizing a scheme employed on other instruments by the Hook brothers themselves. I recycled the original thirteen-note pedalboard as a hall ornament in my home.

With the exception of the fourteen added pedal pipes, all the speaking pipes are original. The *Stop'd Diapason* 8-foot and the *Flute* 4-foot are both metal chimney flutes. Non-speaking pipes in the case front are new, the originals having been lost some years ago.

After serving the Covenent Church for some time, the congregation moved to a larger building which already contained a pipe organ. Having no need for the Hook, it was sold and moved to St. Mary's Cathedral in St. Cloud, Minnesota where it still gives good service in their basement chapel.

We often think of instruments by Hook and Erben as being the top-of-the line of their time, and so they were. However, more modest builders also made valuable contributions to the trade. While Erben was sometimes referred to as "the Cadillac of the industry," one such as John Hinners built very humble but serviceable organs, many of which were designed for small rural churches. Hinners built many modest instruments, often with only one manual, that are still giving reliable service. Most of the one-manual Hinners have a divided keyboard (usually between b and middle c) with separate drawknobs for the treble and bass of each stop. One such instrument, Hinners Opus 2650, was built and installed around 1920 in what was St. Peter's Lutheran Church in Plato, New York – a church which no longer exists. When the church closed and was sold at auction in the 1950s, one Harold Olmstead bought the organ and moved it to his barn in Sardinia, New York, for storage. Many years later, Mr. Olmstead's survivors gave the organ to Larry Ploetz of St. Paul's Lutheran Church in Ellicotville, New York. I was contacted to come and look at the assortment of parts, and noted that I thought it could make a viable instrument. The rebuilt Hinners was given a central place in the rear gallery. Because the organ was literally brought back from the dead, it was named "Lazarus."

Other Hinners instruments have come under my hands: St. John Lutheran Church, New Baltimore, Michigan, Immaculate Conception Catholic Church,

Lapeer, Michigan, and Our Lady of the Miraculous Medal Catholic Church, North Baltimore, Ohio (this organ almost a twin to the New Baltimore organ).

The North Baltimore Hinners is thought to have been built *ca.* 1915 for a Lutheran Church in Sterling, Nebraska, and relocated to North Baltimore in 1930. Having read about this Hinners, Frank Kuhlman, then of Detroit, contacted me to say that he had been born in Sterling and that his grandfather had been organist when the Hinners was installed there and that he (Frank) would like to play the dedication at North Baltimore. Small world!

The Lapeer, Michigan Hinners is a small two-manual organ which came to Immaculate Conception Church from an unknown church in Detroit. Certain characteristics of the installation suggested practices of an organ technician known to me years before in Ohio – a Frederick Cesander, now long departed. The priest of the Lapeer church obligingly searched old financial records and found that, indeed, I was correct. It was also revealed that the aforesaid Cesander removed an old hand-pumped tracker organ to make room for the Hinners, and gave the pipes to neighborhood children to play with. I was curious to learn the builder of this now defunct organ, but no one could remember the builder's name. However, one day as I was checking some supports from the façade to the Swell box, I noticed something pencilled on one of them. Upon removing the support, I found: "Dudley Jardine, November, 1861." It this became evident that George Jardine was the builder and perhaps Dudley Jardine (his son) helped with the installation. While the Hinners that replaced the Jardine is a fine organ, I suspect that the Jardine might have been the better organ. I surmise that the Jardine may have been only one manual, thus prompting the decision to upgrade. The above mentioned support was replaced with a new piece, and the historic support is in my possession.

Some organs have suffered through many changes, presenting a real challenge for restoration. One such instrument is the 1886 Opus 657 William A. Johnson at Good Shepherd Episcopal Church in Allegan, Michigan, which I rebuilt in 1995. The original double-rise bellows had been replaced with two spring-weighted reservoirs. The flat pedalboard had been replaced with a concave and radiating clavier of twenty-seven notes, the AGO norm being thirty-two. The *Dulciana* had been removed; in its place was a mis-matched

2-foot stop. Since the *Dulciana* had shared its bass notes with the *Melodia*, the *Melodia* now had no bass. The manual chests were cracked. Wooden pedal trackers had been replaced with wire. The organ itself appeared to have been moved back under the arch, so what had once been speaking façade pipes were shortened to fit under the arch and were no longer functional. The front oak casework had been replaced with ugly plywood, with the wind line entering from the front.

How did we deal with these problems? Wayne Warren, my assistant at that time, was fortunate to find a large bellows and a flat pedalboard (both of which we were sure were Johnson parts), the original *Dulciana* was located and the owner persuaded to donate it back to the church, chests were retabled, wood trackers installed for the pedal action, a pedal check designed and built, a new case front constructed in the old style by Elgin Clingaman of the Renaissance Organ Company, and new façade pipes were installed. The organ now looks and sounds as it did originallly.

Another Johnson, not the familiar William A. Johnson but another – one John Johnson. John Johnson was an immigrant farmer from Sweden, who had worked briefly with an organ builder there before coming to America. Some years ago I received a call from Paul Schneider, organ historian, asking me to accompany him to Sparta, Michigan to bring back an old one-manual organ built by Johnson, (now stored in a building on what had been the Johnson family farm). The grandson, Lowell Johnson, described the history of the organ – it was one of two organs built by his grandfather around 1880. It is not known what had become of the first organ, but the second instrument he built for the Mamrelund Lutheran Church, Kent City, Michigan where it served for many years with John Johnson himself serving as organist. Eventually the church built a new, larger building and gave the organ back to the family. By the time Paul and I saw it, the parts were in desperate condition. Paul later discovered that the reason the bellows was so heavy to move was that it contained forty-three pounds of nut shells!

The organ came to my shop, but I was too busy to do anything with it at the time. After not too many years, the Mamrelund pastor called and asked if the church could have the organ back. So back it went and, primarily with the help of Lowell Johnson, the rebuilt organ now sits proudly in the chapel of the Mamrelund Church. This instrument has four ranks of wood pipes, most of which plug directly into the chest without having a rackboard. The pedal has twelve stopped wood pipes and a small twelve note pedalboard. The case, parts of which had rotted away while in storage on the Johnson farm, was replicated from wood found on the Johnson property, from whence had come wood for the original case. While fragile and ill suited for playing elaborate literature, the Johnson organ is a handsome remnant from this church's past, and part of the overall history of organ building in this country.

The one-manual M.P. Möller tracker at St. John's Episcopal Church in Sandusky, Michigan, built in 1889 as Opus 212, was originally installed in St. Mary's Catholic Church in Bath, New York. Not much is known about its subsequent travels, but it is thought that it was moved from Bath, perhaps to a church in northern Michigan, then went into private hands where it was subsequently set up in an outbuilding. From there it became the possession of a piano technician in Lansing, Michigan where it languished in storage in his basement. At some point, needing money, he offered to sell it to me. Two members of the Sandusky congregation came to see it, and the rest is history. It now sits in St. John's Episcopal Church, Sandusky, Michigan, having been restored by Alex Paladi and myself, with the help of other church members. This organ, too, has a divided keyboard.

The organs noted in this paper are but some of the success stories of my endeavors. Sadly, not every situation turns out so well. Perhaps one of the saddest was the 1892 George Jardine in Trinity Episcopal Church, Detroit, Michigan where I was organist for over five years. In August of 2000, I came to church one Sunday morning to find that the plaster ceiling had collapsed into the organ. Because this was a poor church, I obtained permission from the Vestry to begin restoration of the organ, hoping for some monetary compensation in time. Several months later, when the work was nearing completion, my organist position was terminated in favor of a gospel piano player, and payment refused for my work on the organ. Since the church has taken "another path" I can only assume that the organ restoration will never be completed, thus spelling the demise of a wonderful organ in a lovely building.

WINDS OF CHANGE

Jonathan Ambrosino

THOSE OF US CONCERNED WITH OLD ORGANS have an uneasy relationship with change, and perhaps it boils down to a form of addiction. After all, a completely unaltered organ somehow verges on the narcotic. It isn't merely that sense of relief that stems from not having to listen through later changes. Coming into contact with undiluted history can evoke, at least for us, an emotional reaction approaching the sacred.

And yet, historians often campaign for change, in attitude, method or approach. We want builders to respond more passionately to research, we want restorers to be more careful, conscientious and documentary, we want to change outlooks so that the unchanged should remain that way – all growing out of a conviction that the unaltered organ is history's sacrament, handed down to us not for transformation but veneration.

In this context, what are we to make of changes a builder himself carries out? I refer not to those historic American organs revised by the original builder's successors (Church of the Immaculate Conception or Church of the Advent, both in Boston), but to those rarer examples of a builder revising his own work. That it happens is not surprising. However splendid the egos of organbuilders, few leave any organ content in all details, and more than one could be quoted as saying, "organs aren't finished, they are abandoned." Even in instruments of tremendous acclaim, a builder will know only too acutely those details – great or small – that could stand improvement.

For a builder to reconsider his own work, certain conditions need to be in place: desire on the part of the musician, concurrence and willingness of the builder, and, ideally, funding and institutional authorization. With the logistics settled, the builder considers the aesthetic proposition, an arena in which hubris confronts humility. Revisions involve not only acceptance of shortcoming but also the projection of confidence – that the passage of time has allowed both technique and approach to mature into something more refined.

Few of the great builders remain static in style; Gottfried Silbermann stands out as an exception rather than an example. Most builders evolve the style handed them into something more personal. Others create something so personal that any antecedent fades into insignificance. When we see a builder revising his own work, we are witnessing to some extent that friction between youth and maturity, the act of declaration now reconsidered, springing from the same artistic nature, yet now evolved.

AUGMENTATION NO. 1

Grand Avenue Methodist Temple, Kansas City, Missouri
Ernest M. Skinner Organ Co., Op. 190, 1912
Changes 1948 and 1951, Ernest M. Skinner & Son. Co. (Carl Bassett)

Op. 190 was one of Ernest Skinner's first success stories outside the Northeast. In Skinner's first decade of business from 1901 to 1911, most of his prominent work was installed in New York City, with a few examples in Ohio and one in Minneapolis. Kansas City, then a central hub of railway lines and goods exchange, was a propitious locale for a benchmark installation in a new midwestern downtown church. Although containing no new tonal or mechanical feature, Op. 190 was nevertheless a showcase of the budding Skinner ethos, from its pitman wind chests and modern drawknob console (with newfangled adjustable general pistons) to an effective and idiosyncratic tonal philosophy: a small Great paired to a giant Swell, a Solo and Choir sharing windchests, swell box and certain registers, and a Pedal organ of few ranks but big impact. From a modern viewpoint, the noteworthy aspect of this early organ is how the diapasons and chorus reeds are livelier than the more opaque tone that became fashionable in the early 1920s.

In July 1949, now 83, Ernest Skinner was invited back to Kansas City to advise on revisions and additions. His choices are indicative of how time re-figures notions of the necessary and the dispensable.

Swell: replace *Clarabella* with two-rank *Flute Celeste*
          (bottom octave unchanged)
Great: add *Twelfth* and *Fifteenth*
Choir: add *Nazard, Tierce, Larigot* and *Septième*
Pedal: add five-rank *Mixture* (5⅓', 4', 3⅕', 2⅔', 2')

The Great and Pedal additions show that Skinner was not entirely re-actionary to the chorus-oriented developments his own firm had pioneered in the later 1920s. The Choir mutations recall Skinner's fascination with such stops beginning around 1920; here they are of dulciana strength, as they would have been in a Skinner organ thirty years earlier. Finally, it is interesting that Skinner's thinking about diapason and chorus reed tone, which had darkened in the late 'teens and early '20s, then brightened under the influence of G. Donald Harrison in the late '20s and early '30s, had re-arrived in 1949 largely to his attitudes of 1910. Thus, what he heard in Kansas City probably gave him little desire to revise, merely to "complete." In this vein, surely Skinner felt that no organ of his could exist without a *Flute Celeste* (introduced after Op. 190 had been completed); this stop was very likely the alteration Skinner considered most vital.

This type of tonal updating is reminiscent of the periodic software up-grades performed on modern computers. The resulting difference is more in nuance than concept. In Kansas City, Skinner neither revoiced the chorus nor changed the character of the reeds, although there was now greater order to the Great diapason family. Certainly the changes were insufficient to trans-form the ensemble into something constitutionally different; it merely gained a bit of focus, while the color palette broadened at the *piano* and *mezzo* levels. As these are areas in which Skinner had always excelled, the work in Kansas City demonstrates the old man being, fundamentally, himself.

Saint John's Chapel, Groton School, Massachusetts.
Case designed by Henry Vaughan, originally housing a
Hutchings–Votey organ of 1901, with the organist seated in the lower gallery.

COLLABORATIVE CONDITIONS

Saint John's Chapel, Groton School, Groton, Massachusetts
Aeolian-Skinner Organ Co., Op. 936, 1935

Although G. Donald Harrison and Aeolian-Skinner had built a series of progressive organs leading up to it, the Groton organ of 1935 departed considerably even from its immediate predecessors, both in tonal design and in the sophisticated individuality (for its period) of pipe construction. This is the organ containing Harrison's first unenclosed Positiv and reedless Great, no manual windpressure higher than three-and-three-quarter inches, and many other features advanced for its day. Only rarely was Harrison able to devote such attention to concept, detail and execution as prevailed at Groton, and the resulting organ changed the direction of American organbuilding for the next thirty years.

Op. 936 was born of intellectual ideals. Any instrument whose Great contained independent quint, tenth, twelfth, and seventeenth stops, but no 4-foot flute, symbolized a proud commitment to orthodox chorus-building, especially in a period many found unprincipled. In 1941, consultant and journalist Edward B. Gammons became organist at Groton, and his tinkerer's bent led to a number of modifications. While many changes were made after Harrison's death in 1956, Harrison authored and executed many himself. In 1944, Harrison outlined a program to bring the instrument fully up-to-date with the various features that had been introduced in Aeolian-Skinners since the Groton organ's completion. Thus over time, and after much playing, the changes at Groton indicate high idealism being tempered both by daily practicality and the march of progress.

Changes through 1954, Harrison's last involvement with Op. 936:

Great:	replace *Flute harmonique* with capped metal *Rohrflöte* (from Positif)
Great:	replace 3⅕-foot *Gross Tierce* with capped metal 4-foot *Flute Couverte* (new)
Great:	revised *III Cymbel* into *III Scharff* (using pipes from ex-Positif *IV Scharff*)

Swell:	reduce 6-rank *Plein Jeu* to the upper four ranks only; introduce new, mild, low-pitched *III Mixture* in place of the original first two *Plein Jeu* ranks
Swell:	exchange *Trompette II* for an *Hautbois*
Swell:	replace *Echo Viole* with *Flute Celeste*
Swell:	unify *Flûte conique* to play at 16-foot and 8-foot
Choir:	add 4-foot *Rohrschalmei* to create a minor 16-8-4 reed chorus
Choir:	replace 4-foot *Lieblichflöte* with 4-foot *Nachthorn*
Positif:	replace 8-foot flute with ex-Choir *Lieblichflöte*
Positif:	revise *Scharff* into a higher-pitched mixture, using pipes from Great *Cymbel*
Pedal:	add 2-foot flute

Epochal organs start out being grand exercises for the builder. Once complete, the instruments teach lessons that builder, player, and listener experience from the same starting point. The creator may be best equipped to understand his work, but, paradoxically, he may also be the one least able to gauge its importance or force. (Think of the impact of the first organs tuned out of equal temperament in the late 1960s, and the long period it took to come to a fuller understanding of what temperament really means.) Also, can a builder's intent ever perfectly align with the actual artistic result? Constantly saturated with the chore of daily work, the mid–20th-century factory organbuilder was perhaps the least suited to judging his own work in some sort of objective historical manner.

And yet, in the correspondence, Harrison allowed that at Groton, he had created something larger than himself. Authorship did not exempt him from the intellectual, artistic and emotional impact of his own work. Perhaps for this reason, Harrison's initial changes at Groton were limited to color management. For example, exchanging the Swell *Trompette II* with an *Hautbois* mildly adjusted the palette in a way that left ensemble combinations largely unchanged. But in time, Harrison moved beyond the approach that characterizes what Skinner did in Kansas City; he advanced from the transformative to the corrective. While the essential character of the ensemble probably did not change much, its intensity surely did. By raising the pressure on the Great a quarter inch (to such an extent that it required conversion from cone- to slide-tuning) and introducing louder Swell reeds, Harrison was altering not only the power of the manual *tutti*, but de-emphasizing to some extent the contribution of the Pedal and its balance to the manual fluework. Subtle readjustments to the Pedal fluework, and finally the loudening of the Pedal *Trompette* and *Clairon*, seems to have restored, or at least resulted in, balances Harrison found satisfactory.

RECONSIDERATION

Memorial Church, Harvard University
C.B. Fisk, Op. 46, completed 1967

This great, irascible instrument was the first four-manual tracker organ built in the United States in the 20th century. The boldness and enthusiasm of its gesture was paired to ingenuity for a difficult situation. Memorial Church is essentially two separate rooms: Appleton Chapel is both a collegiate-style gathering place for daily services, and the chancel to a larger adjacent room – the Memorial Church. The two are connected (or divided, one might say) by a heavy rood screen. The 1933 Aeolian-Skinner was installed in side chambers above the Chapel pews; from the outset the instrument was viewed as a problematic compromise for its difficult location and the poor acoustics. The Fisk was better sited, on axis at the extreme east end of the Chapel, from where it had to traverse the long Chapel, past large openings into the old organ chambers (which act as sound traps, even as they add a mist of reverberation), and finally into the acoustically indifferent nave that is the Memorial Church. Fisk addressed the situation in two ways, first by placing Great and Positive at the top of the case, to survive the chancel and penetrate the nave, and next by locating the Swell and Choir at floor level, sort of an organ-within-an-organ that constituted a milder counterpart for the sung daily services held exclusively in Appleton Chapel.

Early changes came in the tuning, when the original equal temperament was converted to Werckmeister. In 1981 the organ required cleaning and some mechanical overhaul. Now in his sixtieth year, Charles Fisk suggested certain changes that betray the challenge this "caged animal" (his words) had posed.

Proposed 27 January 1981[1]

Swell: replace *Trumpet* with a new rank patterned after Cavaillé-Coll

Swell: replace 2-foot *Night Horn* with *Hautbois,* also patterned after Cavaillé-Coll

Great: revoice *Trumpet* "for a fuller sound in the bass"

Pedal: increase 32-foot *Contrabassoon* to full-length resonators, "the least satisfactory stop in the organ"

Great: replace the existing Great mixtures and *Twelfth* with the following

    a.   *Mixture V-VIII*

    b.   *Grave Mixture II* (including 5⅓ from f♯')

    c.   *Sesquialter*

Positive: recast two mixtures

    a.   *Sharp* (remain essentially as is)

    b.   *Cymbal* (reworked in the style of Praetorius's *Doppelt Zymbel*)

In the end, only the Great was altered, and not quite to the original plan. The *Mixture* was recast as a five-to-eight-rank stop, primarily to improve tuning stability; the *Twelfth* was replaced with a wide-scale *Nasard;* and a matching wide-scale *Tierce* was introduced in place of the original *Sharp* mixture. The broad scaling and high cut-ups of the existing principals meant that the 4-foot and 2-foot registers were more complementary than antagonistic to the intentions behind the new mutations. Finally, the organ was retuned in Fisk I, a mildly unequal temperament and the instrument's third.

Safe organbuilding is easy to walk away from unscorched. Daring organbuilding – and the Harvard Fisk was one colossal risk – can result in something really striking, in a context that combines experimentation with anticipation. In 1967, Fisk already had several noteworthy organs to his credit, but all the career-defining organs were yet to come. He astutely understood the conditions at work; the expectation that this organ should represent a defining moment for organ reform was set against the unavoidable reality of Memorial Church. Probably knowing that no organ could ever be wholly successfully, Fisk nevertheless responded with an organ of tremendous bravery and vigor. A bold proposition rooted in compromise was bound to produce reflections fifteen years later.

In some ways, Fisk's wish list for Harvard is reminiscent of Harrison's for Groton. Had all Fisk's suggested changes been carried out, the organ would have lost some of its 1960s hard-line qualities in exchange for daily practicalities and the realities of emerging historical understanding. The "completeness" of both low- and high-pitched mixtures on both Great and Positive had, by the early 1980s, graduated into an altogether different approach, while the sounds for both the earlier music (wide-scale mutations, *Doppelt Zymbel*) and Romantic repertoire (*Hautbois,* full-length 32-foot reed) were also being addressed.

AUGMENTATION NO. 2

Christ Church, Tacoma, Washington
John Brombaugh, Opus 22, 1979

Op. 22 is one of three two-manual organs planned, engineered and built in the late 1970s as essentially identical instruments, the others being in Storrs, Connecticut, and Berkeley, California. Tacoma's is a healthy two-manual instrument, entirely unenclosed, the Great and Pedal sharing a common chest at impost level, the Positive above the Great. The organist David Dahl presided over its commissioning and recently celebrated the organ's twenty-fifth birthday. Ten years into its life, it received a few changes.

Pedal: replace half-length *Fagot* with full-length *Posaune*
Positive: add *Erzähler* and *Erzähler Celeste* (t.f through d51)

Brombaugh writes most succinctly about his own work here:

The Pedal 16-foot reed was originally a Fagot, i.e., a half-length reed similar to a Dulcian; that format was used in the original due to costs and because of available space when the original contract was written. As I got into doing the design on Op. 22 in the late 1970s, however, David made some requests for some alterations that took the project away from having its planned Brustwerk to having the upper Positive, so there was room to provide a real full-length Posaune type reed. That great change was whatsoever possible because we also were in the works to make Op. 20 for St. John's Pres. in Berkeley, CA, and Op. 21 at St. Mark's in Storrs, Conn., so building Op. 22 along with them together in a very similar format let David's requests be possible without an impossible price rise – but not enough to have included a Posaune, which he didn't ask for anyway.

Later, however, after hearing the Berkeley organ, he wanted an upgrade and other additional stops, so we went into the big change in '89 when Jeff Smith and the Habedank family provided the funds. The other stops were a set of quiet stops that could have celeste effects. One idea was real strings, but that could have been a real space problem, so I worked out a solution using a very narrow-scaled tapered pipe pair with a "gedackted" bottom octave for the non-celeste rank. Since I knew [Ernest Skinner] had done something like that which his shop colleague gave the name "Erzähler," I thought that would be just the ticket for the additions to Op. 22! Whether or not my Erzähler reminds anyone of what [Mr. Skinner] made, I'd never want to say, but it does give a very different sound to the organ which is usable in many different ways … [2]

Can one be resolute about a principle but elastic in its application? Here, the substitution of *Posaune* for *Fagot* seems little more than exchanging a temporary stop with a permanent one, as if in fulfillment of the original plan. But the presence of string and celeste on a Brombaugh organ reflects a broader context. One aspect is friendship: given the bond between them, John Brombaugh would probably respond to any reasonable request David Dahl might make. Another is shifting trends. In the late 1980s, the canon of organbuilding of which Brombaugh was arguably the head had perhaps eclipsed him in notoriety and advance. While Brombaugh had trained a generation of builders who today command considerable acclaim (George Taylor, John Boody, Paul Fritts, Ralph Richards, Bruce Fowkes, Martin Pasi), the late 1980s was a tough and shrinking market for the narrow swath Brombaugh had channeled for himself. Realities led to a reconsideration of eclecticism, and in organs such as Christ Church, Christiana Hundred near Wilmington, Delaware and Lawrence University in Appleton, Wisconsin, Brombaugh was clearly open to the lines of thinking that Fisk and Rosales had promulgated to such success and popularity. It may well have been that such prodding as Dahl's for stops both churchly and practical helped to inform Brombaugh's developing new modes.

CHANGE OF HEART

First Lutheran Church, Boston
Richards, Fowkes & Co., Op. 10, 2000

Some changes that appear minor have the effect of lines drawn in the sand. In two recent Richards, Fowkes & Co. organs, the voicer Bruce Fowkes has returned of his own volition to revise a key detail: the voicing of the 8-foot *Principal*. Fowkes' original voicing work was modeled upon the Brombaugh approach, with very high cut-ups and "a traverse flute quality, very elegant, very beautiful," in Fowkes' words. But over time, Fowkes realized that he was after a different sound, one with less overt articulation, keener, perhaps something more orchestral. His work over the last ten years has been moving toward this new, personal objective.

On a study trip to Germany, Fowkes brought along one of his pipes to show Christian Wegscheider, the noted specialist in the work of Hildebrandt and Silbermann. Fowkes realized that the pipes as his company was building them were architecturally unsuited to the more relaxed tone Fowkes was now after. He relayed:

> I went back to two of our organs, in Boston [First Lutheran] and New Brunswick [Op. 9] and was unhappy with the 'tight' sound of the 8-foot Principals. Once attuned to this quality, I became increasingly determined to move beyond it, not only in our new work but in these recent organs with which, in almost every other respect, I was fairly well satisfied.[3]

First Lutheran Church, Boston, Massachusetts.

In the above examples, the builders seem to have struck respectable balances between original and evolved perspectives. Perhaps the most difficult situations are the ones in which – at least to our present-day ears – the builder changed his own work in such a way as to diminish its worth. What if the new vision was less compelling than the original – if a builder, in his new mode, was being current without being timeless? G. Donald Harrison left several such examples. At what point is the builder's work the sole point of reference for the precise manner of its perpetuation?

: : N O T E S : :

[1]   Letter from Charles Fisk to Peter Gomes, 27 January 1981

[2]   E-mail to the author, 9 December 2004.

[3]   Telephone conversation between author and Bruce Fowkes, 6 December 2004.

MANUEL ROSALES AND THE LOS ANGELES ORGAN RENAISSANCE

❧

Orpha Ochse

FROM GOLDEN AGE TO RENAISSANCE

A CENTURY AGO Los Angeles enjoyed its first Golden Age of the organ. From 1894 to 1913 the small but growing Southern California city prided itself on having an organ-building shop: one that could fill the city's churches with organs equal in quality to those of highly-respected builders on the East Coast. From time to time newspaper articles described in detail the various departments in the shop, and the completion of a new organ was hailed as an achievement of front-page significance. Crowds flocked to hear shop demonstrations of new organs, as well as inaugural recitals in the churches. Each new instrument was another star in the crown of civic pride, and one more solid piece of evidence that Los Angeles was no longer just a little Spanish town built of adobe. The organ company became a symbol of art and culture as well as a business enterprise, and a large portion of the general population was interested in seeing and hearing what it could produce.

The central figure in raising the organ to a high level of visibility in the community was Murray M. Harris, regarded today as the father of organ building in Los Angeles. Although Harris's personal involvement in organ building fluctuated (as did the financial condition of his successive firms), he was an unusually successful advocate for the organ. Initially, it was the Harris vision and ability to inspire confidence that sparked a Golden Age for the organ and provided many churches up and down the California coast with wonderful instruments. His reputation spread nationwide when he signed a contract in 1903 to build the "World's Largest Organ." That instrument today forms the core of the famous Wanamaker organ in Philadelphia.

Since the Murray M. Harris days the organ profession in Los Angeles has experienced other noteworthy high points. In the prosperous period just before the Great Depression many fine new Los Angeles church buildings installed equally fine new organs purchased from organ builders in the East and Midwest. The 1962 National Convention of the American Guild of Organists, sponsored by three Los Angeles County AGO chapters, was another time of particular importance. But in general, these high-water marks attracted only peripheral attention outside the organ profession.

Recently, Los Angeles has been reawakened to an awareness of pipe organs. In 2002 the opening of the new Cathedral of Our Lady of the Angels attracted throngs of tourists, and performances on its 105-rank Dobson organ were an important part of the inaugural events.[1] Completion of a new cathedral is a rare event in any age. In this particular case it was the spectacular curtain raiser for a new focus on downtown Los Angeles as a cultural center. Significantly, the new Cathedral is diagonally across the street from the Music Center, the city's home for the performing arts since 1964.

Meanwhile, just south of the Music Center, a seemingly random jumble of steel beams was finally beginning to take shape as the Walt Disney Concert Hall. As if to challenge the austere lines of the Cathedral, Frank Gehry's audacious design for the new hall is a study in curved lines and unexpected angles. Gehry's visual design for the organ, as unconventional as the building, had already astonished the organ world and elicited more than a few nicknames and clever comments. Seen in the hall itself, the organ's curves and angles are right at home, mirroring those of the building itself.

The Walt Disney Concert Hall, new home of the Los Angeles Philharmonic Orchestra, opened in October 2003. The Rosales/Glatter-Götz organ had been installed, but tonal finishing was only in its initial stages. Sold-out concerts marked the first season, giving some 2000 patrons at each performance the opportunity to speculate about the strange array of organ pipes so prominently displayed above the sight-line of the orchestra. Were they real? How did they work? Was that the whole organ? Would it be deafening?

Information about the organ was frequently included in media reports, and during 2003 and 2004 the name of Manuel Rosales became known to a larger public as he explained some of the basics of organ construction and related them to the dramatic new organ in Disney Hall. Rosales, the tonal designer of this organ, is its acknowledged authority. As articulate as he is knowledgeable, he has been remarkably successful in describing this complex instrument in terms intelligible to the non-organist.

In April 2004, a two-segment review of the hall and its architecture was presented on the popular PBS television program, "Life and Times." The organ was one of the features reviewed, and as in various other news reports, the spokesperson for the organ was Manuel Rosales. During this presentation the Los Angeles Philharmonic Orchestra's distinguished Music Director, Esa-Pekka Salonen, discussed the opening of the hall as the high point in his career, remarking that he did not envision having another opportunity of similar magnitude. In the same way, the organ marks a unique high point in the career of Los Angeles organ builder Rosales. But the uniqueness of this event isn't limited to individuals and careers. For the first time in a century the organ is clearly in the mainstream of musical events in Los Angeles. For the first time ever the 2004-2005 program book of the Los Angeles Philharmonic Orchestra offered the orchestra's patrons eleven concerts featuring the organ with orchestra, and an Organ Recital Series of six solo programs. Thus the concert-going public was invited to experience the musical delights that all too often have been the exclusive pleasure of a few. The response was almost overwhelming. Following the inaugural recital played by Frederick Swann, an amazed *Los Angeles Times* music critic headlined his review "*Organissimo!*"[2]

Because he has played a central role in recent Los Angeles organ developments, it seems a fitting time to review the career and achievements of Los Angeles's best-known contemporary organ builder, Manuel Rosales.

GROWING UP

A New Yorker by birth, Manuel Rosales (b. 1947) has been a Southern Californian since early 1953, when he moved to Los Angeles along with his mother, father, and sister. He attended parochial schools: St. Francis of Assisi grade school, and Pater Noster High School.

His musical interests began to develop early in his school years. His mother played the piano, and when Manuel was still in grade school he took accordion lessons for three or four years. Mother and son sometimes combined their talents in piano and accordion duets. However, it wasn't until later, when Manuel was in high school, that exposure to a wider world of music steered his interests toward a life-long career.

Manuel Rosales in 1955.[3]

In his early years Manuel had no interest in the organ, and the uninspiring Baldwin Model 4 in his home church did nothing to whet his appetite for organ music. Later, some fortunate coincidences proved to be pivotal events. When he was twelve years old his father took him to see Disney's 1940 film, *Fantasia*. The film score, conducted by Leopold Stokowski, included an orchestrated arrangement of Bach's Toccata and Fugue in d minor, played by the Philadelphia Orchestra. Manuel was so captivated with this music that his father took him to a record store. There they found the organ version of the Bach work, and as luck would have it, the recording they bought was performed by E. Power Biggs on the 1958 Flentrop organ at the Busch-Reisinger Museum, Harvard University.

A few years later another coincidence further spurred his interest in the organ and its music. When he was about fifteen or sixteen years old, Manuel began attending St. Finbar's Church in Burbank with some of his high school friends.[4] There he joined the choir (an important musical experience, as he later recalled). This church had a real pipe organ: an eighteen-rank WurliTzer (opus 1541), transplanted from Grauman's Chinese Theater in 1959 by a retired organ builder, Lee Haggart.

Manuel soon became involved in a small circle of organ enthusiasts at the church. Joseph Hunziker, an assistant organist, had an organ in his house, and Manuel gladly helped him work on it. Sometimes they would be joined by Lee Haggart, who decided to train Manuel as a voicer.[5] Thus began a series of lessons in Haggart's studio, with the teacher demonstrating both reed and flue voicing techniques to an eager and apt student.

Meanwhile, Haggart had been banned from St. Finbar's Church for playing secular music on the organ. Lloyd Davies, who was then the West Coast representative for Welte, succeeded him as tuner at the church. Davies asked Manuel and one of his friends to help with cleaning and repairing the church organ, a project that stretched into two years. All that time Manuel continued to take occasional voicing lessons from Haggart, and continued to work on Hunziker's organ.

Having taken advantage of the available opportunities, by the time he had finished high school Manuel had already absorbed some fundamentals about organ construction, and had acquired some very valuable voicing skills. These experiences had served to increase his interest in organ lore, and he spent many evenings in the Los Angeles Central Library exploring the library's generous supply of organ recordings and books. Manuel Rosales was among the fortunate who manage to fall in love with a career early in life, and become ever more enamored with it in later years.

After graduating from high school in 1965, Manuel enrolled in a Liberal Arts program at Los Angeles City College. There he sang in the college choir and met some musicians who would influence his future. One was his ear-training teacher, early-music specialist John Biggs (son of organist Richard Keyes Biggs). He also found a kindred spirit in his music history teacher, organist Anita Priest.[6] His studies with John Biggs continued at Immaculate Heart College in an intensive team-taught course in Medieval and Renaissance music. As a part of this "total-immersion" experience Manuel learned to play the recorder and bass gamba. His academic training was rounded out with a course in German at the University of California, Los Angeles.

THE SCHLICKER EXPERIENCE

In 1968 Manuel found another opportunity that fitted his interests and goals. The Schlicker Organ Company was installing large, new organs in two Los Angeles churches: First Congregational Church, and White Memorial Church, and he found work helping with the installations. The following year he moved to Buffalo, New York, to begin an apprenticeship in the Schlicker factory. He stayed there until late 1972.

Manuel Rosales in 1969.

In the factory his work was primarily in the woodworking and pipe shops. While he learned basic woodworking, more advanced fancy woodworking was not part of his training, nor was the physical design of organs. Instruction in voicing took place when he was sent to various locations for on-site finishing of new installations. At those times his chief instructors were Donald F. Bohall and Walter Guzowski. He found, however, that some of the techniques he had already learned from Lee Haggart were generally more advanced than those he acquired from the Schlicker men, particularly when it was a question of voicing string pipes.

Herman Schlicker himself was a familiar presence in the Schlicker factory. Although he did not instruct his apprentices, he regularly visited each employee every day, observing the work that was being done.

THE ROSALES COMPANY

In 1973 Manuel returned to Los Angeles where he established his own firm, "Manuel Rosales Pipe Organ Service."[7] For two years he remained associated with the Schlicker Organ Company, doing all the Los Angeles area service and guarantee work for that firm. For his own company, major projects during that time were the rebuilding of the large E.M. Skinner organ in the First Methodist Church, Pasadena (Rosales opus 1), and revoicing the Aeolian-Skinner organ in Grady Gammage Memorial Auditorium, Arizona State University, Tempe, in collaboration with John DeCamp.

Within a year after Herman Schlicker died in December 1974, Manuel ended his relationship with the Schlicker firm. Through the rest of the 1970s his work was fairly equally balanced between new organs and renovations (opus numbers 2 through 8). In 1980 the company name was changed to "Rosales Organ Builders, Inc." During the next fifteen years a succession of new organs was built in the Rosales shop (opus 9 through opus 19). Opus 21, completed in 1997, initiated a practice of building organs cooperatively with another organ company. While the Rosales firm would complete five more organs independently, the cooperative plan has subsequently dominated the company's work.

Among the organ builders who have worked in the Rosales shop through the years, several deserve special mention for their roles in the development of the firm's techniques and reputation.

Richard Bond's skill in all aspects of organ building was a great asset in the early years, contributing specifically to the success of opus 1 and opus 2, and to the initial stages of opus 4. In 1976 Richard and Roberta Bond opened their own organ firm in Portland, Oregon: Bond Pipe Organs, Incorporated.

John DeCamp, a long-time friend and colleague, was not actually a member of the Rosales staff, but he assisted with many Rosales organs through opus 16, both as a tonal finisher and as a trusted advisor.

David Dickson was with the Rosales firm for ten years, 1975 to 1985. Not only a fine voicer, Dickson also had a background in engineering. He developed the mechanical details of the firm's tracker action.

Phillip Schlueter worked for Rosales during the late 1970s (opus numbers 3, 4, 5). He later assisted with the installations of opus 11 and opus 15.

William Visscher was instrumental in establishing good cabinetmaking principles, particularly in regard to the construction of cases and consoles. After Visscher left to establish his own firm, Bruno Lagarcé continued to raise the woodworking standards to ever higher levels.

Steuart Goodwin brought three organ projects to the Rosales shop, two of which he completed under his own name. The third, listed as Rosales opus 8, was designed by Goodwin and Visscher. Goodwin was also responsible for the visual design of opus 7.

Michael Van Dyke added his talents to the Rosales staff both as a woodworker and as a project coordinater during the construction of opus numbers 10 through 15.

Mark Hotsenpiller, now with Schoenstein & Co., was a valuable addition to the Rosales staff during the construction of opus 17.

Jonathan Ambrosino has worked with Rosales on several specific projects: opus numbers 16, 17, 21, and 24. He has had administrative responsibilities and has contributed to decisions regarding artistic design. Particularly important for the company have been his descriptions of Rosales organs published in the national journals.

Sean O'Donnell, a former employee, returned to the Rosales company in 2003 as a project manager for releathering and rebuilding.

Socorro Trinidad continues with the Rosales firm as an expert in leathering and releathering bellows and electro-pneumatic organ parts. She is Rosales-trained but has developed her own techniques for this intricate work since entering the firm in 1987.

Kevin Gilchrist holds the record for the longest tenure with Rosales. He entered the firm in March, 1977, having had previous electrical and shop experience as well as a musical background (playing the oboe). He learned organ building in the Rosales shop and has participated in every project from opus 4 to the present. Proficient in all aspects of organ building, Gilchrist is now Manuel Rosales's principal associate.

EARLY CONNECTIONS: FISK AND OWEN

In September 1976 Manuel Rosales attended a three-day conference in The Old Church, Portland, Oregon. Organized by Douglas Butler (1944-1990) and entitled "The Organ in America," it included workshop sessions, lectures, and panel discussions.[8] Particularly important for Rosales was the opportunity to meet Barbara Owen (b. 1933) and Charles Fisk (1925-1983), two people whose work he particularly admired. Many years later he recalled how gratified he had been to discover that neither was aloof; quite on the contrary, both Owen and Fisk were interested in the emerging career of a young organ builder seeking to define his own path in the American organ jungle. Here were formed the initial links with people who would later play significant roles in Rosales's career.

Further connections with Charles Fisk were soon to follow. Two years before the Portland conference, Rosales had been engaged as a consultant for an organ project at Stanford University. The 1901 Murray M. Harris organ in the University's Memorial Chapel was in poor condition, and something had to be done about repairing or replacing it. In consultation with University Organist Herbert Nanney (1919-1996), Rosales worked out a plan to renovate the Murray M. Harris organ, and to install a new organ in the rear gallery between the two widely-separated organ cases of the Harris instrument. Initially Rosales recommended that the Schlicker Organ Company build the new organ. However, changes in the firm following the death of Herman Schlicker prompted him to reconsider that choice.

It is not surprising that Herbert Nanney endorsed Rosales's recommendation that the contract for the new organ should go to C.B. Fisk, Inc. Charles Fisk was not only one of the most experienced and successful of the American organ builders following historical building traditions, but he was also a Stanford alumnus.

In the winter of 1982 Manuel Rosales, Charles Fisk and Harald Vogel embarked on a research tour to study historic organ styles and temperaments, particularly in North Germany and East Germany. The design of the new Stanford organ (Fisk opus 85) reflected the results of that trip and the subse-

Opus 11, Rosales Organ Builders, Trinity Episcopal Cathedral, Portland, Oregon.

quent deliberations of the three participants. Charles Fisk died in December 1983 before the organ was finished, and Rosales undertook the responsibility of seeing the organ through to completion, in cooperation with the staff of the Fisk company. It was inaugurated in May, 1984.

Concurrent with the Stanford project, Rosales was working on a new organ for Trinity Episcopal Church, Portland, Oregon.[9] It would be opus 11 for Rosales Organ Builders, and would be larger and more demanding than any organ the company had then built. The contract was signed in 1981, but with Rosales's involvement at Stanford as well as other work then in progress, opus 11 fell far behind schedule.

Growing concern prompted the church to engage Barbara Owen as an independent advisor. She convinced the church authorities that patience and sympathetic negotiations would be rewarded in the end by a musical instrument of high quality. She also worked out a realistic plan for the completion of the organ. When it was finally completed in 1987, Owen was invited to write an article for the inaugural publication. She predicted: "Years from now the trials will have been forgotten, and the members of Trinity Church will only know that, back in A.D. 1987, they dedicated and took into their lives a very special musical instrument."[10]

In discussing the eclectic style of the organ, Owen wrote: "The 'Romantic gesture' has become a foundation, and yet it is not merely a Romantic organ with a Classic caboose, any more than it is a Classic organ with Romantic appendages. It is rather that most difficult-to-achieve thing, an integrated eclectic organ that will not do quite everything, yet will do a significant amount of musically important things authentically and with style."[11]

Owen's prediction about the future of opus 11 was justified. This organ proved to be a turning point for the Rosales company, as it resulted in a level of national recognition the company had not previously experienced. Barbara Owen, glad to have helped the participants resolve their problems, remembered the episode as particularly "cliff-hanging."[12] As for the organ builder, he recalls how much it meant to him at the time to have the encouragement of one of America's most respected organ experts, and how grateful he is today for her appreciative evaluation of the completed opus 11.

LATER CONNECTIONS, 1992 TO 2005

In view of the cordial relationship that already existed between Manuel Rosales and the staff of C.B. Fisk, Inc., it is not surprising that the Fisk company was Rosales's choice for collaboration in a project that outgrew the capacity of his own shop. In 1992 Rosales Organ Builders was engaged to build a recital hall organ for the Shepherd School of Music, Rice University, Houston, Texas. The following year the Fisk company was brought into the project, and became the primary contractor. As the specification was to be oriented toward nineteenth-century French characteristics, preparations for the design and construction of the 83-rank organ included a two-week study trip in France, as well as detailed planning by the two companies.[13] The organ was completed in 1997 and bears the opus numbers 109 (Fisk) and 21 (Rosales).

A joint project of a different type had its birth in the spring of 1995, when the United Church of Christ, Congregational, in Claremont, California, signed a contract with Glatter-Götz Orgelbau of Owingen, Germany, for a new organ. Caspar Glatter-Götz (formerly with Rieger Orgelbau, Austria) wanted the organ to be an international project. He first chose Thomas Itten of Switzerland to prepare the preliminary design and concept. He then engaged architects from Scotland, Douglas Laird and Graham Tristram, to prepare the visual design. To complete the team, Rosales was invited to take charge of tonal work. Starting from an initial tonal design by Glatter-Götz, and in consultation with Carey Coker-Robertson, organist of the church, Rosales designed the final specifications and was responsible for on-site tonal finishing. The Claremont organ was quickly followed by another joint project: an organ for Neighborhood Congregational Church in Palos Verdes, California. Construction and installation were carried out by the Glatter-Götz firm, while Rosales Organ Builders had charge of tonal design, voicing and finishing.

Manuel Rosales was able to return the compliment by inviting Glatter-Götz to join Rosales Organ Builders in providing an organ for Walt Disney Concert Hall, the new home of the Los Angeles Philharmonic Orchestra. Plans for the building had been initiated in 1988, and late that year Frank O. Gehry had been chosen as architect. A committee consisting of Michael Bar-

The Walt Disney Concert Hall organ provides the setting
for this 2004 picture of Manuel Rosales.

one (chair), Cherry Rhodes, and Robert Anderson selected Rosales Organ
Builders to create all aspects of an organ for the hall except the visual design,
which was entrusted to architect Gehry. An agreement was signed with Rosales Organ Builders in July, 1990.

All design work on the hall was halted after the Northridge earthquake
in 1991, and for a time it seemed doubtful that the hall would ever be built.
However, in 1998 heroic fund-raising efforts, and the enthusiastic leadership

of Los Angeles Mayor Richard Riordan and businessman Eli Broad put the project back on track. By this time Glatter-Götz and Rosales had successfully completed the Claremont organ and were working on the design of the Palos Verdes organ. Rosales's proposal that they jointly build the Walt Disney Concert Hall organ was accepted by the hall's management. A contract was signed in 1999, and Michael Barone was engaged as consultant and liaison for the project. Installation began in October, 2002, and was completed a year later; voicing began in October, 2003. The first public performance on the organ took place at the National Convention of the American Guild of Organists, July 8, 2004; inaugural programs for the general public followed in October, 2004. The Walt Disney Concert Hall organ bears the opus numbers 24 (Rosales Organ Builders), and 9 (Glatter-Götz Orgelbau).

As these projects developed, it became increasingly clear to Manuel Rosales that it was advantageous for a small firm to specialize in one facit of organ building. For him, leaving the construction and installation in the hands of a respected colleague freed his own time and resources for the part of organ building in which his interests were particularly focused: seeing the tonal design through from initial concept to musical fulfillment. Thus, later additions to the Rosales opus list follow a path of joint projects, not only with C.B. Fisk and Glatter-Götz, but also with Parsons Pipe Organ Builders of Canandaigua, New York, and Dobson Pipe Organ Builders of Lake City, Iowa.[14] Rosales affirms: "I believe in collaboration, and that the results can be better than either firm could create on its own."[15]

LINKS WITH THE PAST

Throughout his career Manuel Rosales has been a champion for the preservation of historic organs in the Los Angeles area. While his work has involved the relocation and restoration of organs by William B.D. Simmons and Woodberry & Harris, his greatest influence has been in saving the remaining work of early Los Angeles organ builders, specifically that of the Murray M. Harris Organ Company and its successors (the Los Angeles Art Organ Company and the Murray M. Harris Company).

Opus 30, Rosales Organ Builders, St. James Cathedral, Seattle, Washington.

His first major contract involving an early Los Angeles organ was for the renovation of a 1904 Los Angeles Art Organ Company instrument. This organ had originally been installed in Christ Church, Los Angeles, but in 1919 it had been reinstalled in a much larger edifice, the Church of the Open Door, Los Angeles. Rosales relocated the Great *Mixture*, added a 4-foot *Clarion* and re-placed a missing *Vox Humana,* but otherwise restored the organ to its 1919 state.

In the 1980s, having long advocated the preservation of the Murray M. Harris organ in Stanford University's Memorial Church, Rosales participated in its restoration. Rosales Organ Builders furnished a new console in the style of the original one, restored several reed stops, and upgraded the design of the Fleming valves.[16] Robert Newton (1941-1987), then Curator of the Stanford Memorial Church organs, was in charge of other aspects of the restoration.[17]

His influence played an important role in saving the 1911 Murray M. Harris organ in St. Paul's Cathedral, Los Angeles. When an announcement was made in 1979 that the Cathedral building was to be razed, Rosales was among those who persuaded church authorities to save the organ and place it in storage. He was consultant for this organ's later renovation and re-installation in St. James' Church, Los Angeles: work that was completed in 1995.

When asked to comment on his continuing efforts to preserve the work of the early Los Angeles builders, Rosales noted both their tonal and structural excellence. "These organs," he said, "are beautifully voiced. They have clarity and brilliance, and a cohesive ensemble that bridges the line between classical and romantic styles. Their construction is heroic! There was no cutting corners to save money; nothing was done cheaply, and the craftsmanship is excellent."[18]

Viewing these high standards as models worthy of preservation and ideals worthy of emulation, Rosales links his own work with Los Angeles history: "I see myself as the inheritor of a fine organ-building tradition going back to Murray M. Harris."[19] With his own firm now embarked on its fourth decade, Rosales, too, has created a legacy of craftsmanship and artistic achievements to challenge, inform and inspire future generations of Los Angeles organ builders.

ROSALES OPUS LIST

MANUEL ROSALES PIPE ORGAN SERVICE
(1973-1979) [20]

1.   1974 – *First United Methodist Church, Pasadena, California.*
E. M. Skinner, Opus 430, rebuilding, additions, new console.
4m, 63 ranks.

2.   1976 – *Church of the Open Door, Los Angeles, California.*
1904 Los Angeles Art Organ Company, renovation, one addition.
3m, 45 ranks.
Organ removed to storage, 1985; sold and broken up, 1988.

3.   1976 – *Grace Episcopal Church, Glendora, California.*
New organ and console.
2m, 25 ranks; electric action, slider chests.

4.   1977 – *Los Altos United Methodist Church, Long Beach, California.*
1852 Wm. B.D. Simmons, restoration, additions, relocation.
2 m, 31 ranks; mechanical action.

5.   1977 – *Avalon Community Congregational Church, Avalon,*
California.
1889 Woodberry & Harris, restoration, relocation.
2m, 12 ranks; mechanical action.
Now in First United Lutheran Church, San Francisco.

6.   1979 – *First Christian Church, Whittier, California.*
New organ, rebuilt console.
4m, 55 ranks; electric action, slider chests.

7. 1980 – *First Presbyterian Church, Marysville, California.*
    New organ created from parts of 1869 E. & G.G. Hook organ.
    2m, 23 ranks; mechanical action.

8. 1981 – *St. Anthony Roman Catholic Church, Upland, California.*
    New organ.
    2m, 17 ranks; mechanical action.

ROSALES ORGAN BUILDERS, INC.
(SINCE 1980)

9. 1982 – *First Presbyterian Church, Granada Hills, California.*
    New organ.
    2m, 45 ranks; mechanical action.

10. 1983 – *St. Andrew's Episcopal Church, Ojai, California*
    New organ.
    2m, 17 ranks; mechanical action.

11. 1987 – *Trinity Episcopal Church (now Cathedral), Portland, Oregon.*
    New organ.
    3m, 85 ranks; electric stop action, mechanical key action.

12. 1986 – *Valley Presbyterian Church, Scottsdale, Arizona.*
    New chapel organ.
    2m, 16 ranks; mechanical action.

13. 1987 – *St. Francis of Assisi Catholic Church, Concord, California.*
    New organ using parts of an 1854 Wm. B.D. Simmons organ.
    2m, 25 ranks; mechanical action.

14. 1989 – *Mission San José, St. Joseph's Parish, Fremont, California.*
     New organ.
     1m, 19 ranks, Iberian style, divided; ¼ comma meantone tuning;
     mechanical action.

15. 1990 – *University United Methodist Church, San Antonio, Texas.*
     New organ.
     2m, 47 ranks; mechanical action.

16. 1993 – *First Presbyterian Church, Oakland, California.*
     New organ.
     3m, 75 ranks; electric stop action, mechanical key action.

17. 1995 – *King of Glory Lutheran Church, Dallas, Texas.*
     New organ.
     3m, 48 ranks; electric stop action, mechanical key action.

18. 1990 – *Emory University Department of Music, Atlanta, Georgia.*
     New practice organ.
     2m, 3 ranks; mechanical action.

19. 1992 – *Trinity Episcopal Cathedral, Portland, Oregon.*
     New continuo organ.
     1m, 4 ranks; mechanical action.

20. [organ not built]

21. 1997 – *Rice University Shepherd School of Music, Houston, Texas.*
     New organ; joint project with C.B. Fisk, Inc. (Opus 109).
     3m, 83 ranks; electric stop action, mechanical key action.

22.   2000 – *Saint Paul's Episcopal Church, Richmond, Virginia.*
New organ; Greek Revival casework.
3m, 51 ranks; electric stop action, mechanical key action.

23.   1998 – *Saint Cyril of Jerusalem Church, Encino, California.*
New organ.
3m, 45 ranks; electric stop action, electric slider chests.

[23a.][21] 1998 – *Claremont United Church of Christ, Congregational, Claremont, California.*
New organ; joint project with Glatter-Götz Orgelbau (Opus 2).
3m, 78 ranks; electric stop action, mechanical key action.

[23b.] 1999 – *Neighborhood Church, United Church of Christ, Palos Verdes Estates, California.*
New organ; joint project with Glatter-Götz Orgelbau (Opus 4).
3m, 34 ranks; electric stop action, mechanical key action.

[23c.] 1999 – *West Market Street United Methodist Church, Greensboro, North Carolina.*
New organ; joint project with Dobson Pipe Organ Builders (Opus 71).
3m, 57 ranks; electric stop action, mechanical key action.

24.   2004 – *Walt Disney Concert Hall, Los Angeles, California.*
New organ; joint project with Glatter-Götz Orgelbau (Opus 9).
4m, 109 ranks; two consoles; electric stop action, attached console with mechanical key action, stage console with electric key action.

25.   [organ not built]

26.   [organ not built]

27.   2001 – *Indiana University School of Music, Bloomington, Indiana.*
       New organ.
       3m, 63 ranks; electric stop action, mechanical key action.

28.   [organ not built]

29.   2003 – *St. Bartholomew's Episcopal Church, Atlanta, Georgia.*
       New organ.
       2m, 35 ranks; mechanical action.

30.   2000 – *St. James Cathedral, Seattle, Washington.*
       New organ.
       3m, 47 ranks; electric stop action, electric slider chests.

31.   *Pacific Palisades Presbyterian Church, Pacific Palisades, California.*
       New organ; joint project with Parsons Pipe Organ Builders.
       2m, 30 stops; electric action.
       Design in progress.

32.   2004 – *First Lutheran Church, Venice, California.*
       New organ; joint project with Parsons Pipe Organ Builders.
       2m, 6 ranks; electric action.

33.   *St. Stephen's Lutheran Church, Monona, Wisconsin*
       New organ; joint project with Parsons Pipe Organ Builders.
       2m, 32 ranks; mechanical action.
       Now under construction.

34.   *Louisiana State University School of Music, Baton Rouge, Louisiana.*
       New organ, to be built jointly with Glatter-Götz Orgelbau.
       4m, 73 ranks; mechanical action.

35. *Augustana Lutheran Church, West St. Paul, Minnesota.*
     New organ, to be built jointly with Glatter-Götz Orgelbau.
     2m, 50 ranks; mechanical action.
     Now under construction.[22]

: : N O T E S : :

[1] This organ is opus 75 for Dobson Pipe Organ Builders. The consultant was Manuel Rosales.

[2] Review by Mark Swed, *Los Angeles Times* October 2, 2004, pp. E1, E6.

[3] The author is indebted to Manuel Rosales and William Van Pelt for furnishing and preparing illustrations for this article.

[4] Burbank is located about 12 to 14 miles north of the central part of Los Angeles.

[5] Haggart himself had learned his craft from Hope-Jones-trained James H. Nuttall.

[6] Anita Priest was then organist for the Los Angeles Philharmonic Orchestra, and organist at First Methodist Church, Pasadena, where Rosales would later rebuild the organ as his opus 1.

[7] The name "Manuel Rosales & Associates" was occasionally used by the company during the 1970s, but was not actually an official designation.

[8] Workshop leaders were John Brombaugh, Douglas Butler, Charles Fisk, Lee Garrett, John Hamilton, Margaret Irwin-Brandon, Wayne Leupold, Orpha Ochse, and Barbara Owen.

[9] Now (since 1993) Trinity Episcopal Cathedral.

[10] Inaugural publication, Rosales opus 11, Trinity Episcopal Church, Portland, Oregon.

[11] *Ibid.*

[12] Correspondence with the author, 11 May 2004.

[13] This trip was one of nine that Manuel Rosales has made to France since 1989 to study classic and symphonic organ styles.

[14] A major Dobson/Rosales project is the organ currently being installed in Verizon Hall of the Kimmel Center for the Performing Arts, Philadelphia.

Manuel Rosales collaborated with Dobson in the initial stages of the project and in the tonal design. He will participate in shop voicing and on-site tonal finishing. Dedication of the organ is planned for May, 2006.

[15] Correspondence with the author, 25 May, 2004.

[16] The Rosales upgraded valve design has been adopted in restorations of other Murray Harris and Los Angeles Art Organ Company instruments.

[17] After the Loma Prieta earthquake in 1989, further repairs and restoration were undertaken by John DeCamp and Mark Austin.

[18] Conversation with the author, 7/24/04.

[19] Correspondence with the author, 5/10/04.

[20] The name "Manuel Rosales & Associates" was also used during part of this period.

[21] Rosales did not assign opus numbers to the joint projects listed here as [23a], [23b], and [23c].

[22] In addition to work in progress on new organs, Rosales Organ Builders is currently engaged in rebuilding the 1923 E.M. Skinner organ, opus 446, in St. John's Episcopal Church, Los Angeles.

SELECT LIST OF PUBLICATIONS
1956–2005

❀

Barbara Owen

ACADEMIC PAPERS:

Owen, Barbara. *Organ building in New England in the eighteenth and nineteenth centuries.* Thesis (M.M.) Boston University, 1962.

BOOKS AND MONOGRAPHS:

Douglas, Fenner, Owen Jander and Barbara Owen [editors]. *Charles Brenton Fisk : organ builder : volume one : essays in his honor.* Easthampton, Massachusetts: Westfield Center for Early Keyboard Studies, 1986.

Owen, Barbara [compiler]. *Charles Brenton Fisk : organ builder : volume two : his work.* Easthampton, Massachusetts: Westfield Center for Early Keyboard Studies, 1986.

_____. *E. Power Biggs, concert organist.* Bloomington and Indianapolis: Indiana University Press, [c. 1987].

_____. *Mormon Tabernacle Organ : an American classic.* Salt Lake City, Utah: Temple Square [Church of Jesus Christ of Latter-day Saints, c. 1990].

_____. *Organ in New England : an account of its use and manufacture to the end of the nineteenth century.* Raleigh: Sunbury Press, 1979.

BARBARA OWEN

_____. *Organ works of Johannes Brahms.* [Forthcoming, 2006].

_____. *Organs and music of King's Chapel, 1713-1964.* [Boston: King's Chapel, 1966].

_____. *Organs and music of King's Chapel, 1713-1991.* Second edition. Boston: King's Chapel, [c. 1993].

_____. *Registration of Baroque organ music.* Bloomington and Indianapolis: Indiana University Press, [c. 1997].

_____. *Social history of the 'Great Organ.'* [Forthcoming, 2008].

Williams, Peter, and Barbara Owen. *New Grove organ.* New York and London: W.W. Norton & Company, [c. 1980-88].

DICTIONARY ARTICLES:

Musik in Geschichte und Gegenwart : allgemeine Enzyklopädie der Musik begründet von Friedrich Blume. Zweite, neubearbeitete Ausgabe. [Kassel, Basel, London, New York and Prag: Bärenreiter, c. 1994+.]

New Grove dictionary of American music. Edited by H. Wiley Hitchcock and Stanley Sadie. Four volumes. [London: Macmillan Press Limited, c. 1986.]

New Grove dictionary of music and musicians. Twenty volumes. Edited by Stanley Sadie. [London: Macmillan Publishers Limited, c. 1980.]

New Grove dictionary of music and musicians. Second edition; twenty-nine volumes. Edited by Stanley Sadie. [London: Macmillan Publishers Limited, c. 1991.]

New Grove dictionary of musical instruments. Three volumes. Edited by Stanley Sadie. [London: Macmillan Publishers Limited, c. 1984.]

ARTICLES IN JOURNALS AND FESTSCHRIFTEN:

Owen, Barbara. "American Guild of Organists' centennial : the founders of the AGO–who were they?" *American Organist* 30:2 (Feb., 1996), 91-96.

_____. "American Guild of Organists' centennial : the guild grows," *American Organist* 30:3 (Mar., 1996), 45-47.

_____. "American organ music and playing from 1700," *Organ Institute Quarterly* 10:3 (Autumn, 1963), 7-13.

_____. "Bay psalm book and its era," *Hymn* 41:4 (Oct., 1990), 12-19.

_____. "Boston's heritage of organbuilding and playing," *American Organist* 24:5 (May, 1990), 222.

_____. "Brother Klemm," *Moravian Music Journal* 40:1 (Spring, 1995), 3-15.

_____. "Colonial organs: being an account of some early English instruments exported to the Eastern United States," *Journal of the British Institute of Organ Studies* 3 (1979), 92-107.

_____. "Dr. Edward Hodges of Bristol and New York: an 'organ expert' on both sides of the Atlantic," *Journal of the British Institute of Organ Studies* 14 (1990), 48-61.

_____. "E. Power Biggs: a profile," *Music* 5:6 (June, 1971), 24-26.

_____. "The earliest extant Appleton? An early New England organ on the West Coast," *Tracker* 27:4 (1983), 16-20.

_____. "Early organs and organ building in Newburyport," *1635-1985 : Newbury, Newburyport, West Newbury : 350ᵗʰ anniversary essays.* [Originally published in the *Essex Institute Historical Collections* 121:3 (July, 1985)]. Salem, Massachusetts: Essex Institute, 1985, 172-95.

_____. "Early seventeenth-century organ in St. Nicholas, Stanford-on-Avon," *Organ Yearbook* 19 (1988), 5-30.

_____. "Edward Little White, professor of music," *American musical life in context and practice to 1865.* Edited by James R. Heintze. New York and London: Garland Publishing, Inc., 1994, 133-147.

_____. "Eighteenth-century organs and organ building in New England," *Music in Colonial Massachusetts : 1630-1820 : II : music in homes and in churches : a conference held by the Colonial Society of Massachusetts, May 17 and 18, 1973.* Edited by Barbara Lambert. Boston: Colonial Society of Massachusetts, 1985, 655-714.

_____. "An Elliot organ in Boston, Massachusetts," *Fanfare for an Organ-Builder: Essays presented to Noel Mander to celebrate the sixtieth anniversary of his commencement in business as an organ-builder.* Oxford: Positif Press, 1996, 117-131.

_____. "Evidence for Trompes in the sixteenth century English organ," *Visitatio organorum.* Two volumes. Edited by Albert Dunning. Buren (GLD), The Netherlands: Frits Knuf, 1980, 489-98.

_____. "The Goodriches and Thomas Appleton : founders of the Boston organ industry," *Tracker* 4:1 (Oct., 1959), 2-6.

_____. "Hail and farewell: the Biggs memorial service," *Diapason* 68:6 (May, 1977), 5.

_____. "Henrician heyday of the regal," *Continuo* 7:10 (Sept., 1984), 2.

_____. "An historic organ in the Metropolitan Museum," *Diapason* 74:2 (Feb., 1983), 6, 9.

_____. "Historical and cultural importance of David Tannenberg and other Pennsylvania German organ builders," *"Pleasing for our use" : David Tannenberg and the organs of the Moravians.* Edited by Carol A. Traupman-Carr.

Bethlehem: Lehigh University Press; and London: Associated University Presses, [c. 2000], 49-67.

_____."Hook & Hasting: the Boston years," *Tracker* 45: 3-4 (2001), 22-31.

_____."How can we reach Middle Haddam?," *Tracker* 1:2 (Jan., 1957), 2-3.

_____. "Hymn tunes from an American barrell-organ of 1842," *Hymn* 11:3 (1960), 69-72, 74.

_____."John Henry Willcox, organist and organbuilder," *Tracker* 36:4 (1992), 13-24.

_____."Joseph Alley and Richard Pike Morss : early organbuilders of Newburyport," *Tracker* 31:1 (1987), 30-39.

_____."Legacy of Alan Laufman," *Tracker* 44:3 (2000), 3, 5.

_____."Meantone temperament: a 'new' horizon," *Diapason* 73:11 (Nov., 1982), 15.

_____."New light on the Bach organ trail," *Early Keyboard Studies Newsletter* 5:4 (July, 1991), 1, 12-17.

_____."New York pilgrimage," *Tracker* 1:1 (Oct., 1956), 2-4.

_____."Œuvres pour orgue seul de Daniel Pinkham," *L'Orgue* nr. 262 (2003), 131-141.

_____."Organ in Japan," *Diapason* 68:9 (Aug., 1977), 1, 12-14.

_____."Organ in Colonial America," *Journal of Church Music* 18:4 (Apr., 1976), 2-4, 48.

_____."Organ preservation is alive and well 'down under,'" *Tracker* 39:3 (1995), 18-23.

____. "Organbuilding in Connecticut in the nineteenth century," *Tracker* 38:1 (1994), 23-30.

____. "Organs at Harvard," *Tracker* 12:2 (Winter, 1968), 4-5, 14.

____. "Organs at the centennial," *Bicentennial tracker : in commemoration of the bicentennial of the United States of America 1776-1976 and the twentieth anniversary of the Organ Historical Society, Inc., 1956-1976.* Wilmington, Ohio: Organ Historical Society, 1976, 128-135.

____. "The other Mr. Selby," *American Music* 8:4 (Winter, 1990), 477-82.

____. "A 'Payer of Organs' and a 'Voyall,'" *Tracker* 41:2 (1997), 4-11.

____. "Pitch and tuning in eighteenth and nineteenth century American organs," *Organ Yearbook* 15 (1984), 54-59.

____. "Salem chamber organ," *Essex Institute Quarterly* 110:2 (April, 1974), 111-119.

____. "Second Oaxaca conference," *Journal of the Westfield Center* 15: 3-4 (Jan., 2003), 11-13.

____. "Sophia Hewitt Ostinelli : a 'professional lady' in the early 19th-century American music world," *American Organist* 25:5 (May, 1991), 50-52.

____. "Tale of two organs : some historic notes on the organs in the Unitarian and Methodist Churches in Nantucket," *Historic Nantucket* 10:4 (April, 1963), 4-13.

____. "Technology and the organ in the nineteenth century," *The organ as a mirror of its time : North European reflections, 1610-2000.* Edited by Kerala J. Snyder. Oxford: Oxford University Press, 2002, 213-229.

____. "Thomas Appleton (1785-1872)," *An Appleton anthology : seven pipe organs*

built 1812-1843 by Thomas Appleton. Notes to a CD recording by Lois Reg-
istein. [Richmond, Virginia: Raven, c. 2001], 12-23.

_____. "Towards a definition of the English Renaissance organ," *Early Keyboard
Studies Newsletter* 3 (1986), 1-7.

_____. "Tracing an English chamber organ," *Tracker* 22:2 (Winter, 1978), 1, 3-6.

_____. "Two Richard Bridge organs in New England," *Organ* 68:269 (July, 1989),
113-23.

MUSICAL EDITIONS:

Buck, Dudley. *Six chorale preludes on familiar church tunes,* Opus 49. Edited by
Barbara Owen. Mellville, N.Y.: Belwin Mills Publishing Corp., c. 1995.

Owen, Barbara [compiler]. *A century of American organ music.* Four volumes.
Dayton, Ohio: McAfee Music Corporation, 1975-91.

_____ [compiler]. *Four centuries of Italian organ music.* Miami, Florida: CPP/Bel-
win, Inc. 1994.

_____ [compiler]. *International collection of nineteenth century hymn preludes.* Mellville, N.Y.: Belwin-Mills Publishing Corp., c. 1982.

_____ [compiler]. *A romantic Christmas : twenty pieces from the 19th century.* Miami,
Florida: Belwin-Mills, c. 1995.

MISCELLANEOUS:

Owen, Barbara. *Timeline of the organ : 2600 years of history.* [Easthampton, Massachusetts: Westfield Center, c. 1995.]

Compiled by Stephen L. Pinel

Geschichte:

The cat was originally drawn on a small piece of paper by Barbara Owen while the latter was seated in the smallest room in the old workshop (Maplewood Ave.) Originally it was simply washing itself. Someone later added voicing tools to the original cat drawing, thereby turning it into a self-portrait of Barbara herself. (She was always thought of as being cat-like, and was a lover of cats.) The original drawing was glued to the glass of the door to the voicing room that Barbara used. When the company moved to Kondelin Road, efforts were made to detach the cat drawing from the glass, to no avail. Shortly after the move, this rendering (and enlargement) of the original appeared on the office wall of the new shop. Bob Cornell had copied the original, and had framed it for posterity. This may be the most sensitive portrait of Barbara Owen in existence, seen, as it is, through the humorous affections of several of her colleagues at C.B. Fisk, Inc.

Charles Fisk
March 1980